Guitarist's Guide to Computer Music

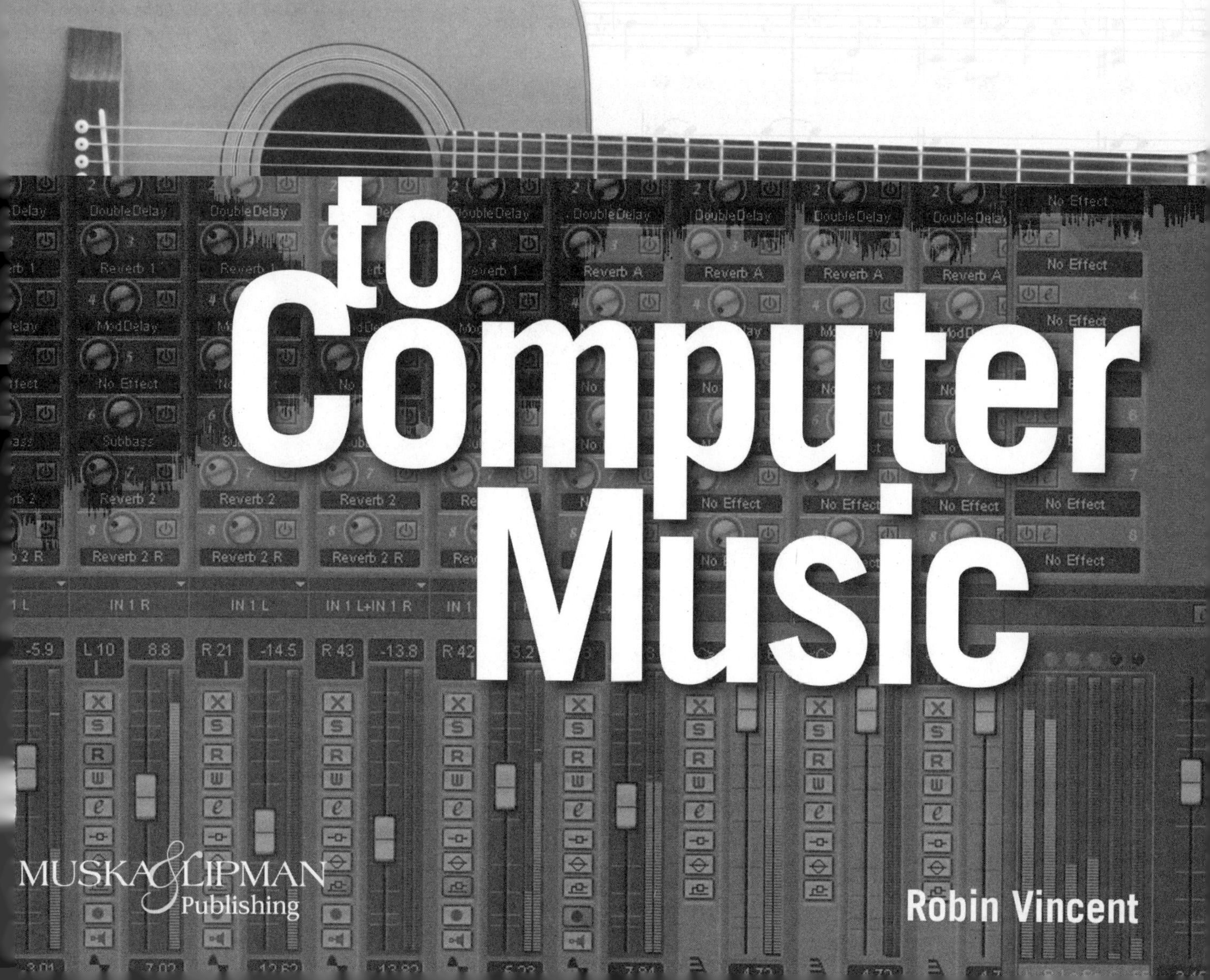

Robin Vincent

MUSKA & LIPMAN Publishing

Guitarist's Guide to Computer Music

Senior Vice President, Retail Strategic Market Group: Andy Shafran

Publisher: Stacy L. Hiquet

Credits: Senior Marketing Manager, Sarah O'Donnell; Marketing Manager, Heather Hurley; Manager of Editorial Services, Heather Talbot; Acquisitions Editor, Todd Jensen; Senior Editor, Mark Garvey; Associate Marketing Manager, Kristin Eisenzopf; Retail Market Coordinator, Sarah Dubois; Production Editor and Proofreader, Megan Belanger; Cover Designer, Mike Tanamachi.

Library of Congress Catalog Number: 2003108384

ISBN: 1-59200-133-5

5 4 3 2 1

Muska & Lipman Publishing,
a Division of Course Technology
25 Thomson Place
Boston, MA 02210
www.muskalipman.com
publisher@muskalipman.com

Introduction

The first time I used a computer with a guitar was back in 1988. It was my first gig at the tender age of 18. My trusty Commodore 64 sequenced all the drums and keyboard parts while I played guitar and sang over the top. The crowd (made up of friends and family) went wild, and it all worked fantastically well, although it took three minutes to load each song onto the computer. At that time, the relationship between the computer and the guitar was nonexistent. The computer dealt with MIDI, synths, electronic noises, and controlling drum machines while the guitar got on with rockin' very loudly alongside. It would take a good ten years or so before they started to flirt with each other with more than a passing interest.

Other than playing live, which I could have done just as well with a backing tape, the main interest for the guitarist is home recording (as a natural step toward ultimate rock stardom and 'real' studios). The essential piece of gear for this has always been the four-track cassette PortaStudio, and I was no different, getting years of demo-making creativity out of those four tracks. Combine that with a microphone, a nice drum machine like the Alesis SR-16, and maybe a digital effects box, and your home studio is complete. Given a bit more cash and a leaning toward technology, you might find yourself with an 8-track Minidisk recorder, or 16 tracks of hard disk recording on a Roland or Fostex digital recorder. All fabulous recording tools.

If I were to tell you that for the price of the smallest 4-track you could get some software that could surpass all your creative expectations, could provide you with almost limitless track counts of the highest quality recording, racks of effects to rival even the poshest external box, built-in drums with the most realistic grooves, virtual bass guitar and unlimited amount of synth and sampled sounds and textures, mixing, processing, and mastering, and, if you want, all mixed to a CD ready for playing in your car – would this surprise you? 'Yeah, but you've got to use a computer' I hear you say, which is true. It does involve a computer, but it's easier and more intuitive than ever before. I can guarantee that by the end of this book, you'll be wondering why you didn't do this years ago, and you'll see computers not as an obstacle but as a phenomenal creative tool. That professional studio you've always dreamt of trying out is available right on your desktop, and it couldn't be easier to use.

A computer can be the most amazing recording machine you'll ever come across, and recording is just the beginning. You'll find yourself taken to places and ways of working you've not even considered. My personal 'road to Damascus' moment was back in '96 when I first started working in the music industry. I was given a simple piece of recording software to try out. I installed it on my painfully slow PC, which I'd used previously only for writing letters and playing games, and plugged my

Telecaster into my Zoom effects box and plugged the output into my soundcard. I loaded up a simple 4/4 drum pattern, which played drum sounds on my soundcard I didn't realize I had, hit record, and began to play a few riffs. Fabulous, I thought. So far, so 4-track. Now I'm a terribly sloppy player and my riffs were all over the place, and before I tried to re-record the track (as I would have done on the 4-track), I began playing around with the mouse. I found that I had played the riff perfectly for one of the bars, so I cut around that bar and deleted the rest of the track. Then I copied and pasted the perfect bar throughout the song – just like you can do with text in a Word document. Selected track 2, hit record, and I could play along to a wonderfully competent rhythm guitarist for the first time in my life. That was the 'moment' – I was hooked. A couple of tracks later, I was rearranging the song by moving blocks of stuff around on screen and producing ideas and possibilities that I couldn't believe had come from a 12-bar blues riff. I never used my 4-track again.

This was all before virtual effect 'plug-ins', real-time mixing and mastering - this was just the beginning. Today my computer is a recording, editing, producing, sound-wrangling, effect-processing, mixing, and rockin' mother of a studio. You can have one too, if you like, and in the following pages, I'll show you exactly what you need and how to make it all work with none of the problems your computer-savvy friends tell you about. It's not scary, it's just a computer.

We'll be looking at what all this MIDI and audio stuff is about, what it all means, and how we use it. We'll be getting into the guts of soundcards so that you can make the perfect choice for your own studio. Then we'll follow all the connections around our studio to see how it all fits together, where you plug your guitar, and how to combine your existing gear with the computer. I'm sure you're dying to know how I intend to get the computer to make your guitar sound like a Marshall Stack – we'll look at software plug-ins in great detail. Next we'll take a practical look at using your software studio, with full tutorial step-by-step instructions to get you recording in no time at all. We'll then start to dispense with the useful, but cumbersome, mouse and get into controlling your music from guitarist-friendly MIDI floorboards and other controllers. We'll start to get real and talk about the possibilities of taking computers out when playing live. Finally, we'll have a look at the vast array of products available to show you what would be ideal for your setup.

I'll assume that you have pretty much no prior knowledge of music software and I'll take you through every step of installing it and using it. You may have come across interactive CD-ROMs and cool guitar tuition software that helps you improve your skills - undoubtedly a fabulous use of computers but not something that I'll go into. This is about recording and making music rather than learning about it. You don't have to be able to read music or know about computers in any depth. If you can use a mouse, then we'll get along fine.

If you feel that you already know some of the stuff that I'm talking about, then I'd still advise you to read through it anyway. There are so many misconceptions and misunderstandings about computers and music technology in general that I just might be able to set you straight on a couple of things. The book follows a straight line, building up knowledge and experience along the way, so I'd urge you not to skip to chapters you're more interested in, but to start at the beginning and work through.

Acknowledgments

I would like to thank everyone who was interested enough to make a contribution to the creation of this book, with particular thanks to the kind people who let me include their software on the CD-ROM.

I'd especially like to thank Bill, Neil, and Mark at Steinberg, Angus, at Fxpansion, and Paul at IK Multimedia for their friendship and support of this project.

I'd also like to thank Maria, who so foolishly believed me when I said it would only take a couple of weeks, some three months ago. Your support and encouragement was more essential than you know.

Lastly, I'd like to thank Johnny, Media Tools, and Carillon Audio Systems for continuing to give me the opportunity to play around with all this stuff. Long may it continue.

Contents

1 Starting with the familiar 1
The average guitarist's home studio 1

2 Installing the software from CD-ROM 4
Setting up the tuner 6
Setting up Cubase SX 7
Setting up Amplitube 12
Play the demo song 12

3 Let's record some guitar 15
Plugging the guitar into the computer 17
Using the line input 18
Using the mic input 18
Getting the right signal 19
Recording your first track 20
Multitrack recording and playing along with yourself 23

4 Getting the right hardware 26
Talking about soundcards 26
Dealing with latency 30
The 'right' hardware 32

5 Virtual effects processing 34
Talking about plug-ins 34
Using Amplitube 38
Recording with effects 43

6 Bring on the drums 44
Virtual drum machines 44
Loading VSTis 46
Native Instruments Battery 46
Velocity layers 48
Fxpansion's DR-008 49
Playing and programming drums in Cubase 53
Understanding MIDI 53
Connecting MIDI to the computer 54
Playing drums in Cubase 57
Recording a drum track 60

Quantization 63
Groove Quantize 64
Using the drum editor 65
Arranging patterns 67
Preset patterns 68
MusicLab's SlicyDrummer 70
MIDI files 74
Using drum loops 75
ACID 75
Loops in Cubase 78

7 Creating a virtual band 84
Talking about software synths 84
Development 84
Software samplers 86
Creating a VSTi bass line in Cubase 89
Using the Key Editor to create notes 91
Using effects with VSTis 93
Adding other instruments 94
CPU performance 96
Adding and editing a guitar track 96

8 Hands- and feet-on control 99
Talking about MIDI control 99
Knobs 101
Drum control 102
MIDI floorboards 103
Controlling stuff in Cubase 104
Controlling the mixer 104
Controlling effects 107
Controlling VSTis 108
Using a MIDI floorboard with Cubase 110
Basic floorboard control in Cubase 111
Floorboard control of Amplitube in Cubase 113
All-singing and all-dancing control of Amplitube in Cubase 114

9 Mixing and automating 123
Mixing in Cubase 124
VST channel editor 126
Track mixer 126
Applying effects 127
Level adjustment 130
Panning 130
Effects 130
EQ 131
Dynamics 132
Automation 133
Automating effects 135
Automating VSTis 135
Tidying up 136

10 Creating a finished product 138
Mixing down in Cubase SX 139
Mastering software 140
Putting your mix onto CD 143
Creating MP3s of your music 145
What is MP3? 145
Making your own MP3s 147
Publishing your music on the Internet 147
Copyright 152
Other Internet music formats 152

11 Studio setups 154
Basic setup 154
Enhanced basic setup 155
Basic mixer setup 156
8-bus mixer setup 158
Digital mixer setup 160
The virtual studio 161
Virtual studio with real control 162

12 Taking it on the road 164
Using software effects live 165
RT Player 168
Getting sound into and out of a laptop 168
USB and Firewire audio 169
Getting the right laptop 170

13 A round-up of computer hardware and software 172
Deciding what's right for you 172
Soundcards 172
Recording software 184
Effects plug-ins 192
Drum software 194
Software synths and samplers 196
MIDI controllers 201

14 What about the computer? 208
What to look for 208
Where to buy 211
The great 'PC versus Apple Mac' debate 212
Example specification 213
Windows? 213

15 Looking back through what we've learned 214
What the future holds 214

Appendix A **Understanding the difference between MIDI and audio 216**
Appendix B **Setting up Windows XP for music 220**
Appendix C **Internet resources 226**
Appendix D **Glossary 227**

Index 234

1 Starting with the familiar

Shortly, we're going to be plowing right into the rock 'n' roll of recording onto the computer, and you'll be amazed how easy it is. Before we do, I would like to take a few minutes to explain how this book is going to deal with this notoriously troublesome arena of computer music. At the moment, I'm sure that to you, a computer couldn't look less like a recording studio if it tried. It's probably a boxy beige-colored thing that roars on, or under, your desk, whirring unexpectedly and occasionally refusing to do the most basic of tasks, such as printing out something you've been working on for days. Worry not, appearances are unimportant (a scary thought for a guitarist!) and more importantly, deceptive. Hidden within that cheap plastic shell is the living, breathing, and sweating powerhouse of the ultimate recording machine. Your cobweb-strewn CPU, memory, and hard drives are about to start earning their keep.

The average guitarist's home studio

Well, we've all been there, and I would certainly consider myself no more than an average guitarist, so let's look at the kind of studio equipment you may have been using up to now.

Most guitarists will be familiar with some form of hardware-based recording. By that I mean using a dedicated box of some kind as a little recording studio. The most common is the 4-track cassette-based PortaStudio (a term coined by Tascam

Figure 1.1
Tascam PortaStudio 424 cassette-based recorder/mixer.

who invented the first one), and if you don't own one, then you've probably come across one. It's like a cassette player with a little mixer built in. In recent times, these have gotten quite clever and have moved to Minidisk rather than cassette, arguably increasing the quality, certainly removing the hiss, and recording suddenly becomes digital. 'Digital' simply means that the sound goes through a conversion process into data, like what CDs have on them. This conversion process is so accurate that you get very high-quality recordings. On the other hand, 'analog' is the traditional tape-based recording which deals with electrical charges, which come from a microphone or pickup, written onto magnetic tape. We'll look at the differences between 'analog' and 'digital' later on.

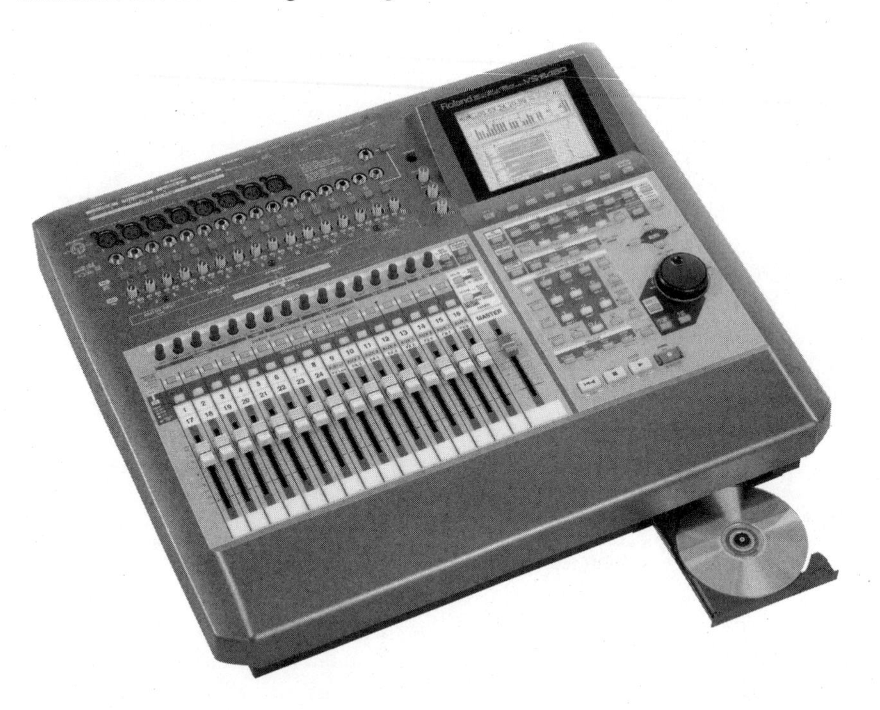

Figure 1.2
Roland VS2480CD. Digital recording for guitarists.

Competing with Minidisk is hard-disk recording, and these are becoming cheaper and more feature-laden by the minute. Roland started the whole home hard-disk recorder thing off with their VS880 8 track recorder, and now you can get 24-track machines, packed with effects and automated faders, and you can even connect them to a screen to edit tracks – phenomenal.

The next bit of essential hardware is the drum machine, that rhythm-making companion to play along to. For some reason, the Alesis SR-16 has been the favorite for years and years, probably because it's easy to program and sounds fabulous.

You can select a number of patterns to create a song, painstakingly entering numbers and playing it through over and over to make sure you've got all the right bits in the right places. Some drum machines also give you the option of a bassline, a handy extra and a great tool for the low frequency challenged.

Figure 1.3
Alesis SR-16. Easy to program – sounds great.

The final bit, or bits, of equipment, is the guitar effects boxes, be these stomp boxes or digital effects units, or something grander like a combined amp modeler and effects processor. These are undoubtedly useful in performance as well as recording, and essentially shape your guitar sound, along with your amp/stack/combo.

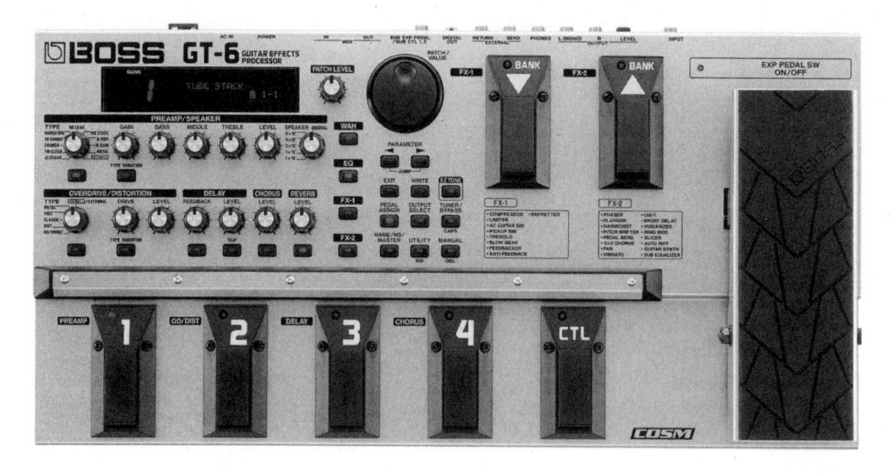

Figure 1.4
The Boss GT-6 guitar effects processor – does what it says on the box.

This is all very familiar and indeed was the basis of my own studio up to a couple of years ago. So why change? Well the fact that you bought this book means that you have a niggling feeling that maybe there's something you're missing out on.

An average computer could probably do, oh let's say 100–200 tracks of audio, can have built-in drum machines with hundreds of different kits, and thousands of patterns, has access to an increasing pool of studio quality effects, and is as easy to edit as it is to move text about in a Word document. Don't be deceived; a computer can be every bit as 'hands-on' as a hardware recorder, every bit as instant, every bit as portable (laptops anyone?) and can do so much more.

In the following chapters, I'll use our 'average home studio' as a direct comparison to the average computer software and hardware and show you how, although you probably don't see it yet, a computer can work in exactly the same way. It may take a little imagination to begin with, but I promise you'll slap yourself that you didn't use a computer for music making years ago.

Installing the software from CD-ROM

Info

If you experience any problems with the CD-ROM, please visit us at *www.muskalipman.com.*

In order to help me get across the wonders of recording onto a computer, I've included a CD-ROM with a few bits of software on, and some example songs, or 'Projects' to illustrate the points. Don't get too excited: the programs are demo versions, which means that they have some features missing and have been disabled in some way. However, we can do enough with them to get your juices flowing and they are also some of the best bits of software currently available.

Pop the CD-ROM into your CD-ROM drive and let's have a look at what we find. You can get to the CD-ROM through the 'My Computer' icon on the desktop or under the Start menu, or if it tries to open automatically, select 'View Contents'. There will be four folders:

Cubase projects

This contains a number of demo songs and tutorial projects that we'll use throughout the book. Copy this folder onto your hard drive. You can do this by simply dragging the folder onto your desktop. These projects contain audio tracks that need to be run from the hard drive. (Your CD-ROM drive is too slow and would not allow for any editing to take place.)

Loops

A selection of drum loops that we'll use in the chapter on drums.

Mixes

Some mixes that I'll talk about in the mixing and mixdown sections.

Software

This contains the software that we will install onto the computer and use throughout the book. Some of it we'll install now, some of it can wait until later:

Amplitube

An amp modeling and effects processor plug-in that is one of the best software guitar effects currently available. It does indeed sound fabulous.

Audio Phonics Guitar Tuner

A useful software guitar tuner, so that you don't have to unplug your guitar to keep it in tune.

Battery demo
Serious drum sampler from Native Instruments (we'll install this later).

Cubase SX demo
A demo version of Steinberg's leading software recording studio. This is where we'll discover computer recording, use effects, write music and generally mess around.

DR-008 Demo
Comprehensive 'Advanced Rhythm Production Station' drum machine from Fxpansion (we'll install this later).

DSound GT Player
A performance multi-effects box that we'll install later.

LM7
A drum machine for Cubase that Steinberg have given us special permission to use. We'll install this later.

MIDI-OX
A MIDI utility that we'll use in the MIDI control section.

MIDI Yoke
A companion to the MIDI-OX. It'll all become clear later.

Music Lab
Slicydrummer and Fill-indrummer plug-ins for the DR-008 (we'll install these later).

Sonic Foundry ACID
A loop-based program that we'll install later.

The software

I've chosen Cubase as the software I'll concentrate on for the purposes of this book. Cubase SX is one of the best pieces of recording software available. The 'SX' version is the latest and top version of the Cubase family of products and has an enormous selection of features, some of which we'll touch on, many of which we won't. The less expensive Cubase SL version is capable of everything you'll find in this book, so you don't need to fork out for SX if you decide Cubase is for you. What I've tried to do is keep all my tutorials as simple as possible so that the process behind them would be similar regardless of the software you're using. Cubase is designed for Windows XP, and my screenshots will reflect this; however, it can also be run on Windows 98. There are many alternatives to Cubase, from shareware through to integrated hardware solutions, and all of them can handle pretty much everything we'll be covering. Toward the end of the book, there'll be a summary of the most common recording programs to give you a rounded idea of what they offer and how much they will hurt your pocket.

Your computer

Before we install anything, we'd better check that your computer is up to the task of running these programs.

For Cubase, here's the minimum specification you will need:

Processor
Pentium III 500 MHz or AMD K7 (Pentium III or AMD Athlon 1GHz or faster recommended).

RAM
256MB (512MB recommended).

Operating system
Windows 98, 2000, XP Home or Professional.

Sound card
Windows MME and DirectSound (ASIO-compliant audio card recommended). Amplitube is much less than that, and the tuner needs hardly anything at all.

If your computer is not up to scratch, don't worry. The usefulness of this book is not based entirely upon the included software. All the tutorials are fully illustrated, so you will get a very clear idea of what's going on whether you have the software open in front of you or not. Also, at the back of the book, I've included loads of links to other downloadable software that may be more suitable for your computer.

Setting up the tuner

The simplest piece of software is the Audio Phonics Tuner – it should run on anyone's computer. So let's install that first. It's also an easy way of testing whether your guitar is connected correctly – we'll deal with that in the next chapter.

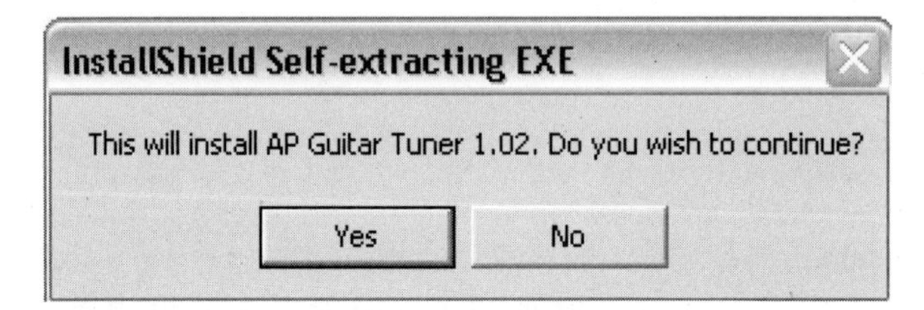

Figure 2.1
Installing the tuner.

Within the Audio Phonics Guitar Tuner folder is a setup file called 'apguitarsetup.exe'. Double-click the file to install the software.

Follow the on-screen instructions – it's best to install it using the default settings for simplicity. Once installation is complete, you can launch the tuner from the Programs menu.

The Audio Phonics Tuner has lots of different tunings to choose from, Standard E tuning being the default. You can use it in two ways. You can click on the six strings at the top left and they will play the pitch of that string so you can tune to it, or more usefully, you can plug your guitar into the computer and the tuner will tell you exactly how far away you are from the correct pitch – just like a hardware tuner. We'll come back to this in the next chapter once we've connected the guitar.

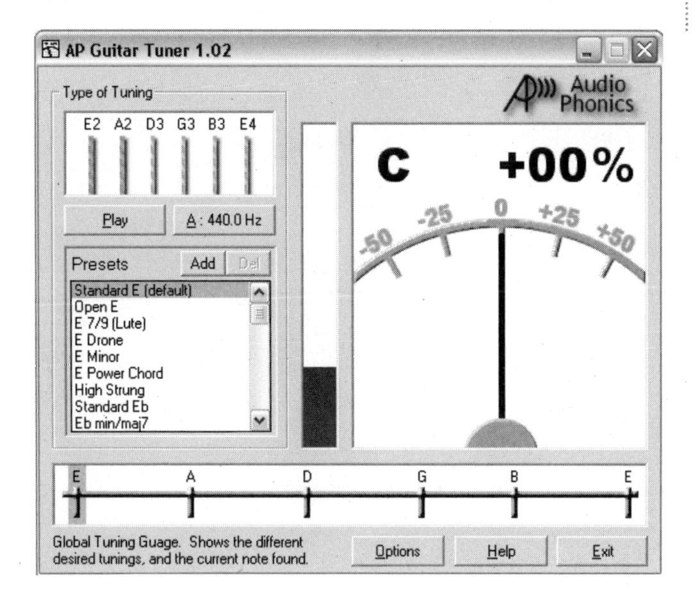

Figure 2.2
AP Guitar Tuner – very visual and lots of different tunings.

Setting up Cubase SX

Within the 'Software' folder you'll find a folder called 'Cubase SX Demo'. Double-click the setup file you find in there to install the software. Again, all the default settings should be fine.

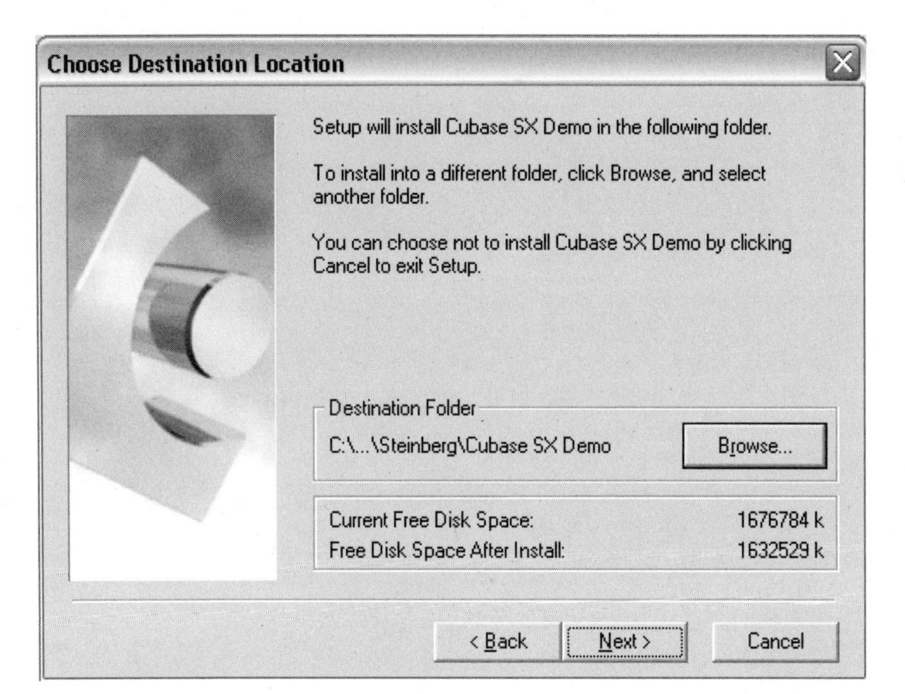

Figure 2.3
Choosing the destination to install Cubase.

Once installed, you can launch Cubase by double-clicking the icon that will have appeared on your desktop.

Figure 2.4
Cubase SX Demo icon.

As Cubase initializes for the first time, it will do a number of tests on your system. The most important one is on your soundcard to try to determine its suitability and which drivers it should use. However, we know better and would rather that it didn't try to do this automatically. So, when asked if you want to test the sync reliability of this new configuration, select 'No'.

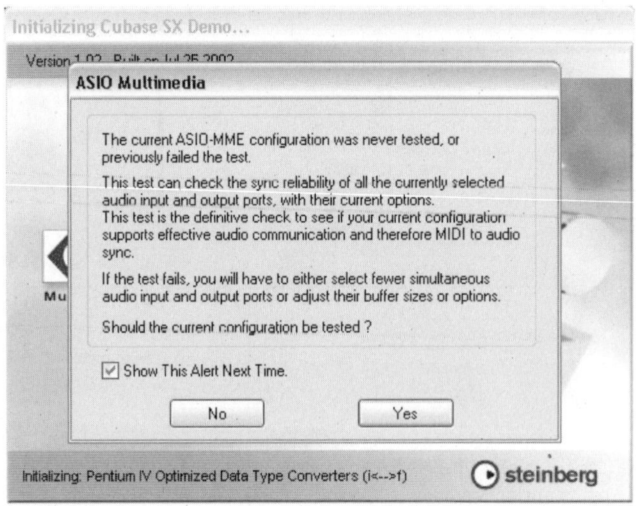

Figure 2.5
Cubase tests your soundcard. We want to ignore this.

Cubase will now open and present you with a very uninspiring blank gray/brown screen. Being a 'pro' bit of software, Cubase would never presume to suggest what you should do with it and so opts for showing you nothing. We will deal with that shortly. First we need to sort out the audio engine side of things so that we'll be able to play and record successfully.

Steinberg (the creators of Cubase) invented their own driver architecture, which is like a special method of communication between the software and the soundcard, to ensure the best possible performance. That architecture is called Audio Stream Input/Output or 'ASIO' (as-ee-oh). In order to achieve the best possible performance, your soundcard needs to have specific ASIO drivers written expressly for Cubase. Most simple soundcards, like those built onto the motherboard or those designed for games and multimedia, will not have these drivers. However, Cubase also supports simpler DirectX or MME multimedia drivers that will certainly do the job for our purposes. In another chapter, I'll talk about soundcards designed for music in great detail and highlight the sort of card you'd need if you wanted to take Cubase to another level.

Info

A soundcard with special 'ASIO' drivers will work best with Cubase.

For now, I'm going to assume that you have some kind of soundcard in your computer. If you usually play music or video on your computer and you have a pair of speakers or headphones attached, then it's a safe bet that you do.

In Cubase, from the 'Devices' menu, choose 'Device Setup'.

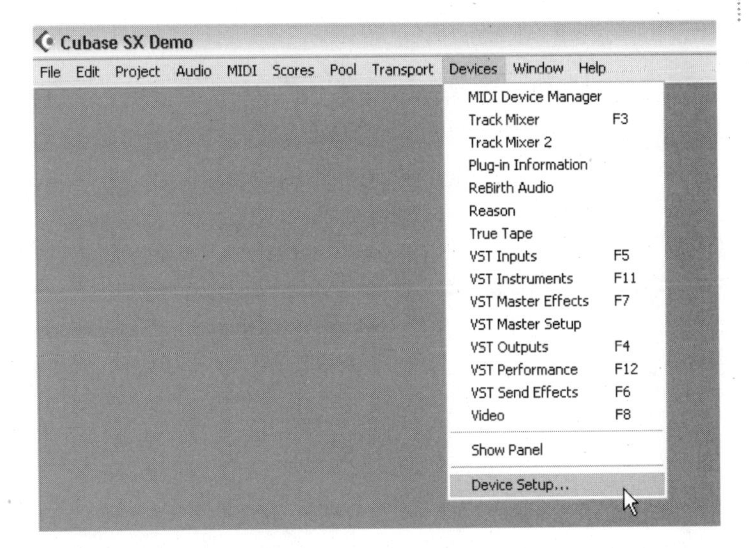

Figure 2.6
Selecting Device Setup from the Device menu.

When the Device Setup window appears, click on 'VST Multitrack' from the list on the left. On the right there's a drop-down menu labeled 'ASIO Driver'. By default it will read 'ASIO Multimedia Driver', which is the Windows basic soundcard

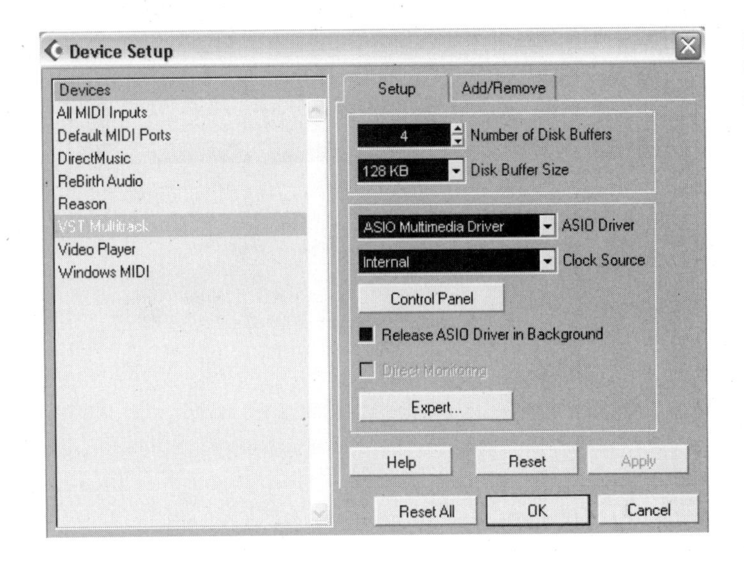

Figure 2.7
Device Setup – VST Multitrack, where the audio drivers are selected.

driver. Although this will work, there is a better driver we can choose that will make Cubase work much faster. Click on the menu and select 'ASIO DirectX Full Duplex Driver' (Figure 2.8).

If you happen to have a soundcard with a proper ASIO driver, as you can see I do, then it will be listed here. The Creative Labs Audigy does now have an ASIO driver, so if you have one, then select it. If not, then the DirectX one will do fine.

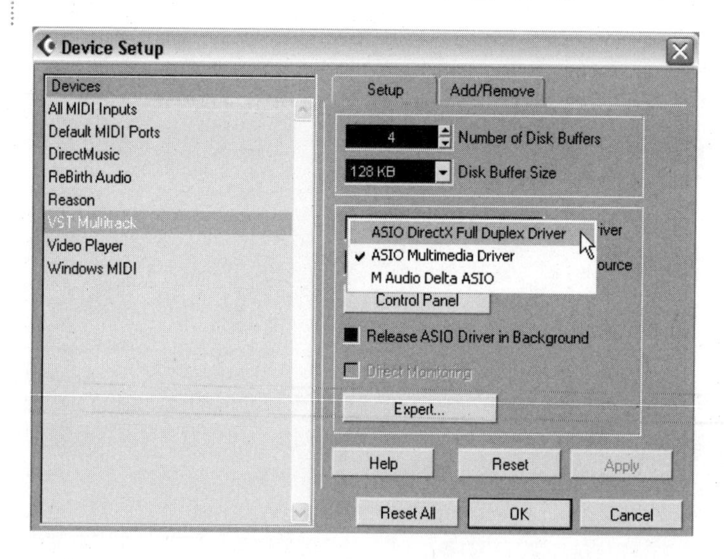

Figure 2.8
Device Setup – select driver.

Once selected, click on the 'Control Panel' button to make sure that you have selected the right soundcard, and not the modems wave driver or something as silly.

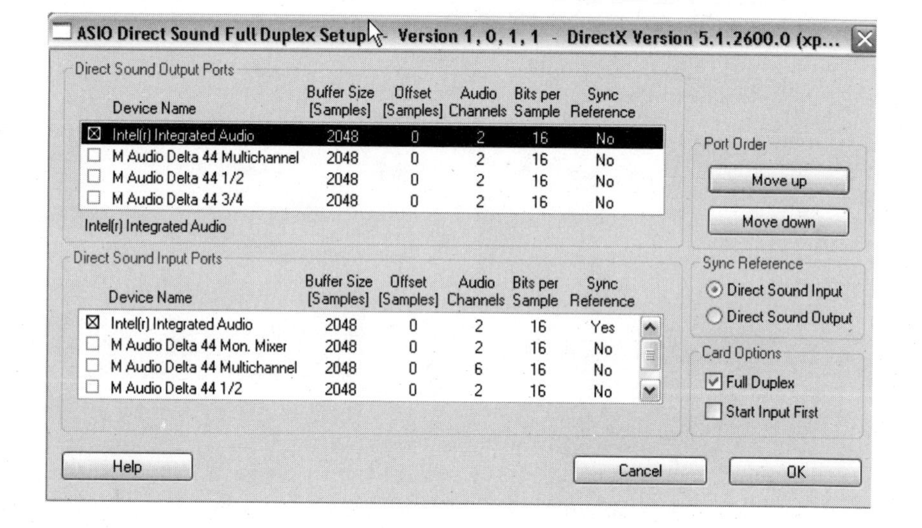

Figure 2.9
ASIO DirectSound Setup for soundcards without proper ASIO drivers.

For the purposes of this book, I'm going to be using the soundcard built onto my motherboard. A very simple Intel device, as shown in Figure 2.9. All you need to do here is make sure that only one box is checked for each input and output port and that it refers to your soundcard. If you have only one choice, then it must be right!

Click 'OK' in this window and in the Device Setup window to get us back to our gray/brown blank screen.

Now to make Cubase a little nicer to look at, we'll set the default 'Project' to open on startup – it will make things infinitely simpler for us. Click on the 'File' menu and select 'Preferences'. From the menu on the left, select 'User Interface'.

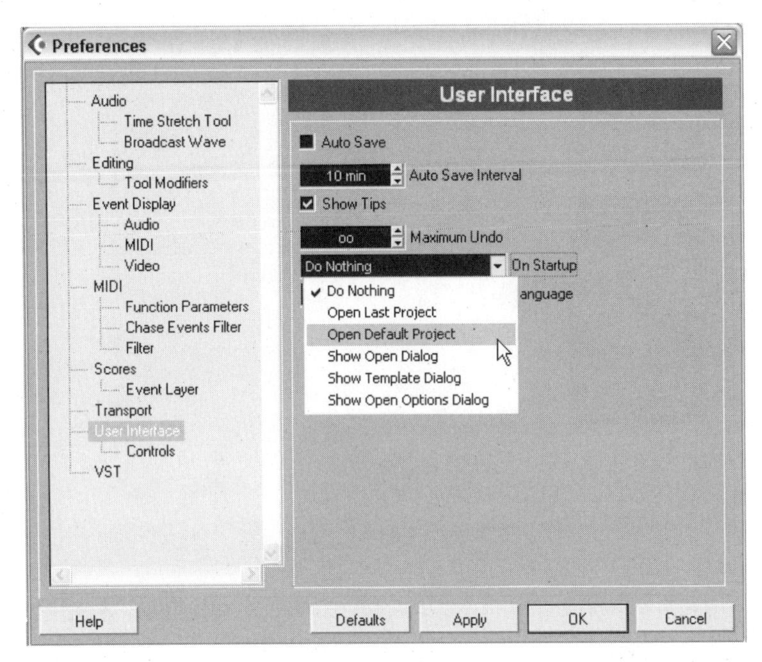

Figure 2.10
Setting the default project to open on startup in Cubase Preferences.

There's a drop-down menu called 'On Startup'; select 'Open Default Project' and click 'OK'. To see the effect, close Cubase. You can either click the red cross at the top-right of the Cubase window, or click on 'File' and then 'Exit'. If Cubase ever asks you if you want to save anything, click 'Don't Save', because you can't – this is a demo version! Open Cubase again, and this time it should look far more interesting.

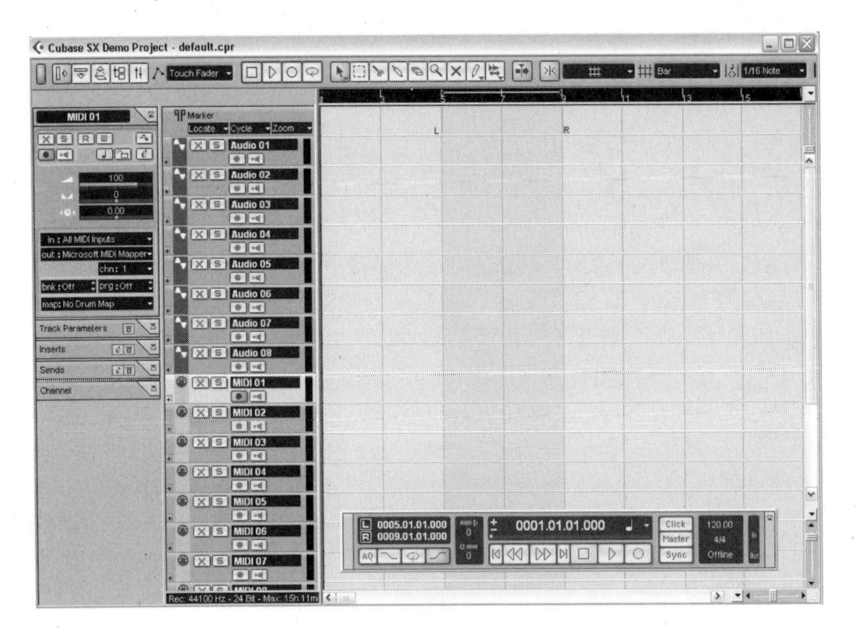

Figure 2.11
Cubase Default Project.

Setting up Amplitube

Make sure that Cubase is closed before installing Amplitube. In the Software folder, you'll find a folder called 'Amplitube'. Within that folder there's a file called 'Setup.exe'. Double-click it to install Amplitube.

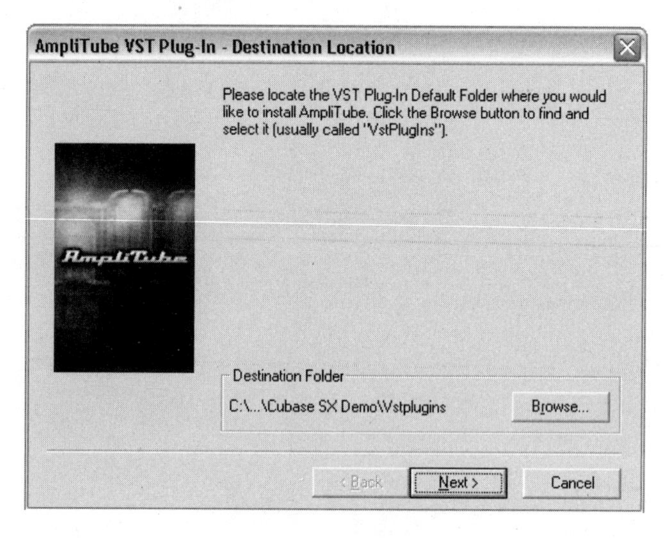

Figure 2.12
Installing Amplitube.

Now, Amplitube needs to be installed within the 'Vstplugins' folder, which is in the 'Cubase SX Demo' folder. Assuming you installed Cubase in its default directory, then it should find this automatically.

Once installed, please restart your computer before you do anything else.

Play the demo song

We've come so far, we've set everything up, and now we want to hear some music. Let's open up the Cubase demo project, which will give you a good idea of what it's all about.

Open Cubase and click on the 'File' menu and select 'Open...'. Now you should have copied the 'Cubase Projects' folder onto your hard drive. Look in that folder, and you'll see the aptly named 'Heaven and Hell' folder. Inside that, you'll find the Project we are after – 'Heaven_and_Hell.cpr'.

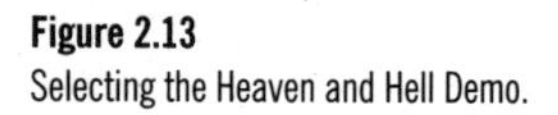

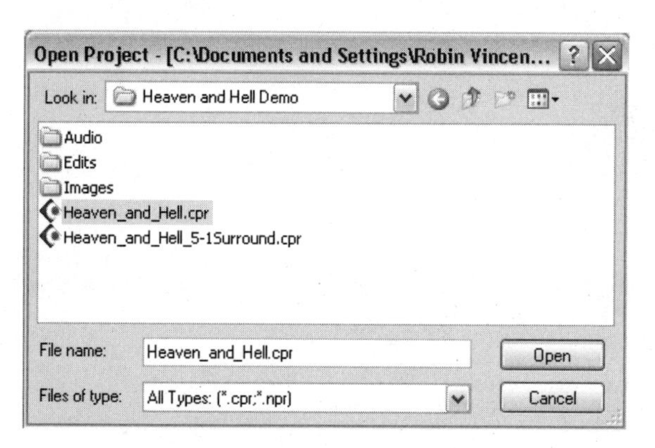

Figure 2.13
Selecting the Heaven and Hell Demo.

Select it and click 'Open'. The project will load up, and the first thing you'll see is an error message.

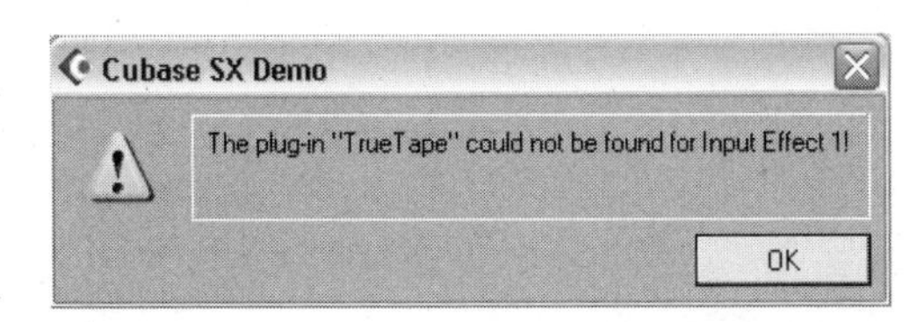

Figure 2.14
TrueTape error. Ignore this.

Don't worry. The 'TrueTape' plug-in is disabled in the demo version. It's a tape saturation plug-in that emulates the warmth of analog tape. Click 'OK' to continue. Unfortunately, this will happen every time you load up a project.

This is your first glimpse at what music looks like inside Cubase. To hear it play back, click the 'play' button on the transport bar or press your space bar.

Figure 2.15
Transport controls – play.

You'll see the song position marker move across the screen, and you'll hear various tracks play back as it reaches them. Pretty cool, eh? Doesn't sound very computerized, does it? Lots of live guitar in there, effects, and odd noises.

Figure 2.16
The Heaven and Hell demo.

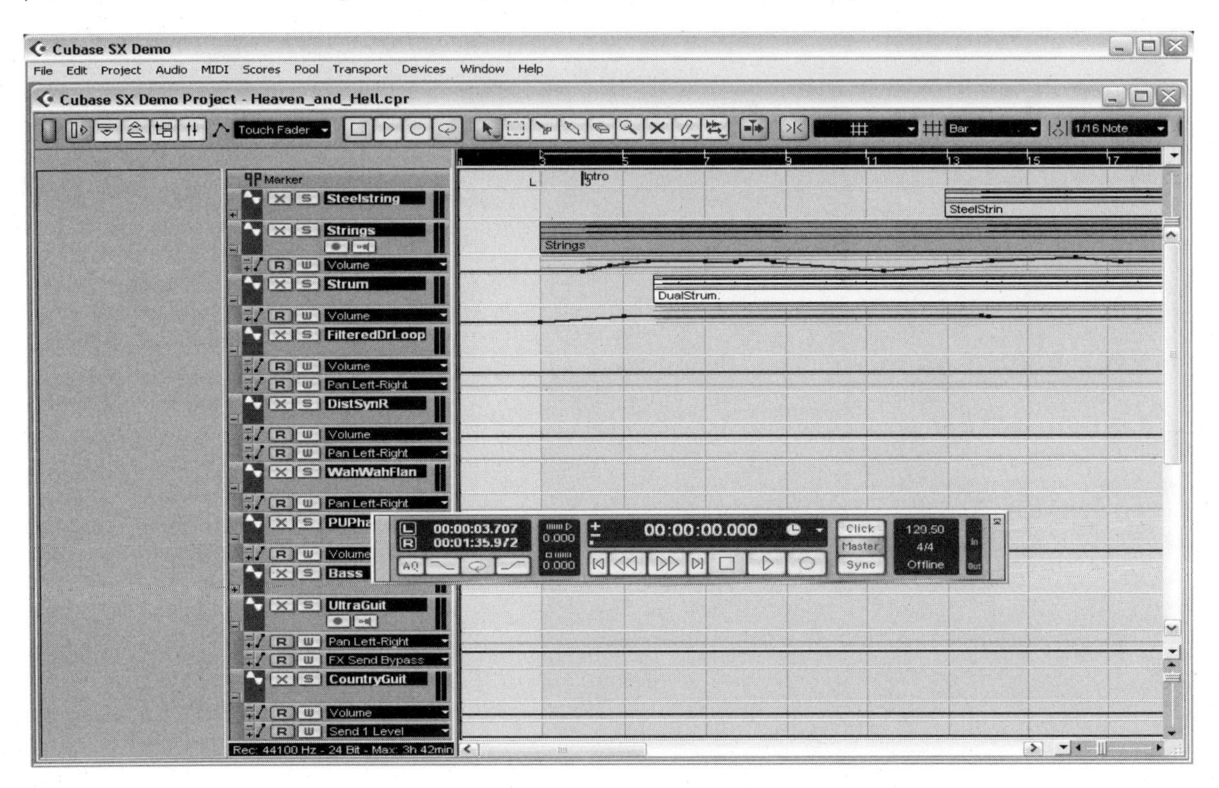

While the demo is playing, have a look around. You'll find scroll arrows on the edge of the windows and also zoom in/out drag handles that'll let you see more of the screen. If you press the F3 key on your keyboard, it will bring up the mixer. You can adjust the level of each track and its panning position just like a real mixer. It's even got a 4 band EQ on top of each channel. You may notice that some of the faders move around by themselves. This is 'automation', and we'll deal with that later.

Figure 2.17
Heaven and Hell Mixer, showing level faders and EQ.

Your computer is now sorted and ready to go. Everything is installed and you've got Cubase to play back its demo song. Feel free to spend some time messing around with it and investigating menus – you can't break anything because this is a demo version. If you find that Cubase stutters or runs really slowly, then check out the appendix on setting up Windows XP for music, which might help your computer cope with Cubase better. When you're ready, we'll move on to making your own music.

Let's record some guitar

Recording your guitar onto your 4-track machine is simply a matter of plugging it in and pressing record. With the computer, it's exactly the same, except now you're plugging your guitar into the soundcard and pressing record in a piece of software like Cubase.

Before I continue I just want to check that we all understand what I mean by 'soundcard'. A soundcard is a bunch of electronic components on a piece of printed circuit board (PCB), about the size of a CD case, the bottom edge of which is slotted into the motherboard inside your computer. This 'card' provides the necessary connections to allow 'sound' to flow into and out of the computer. It has at the very least an input for recording and an output for connecting speakers. Comparing this to the 4-track, you have an input where you plug in your guitar, and a monitor output that allows you to hear the playback. To take the comparison further, the computer's hard disk records in the same way the cassette does. The transport controls and level meters are to be found in Cubase.

So, Figure 3.1 shows the familiar basic functions of a 4-track, in this case a Tascam Porta 02:

Info

Motherboards, the huge chunk of PCB into which all the parts of the computer connect together, usually have a few slots for cards. These 'expansion' slots are called 'PCI' (Peripheral Component Interconnect) slots and can take things like modems, network cards, and video capture cards.

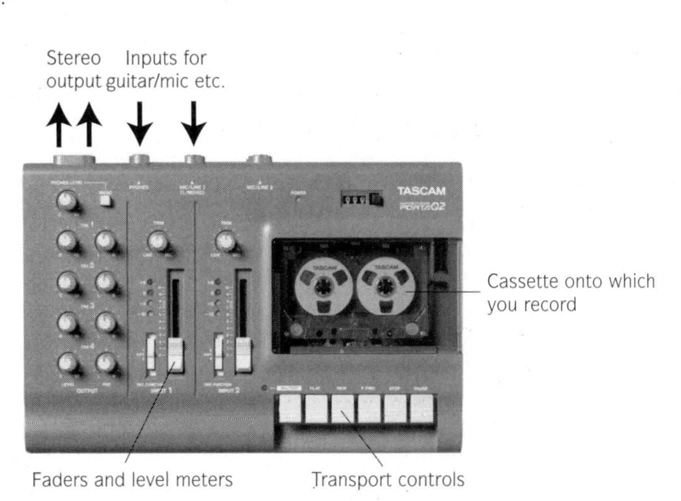

Figure 3.1
Ins and outs of the humble 4-track.

Figure 3.2
The recording parts of the computer.

Let's compare this to our computer:

Inside the computer we have a soundcard that provides the stereo output and the mic/line inputs for recording:

A hard disk onto which you record:

and software, which contains the transport controls, faders, and level controls.

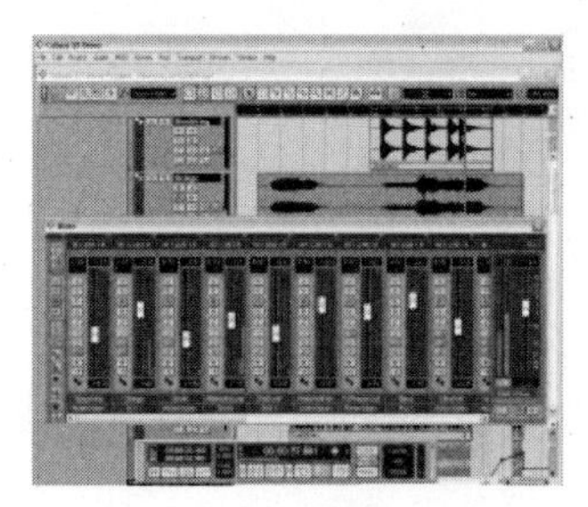

There's nothing mysterious about recording onto the computer. You are using different technology, but the tools are the same.

Plugging the guitar into the computer

This can be a little bit more difficult than your 4-track. A 4-track is designed for recording and so has the right input sockets for things like microphones and guitars. Your computer was probably purchased for surfing the Internet, writing the occasional letter, and playing games, so it might not have exactly the right inputs we need right away. I'll talk about getting the 'right' inputs in the next chapter, so for now we just want to keep things simple and make do with what we have.

You may have a flashy soundcard that has all sorts of inputs and exciting features, even a guitar input. If you do, then plug your guitar in and move onto the next section. If not, and I'm assuming that's most of us, then I'll try to describe how we go about it.

I have no way of knowing exactly what the connections on your soundcard are like; however, there is a bit of a convention regarding soundcards, so my illustration should be very similar to what you actually have.

Figure 3.3
Sockets on your average soundcard.

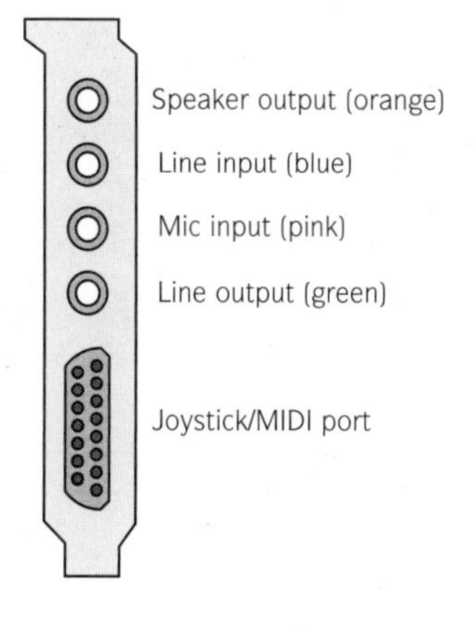

The colors are dictated by the PC99 specification, which is a document created by a bunch of people who said that it would be awfully nice if the computer manufacturers could adopt some kind of standard convention on things like soundcards. The result being that the majority of basic soundcards have their sockets colored as above. This isn't a law as such, it's just a recommendation, so yours may be colored differently or not at all. Please consult your soundcard's documentation to be sure.

There are two inputs available to us: one at 'Line Level' suitable for the output of something like a CD player or tape machine, and one at 'Microphone Level' suitable for simple microphones, like a telephony headset mic or the little mic that may have come with your soundcard. Neither of these are perfect for guitar, as a guitar signal is too weak for line level and a bit strong for a microphone. The best input to use is the line input, but to do this we will need some kind of preamp to get the guitar up to the right level. If you don't have a preamp then don't worry, we can get away with using the mic input for now and it'll sound pretty good, and we'll worry about the sound quality later on.

Throughout this book, I am making the outrageous assumption that you have either an electric guitar or an acoustic guitar with a pickup. If you have an acoustic guitar without a pickup, that's fine, just stick a microphone in front of it and the rest of the book will be pretty much applicable, I just won't be referring to a mic'ed guitar.

Figure 3.4
1/4-inch jack plug.

One of the biggest areas of confusion I come across is the naming and understanding of audio plugs and sockets. Ignoring my fear of being patronizing for a moment, you'll find that it really is simpler than you'd think. An audio cable consists of two wires, one which carries the signal and another which is earth. The connector at each end doesn't really matter provided that it keeps the two wires apart and can be plugged into something. So any plug you have on the end of your audio cable can be exchanged for any other audio plug. You can do this by getting your soldering iron out, or by using an adapter.

Figure 3.5
Mini-jack adapter.

Here's the plugs we'll be talking about: A 1/4-inch jack plug (Figure 3.4), like the one found on the end of a guitar cable. You can't plug the other end into the soundcard as it's too big. The soundcard uses the 3.5mm or 'mini-jack' size of socket, so you'll need an adapter (Figure 3.5).

Figure 3.6
Phono plugs.

If you want to plug straight in then this fits on the end of your guitar cable to bring the plug down to the right size. You can also get a cable made up with a normal jack on one end and a mini-jack on the other.

If you would like to use a preamp, then we have RCA Phono plugs (Figure 3.6) which usually come in pairs on the end of a stereo cable. Again, you can get an adapter to have phonos on one end and a mini-jack on the other, or you can buy a cable that's already made up that way. You'll also find that the color of these plugs varies with the red or white one often replaced by a black.

Using the line input

We need to get the guitar signal up to line level. You can do this with a number of things:

Guitar amp or preamp
Digital effects processor
Mixer
Your 4-track recorder.

The key to this is that they have an input for your guitar and a line level stereo output, so the output will be the right level to plug into the line input on the soundcard. It may seem weird using your 4-track like this, but essentially you are using it as a mixer and preamp.

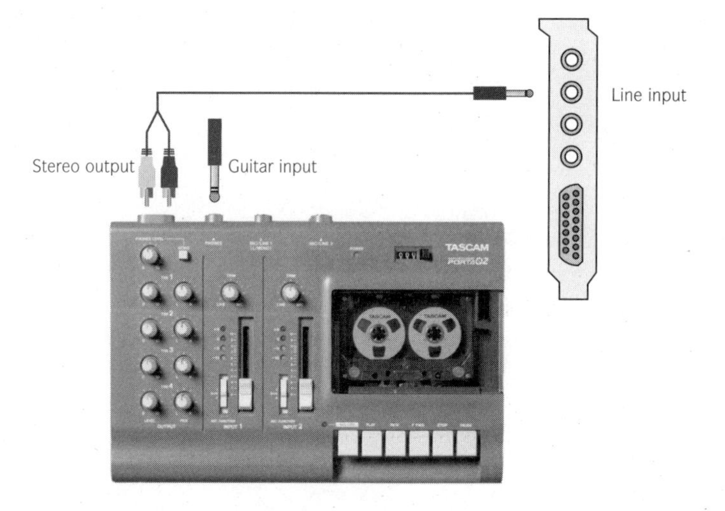

Figure 3.7
Connecting a 4-track to the soundcard.

So plug in your guitar and adjust the input trim to get a good level, then plug the stereo output into the line input on the soundcard. You could use a mixer, or preamp, or effects processor in exactly the same way. We'll talk more about connecting up your existing gear to the computer in a later chapter.

Using the mic input

If you've just got a guitar and a cable, then we'll do it the easy way and plug it straight into the mic socket. To do this, you'll need an adapter to turn the guitar jack cable into a mini-jack that'll fit into the hole.

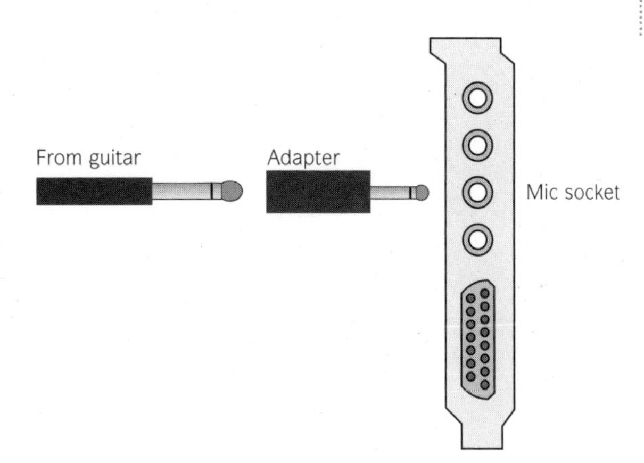

Figure 3.8
Adapting the guitar jack to the soundcard.

Getting the right signal

With the guitar plugged in, we need to make sure that the computer is receiving the signal. The best way to test this is with our virtual guitar tuner.

Open the tuner and pluck a string on your guitar.

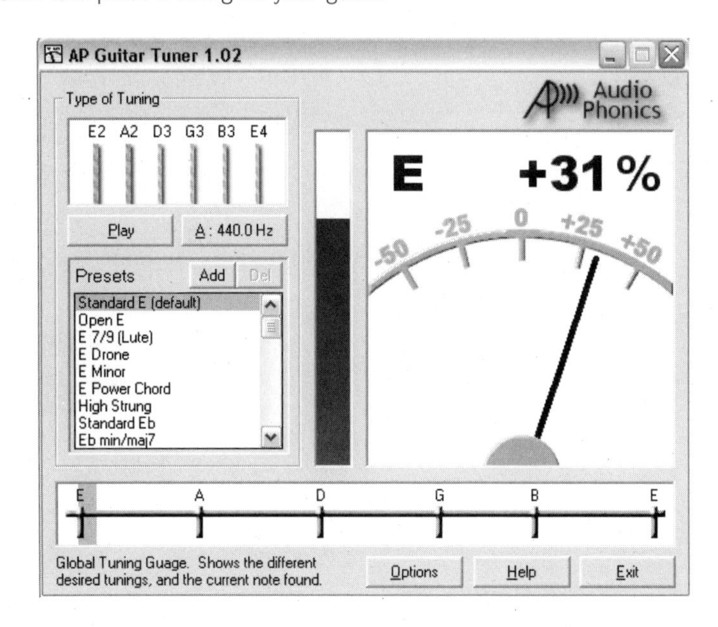

Figure 3.9
Tuner with input. A little bit sharp here, I think.

You should see the needle move and the bar in the middle shoot up into blue, and the tuner will display the current tuning of the string you plucked.

If you are not getting anything, then it will be one of two things. First click on the 'Options' button and then the 'Devices' tab, and check that your soundcard is selected as the recording device (Figure 3.10).

Second, we need to look at the soundcard's volume controls, as often the inputs are muted by default. Your soundcard may have its own software regarding the input and output controls. If so, then take a look at them and make sure that the input you are using is active and the fader is up. If, like me, you have just the Windows volume control, then open it up (Figure 3.11).

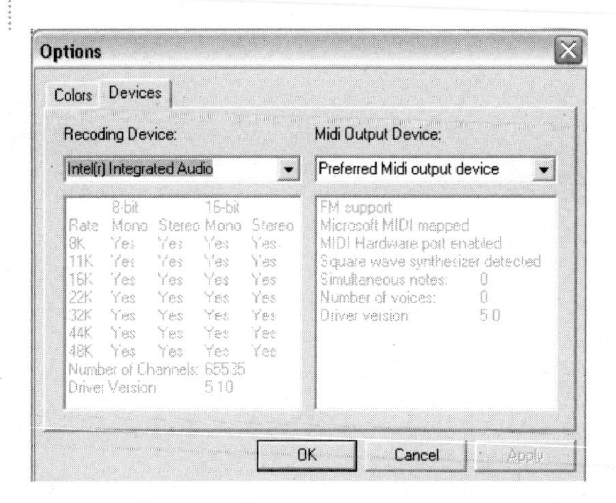

Figure 3.10
The Tuner's Device Setup Window.

If you can't find a fader for Line In or Microphone, then click the 'Options' menu and select 'Properties'. You should then be able to tick a box to show the input you need.

The sort of signal level we're after is so that the colored bar in the tuner almost reaches the top. Adjust the controls on your guitar and in the volume panel to get the right level. If you can't seem to get a very high level, don't worry for now, as long as you get a response in the tuner you'll be able to record your guitar.

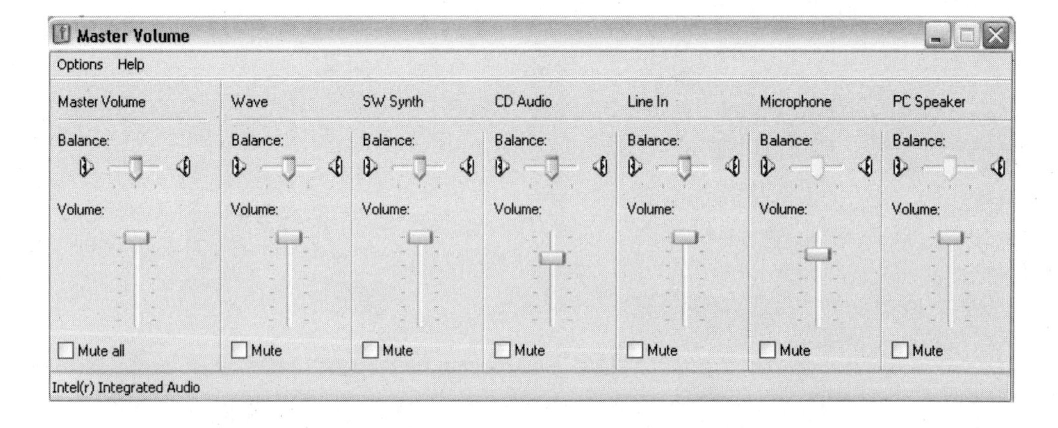

Figure 3.11
Windows soundcard mixer.

While you're here, tune up the guitar ready for recording.

Recording your first track

Once you're tuned, close the tuner and open up Cubase SX. So here we go, already three chapters in and finally we get to make some music!

Provided you've set the preferences that I mentioned earlier, Cubase should open with the default project. Let's point a few bits out:

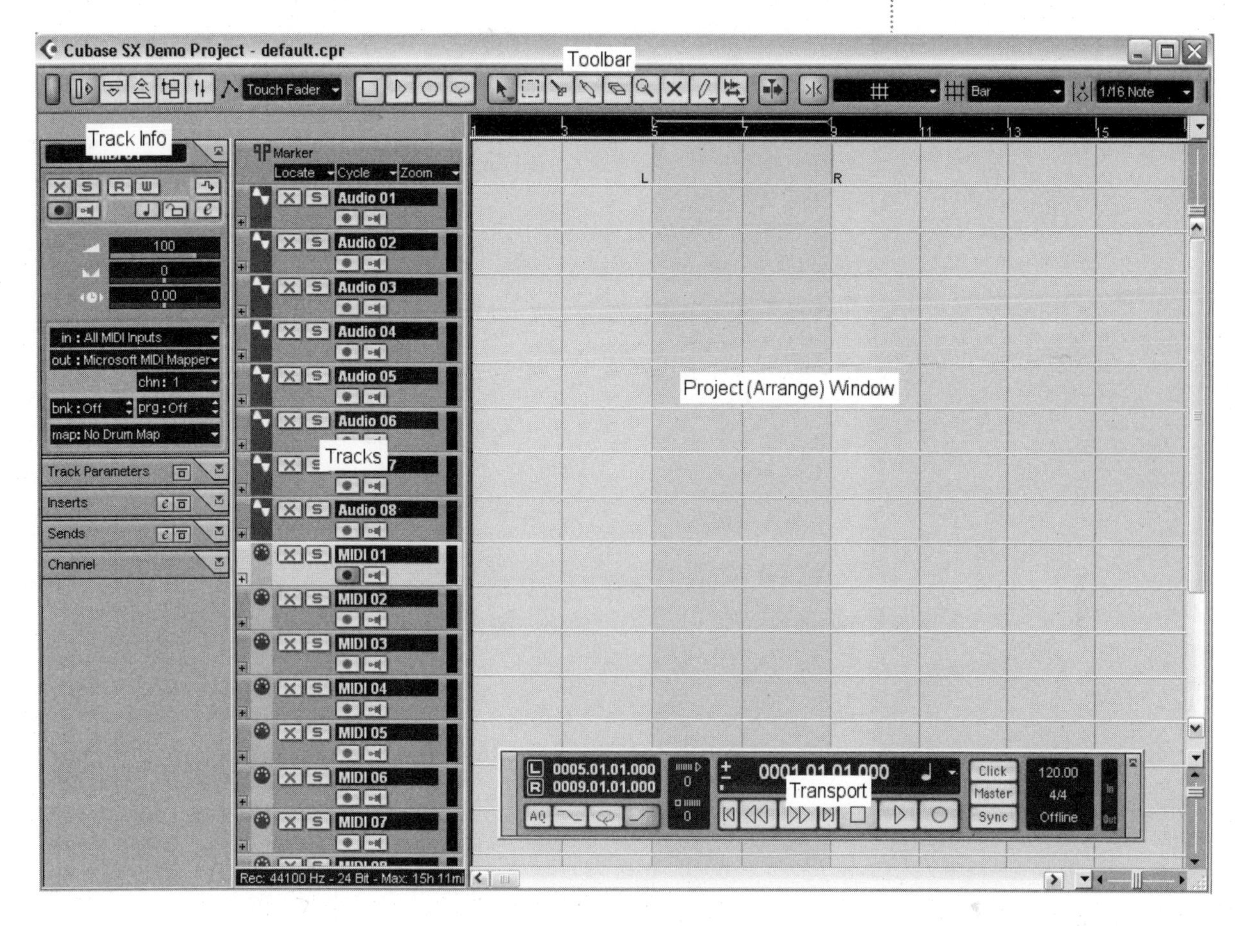

Figure 3.12
The various parts of Cubase.

Project Window – Also know as the 'arrange' window. This is where the recorded data, MIDI or audio, is displayed and can be arranged or moved around. It has a timeline at the top that can show seconds, frames, or bars and beats.
Tracks – Lists the currently available tracks. Here we have 8 audio tracks, with some MIDI tracks underneath. You can add and remove as many tracks of whatever type you like.
Track Info – This shows relevant information for the currently selected track. Inputs and outputs and routing, you can also see level and pan and insert effects here.
Toolbar – Various tools for selecting and editing blocks of recorded data, or 'events', in the Project Window.
Transport – Controls for Play, Stop, Record, tempo, metronome, etc.

Click on the first audio track labeled 'Audio 01'. The 'record enable' button will light up red, and if you now strum a few chords, you'll see a green level indicator next to the track light up. This shows your input signal. If you look at the track info column, you can check which input is being used ('in'), so if you're not getting a signal, try changing the input to see if that helps.

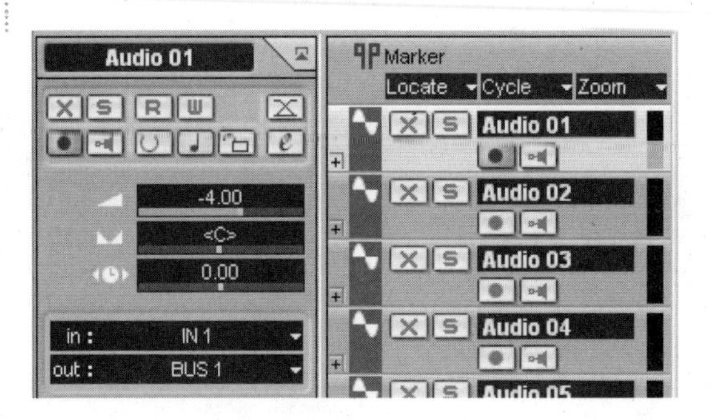

Figure 3.13
Getting an input into Cubase.

- Don't concern yourself with tempo or metronomes or anything at this stage, we just want to record.
- Locate the transport bar. If you can't see it, press the F2 button on your keyboard to bring it to the front.
- Make sure that the two 'punch in' and 'punch out' buttons on the left of the transport are not lit.

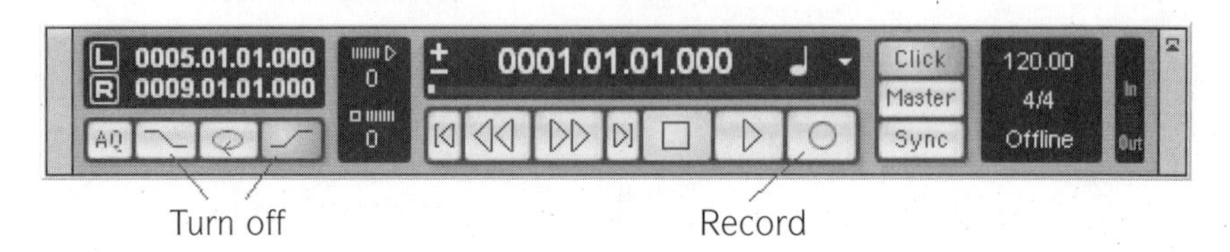

Figure 3.14
Transport bar – Record.

You've got the first track selected, you're seeing a signal indication, now press the record button and play from deep within your soul – or strum a few chords if you like.

In Cubase, as you play you'll be able to see stuff emerging behind the song position line. Play for as long as you like and click the stop button to er... stop – or press the space bar.

Congratulations, you've made your first digital recording onto a computer! I know what you're thinking: 'So far, so 4-track'. There's nothing new going on yet; in fact, you probably feel it's all been a bit complicated so far. Sure, it's true that setting it all up is a bit of a hassle, but once it's set, you won't have to do it again, just launch the software and off you go. So now that we've recorded our first track, I'll begin to sneak in various simple features that'll make your 4-track look as obsolete as a wax cylinder.

> **Info**
>
> It's true that setting it all up is a bit of a hassle, but once it's set, you won't have to do it again.

Press the stop button again to return the song to the beginning and press Play to hear yourself back. Did you notice how long it took to rewind itself back to the beginning? No time at all! It was instant. In fact, by clicking in the timeline at the top, you can start playback from wherever you like, instantly. You can even do this while it's playing. No more time wasted waiting for tape to rewind – how cool is that?

If you don't hear anything on playback, make sure the monitor button on the audio track is *not* lit. It looks like a little speaker next to the record enable button.

Let's have a closer look at what you recorded.

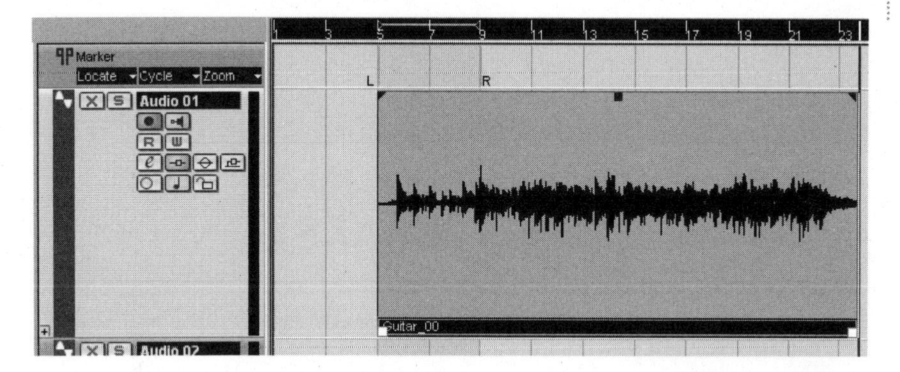

Figure 3.15
Closeup of recorded audio.

If you move your mouse to the bottom of the track in the track column, onto the line between the first and second tracks, the cursor turns into an up/down arrow. If you click and drag downward, you'll be able to enlarge the track. Within the 'event' (recorded section) you'll see a black mess of stuff. This is a graphical representation of the audio you recorded. What it shows is amplitude, or volume, over time. It's the same thing as seeing a sine wave on an oscilloscope at school. In fact, audio files on a computer are known as 'Wave' files for the reason that they are essentially a bunch of sine waves. You can see this much clearer by zooming into the event. There's a slider in the bottom right of the screen, and if you pull it to the right it'll zoom in.

Multitrack recording and playing along with yourself

Let's record another track. Click on the second track labelled 'Audio 02'. Now you may not be able to see a level right away, and this is because track two is set to input 2. A soundcard's inputs are usually stereo, which actually means two channels, left and right. If you are using the microphone input straight from guitar, then your input is in mono, just one channel. Cubase sees the input as two distinct channels, so if your input is mono, then it'll only appear on input 1, not input 2. So, to get our guitar to record onto track 2, we need to change the input allocation to 'Input 1' (or whatever input enabled you to record last time) in the track info column.

Before we record the second track, we can play along with the first track to get a bit of practice in. What would be useful would be to get the first track to play back continuously so we don't have to take our hands off the guitar to click stop, rewind, and play again. Click on the event you recorded on the first track and then press the 'p' key on your keyboard. You'll see that a blue line has appeared above the event in the timeline, and two green lines marked 'L' and 'R' have appeared at the beginning and end. The L and R are left and right markers, and we can loop playback between these two markers by pressing the loop button on the transport bar (Figure 3.16).

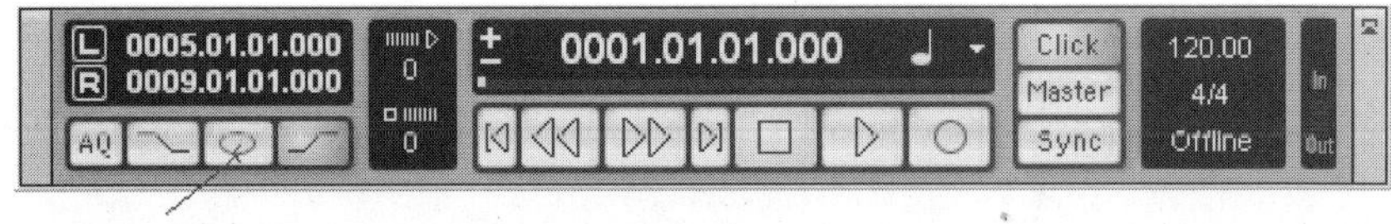

Figure 3.16
Transport bar – loop on/off.

Once you're ready, make sure the second track is selected, hit the record button, and play like the ghost of Hendrix – or strum a few more chords if you like.

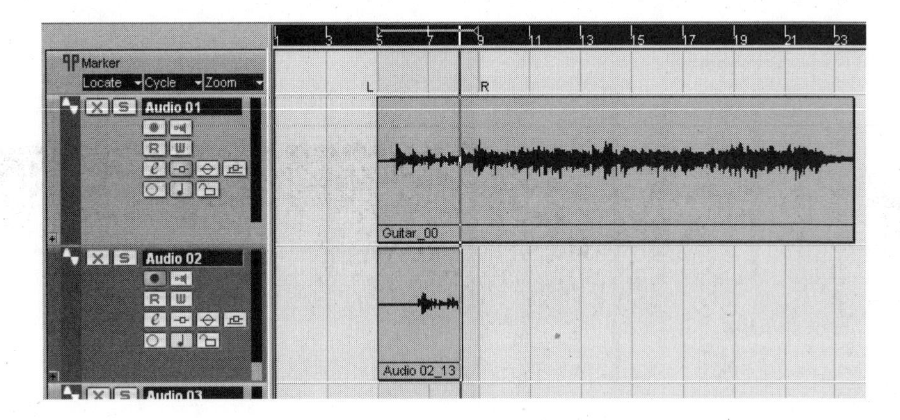

Figure 3.17
Recording a second track.

> **Info**
>
> With Cubase's 'Undo' feature, if you accidentally delete something you can always bring it back.

Press 'stop' when you're done, 'stop' again to rewind to the beginning, and 'play' to hear yourself. Well if it's anything like I've just done then it's a load of inept rubbish. Fortunately, we don't have to settle for the first take. If you click on the Edit menu and click 'Undo record', it'll remove your last effort and allow you to try it again. Alternatively, you can click on an event and press 'delete', and it's gone.

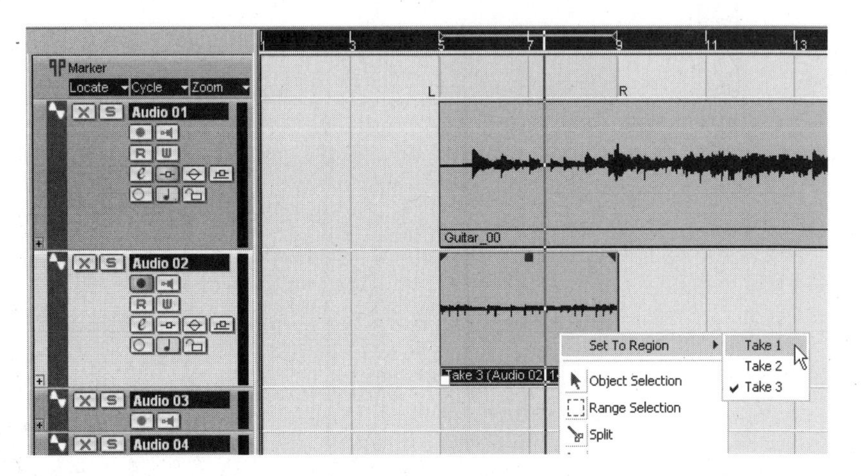

Figure 3.18
Selecting different takes.

Talking of 'takes', one cool feature of Cubase worth pointing out at this point is its ability to do multiple takes while loop recording. To see what I mean, set up your first track looping again, either the whole event or you can move the ends of the blue line to loop a smaller part. Hit record and play your guitar. Each time it loops back, it will record a separate take. Then you can choose which take you want to hear by right-clicking on the new event and selecting it from the menu.

All the takes you do will remain intact, so even if you come back to the project at a later stage, you still have all the various takes available to you.

If you want, you can now select track 3 and record another track alongside, then another and so on for as many tracks as you want. If you need to add tracks to the project, click the 'Project' menu and select 'Add track' and the type of track you wish to add. I was doing some performance testing recently and I quite happily got over 180 audio tracks out of Cubase on a regular Pentium 4-based desktop PC. It could have handled more, but if I had to think up another track I probably would have killed myself!

Getting the right hardware

Most 4-tracks let you record up to four inputs at once, so you could record, for instance, two guitars, vocals, and harmony all at the same time. It would be nice if we could do the same with the computer, but so far our standard soundcard only has a stereo input and at best this could be two separate inputs.

The sound quality of what you've recorded so far may not be that inspiring, and what's all this business with mini-jack connectors – hardly professional now is it? And then there was this talk of ASIO drivers to get the best out of Cubase – how do we get some of them?

Well, we now need to start looking at soundcards that are designed for music recording and production. There's a whole industry of recording soundcards above and beyond even the best Sound Blaster card Creative Labs can offer. I'm talking about pristine studio recording quality and all the inputs and outputs you could possibly need.

What's the right soundcard for you? A question I get asked a lot. The simple answer is the one that has the features you need to do your recording.

- Guitar inputs? No problem.
- Mic preamps? Sure, how about eight in a row?
- Multiple inputs? At last count, you can get 72 individual inputs simultaneously into Cubase.
- Professional 24bit 96kHz quality? Pretty much as standard these days.

It's exactly the same as going out to buy yourself a new multitrack recorder. You choose the one that fits your requirements and your budget. With a soundcard it's the same.

What I think I should do is explain a bit about how soundcards work and what they do so that you'll be able to make a more informed choice when it comes to choosing one.

Talking about soundcards

I am not going to go into terrible detail about this as it's all dreadfully dull and there are plenty of books out there that will delve into the depths if you feel so inclined. What I'll do is give you the gist of what it's all about so that you can get by at dinner parties.

Soundcards are mostly about dealing with audio, sound, stuff you can hear, and about recording it and playing it back. Many soundcards also have a MIDI (Musical Instrument Digital Interface) part consisting of either just an interface for connecting to other MIDI devices like keyboards and synths and such, or a little MIDI synth as well. We're not going to worry about the MIDI side of things just yet, so let's concentrate on the audio.

What a soundcard does when recording is to 'digitize' or convert sound into data and store it on your hard drive. On playback the soundcard converts that data back into analog sound that we can hear through our speakers. There are two, very aptly named components on a soundcard that handle all this digitizing/un-digitizing business, which are called 'Converters'.

When recording, the soundcard uses an Analog-to-Digital converter, or ADC, and on playback it uses a Digital-to-Analog converter, or DAC. So, when you hear people talking about the quality of their soundcard's converters, it's these two components that they are talking about.

The process of digital recording, taking sound through an ADC is known as 'sampling'. Sampling is a word that gets thrown around quite a bit and is often applied to big chunks of external gear called 'Samplers' usually made by Akai or Emu. Samplers are digital boxes that have ADCs through which you can 'sample' bits of sound. These 'samples' are stored in RAM (memory) and can be played back instantly from a keyboard connected to the sampler. With a soundcard in a computer, the same conversion is going on, but the samples are stored (or recorded) onto the hard drive and are then played back in software, like pressing play on tape. It's simply the process of digitizing sound through an ADC that's called 'sampling', so there's no need to get confused by it regardless of what it's applied to.

With sampling there are two important factors – bit depth and sample rate. These two factors determine the accuracy (or 'quality' if you like) of the recording. You've probably heard people talk about sample rates and bit rates; for instance, you're probably aware that a CD is recorded with 16 bits at 44.1kHz, even if you don't know what that means. What it really means is probably quite complicated, and you're probably wondering why you should care; well, these numbers will keep cropping up when recording with a computer and, more importantly, have an awful lot to do with your decision on which soundcard you should buy. So here's my stab at a simple and relatively accurate explanation.

Sound in air, analog sound, is a bunch of vibrations that we describe as sine waves of certain frequencies. We measure these frequencies in cycles-per-second or Hertz (Hz), after some guy who first thought it up, and this denotes the pitch. For instance, the note 'A' to which we tune our guitars has a frequency of 440Hz – the sine wave cycles at 440 times per second.

Got that OK? When this sound is sampled, it's converted into digital audio. Now, a computer can only deal with whole numbers and cannot understand the continuingly varying curves of a sine wave, so when it looks at, or 'samples', the sine wave, it has to give it a value for that moment in time. There can be no fractions, no half values: it has to deal with the ones and zeros of binary, so it has to give it a whole number value.

Figure 4.1
Analog sound sampled into digital audio by the soundcard.

The bit depth (or bit rate) specifies the range of values that the computer can use to describe the sine wave at a particular moment in time. The number of times a second the computer looks at (samples) the sine wave is specified by the 'sampling rate', measured, as with frequency, in cycles per second or Hertz (Hz).

So, it's logical to assume then that the higher the bit rate, the more values the computer has to describe the sine wave and so the more accurate the conversion will be. Similarly it's also logical to assume that the more times the sine wave is sampled per second, the more accurate it will be.

Imagine trying to draw a half circle by joining up dots on a page with straight lines.

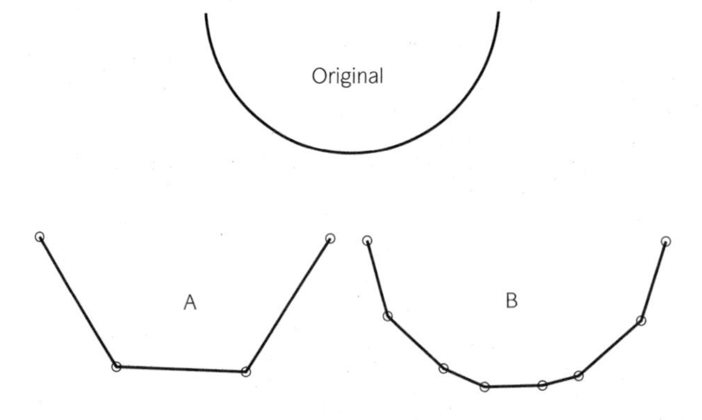

Figure 4.2
Drawing a curve by joining dots.

You can see straight away that the more dots you have, the more accurate your representation of a curve. So you should be able to see that the more bits you have available and the more times you sample per second, the more accurate the representation of our sine wave will be over time.

So, what sort of numbers are we talking about? If we look again at our example of what a CD is recorded at, also known as 'CD Quality' it's 16-bit and 44.1kHz. A 'bit' is a binary value, so 16 bits is not 16 values, it's 2 to the power of 16, which equals 65,536 actual values. 44.1kHz means that the audio is being sampled at 44,100 times per second. This level, or 'resolution' of bit and sample rate, as we know from listening to CDs, produces a pretty good recording.

The resolution that everyone is aiming for at the moment is 24-bit at 96kHz; that's 16,777,216 possible values sampled at 96,000 times per second. After that, the next milestone, reported to be called 'DVD-Audio quality', is 32-bit at 192kHz, but I wouldn't worry about that any time soon.

But if CD quality sounds fabulous, why would we need to go any further? Well, one of the criticisms laid on digital recording is its tendency to sound 'cold' or slightly metallic or just plain 'digital'. This is down to the computer only being able to handle whole numbers. For instance, if a sound is sampled and its value is found to be 502.6, the computer has to move the value to the nearest whole number – 503, so a certain amount of 'error correction' is going on. Remember that regardless of the number of dots, our curve is still made up of straight lines. It's this error correction that makes digital recording sound, well, digital. Increasing the bit depth and sample rate make this error correction so small that you really cannot tell the difference between a digital recording and the real thing. This is a really simplistic explanation and there are all sorts of magical technological wizardry that goes on with filters and stuff that smoothes it out somewhat, but it is essentially true.

However, can we really tell the difference between a 16-bit recording and a 24-bit recording? What about between a recording made with a sampling rate of 44.1kHz and 96kHz? To be honest, after all the years of going to, and playing at, very loud live gigs, my ears are so traumatized that I really struggle to appreciate the benefit. There's another fly in the ointment that causes lots of arguments among the elite Hi-fi buffs which is the mathematical theorem of the extraordinarily named 'Nyquist', who proved that to reproduce any sine wave with complete accuracy, you only need to sample it twice during its cycle. So, to accurately reproduce our 440Hz 'A' pitch, we'd only need a sampling rate of 880Hz. Therefore, in order to accurately sample every frequency within our hearing range – arguably up to 20kHz, we only need a sampling rate of 40kHz. 44.1kHz was chosen for exactly this reason, and the extra was bolted on to give us a bit of leeway. So, you could say that using a sample rate of 96kHz gives us no advantage whatsoever. This will be argued about forever, with people talking about the effect of frequencies outside our hearing range reflecting onto ones we can hear, and the accuracy of the sampling clock in the first place and all sorts of other nonsense. Ultimately, it's up to what you can hear – or not. Still, everyone likes the idea of something being 'better', even if you can't really hear it.

Increasing the bit depth, on the other hand, does have a positive effect on the quality of recording. The increased number of values available does indeed seem to make digital recordings sound 'warmer'. More importantly than that, it does have one definite advantage for us home recordists and that's its ability to do 16-bit recordings much better than if we recorded at 16-bit in the first place. 16-bit is generally our aim, as, at the end of the day, we want to get our music onto CD. Recording at 24-bit sounds much better when dropped down to 16 bits for CD, than recording straight at 16-bit. Here's why:

Bit rate is essentially measuring the amplitude, or volume, of the sine wave. In order to fill all 16 bits available to us, we need to record at the highest possible level before distortion. Now, if you hit distortion when recording digitally, the sound is not like that nice overdriven tape distortion, it's nasty digital noise, so when recording we do not want to peak into the red at any stage. So, when recording digitally we tend to shy away a little from the maximum, so really we'll probably only fill up 12-14 bits. If we record in 24 bits, then the peak point is so much higher that even if we under-record a little, we're still easily filling at least 16 bits. When we come to convert down, or 'dither' to 16-bit from 24-bit, all 16 bits are used to their full potential. A useful analogy would be that of an LED meter, like one you

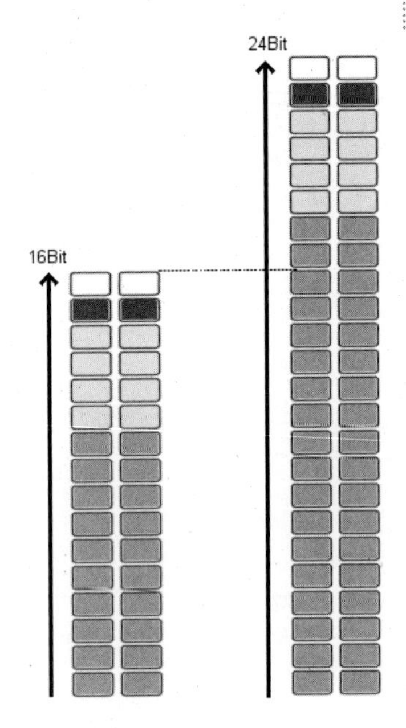

Figure 4.3
Bit depth seen as level LEDs.

might use to measure the input level into the computer. The one on the left shows the input using 16 bits and not quite using them. The one on the right shows input using 24 bits and you can clearly see how much more headroom you have for your recording.
It's not a completely accurate explanation of what's going on, but I hope it's helpful to you and not too mind-numbing.

One more factor involved in the question of resolution is file size. If you double the sample rate, then you've doubled the amount of values generated within a second, and so doubled the amount of data stored on the hard drive. Recording in 16-bit 44.1kHz uses up about 5MB per minute per track, so that's 10MB per minute for stereo and 40MB per minute for 8-track recording. Recording in 24-bit 96kHz uses up about 3 times that amount. Also the computer has to work harder in processing all the extra data, so these are things to consider.

Dealing with latency

Now there's a term you've probably heard, and it always seems to refer to some sort of problem. 'Low Latency' is a term that's generally considered to be a good thing – but what does it all mean?

Latency, in a nutshell, is the amount of time it takes for the computer, and the soundcard, to process the audio going through it. It's the time between pressing 'Play' in Cubase and the audio actually playing back. It's the time between plucking your guitar string and hearing the sound back monitored through Cubase (or any other software). Latency is present in all computer systems, as nothing can happen instantaneously, and there comes a point at which this latency becomes a noticeable 'lag'. We experience latency as a 'delay' between what we do and what we hear – it's like a response time.

Now, latency only causes trouble in two areas of computer music:

Monitoring an input signal (your guitar) through software

This never used to be a problem because it never occurred to anyone to try to monitor the input through the software – that's what your mixer was for. You monitor your guitar before it hits the computer. However, the software has gotten so good nowadays that you can now use software effects on inputs and monitor the whole thing through the computer. If there's a noticeable delay between playing your guitar and hearing it, then this is definitely a problem and renders monitoring through the software useless.

Software synths

This is where we first really became aware of latency. When soft synths arrived, we thought 'brilliant, all these cool sounds at my fingertips' only to find that when we pressed a note on our keyboard, we didn't hear the sound until about half a second later.

The issues that latency creates are completely solved by using a soundcard with good, 'low latency' drivers. A soundcard where the latency is so low it's no longer noticeable and so no longer matters. People go on and on about latency figures and buffer sizes, but at the end of the day, if you can't hear it then it doesn't matter. This is one of those things that these ASIO drivers I mentioned earlier provide with Cubase.

You may not have encountered latency in any form yet, but if you have a normal soundcard, without ASIO drivers, then you will encounter it in the next chapter when we talk about using effects.

I know this all sounds awful right now, and that latency is going to screw up your whole idea about using a computer for music. Don't worry, we've been working around it for years and it certainly doesn't have to be a problem. Shortly I'll be talking about getting the 'right' hardware so that it removes the issue of latency for good, but first I want to explain what causes latency in computer recording so that you'll understand how to minimize it.

The latency time is dictated by the soundcard's drivers. The drivers use a chunk of memory, called a 'buffer', which fills up with audio data for processing and is then released. The size of this buffer determines how long it takes for the audio to get into and out of the computer. So, the bigger the buffer, the longer it takes to fill, which results in a longer latency. You could see the buffer as a little bucket, getting filled by a stream of audio data. While the data is in the buffer, the computer, or the CPU, can process it, for example applying effects, level changes, or routing it to the hard drive. So the CPU essentially looks into the bucket and sorts out everything that's in there. If the buffer is large, then the CPU has loads of time to process it and idles along twiddling its silicon thumbs. If the buffer is small, then the CPU has to work up a sweat processing the audio into a nice constant stream.

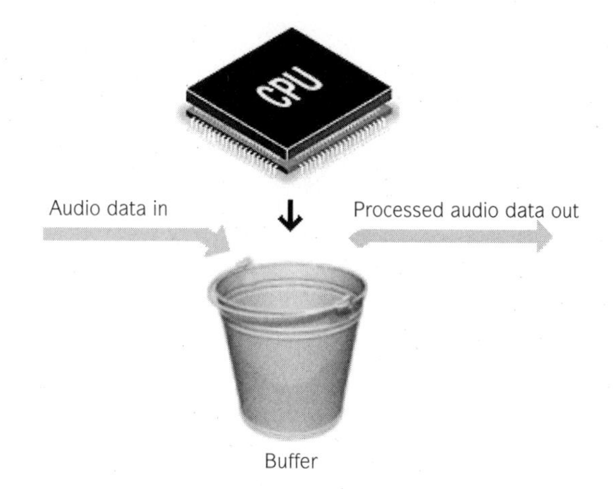

Figure 4.4
Audio flowing through the soundcard's buffer.

If the buffer is too small, then the CPU can't cope with the workload and the output ends up full of glitches, clicks, and pops. So, you can see that the power of your CPU also has a bearing on all this. Buffer size can be changed within Cubase, by how much depends on the soundcards drivers.

Before Windows XP, the standard soundcard drivers were called MME (Microsoft Multimedia Extensions) drivers, and these were designed for multimedia applications, like playing back little sounds in Windows, games, and the like, and were designed to work with pretty much any power of computer. The idea of doing studio recording and monitoring through the computer had never occurred to them, and consequently the buffers were huge to ensure it all worked ok. Using MME drivers with Cubase would usually produce a latency of about three-quarters of a second. Imagine playing your guitar and not hearing the sound until nearly a second later! Some delay stomp boxes don't have delay times as long as that.

With Windows XP, Microsoft brought along new audio technology called WDM (Windows Driver Model), which is much faster than the MME drivers and is capable of getting latency down to unnoticeable levels with the 'right' soundcard and the 'right' software.

It was the demand for lower latency and better performance that prompted Steinberg to develop their ASIO protocol which enabled soundcard manufacturers to write drivers that bypassed Windows all together and dealt directly with the software. This finally gave musicians the ability to use soft synths and monitor through software without any noticeable delay whatsoever – hurrah!

So, now that I've filled your heads with all this knowledge about buffer sizes and buckets, is there anything we can actually do about it right now with our current soundcard? Yes there is, a little. In the next chapter, we're dealing with using effects in Cubase, and we'll look at how good your soundcard drivers are and how we can go about getting the best out of them.

The 'right' hardware

I keep mentioning getting the 'right' hardware as if to assume that what you already have is rubbish. I don't really mean that, but what I do mean to do is show you that there is a huge difference between the quality of soundcards, and, the speed and performance of the drivers that come with them.

Not all soundcards are the same. When I talked earlier about converters (ADC/DAC), the quality of those chips can vary enormously, so then can the other circuitry, and the connectors and sockets into which you plug your guitar. You probably already know that there is a difference between a guitar lead and really good guitar lead, between a cheap guitar amp and a nice Vox or Marshall. Soundcards are no different.

Soundcard manufacturers often play a numbers game, throwing around numbers such as '24/96', '16', '32', '64' all popular numbers splashed across their boxes, but they are not always as they appear. '24/96' we now know refers to 24-bit 96kHz sampling, but is it for recording or just for playback? The Creative Labs Audigy card fooled many with its claims of being 24-bit capable, and indeed it is, but only on playback. It still records in 16-bit. Thankfully they have sorted this out with the version 2.

A few years ago, Creative brought out the Sound Blaster 16, which was their first 16-bit card. They then followed it up with the AWE 32, which leads you to believe it was a 32-bit card when in fact the 32 refers to the number of voices its on-board synth can handle. Many other manufacturers do the same sort of thing. Make sure you read the small print on the back of the box.

As we all strive to get the best quality stuff we can, we still find that professional, high-end converters running at 16-bit can sound better than the 24-bit converters we find on more entry-level soundcards. Unfortunately, as with most things in life, you get what you pay for.

This, however, doesn't mean that you have to spend loads of money getting a really posh soundcard, you just need to consider its importance in the recording chain. We now know that a 24-bit soundcard will potentially give better quality recordings than a 16-bit one, and we also know that good drivers make the difference between recording onto the computer and having an entire software studio at your fingertips. The soundcard is the key to the computer-based studio. It provides the inputs and outputs you connect your gear to, it does the digital conversion on the audio, and it dictates the speed and performance of your music software.

In a later chapter, I'll do a roundup of good quality soundcards that you might want to consider and how you go about choosing one for yourself.

Sounds expensive? Well, roughly I would say that for a decent recording soundcard, you would need to be looking at over $150 – not too bad is it? Considering that you'd probably spend $650 on a cassette-based 4-track, over a thousand on a hard disk recorder, and maybe a thousand on your computer in the first place. If it's the most important part of your setup, then it's worth investing in.

Virtual effects processing

Info

Currently there are thousands of plug-ins available out there from simple things like chorus through to filters, compressors, distortions, overdrives, delays, and the lushest of reverbs. There's also stranger effects like bit crushers, metalizers, quad filters, pitch wranglers, amp modelers, spectrographic enhancers; in fact, pretty much anything you can think of – and many more that you can't.

Back to the fun stuff. No more theory: the rest of the book is about practical application, the first of which is using software effects. These are really cool and you'll be very impressed, I promise.

Talking about plug-ins

Virtual effects are one of the wonders of recording software. They take your software studio far beyond the capabilities of the humble 4-track and enable you to create finished products on your computer rather than just demos. Of course, you may have an effects box already, or even a digital recorder with effects built in. However, with the open architecture of recording software, there are new virtual effects appearing all the time, and many of them are free.

Virtual effects appear in your software as 'Plug-ins'. This simply means that they plug into your recording software and run within it. They are not a separate pro-

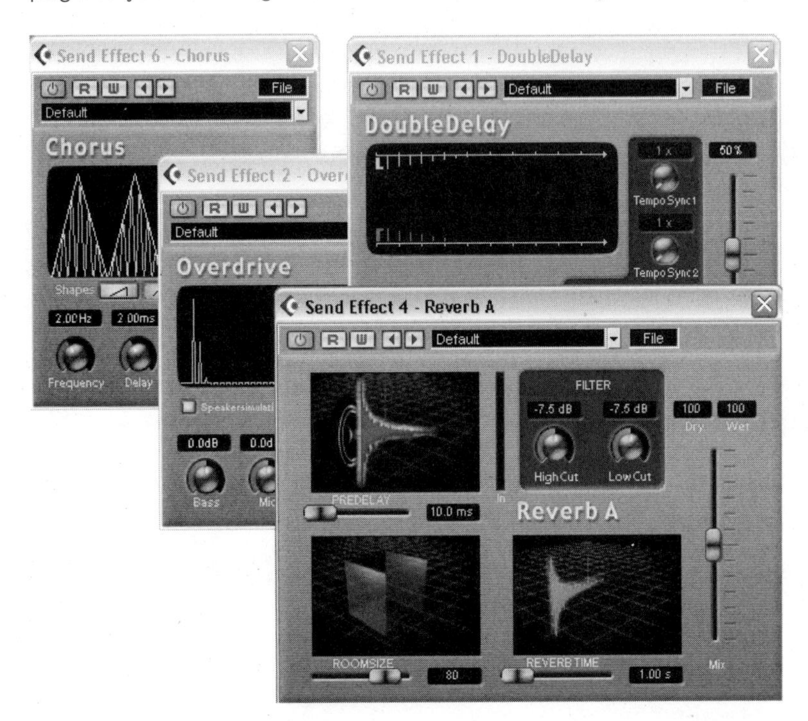

Figure 5.1
A selection of Cubase effects.

gram, they run within a 'host' program like Cubase. They are very much like plug-in filters that you can get for Photoshop and other graphics software – same sort of thing.

There are two main formats for plug-ins: VST and DirectX.

VST – Virtual Studio Technology

This format was invented by our friends at Steinberg and is the center of the audio engine in Cubase. It's an open format that allows anyone to write plug-ins that will work with Cubase. They also allow other recording software manufacturers to use the technology so that many other products are 'VST Compatible'. This is overwhelmingly the largest-supported format.

DirectX

This is based upon Microsoft technology and was originally used by audio editing programs like Sound Forge. Again, these plug-ins will turn up inside any software that supports DirectX plug-ins. Cakewalk's Sonar software is a good example, although Cubase also supports this format.

The best way to learn about plug-ins is to play with them. Load up Cubase and the 'Heaven and Hell' demo song and we'll have a go (if you look under the 'File' menu in Cubase, you'll see a 'Recent Projects' field, and you should find the demo song listed there for easy access).

What we should do is listen to a single track and have it loop so that we can fully appreciate the effects. Select the 'Strum' track and click the 'S' button. This will 'Solo' the strum track so only it will be heard on playback. Next click on the 'DualStrum' event and press the 'P' key on your keyboard to move the left and right markers around it. Make sure the loop button is lit on the transport bar and click play.

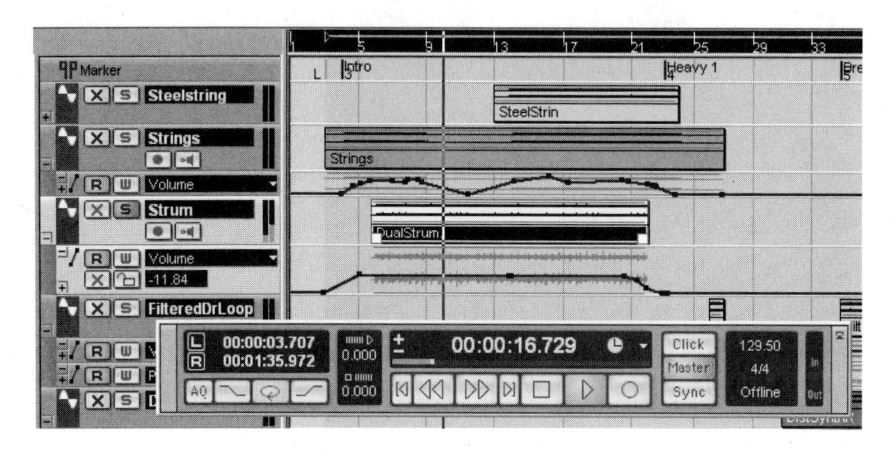

Figure 5.2
Soloing the Dualstrum track.

There are two ways of adding an effect. The mixing side of Cubase acts just like a mixer console, so if you've ever used a mixer, then most of the terms and features should be familiar to you. As with a mixer, effects can be used on 'Inserts' and 'Sends'. If you're not sure what these mean or what the difference is, let me explain.

Insert

This is where an effect is placed directly in the path of the audio channel, so that the signal passes directly through the effect and you get the effected signal coming out the other side.

Figure 5.3
Audio passing through an insert effect.

Send

This is where part of the audio signal is 'sent' to an effect. The part of the signal that was sent to the effect is then 'returned' and mixed with the original.

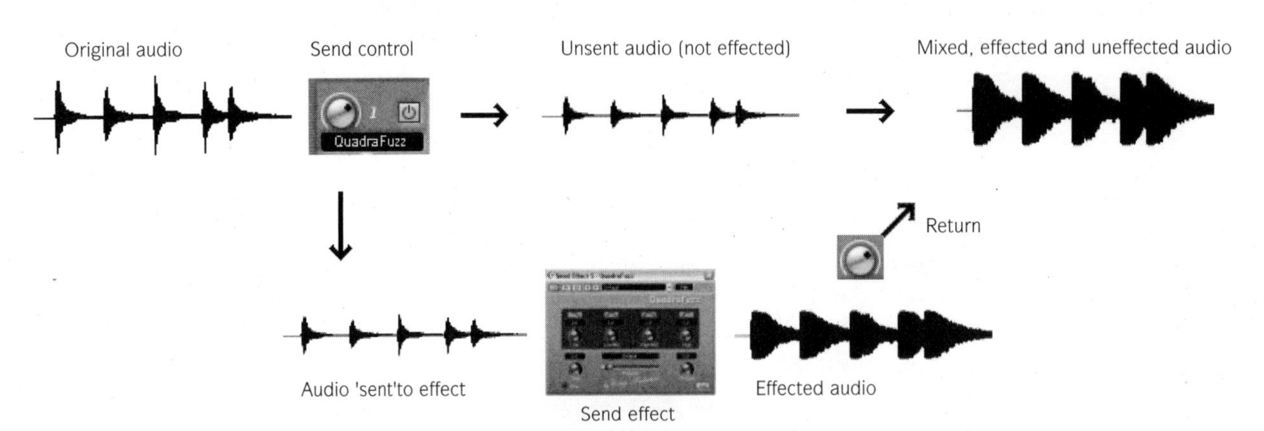

Figure 5.4
The path of audio through an effect send.

So, if you insert an effect, the whole channel is affected, and if you use a send effect, then only part of that signal is affected – although you can always send all of the signal.

The simplest way of looking at them is that if you want to apply an effect to a single channel, then use it as an insert. For instance, putting a distortion effect on a guitar track. If you want different channels to be affected by the same effect, then use a send. For instance, you could put a reverb on a send and route a small amount of different channels to it so that they all use the same kind of reverb.

Right, let's get effecting. Best place to start is with an insert, as all the signal is going through it the effect is very obvious. In Cubase you'll find the inserts for a track in two places: in the Track Info column or in the Track Mixer. We'll come to the mixer later, so for now, with the strum track selected, look on the left at the Track Info column.

You'll be able to see a bar called 'Inserts'. The top-right corner of the inserts bar is a button. Click it to reveal the 8 inserts. Currently, none of the inserts have any effects loaded. Click on the first one, where it says 'no effect', and a menu will pop up allowing you to choose from a whole range of available plug-ins.

Choose the very first one, 'DoubleDelay' (Figure 5.5) and you'll instantly hear the effect.

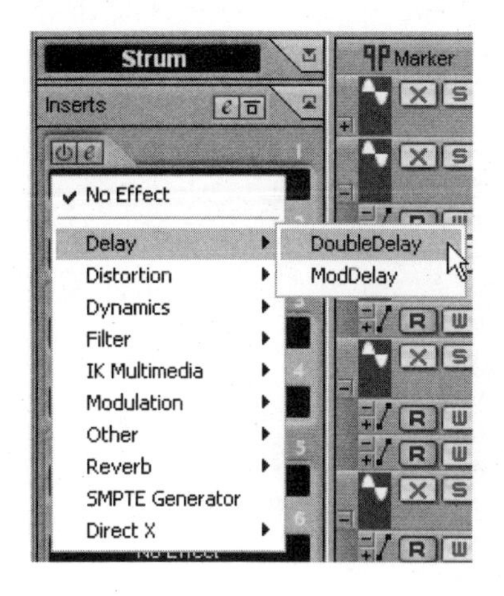

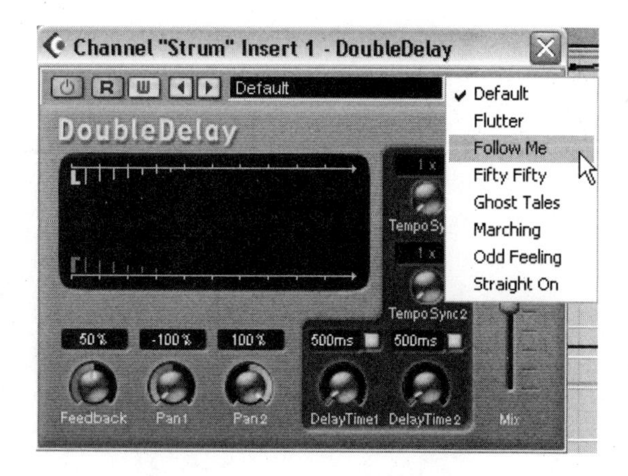

Figure 5.5 (left)
Inserting a delay effect.

Figure 5.6 (right)
Presets of the DoubleDelay.

Every effect has an editor window where you can change various parameters. The DoubleDelay editor should come up automatically (Figure 5.6). If not, then click the little 'e' button next to the insert to bring it up.

Most effects also come with a number of presets found under where it currently says 'Default'. Try moving some of the knobs and sliders to hear what happens. Graphical interface, eh? How nice is that?

You'll find all sorts of effects available to you as standard in Cubase; some you'll recognize, some you won't.

Try inserting the 'StepFilter' from the 'Filter' menu into insert number 2. Sounds interesting, doesn't it? Try moving the 'PatternSelect' knob to see different examples of what it can do (Figure 5.7).

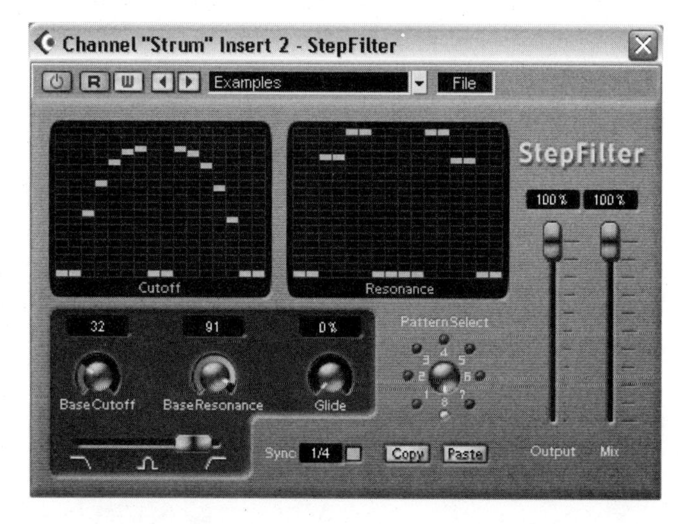

Figure 5.7
The StepFilter effect.

You can insert up to eight effects on a single channel and every knob movement you make can also be recording in the form of 'automation' – we'll look at this later.

Each effect can be bypassed, or turned off, by clicking the little button that looks like a stand-by power button, in the top left of the editor window, or just above the insert itself. You can remove them completely by clicking on the insert and selecting 'No Effect'.

Let's have a look at using a send effect. The demo song already has some effects loaded up as sends. Press the F6 button on your keyboard to bring up the sends window.

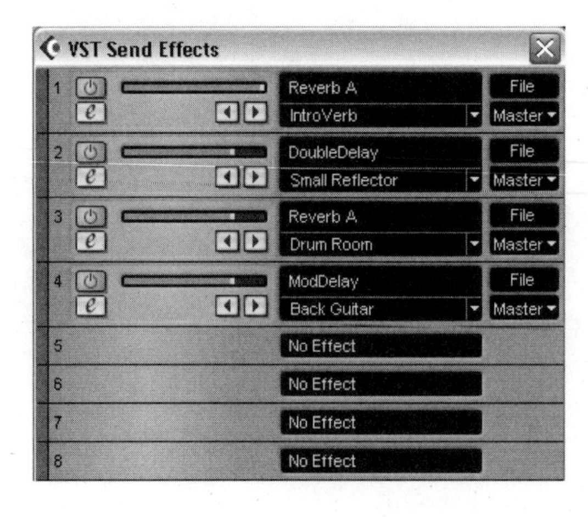

Figure 5.8
The Send Effects window.

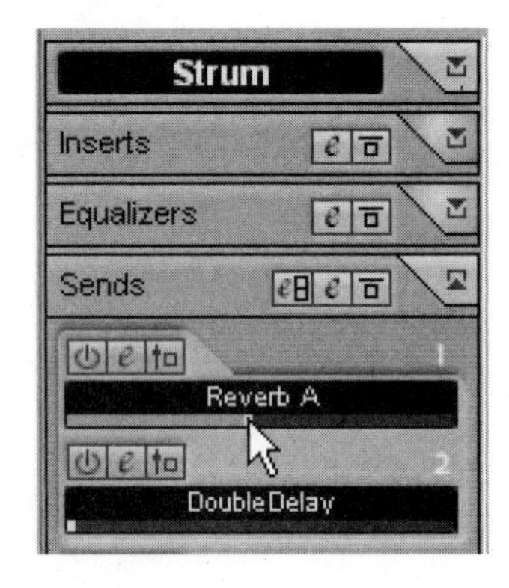

Figure 5.9
Altering the send amount.

Adding an effect to a send is exactly the same as with the inserts, and the same effects are available to us. This time, rather than hearing the effect straight away, there are two settings that affect how much of the effect we can hear. Back to the Track Info column and you can see a bar with 'Sends' written on it. Click the button on the top right of the bar to bring up the sends for that track.

You'll see the same effects there as are loaded in the main sends window. Here again you can select effects like we did with inserts, but this time, only the effects loaded into the main sends window will appear. First you need to turn the sends on by clicking the little stand-by button. The first parameter is the 'send amount'. This means how much of the audio signal do we want to send to the effect. Just under where it says 'Reverb A' is a thin blue line, and this shows the send amount. Click into the line and drag left and right to see how you change the send amount (Figure 5.9).

Then we have the 'return amount', which is found on the main sends window and dictates the level of signal returning from the effect. The returns are already set nice and high, so turn on the sends and increase the send amount to hear the effect. Send effects are generally subtler than inserts as you can probably tell right away.

Let's get on with using our guitar with some effects, and the best effect for that is Amplitube.

Using Amplitube

IK Multimedia's Amplitube is probably the best amp modeling/effects plug-in available. In a recent roundup review in *Future Music* magazine, it came out on top, beating even the superb Line 6 Pod. So let's try it out.

Close any projects you have open and then open the 'Amplitube Demo' project which is in the 'Cubase Projects' folder that you copied off the CD-ROM. You'll see a single track labeled 'Guitar' and some curiously named events. Press play and you'll hear various guitar licks played with a clean guitar. What this demo does is show you that Amplitube can recreate the guitar sound of pretty much anything you want. Let's do it.

The Guitar track is already selected, so bring up the inserts and select the Amplitube plug-in which is to be found under the IK Multimedia menu.

Audio 01
Marker
Locate
Inserts
No Effect
Delay
Distortion
Dynamics
Filter
IK Multimedia
Amplitube
Modulation
Other
Reverb
SMPTE Generator
Direct X

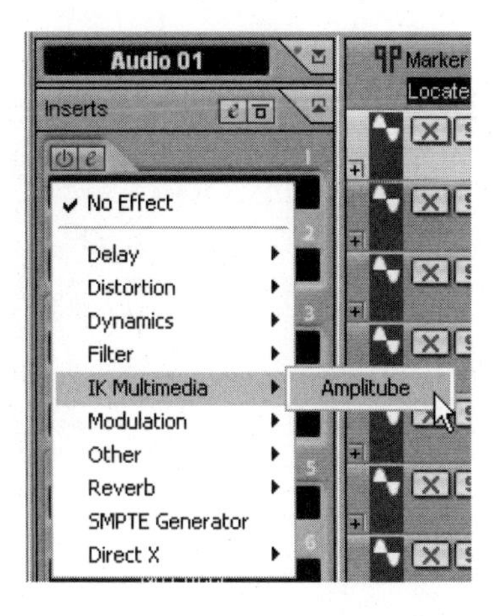

Figure 5.10
Inserting Amplitube onto an audio track.

Unexpectedly, a big window appears.

Figure 5.11
Amplitube Registration form.

Amplitube - Registration form
Thanks for using AmpliTube plug-in.
Until eventually authorized, AmpliTube will only work in demo mode inserting random white noise during processing.
- If you're evaluating AmpliTube click on the 'Demo' button.
- If you've purchased AmpliTube follow the procedure below for the authorization of your new software.
----
1) In this window you see:
-|a Serial Number field: this is written on a registration card included in the package.
-|a Digital ID field: this is a code generated by AmpliTube based on your system's characteristics. The Digital ID is unique to your computer. If you try to install AmpliTube on another system you will get a different Digital ID.
-|an Authorization Code field: this is generated by each user registration, and is linked to both the
Digital ID R6PDBHWY-KHHS-MMJM-0MH1-LN9LVBLL
Copy
Serial number
Paste
Authorization code
Paste
Demo
Register

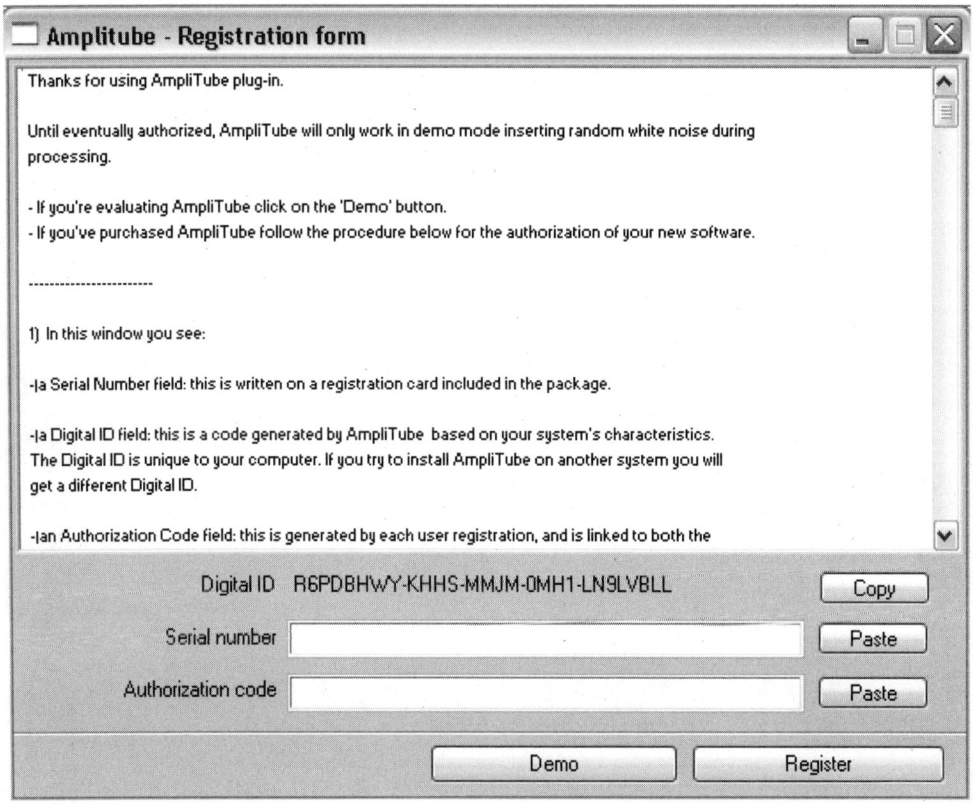

The Amplitube demo is actually the full version of Amplitube but with a little buzz of static that appears every 4 seconds or so, you can probably already hear it. Annoying though it is, it does not prevent us from getting a lot of fun out of the plug-in, and if we want to remove the buzz all you have to do is purchase the program and complete this registration form. In the meantime, click the 'Demo' button and we'll get into Amplitube and try to ignore the buzz.

Figure 5.12
Amplitube's Amp window.

As you can see, Amplitube has a whole array of controls, not unlike the Pod, with choices of preamp model, EQ model, amp and cabinet models along with a few other bits and pieces. On the bottom right there are three buttons: 'Stomp', 'Amp', and 'FX'. Currently we are looking at the 'Amp'. Click 'Stomp' and you'll find a bunch of familiar stomp box style effects.

Figure 5.13
Amplitube's Stomp Box window.

Click the 'FX' button and we have three 'post' effects: Stereo Delay, Stereo Reverb, and a Parametric EQ.

Figure 5.14
Amplitube's FX window.

Yes, yes, yes, but does it sound any good? Let's see shall we? Amplitube has tons of presets, not in the usual place but under the 'Load' drop down menu. The demo track is designed to match certain presets, all from the 'Amp' section where they've modelled different amplifier sounds.

The first one, '4x10 Ambient', is the first 'Amp' preset, so select it from the menu and press play. Then when the '80's Heavy 2' event comes along, select the relevant preset from the 'Amp' menu, and so on. If you need convincing that the plug-in is actually doing what you can hear, then click the stand-by/bypass button to turn the effect off to hear the clean guitar underneath. Sounds pretty good, I reckon.

Now of course, I can tell, you want to be able to play this with your own guitar. Just plug the guitar in and off you go – well, maybe. This is where our old friend latency might make an appearance, but we don't know until we try, so let's have a go.

We already have Amplitube inserted on the first audio track, so plug in your guitar, exactly as we did when we were recording it, select the first track, and make sure that the 'monitor' button is lit. The monitor button looks like a little speaker, and is next to the 'record enable' button.

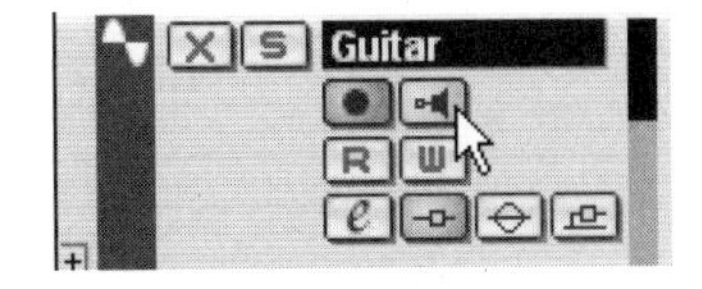

Figure 5.15
Turning on monitoring.

If you now play your guitar, you should be able to hear it going through Amplitube. Pick a suitably distorted preset, like the Aerosmith one, so that you definitely know when you hear the guitar with the effect on it.

Now, if yours is anything like the on-board soundcard I'm using, then you'll hear the clean guitar immediately as you play and the effected guitar about half a second behind. You could see it as a cool delay effect, but really it's just rubbish. However, if you have a soundcard with an ASIO driver, then it might sound great. If not, then let's see if we can improve it.

First of all, we want to get rid of the clean guitar that's being monitored directly through the soundcard and concentrate on the sound going through Cubase.

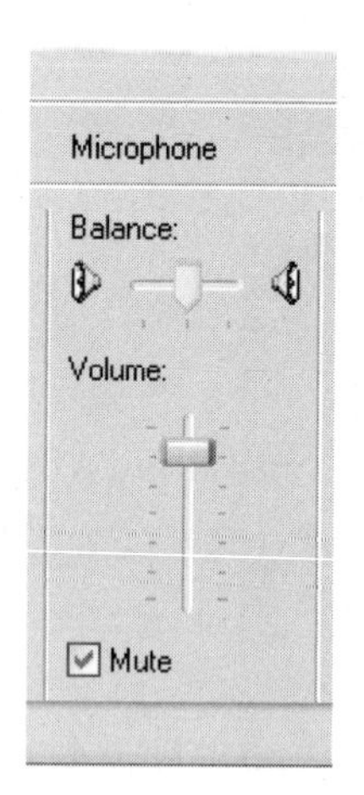

Figure 5.16
Windows Mixer with microphone muted.

Open the soundcard volume control and mute the input you're using for the guitar. In my case, that's the microphone input. Cubase accesses the drivers directly and bypasses the windows mixer. Do note that if you want to use the tuner later on, you must un-mute the input again.

You should now be able to hear only the guitar going through Cubase, about half a second behind your playing.

In Cubase we can alter the soundcard's buffer settings to improve the performance; however, as DirectX drivers are not designed for this sort of thing, we may not be able to get it to a playable level, but let's have a go.

Under the 'Devices' menu in Cubase, select 'Devices Setup' and select 'VST Multitrack' on the left. Click on the 'Control Panel' under the 'ASIO DirectSound Driver'. You may remember this from when we set up Cubase in the first place. The Direct Sound control panel has a buffer size shown for input and output. It's the input one that we want to look at. Double-click it and enter zero to see what the minimum figure is it'll let you have. In my case, it's 512 samples.

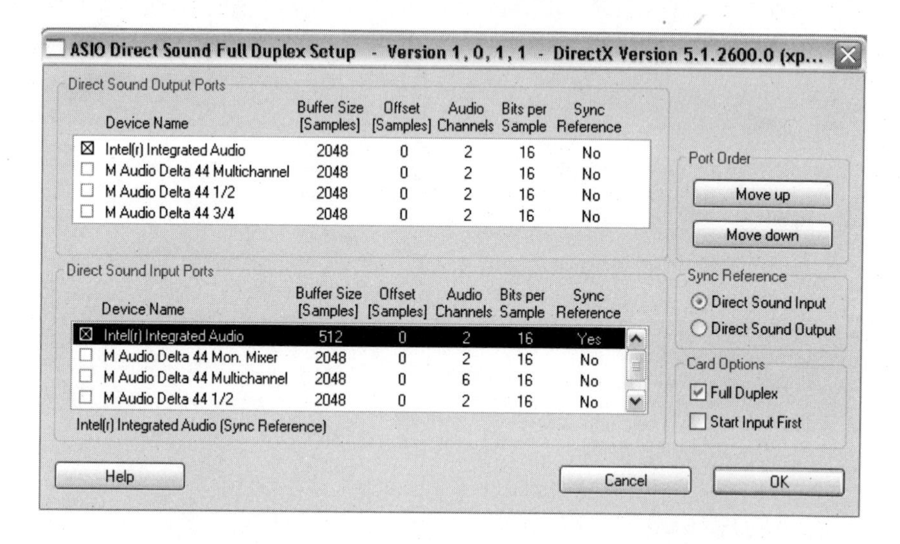

Figure 5.17
Changing the buffer size in the ASIO DirectSound Setup window.

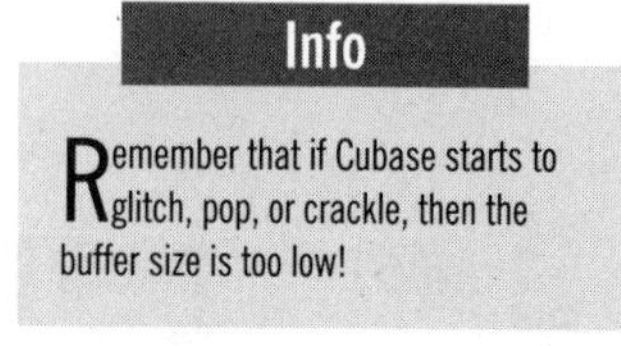

Click 'OK' and the click 'Apply' in the Device Setup window. Cubase's audio engine will then refresh itself with the new settings. This may trigger Amplitube to produce its registration window again – just click 'Demo'. You should now find that the latency has been significantly reduced. However, on my system it's still not quite playable, a bit like a 'double guitar' effect. You may have had better luck than me. If not, then it's probably clear why investing in a soundcard with ASIO drivers would be a really good idea.

As a comparison, if I enable my M Audio soundcard and use its ASIO drivers, I'm able to get down to a buffer size of 64 samples, which is a latency of about 1 millisecond (ms). Generally speaking, I would say that a latency of less than 20ms becomes 'playable'. If you're really into shredding and hammer-ons, then probably less that 10ms is what you're after. The vast majority of soundcards with ASIO drivers can accomplish this without too much trouble.

Recording with effects

If you are getting a playable response from Cubase, or just want to carry on regardless, then you can insert any other effects you'd like.

When it comes to recording, the process is exactly the same as with recording any other track, except that we've put effects on the inserts. Cubase, however, only records the clean guitar input, not the effects, so when you play back you can still remove or change the effects if you want. That's one of the great things about computer recording: few things are 'committed to tape' as it were, or set in stone. You can record a whole song using one guitar sound and then completely change it around afterward.

If you're finding the latency too much to cope with, you can monitor through your soundcard instead, or through your mixer or whatever it is you're using as the input stage for your guitar. In Cubase, turn off the 'Monitor' button for the track, remove the effects, and un-mute your input on the soundcard's volume control. You can now quite happily record your guitar and then apply the wonderful effects like Amplitube on playback.

I'll do a summary of decent plug-ins toward the end of the book, but there's just one that I'd like to mention which is particularly good:

Warp VST from Steinberg, modeled on the 'DSM' technology of Hughes & Kettner, makers of some of the blackest amps around.

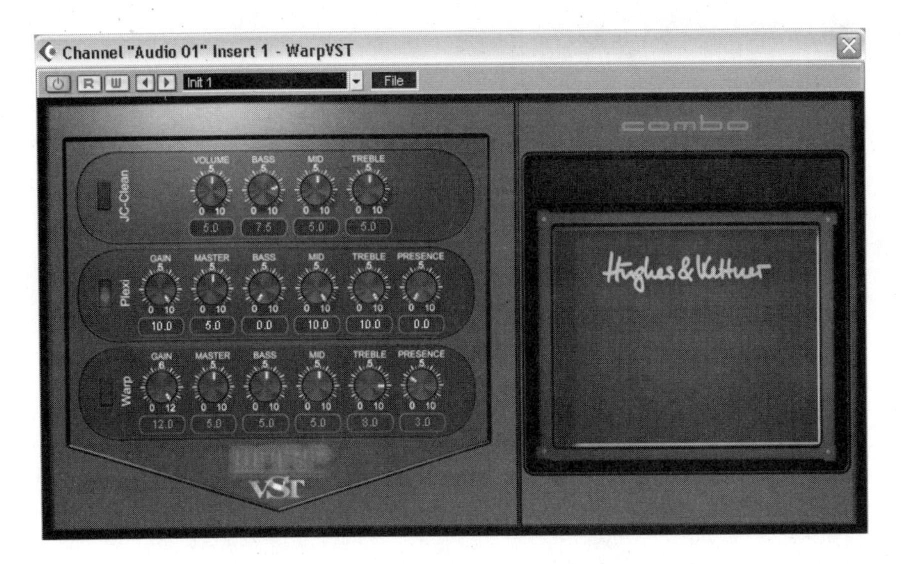

Figure 5.18
Steinberg's Warp VST modeling Hughes and Kettner amp technology.

This is a simple, but serious-sounding, amp model. It has three channels: Jazz Chorus Clean, Plexi Tube Head, and Warp Rectified, and three different cabinet models: Greenback, British, and Combo. The difference between this and Amplitube is like the difference between a Line6 Pod, with a thousand presets, and an old, much-loved, simple guitar amp. Both are fabulous and represent the best guitar plug-ins available at the time of writing, and both have different 'feels' to them.

Bring on the drums

So far we've covered simple recording and using effects to make some great sounds. Now we need to start looking at the other instruments we employ to create our music.

Most guitarists, to some degree, are frustrated drummers, but, let's face it, no one wants the hassle of getting a drummer in to help tinker with your ideas and empty your fridge. So, we use drum machines. Our old friend the SR-16 has been the provider of useful patterns for years, and now we need to look at how we can re-create that sort of usefulness on the computer.

Figure 6.1 Alesis SR-16.

Virtual drum machines

What we need, then, are some decent drum sounds. Most synths, sound modules, keyboards and the like come with drum kits built in. Anything which conforms to the GM (General MIDI) standard will have a couple of drum kits ready to go. If your soundcard has an on-board synth, then it's probably got a drum kit or two. If you've heard your soundcard's drums, they probably sound a bit questionable, at least when compared to something like the SR-16, although they can sound pretty good nowadays. With Windows XP you also get a little 'Microsoft GS Wavetable SW Synth', which has a bunch of sounds on it and half a dozen drum kits. So, without even thinking about it we already have a number of sound sources available to us.

With the miracle of computer and software technology, we have an even better source of drum sounds – software instrument plug-ins.

Similar to the effects plug-ins we've already looked at, you can now get plug-ins which create instrument or synth sounds inside your host program (Cubase). In Cubase and other VST-compatible programs, these are called VSTis (VST

Instruments), and they act like any hardware MIDI synth or sound module. We'll look at software synths in more detail in the next chapter, so for the time being we want to concentrate on drums.

The most realistic drum sounds can be found by using samples. These are actual recordings of drums being hit that are then put together so we can trigger the samples from a MIDI keyboard or from our sequencer (Cubase). There are now some amazing software samplers available as plug-ins giving us access to the most incredible quality of sounds and, more importantly, drum kits. Some of these are designed specifically for drums, others are designed to use samples of any instrument. We can use both.

We're going to look at two of the best drum samplers, Native Instrument's Battery and Fxpansion's DR-008. You'll find demo versions of each of these on the CD-ROM. The reason we didn't install these earlier is because the DR-008 demo has a 4-hour usage limit and I didn't want it to time out inadvertently before you'd had a chance to play with it.

Installing Battery

Make sure Cubase is closed. Inside the 'Software' folder on the CD-ROM you'll find the 'Battery Demo' folder. Double-click the 'Battery demo setup.exe' file within the Battery folder to install the software. Follow the on-screen instructions and all the defaults should be fine.

Installing DR-008

Make sure Cubase is closed. Inside the 'Software' folder on the CD-ROM you'll find the 'DR-008 Demo' folder. Double click the 'dr008demo11.exe' file within the DR-008 folder to install the software. Follow the on-screen instructions and when it asks if you want to install the VSTi version or the DXi version select VSTi.

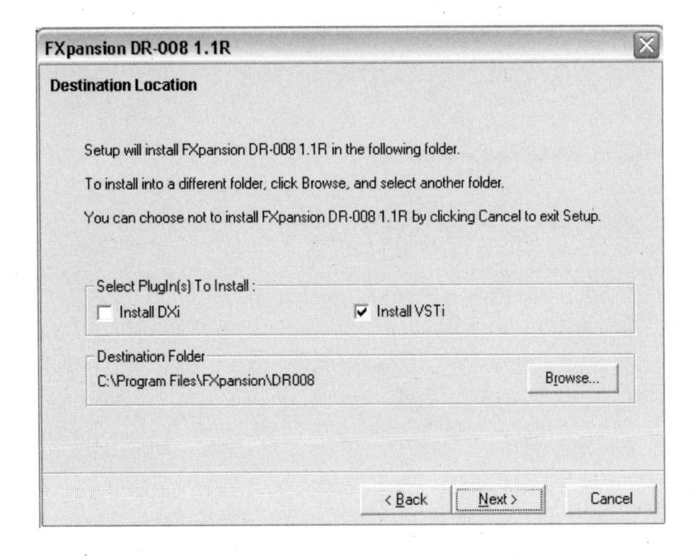

Figure 6.2
Installing DR-008 as a VSTi.

When you're done, let's load up Cubase and have a look.

Loading VSTis

Cubase SX can load up to 32 VSTis, depending on your processing power. As with effects, the more you load, the more work your computer has to do until there comes a point where it can't load anymore. These two VSTis should be no trouble.

Press the F11 key on your keyboard and it will bring up the VST Instrument loading window. It works very much like loading effects plug-ins. In the first slot, click where it says 'No Instrument' and select 'Battery Demo' from the menu that pops up. In the second slot, do the same but this time select DR-008. At this point the DR-008 setup window will appear. You don't need to worry about anything you see there, and just click 'OK'. As with the effects, we click the little 'e' button to bring up the editor window for the plug-in. Let's start with Battery.

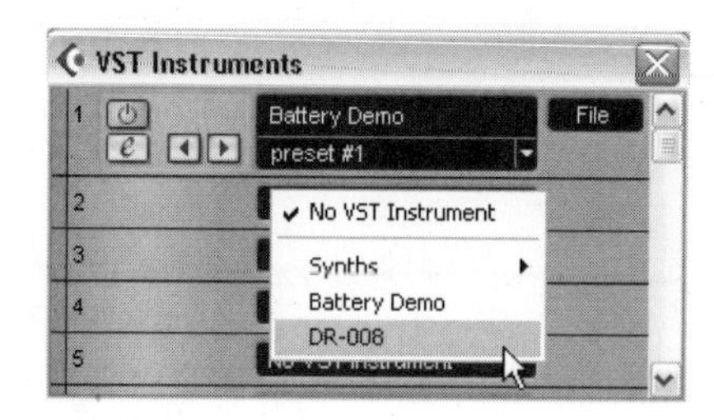

Figure 6.3
Loading the DR-008 VSTi.

Native Instruments Battery

Battery loads up with a demo version splash screen; just click it to remove it once you've found out what's disabled in this demo version.

Battery's interface is basically six rows of nine 'pads', with some editing controls underneath. These are like the pads you'll find on the SR-16 or your drum machine. Each pad can have a drum sound assigned to it, so as you click the pad you hear the sound. At the moment we don't have any drum samples loaded, so we'd best fix that right away.

On the right of the Battery window is a button labeled 'File'. Click on it and select 'Load Kit' from the menu.

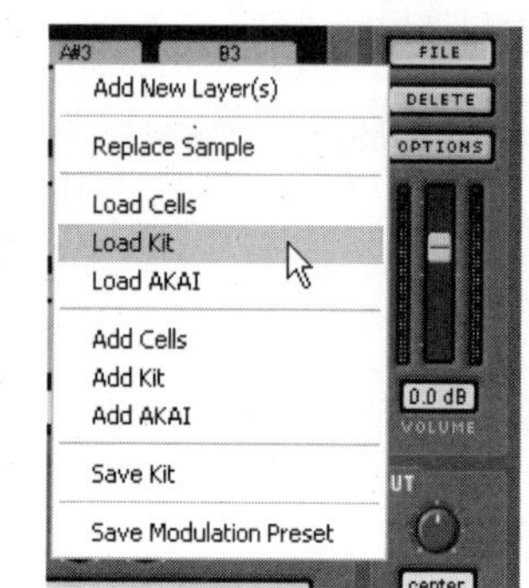

Figure 6.4
Loading a kit into Battery.

A window opens which allows you to select a Battery drum kit. It should default to the Battery Demo folder, but if not you'll need to browse to find where you installed the Battery Demo and select the 'Soul_DEMO.kit'.

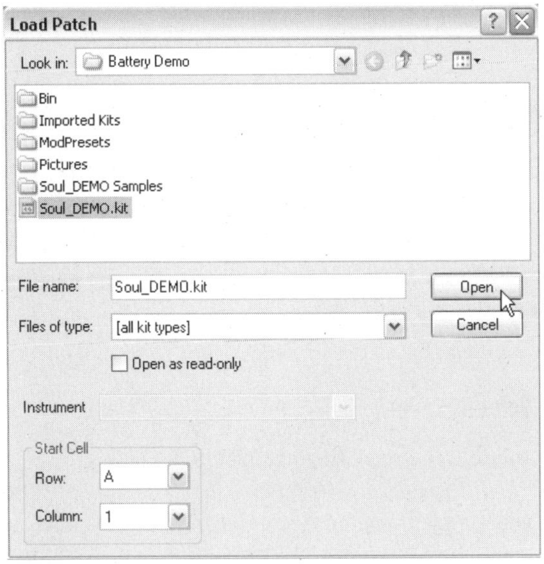

Figure 6.5
Selecting the demo kit.

> **Info**
>
> The Soul_Demo kit is the only kit available to us in Battery's demo version. The full version comes with a whole CD full of drum kits.

If you now click on a pad that contains a drum sound, you'll be able to hear it.

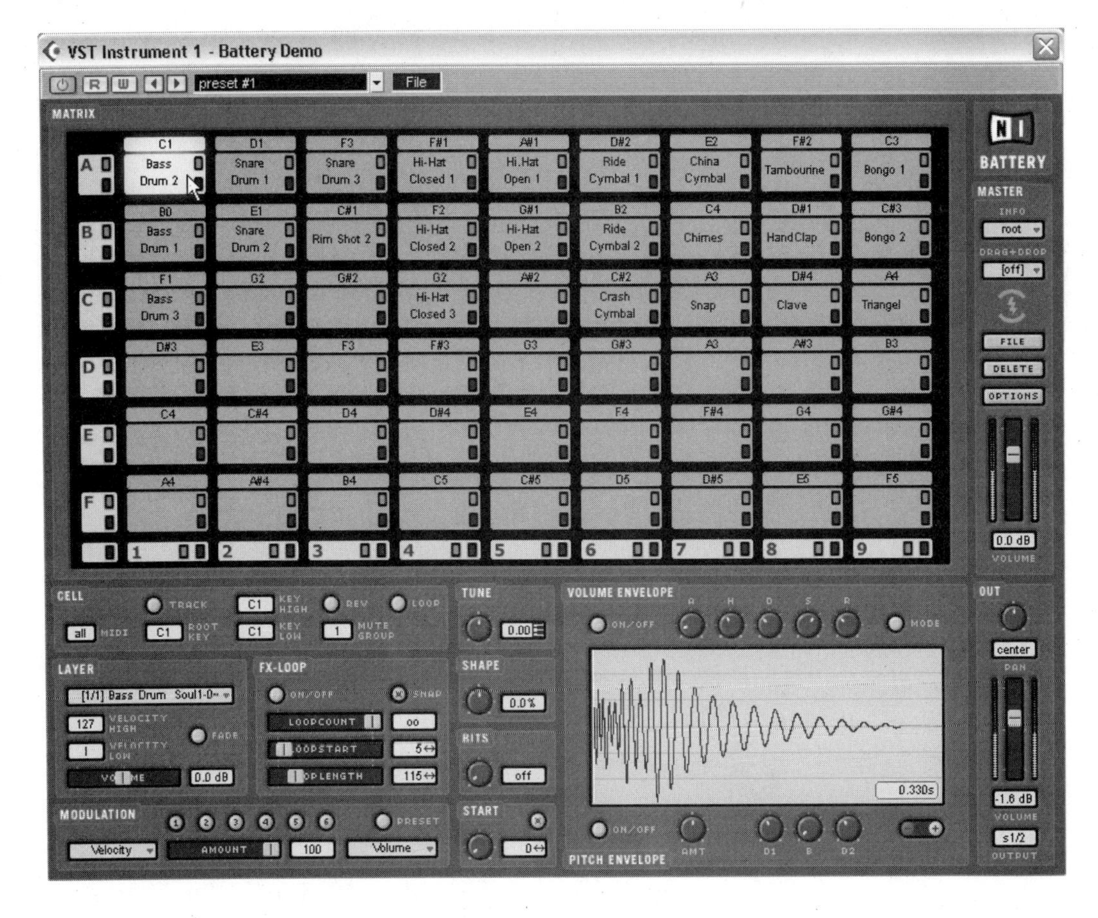

Figure 6.6
Click a pad in Battery and hear the sound.

As you click different pads, you'll notice that the picture in the Volume Envelope window changes. It's showing the sample contained in each pad. The editing controls apply to whatever pad is currently selected. I won't go into great detail but I'll point out a couple of things to try for instant satisfaction. Under the 'Cell' section there's a 'Rev' button: this reverses the sample. Then there's a 'loop' button: this plays the sample over and over again, which is more useful if the pad contains a drum loop rather than just a hit. Next to that we have the 'Tune' section, which allows you to alter the speed of the sample to change its pitch. In the 'Volume Envelope' section, click the on/off button to turn it on and move the knob labeled 'A' a little bit, this increases the 'attack' of the sample – you'll know what I mean as soon as you try it.

Velocity layers

This is a good place to point out something that's very common among all samplers, and that's 'velocity layering'. The idea of velocity layering is to have a different sample triggered depending on how hard the pad, or note, has been struck. If you hit a real drum with different amounts of force, the sound you get is very different, so, rather than just varying the volume drum sample, you would take different samples of the same drum (or instrument) struck with different amounts of force. Clicking on a pad with a mouse would not demonstrate this, but if you were using a MIDI keyboard, or drum pad, then it would be more obvious.

Battery has the ability to layer up to 128 samples on a single pad. MIDI velocity is measured between zero and 127, so that could mean a sample for each possible level of velocity. It's more common just to have a few layers to help the drum sound more realistic. Figure 6.7 shows an example of layering five different snare samples at different velocities. So if the velocity of the trigger falls within the range of one of the samples, it will trigger that sample.

Unfortunately, in the demo version of Battery, velocity layering is not permitted, so you'll have to take my word for it.

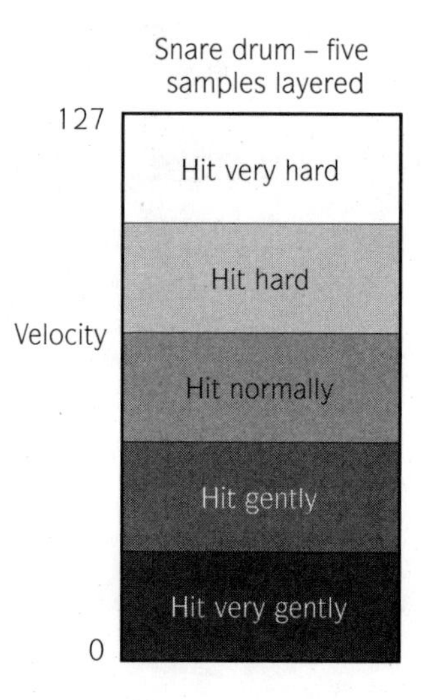

Figure 6.7
Velocity layering within sample instruments.

Let's now look at the DR-008

Fxpansion's DR-008

Press F11 to bring forward the VST Instruments loading window and click the little 'e' next to the loaded DR-008.

Not dissimilar to Battery, but this time we have eight rows of twelve pads, again with nothing loaded. To load up a kit, click the 'Load' button at the top right and select 'Load Settings…'.

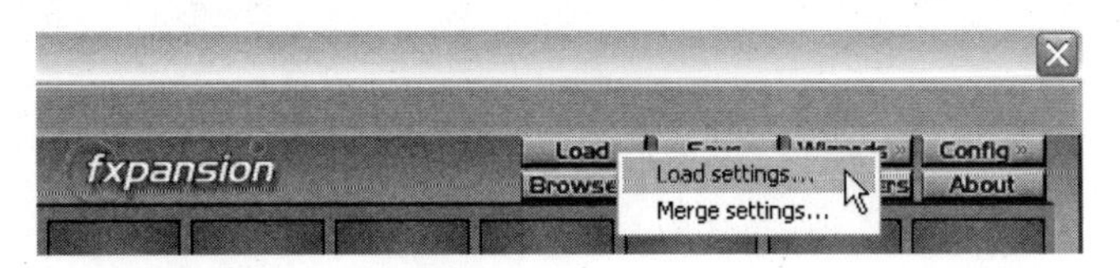

Figure 6.8
Loading a kit into DR-008.

This should open a window into the DR-008 folder where the kits are stored. If not then browse to the folder where you installed it.

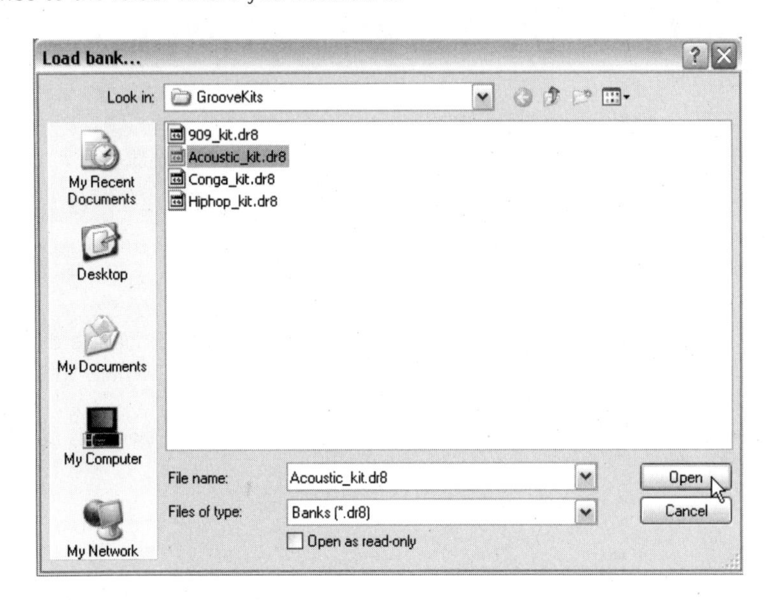

Figure 6.9
Choosing the Acoustic kit.

Info

As with Battery, the full version of DR-008 comes with a CD's worth of kits.

With this demo, we have a choice of four kits. Choose the 'Acoustic_kit.dr8' file and click 'Open'. The kit spreads itself over the pads and you can click on them to hear them (Figure 6.10).

DR-008 does have some editing functions and a cool mixer, which can be accessed through the buttons 'Mix' and 'Edit' at the top of the window, but the DR-008 is far more than just a drum sample player. In fact it calls itself an 'Advanced Rhythm Production Station', and indeed it is. DR-008's power is in its ability to load not just samples onto the pads, but self-contained 'modules' which can do a whole number of useful things.

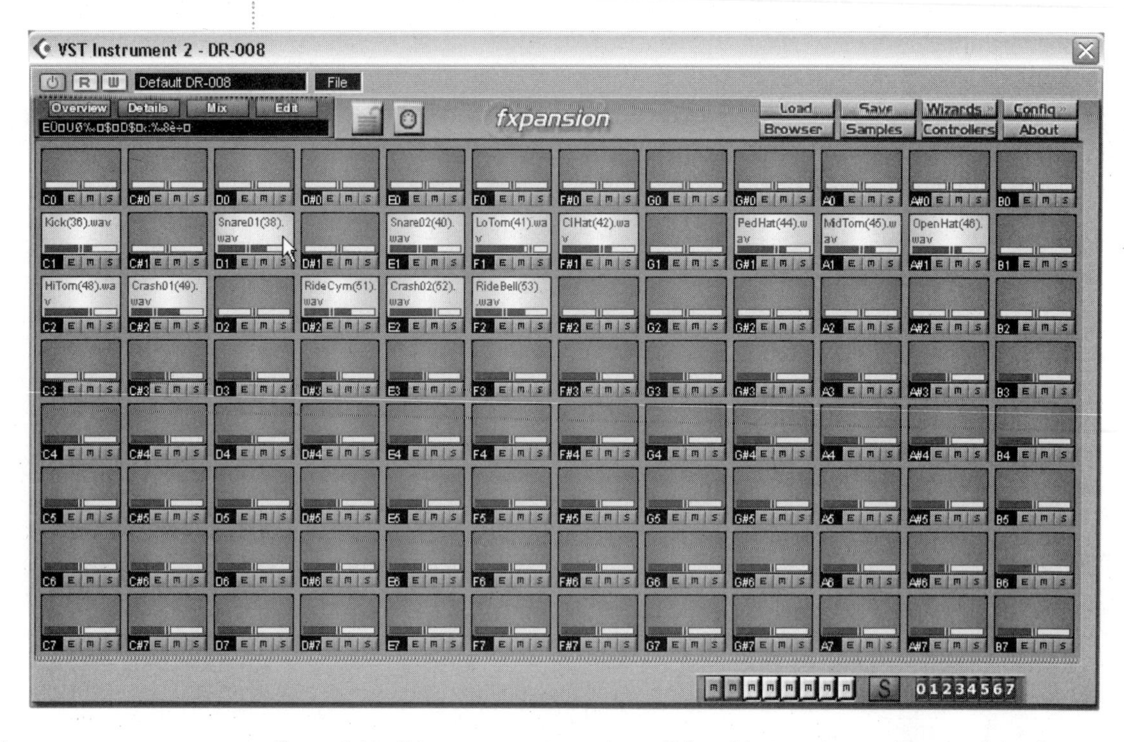

Figure 6.10
Click a pad to play a sound.

If you right-click on an empty pad, you'll be able to select various modules from a menu.

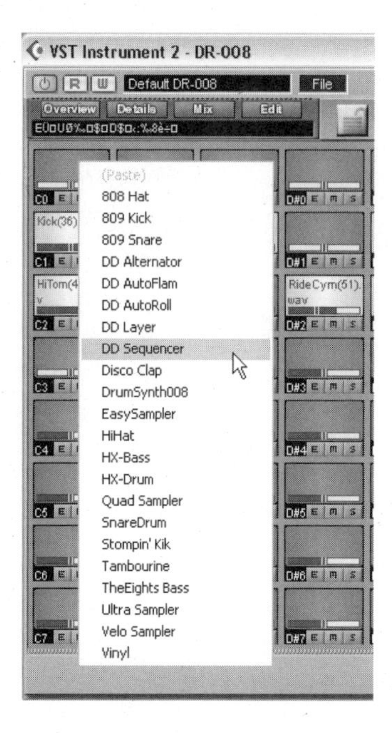

Figure 6.11
Selecting a module or a pad.

There are lots of extra sounds available here as well as editing tools that let you do interesting things to samples, but the main one of interest to us is the 'DD

Sequencer'. The reason this is interesting is because it allows us to generate patterns that play the drum pads for us. Select the DD Sequencer module and then click the little 'E' button under the pad to bring up the editor.

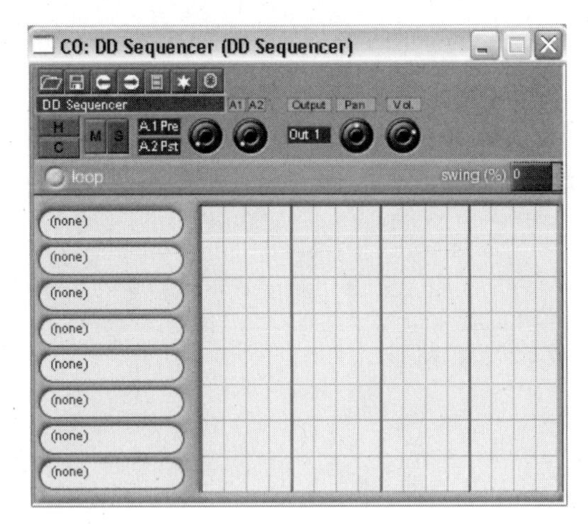

Figure 6.12
The DD Sequencer Editor.

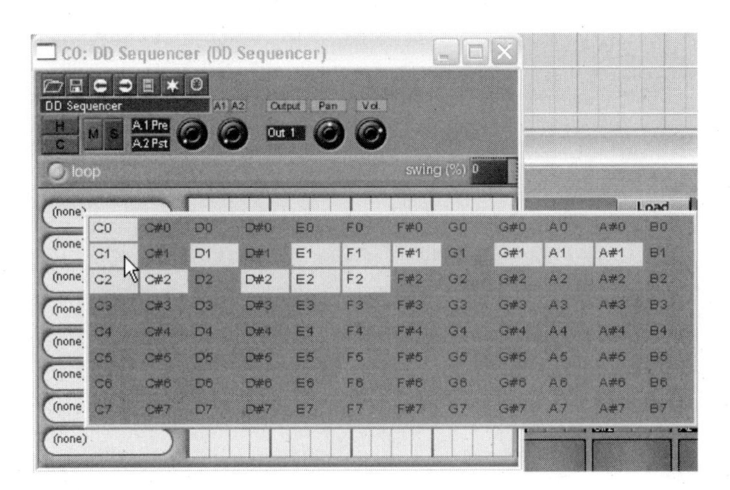

Figure 6.13
Choosing a drum pad for use in the DD Sequencer.

On the left is where we can insert the various drum pads we want to use in the pattern and on the right is a grid where we can write the pattern. Click in each slot on the left, where it says 'none' and select a pad.

I'd recommend loading up:

C1 – Kick drum
D1 – Snare
F#1 – Closed hi-hat
A#1 – Open hi-hat
C#2 – Crash cymbal

We should be able to create a reasonable pattern with those. If you click in the grid, blocks will appear showing where in the sequence the pad will be triggered. If you set the sequence going you'll get an instant playback of your pattern as you add to it. To do this, click the 'H' button, this holds the pad down so it will play back continuously, and click on the pad upon which you inserted the sequencer module.

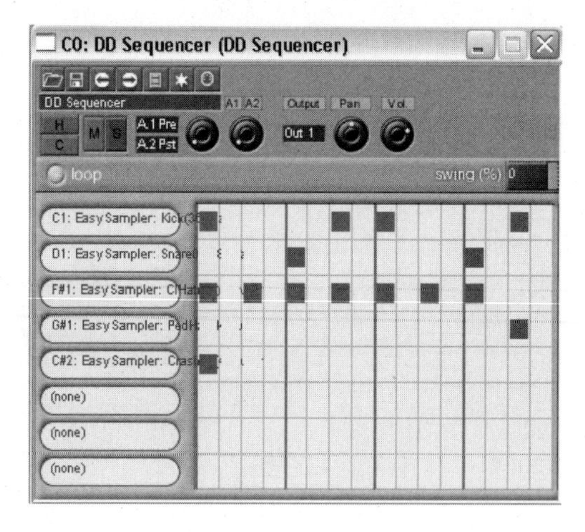

Figure 6.14
A pattern created in the DD Sequencer.

If you're at a loss on what to put where, then try copying my example. These patterns can be saved and recalled later. The full version of DR-008 comes with tons of preset sequence patterns, but the demo comes with one. To load it, right-click on the pad with the sequence module in it and select the preset from the preset menu. Click and hold the pad (or remember the 'H' button) to hear the sequence.

Figure 6.15
Selecting a preset pattern for the DD Sequencer.

Now I've only scratched the surface so far with these drum samplers and I haven't even got to the point of using them in a song. I can also sense that you don't like the idea that you have to click on the pads with your mouse to make a sound; at least with the SR-16 you can bash away at the pads with your fingers. Don't fret, all will be revealed. It might be a good idea to unload the DR-008 to save some of that precious 4-hour time limit while we look at the next bit.

Playing and programming drums in Cubase

The computer has always exceled in drum programming. One of the earliest ways the computer contributed to music was the programming of beats which spawned a whole race of musical genres. Nowadays the genre is irrelevant and we can all benefit.

Understanding MIDI

Well it had to happen sooner or later. We've now got to start talking MIDI (Musical Instrument Digital Interface). MIDI is an instructional language that can be sent between MIDI 'devices'. A MIDI device is anything that can respond to or generate MIDI commands such as sound modules, synthesizers, samplers, electronic keyboards, and drum machines. It might also be a MIDI controlled effects box, mixer, or lighting rig, or even a MIDI guitar or MIDI floorboard controller. The sort of commands that are sent over MIDI are things like note commands:

'Play this note now, this hard and for this long.'

Or control messages:

'Increase volume to this value', or 'Select this patch'.

It enables us to connect up lots of electronic equipment and control it from one place. So, for instance, you could have a MIDI keyboard and send instructions to a number of other sound modules so you can play the sounds from the one keyboard. Cubase, being a MIDI sequencer (amongst other things) can record these commands and play them back through any MIDI device you choose.

The main point to grasp here, before we get on with it, is to understand that MIDI is not sound, it's just a bunch of instructions. It may cause a sound to occur, but it is not in itself sound.

Quick analogy: MIDI information is very much like a sheet of music. The notation on a sheet of music contains information like pitch, duration, expression, and tempo, as does MIDI.

Try to listen to a sheet of music and it'll look at you very blankly and maybe rustle a bit. If you want to listen to the music contained on the sheet then you have to give it to a musician who understands music. The musician will be able to play it back with their instrument. What instrument the musician uses is not necessarily important, and you choose any instrument you like to play back the music. It's the same with MIDI. You can't hear MIDI – if you tried, it would sound a bit like a fax machine – but you can send the MIDI information to a device that understands it and that device would be able to respond to it, i.e., make a sound. The sound it makes is not set, so you can choose any sound available to you, and any other MIDI device for that matter.

VSTis are MIDI devices and so can be played and sequenced using MIDI. So, with our two drum machines, we don't have to click on the pads, we can play them with a MIDI keyboard (MIDI drum pad, or MIDI guitar) connected to the computer.

Info

MIDI information is very much like a sheet of music. The notation on a sheet of music contains information like pitch, duration, expression, and tempo, as does MIDI.

There are three physical connections involved in MIDI:

MIDI IN – receives MIDI instructions from another MIDI device
MIDI OUT – sends MIDI instructions to another MIDI device
MIDI THRU – sends whatever came into the MIDI IN straight back out again.

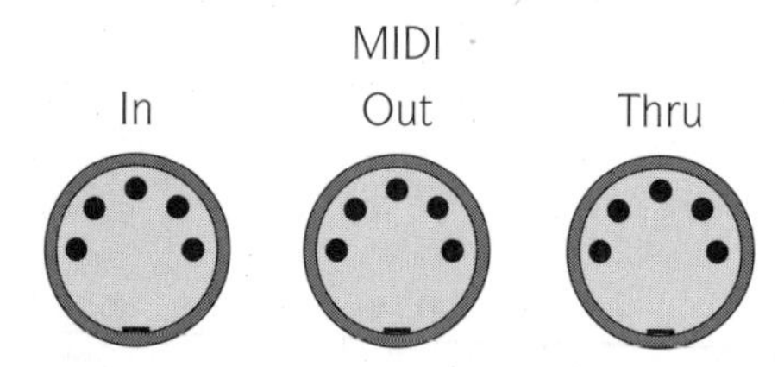

Figure 6.16
The three MIDI ports.

If you have a piece of MIDI gear then you'll find at least one of these connections on the back. These MIDI sockets are connected together using 5 pin MIDI DIN leads, similar to the ancient DIN audio lead but wired differently.

So, as an example, if you had a MIDI keyboard and a separate MIDI sound module, you would connect the MIDI OUT of the keyboard to the MIDI IN on the sound module. Play the keyboard and sound would come out of the module. If you had two sound modules then you could connect the MIDI THRU of the first module to the MIDI IN of the second module and play both at once from the keyboard. Remember that sound is not transferred between the MIDI devices, just instructions, so any sound that's triggered over MIDI will come out of the device which has those sounds.

Connecting MIDI to the computer

As Cubase is full of these wonderful MIDI VSTis, ideally we want to connect up a MIDI keyboard so that we can play them. You might have a MIDI pickup on your guitar, in which case we can use that, although I'd imagine playing drums with strings is quite hard work. Or you could have something like a MIDI drum pad. For now I'll assume that the most likely bit of gear you have, or might be persuaded into getting would be a MIDI keyboard. This might be just a dumb MIDI controller, or it may be an all-singing, all-dancing synth/sampler keyboard like the Korg Triton. Doesn't matter, as long as it has a MIDI output then we're in business.

Figure 6.17
Roland MIDI keyboard.

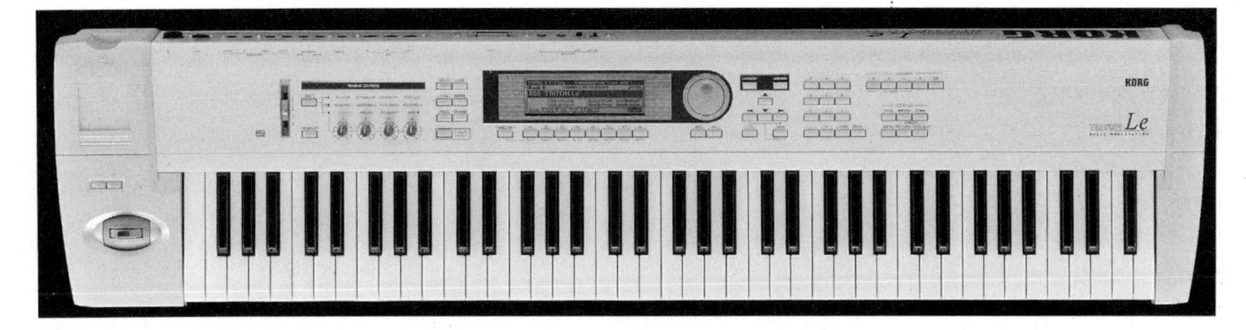

Figure 6.18
Korg Triton LE.

There are three ways of connecting a keyboard to the computer. These are essentially the same thing, but appear to be superficially different. I'm talking about a MIDI Interface.

You can connect a keyboard to the computer via:

A stand alone, hardware, MIDI interface
A MIDI interface attached to the soundcard
USB, on a USB enabled keyboard.

Stand alone MIDI interface

These come in all shapes and sizes and more often than not connect to your computer's USB (Universal Serial Bus) port. Plug it in, install some drivers, and off you go. You can get them with one port, two ports, up to eight ports if you like. Ideally you need a port for each piece of external MIDI gear you want to connect to the computer. So if you have just a keyboard and maybe a sound module, then a one-port interface will do the trick. If you have several keyboards and modules and a MIDI floorboard, then a few more ports would be useful. If you don't have an interface on your soundcard, then you might have to look at this option.

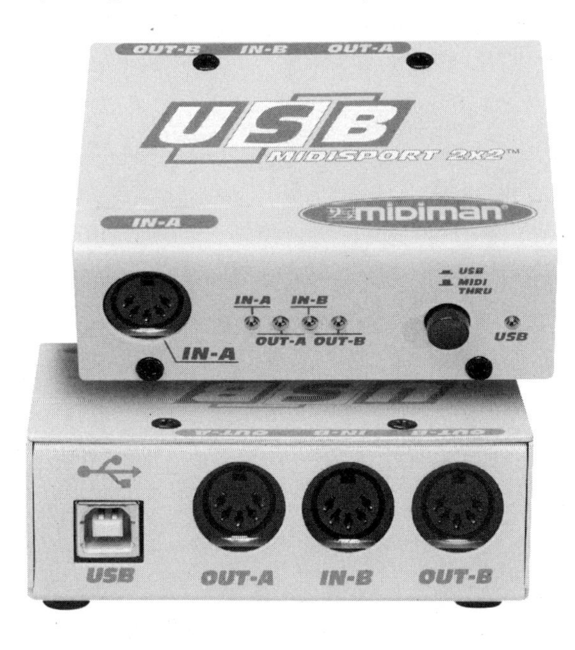

Figure 6.19
Midiman's Midisport 2x2 MIDI interface.

Soundcard MIDI interface

If you have a standard soundcard with a joystick port, then that can act as a MIDI interface.

Figure 6.20
The joystick port on the back of a soundcard with the adapter to convert it into a MIDI interface.

All you need is the right adapter cable, called a 'joystick MIDI adapter'. These either come with longs leads with plugs attached, or short leads with sockets.

USB enabled keyboard

This is essentially the same as the stand alone MIDI interface except that the interface is built into the keyboard and doesn't have any other ports on it. So instead of MIDI sockets, you've just got a USB cable. These are very common nowadays.

Plug the cable into the keyboard and into the USB socket on the computer, install the driver and off you go.

Figure 6.21
Evolution MK 249 USB MIDI keyboard.

So, using either of the first two (a USB keyboard doesn't need a MIDI cable), take the MIDI OUT of your keyboard and connect it to the MIDI IN on the computer.

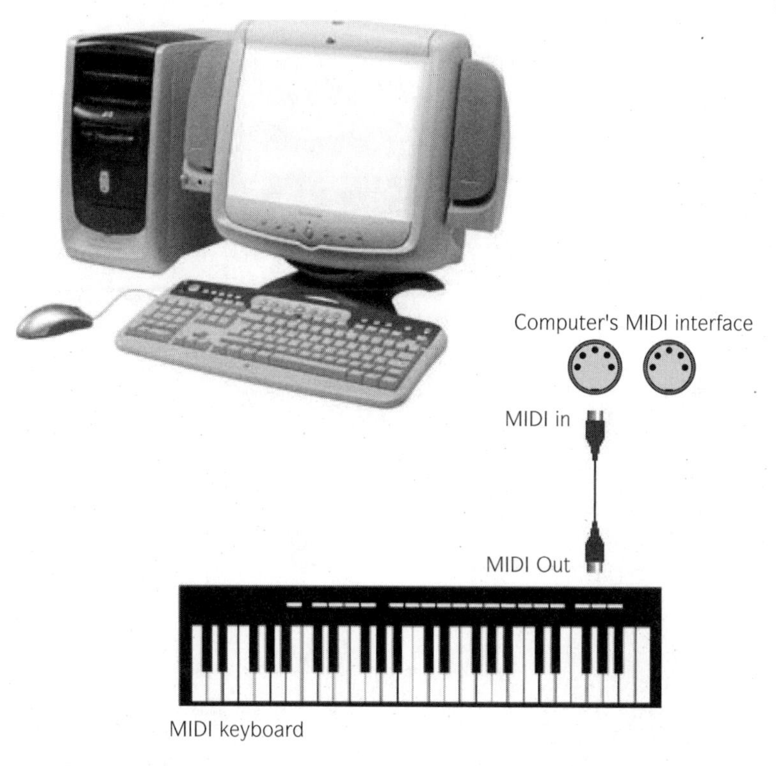

Figure 6.22
Connecting a MIDI keyboard to the computer.

Playing drums in Cubase

Open Cubase and we'll check that you're getting a MIDI input. Hit a few keys and you should see the MIDI IN light flash on the transport bar, and if a MIDI track is selected, you'll see the MIDI activity bar flash as well.

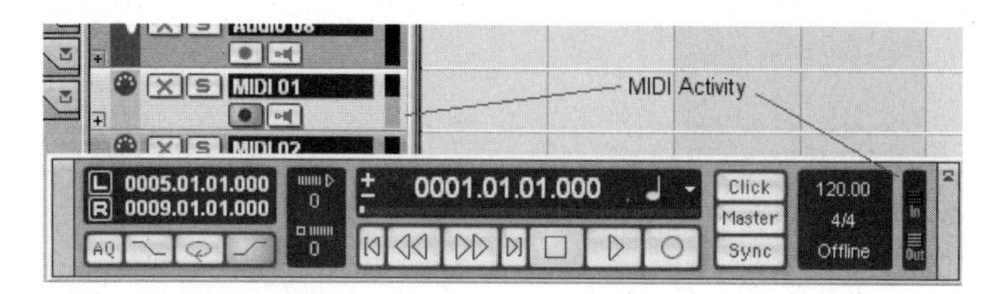

Figure 6.23
MIDI activity in Cubase on the transport bar and on the MIDI track.

You may even hear a piano sound. This would be the Microsoft GS Wavetable synth. You might also notice the 'lag' of the sounds behind your key presses. The Microsoft synth was not designed to be played in real-time, it's for playing MIDI files and music in Windows and suffers from a greater latency than Cubase is providing, so even if you have fast ASIO drivers, it's still not very playable. Let's ignore it for now and concentrate on the good stuff.

The full version of Cubase SX comes with a drum machine built in, but unfortunately it's not included with the demo version. However, my increasingly lovely friends at Steinberg have agreed to let me include their 'LM7 Drum Sample Unit' exclusively with this book for the pleasure of my valued readers.

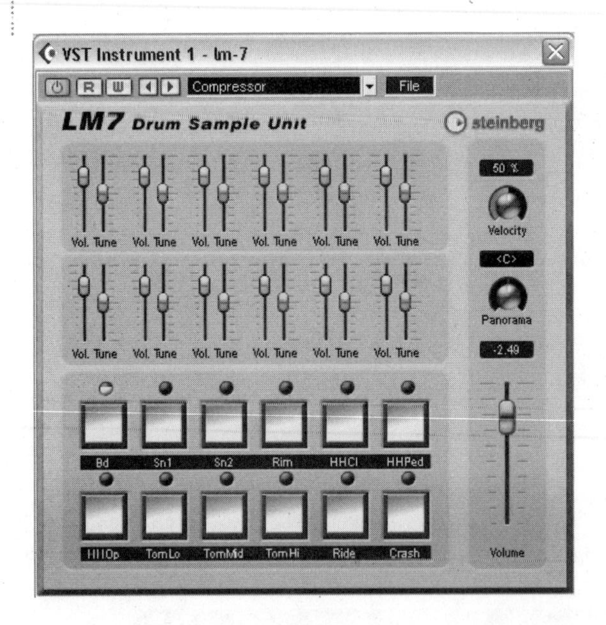

Figure 6.24
Cubase's LM7 Drum Sample Unit.

It doesn't install with the Cubase demo, so you'll have to add it manually. On the CD-ROM, in the Software folder is a folder called 'LM7'. Inside is a folder called 'Drums', this contains the LM7 plug-in and its sample sets and presets etc. Copy the whole 'Drums' folder and place it in the 'Vstplugins' folder which you'll find under:

C:\Program Files\Steinberg\Cubase SX Demo\Vstplugins

Restart Cubase and the LM7 will appear as a VSTi. We'll use the LM7 in a later chapter and for now we'll continue using Battery, as it's very cool and doesn't have a time limit.

Press the F11 key to bring up the VST Instruments loading window and insert the Battery demo into the first slot. Load up the 'Soul' kit as we did before.

VSTis are MIDI devices, and so Battery is a MIDI device. In order to play it from our keyboard, we need to connect the MIDI from our keyboard to Battery; it's a bit like using a virtual cable. Cubase uses MIDI tracks to route MIDI around the place, and any MIDI input into Cubase goes to a MIDI track first – this is so the MIDI information can be recorded. For each MIDI track, you can select a MIDI output that you want to route the MIDI to. This could be a MIDI OUT on your MIDI interface, so you can send the notes from your keyboard back out to an external sound module. Or, as with Battery, we can route it to a loaded VSTi.

> **Tip**
>
> If at any time you don't seem to be getting any sound out of Battery, even by clicking on the pads, then be aware that after it's been loaded for a while Battery will reduce its volume to zero. To get sound back, remove the plug-in and re-load it and the kit.

Click on the first MIDI track (MIDI 01) and look at the track info column on the left (Figure 6.25). It gives access to things like volume, pan, MIDI input and output, MIDI channel number, bank and program numbers. For Battery what we're interested in is the MIDI input and output options.

MIDI input should read 'All MIDI Inputs', that way, regardless of how you've connected your keyboard to the computer, you should get a MIDI input to this track. If you had separate keyboards attached to separate MIDI ports, you may want to select the specific port for the keyboard you're playing.

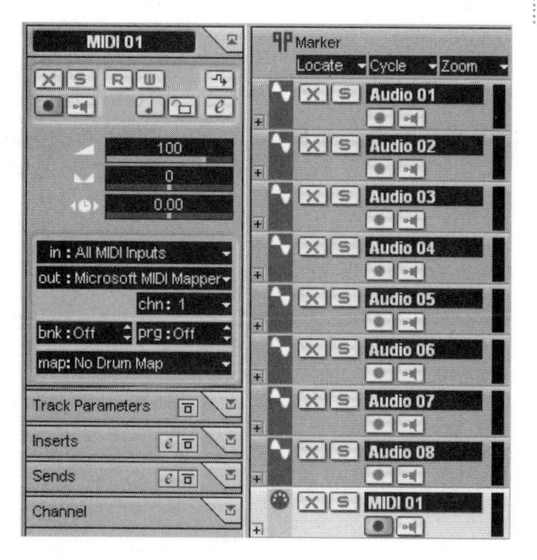

Figure 6.25
The Track Information Column for a MIDI track.

For the MIDI output, we want to select 'Battery'. Click on it and a menu will appear listing all the available MIDI outputs. Near the top will be Battery. You'll notice in my screenshot that I have four listings for something called the 'MT4'. This is my MIDI interface, made by a company called Emagic. It has four MIDI output ports, and I can select any of them from here.

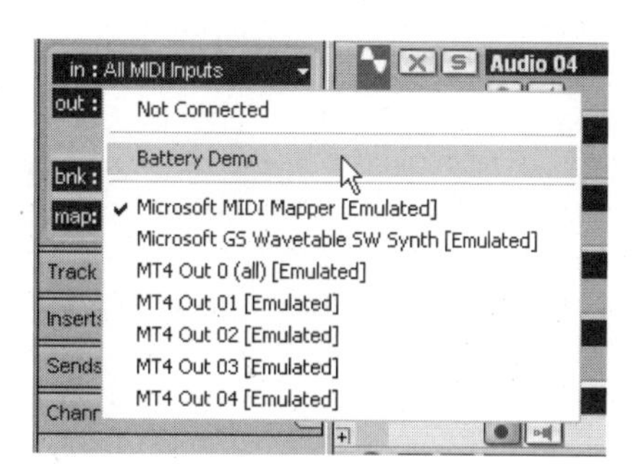

Figure 6.26
Selecting Battery as the MIDI output.

Strike some keys near the bottom of the keyboard and you should see the pads light up in Battery and hear the sounds, provided that you are hitting keys assigned to pads with drum samples loaded.

Each pad has a note assigned to it, and it's written at the top of the pad. The first pad, for instance is assigned to note 'C1'.

The C1 refers to the note C and the octave it's present in. Figure 6.28 shows how notes are described on a keyboard.

Figure 6.27
A Battery pad.

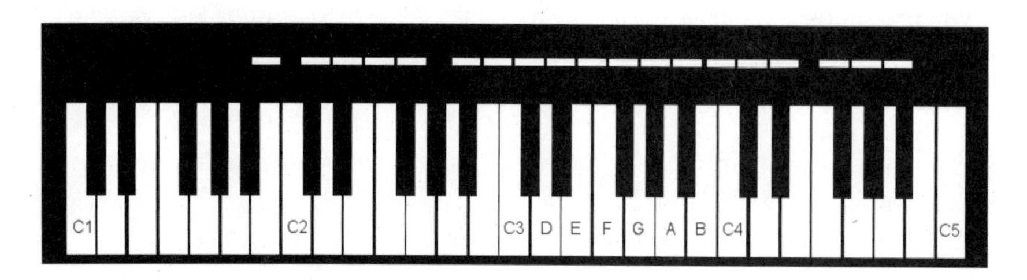

Figure 6.28
Keyboard octaves.

Normally, the middle C note on your keyboard is C3, however, your keyboard may have the ability to move, or transpose, octaves up and down, changing the position of the notes. So you could move C1 up to the middle of the keyboard. This allows you to play a wide range of notes on a small keyboard.

The drum samples in Battery are assigned to C1 upwards. Drum kits usually follow this convention. The other convention they follow is for the layout of the various drum sounds:

C1 – Bass drum
D1 – Snare drum
F#1 – Closed hi-hat
A#1 – Open hi-hat

And so on. This conforms to the General MIDI (GM) standard and is really useful, because regardless of what kit you load, or what drum machine you're using, the notes for the drum sounds are usually in the same place. So, you might write a pattern using one drum machine and then play it back on another without having to edit the notes.

Tip

You can change the note assignment in Battery if you want to by double-clicking the note on the pad and selecting a different note from the keyboard that pops up.

Back to playing Battery, you may notice our old adversary latency making an appearance. If you tried reducing the buffer size during our session of using effects, then the latency shouldn't be too bad. Using my on-board soundcard at the lowest buffer setting, it plays like a drummer who's had far too much to drink – something I'm sure we've all encountered. The latency is there because the audio from a VSTi is created and processed in Cubase's audio engine, and so once again is subject to the speed of the soundcards drivers to move that audio through the computer. If you have a synth on your soundcard, or an external sound module of some kind then there will be no latency at all, because the sound being generated has nothing to do with the computer. In fact if you have an SR-16, MIDI sound module, or other MIDI drum machine, then connect it to the MIDI OUT of the computer, if you have one, select that MIDI OUT for the MIDI track you have selected and try that. If nothing happens try selecting channel 10 for the MIDI track as drums are often on that channel. Remember that the sound will come out of the sound module, not the computer, so make sure you can hear it.

We'll do more on connecting up your existing gear to the computer in a later chapter. For now, let's persevere with Battery.

Recording a drum track

Let's record some live drums, played from our keyboard, into Cubase. If the latency you're experiencing makes it unplayable, then have a go anyway just for fun so that you understand the process. You're probably appreciating now why a low latency soundcard might be a cool idea.

With the first MIDI track selected and Battery responding to your keyboard you're ready to go. Remember if Battery stops making any sound then remove it and re-load it.

In order to keep everything in time, a metronome would be useful. Cubase has one and you'll find it on the transport bar. Click on the button labeled 'Click' so it lights up blue. If you now press play you'll hear a piercing click denoting bars and

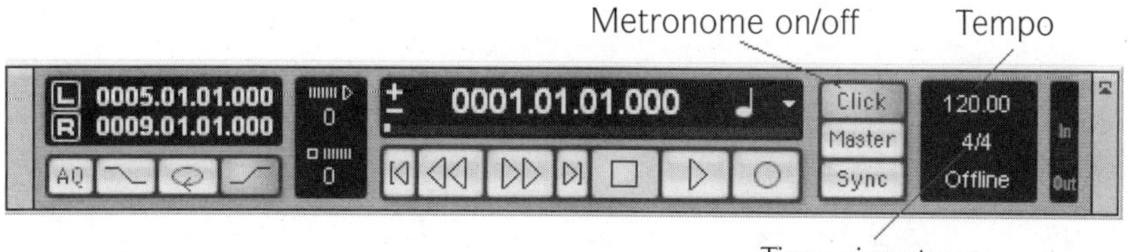

Figure 6.29
The Metronome, tempo, and time signature on the transport bar.

beats. The tempo of the click, and of the whole song can also be set on the transport bar.

The tempo is displayed in beats per minute and you can alter it to whatever speed you are comfortable with. Make sure that the 'Master' button is not lit. This refers to a 'Mastertrack' which is a way of controlling the tempo over time, which I won't go into.

Cubase, by default, records between the left and right markers, this can be changed but let's go with it for now. The timeline at the top of the project arrange window shows bar numbers, click in the top half of the timeline and drag the blue line so it covers 4 bars – this should be enough for our first drum recording.

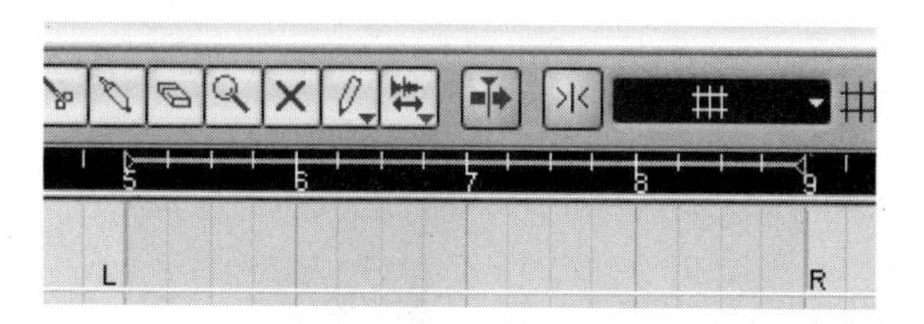

Figure 6.30
Setting left and right markers in the timeline.

When you press record, Cubase will jump to the left marker and give you two bars count-in before recording.

I usually use one hand for playing bass and snare and the other for playing hi-hats so that I can play roughly a whole kit in one go. You can do whatever you like. Press record, wait for the count-in, and play whatever comes to mind, ideally trying to keep in time with the metronome. When the song reaches the fourth bar, it'll stop recording and you'll see that an event has been created with some black lines in it.

I usually use one hand for playing bass and snare and the other for playing hi-hats so that I can play roughly a whole kit in one go.

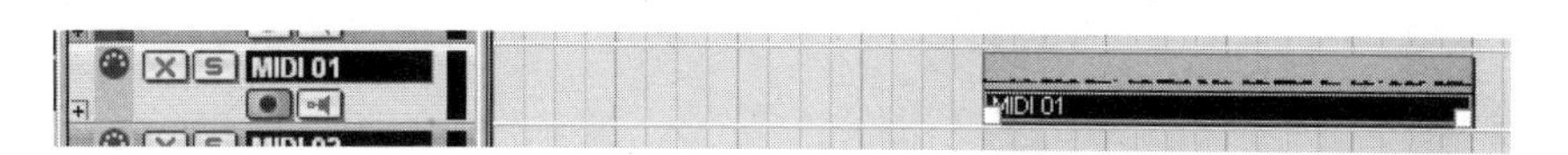

Figure 6.31
A recorded MIDI event.

This event contains all the notes you played on your keyboard. It doesn't contain any 'sound', just the note data. If you rewind Cubase and play it back, you'll hear that the notes are being sent to Battery, which is playing the sounds while you grimace at your terrible lack of timing.

Just to labor the analogy of sheet music, we can see the MIDI information we've recorded as notation in Cubase. It is just a bunch of recorded notes after all. If you right-click on the event and select 'Open Score Editor' from the MIDI menu, you'll be able to see what you recorded as a score. Hang on a minute, it probably looks really weird and very un-notation like. Lots of telephones and mail boxes. What's this all about?

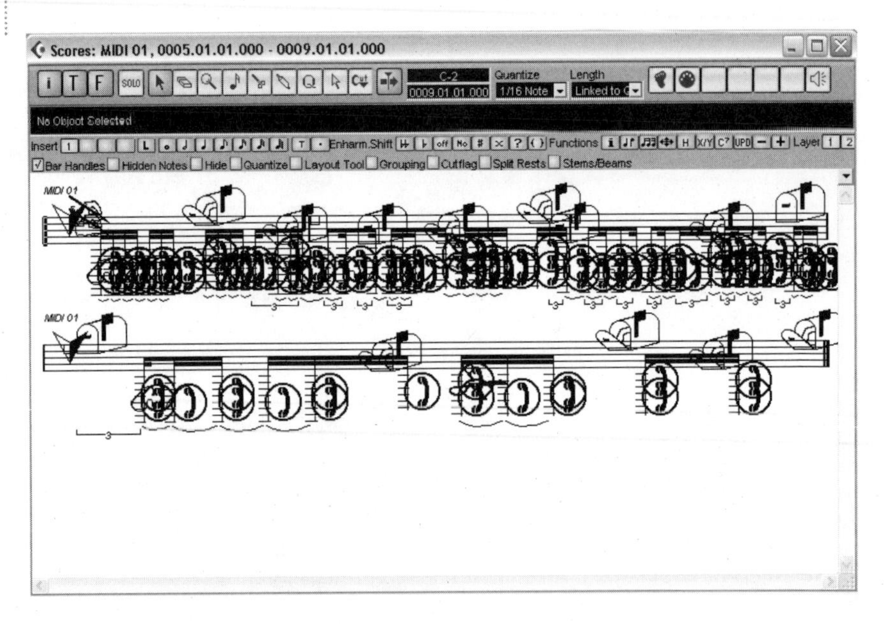

Figure 6.32
Scoring with the wrong font.

This is a stupid bug in Windows where it doesn't see the score font that Cubase installed and instead substitutes 'WingDings'. If you open your 'Fonts' folder (you'll find it in the control panel) and double-click the 'Score Font 4.0', everything will return instantly to normal.

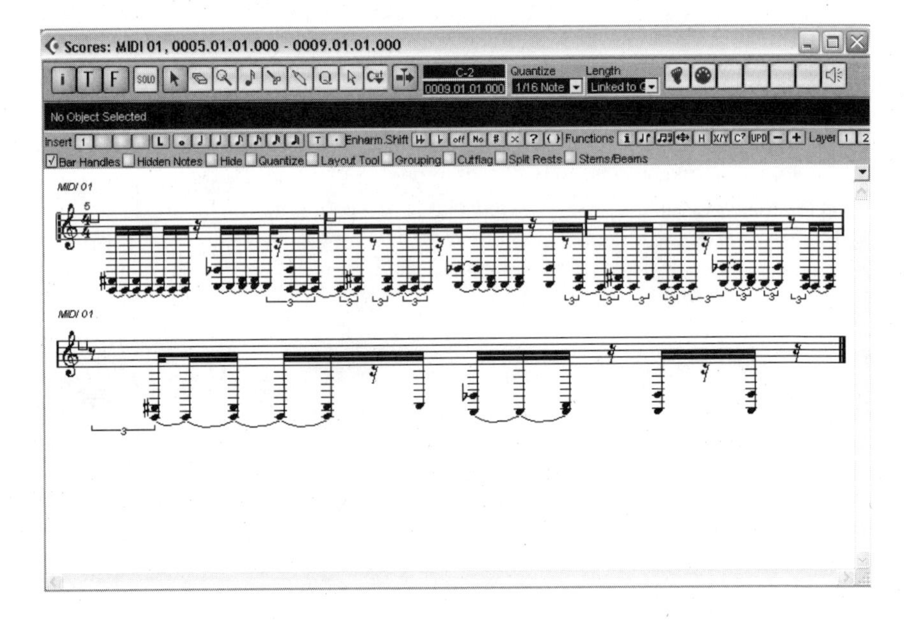

Figure 6.33
Scoring with the right font.

That's more like it. You can close the score window now. It was just an illustration, although useful to you if you like working with notation, I won't dwell on it.

Getting the timing right is one of the things that Cubase is very good at. Our playing may be awful but Cubase has tools to allow us to tidy it up, it's called 'quantization'.

Quantization

With our event selected, press the 'Q' key on your keyboard. You may notice a slight change in the lines within the event. Play back the event again and you'll hear that it's changed. It may not yet sound right, sounds may be out of place, but you'll notice that it now follows exactly on the beat. This is quantization. It snaps the notes to the nearest beat. The quantization parameters are set in the upper-right part of the Cubase window.

Figure 6.34
Quantization options.

Currently it's set to quantize to a 1/16th bar. Try changing it to 1/4 of a bar and press 'Q' again to re-quantize the event. If you hate the change, you can always undo it by going to the Edit menu, or by holding down 'Ctrl' and pressing 'Z' on your keyboard.

To use quantization more effectively, and to try creating a more worthwhile drum pattern, let's split up our drum sounds and record a different track for each. What we'll do is use three tracks, one for bass, one for snare, and one for hi-hats. The first track is already setup for recording, delete our original event (remember that this is a demo version so you can't save anything anyway), hit record, and after the count-in hit C1 to play the bass drum on beats 1 and 3 of each bar.

Next we want to record the snare in time with the kick. Before we do it would be great to have the bass drum bang on the beat; we could probably then lose the annoying metronome and use the kick as our guide.

The bass drum was meant to occur twice in each bar, on notes 1 and 3, so set quantization to 1/2 bar and hit 'Q'. Bingo. Now the bass is on the beat. Select MIDI track 2 (MIDI 02) and for its MIDI output select the Battery Demo VSTi as we did with track 1. You should now be able to play Battery from the second track.

Keeping it laughingly simple, we now want to record the snare, note 'D1', on opposite beats to the bass, 2 and 4. Hit record, if you've turned the click off you won't get a count-in, and off you go. If you would like a count-in but no clicks during the recording, then you need to set it up in the metronome setup window. You'll find that under the 'Transport' menu (Figure 6.35).

Make sure 'Precount' is ticked and under 'Click during', 'Record' and 'Play' are not. Hit 'OK' and you now get a count-in click.

Once you've recorded the snare, select 1/4 note from the quantize options and hit 'Q' to quantize. They should both be playing the rather bland pattern in perfect sync.

Now for the hi-hats. Select MIDI track 3 (MIDI 03), set the output to Battery and record the closed hi-hat (F#1) on every beat, but on the 8th and 16th play the open hi-hat (A#1) instead. When you're done, with the 1/4 note quantize still selected hit 'Q'.

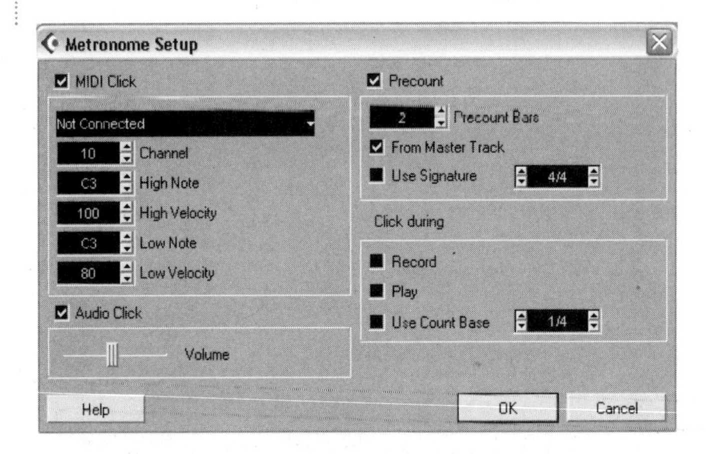

Figure 6.35
Metronome setup.

There you have it. A perfectly in time drum pattern created from your own sloppy playing.

Groove Quantize

A criticism often applied to computerized drums is the lack of 'feel' that you get. This can be true, as we've just seen, we can make our drum patterns stick exactly on the beat, all the time. With a real drummer there would be a certain amount of variation, groove, or swing to drumming. Well, you can remedy that right away by getting a real drummer, mic-ing up the drum kit and recording him playing live on an audio track. Alternatively, you could get a drummer with a MIDI drum kit and record his hits live into Cubase and use Battery or whatever to play the sounds. This all sounds like a lot of hard work though. Luckily Cubase has a solution, known as Groove Quantize.

Groove quantizing essentially moves the notes just off the beat to create a 'swing' feel. You can access this through the quantize select menu, at the bottom, 'setup'. Set Cubase playing and select your hi-hats event. In the quantize setup window, tick the 'Auto' box and move the 'Swing' slider to the right. You'll hear the

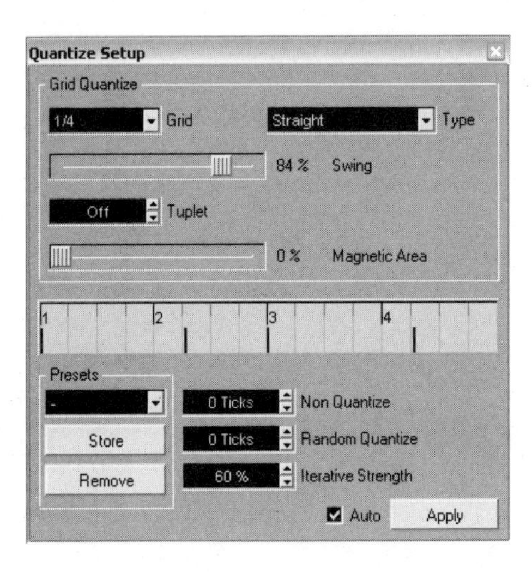

Figure 6.36
Quantize setup window.

hi-hats beginning to sound like they're going all over the place. Move it up 80% or so, and now select the snare event. The hi-hats and snare share the same quantize value, but in order to apply the same swing to the snare you need to move the slide a little for it to register. Set it to the same as the hi-hat. It should now start sounding a bit like a pattern with a time signature of 6:8 rather than 4:4. Obviously the swing we've applied is a bit over the top, but with fine adjustment and practice, you can get some very realistic, human sounding, patterns.

I've only touched on the main features of quantization. There's much more in there for those who want to look.

I want to move on now to another way of creating drum patterns, and for the relief of those experiencing high latencies, you'll be pleased to hear that it doesn't involve playing anything from a keyboard.

Using the Drum Editor

Delete any existing events so that we can have a nice fresh start, but leave Battery loaded. Select the 'Draw' tool, either from the toolbar at the top, or by right-clicking in the arrange window and selecting it from the menu. On the first MIDI track, click and drag from the left marker to the right marker and you'll create an empty event of four bars in length. Now, right-click on the empty event, and from the MIDI menu select 'Open Drum Editor'.

You'll now be looking at Cubase's Drum Editor window which looks like a grid. On the left you'll see a list of drum sounds and corresponding notes, which again follow the GM convention. On the Drum Editor's toolbar you'll notice a little drum stick, select it and click in the grid alongside the bass drum.

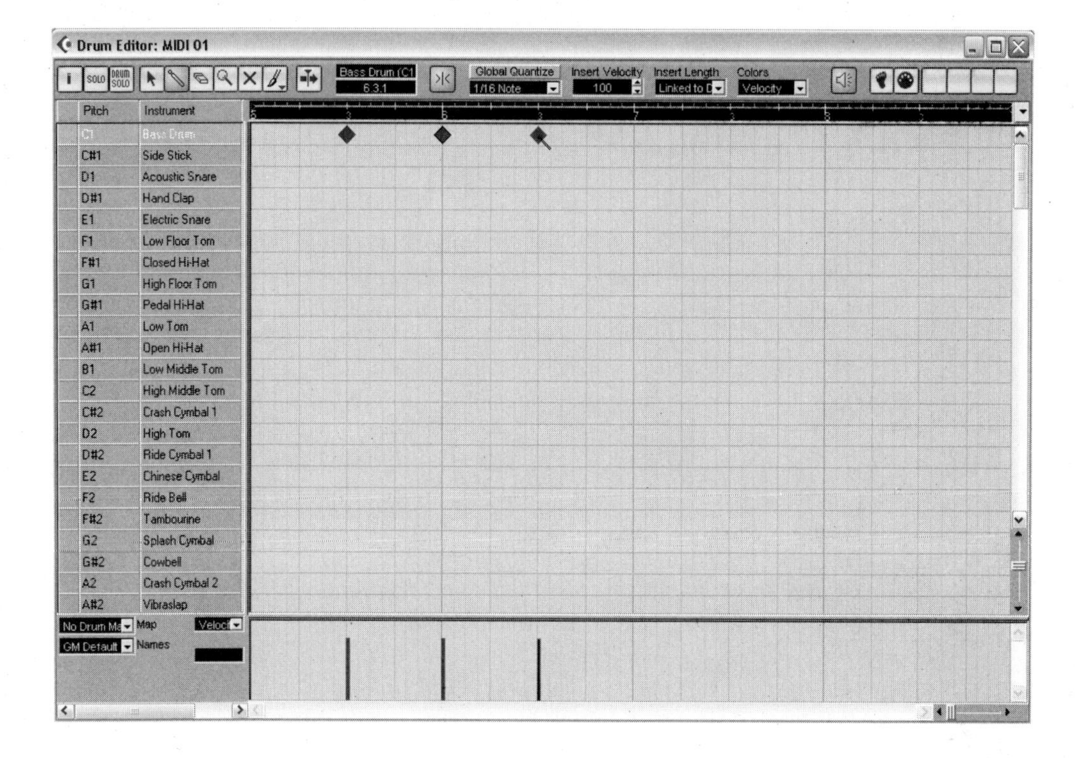

Figure 6.37
Adding hits to the Drum Editor.

Red diamonds will appear and you'll hear the bass drum from Battery every time you add one.

The Drum Editor is marvelously simple and I'm sure you already understand how it works. To create a pattern, simply click in the grid where you want the drums to play. To remove a diamond, click it again.

If you set Cubase to play the four-bar loop, you'll get an instant idea of how the pattern is shaping up as you add diamonds. You can also click and drag to paint diamonds onto every gridline.

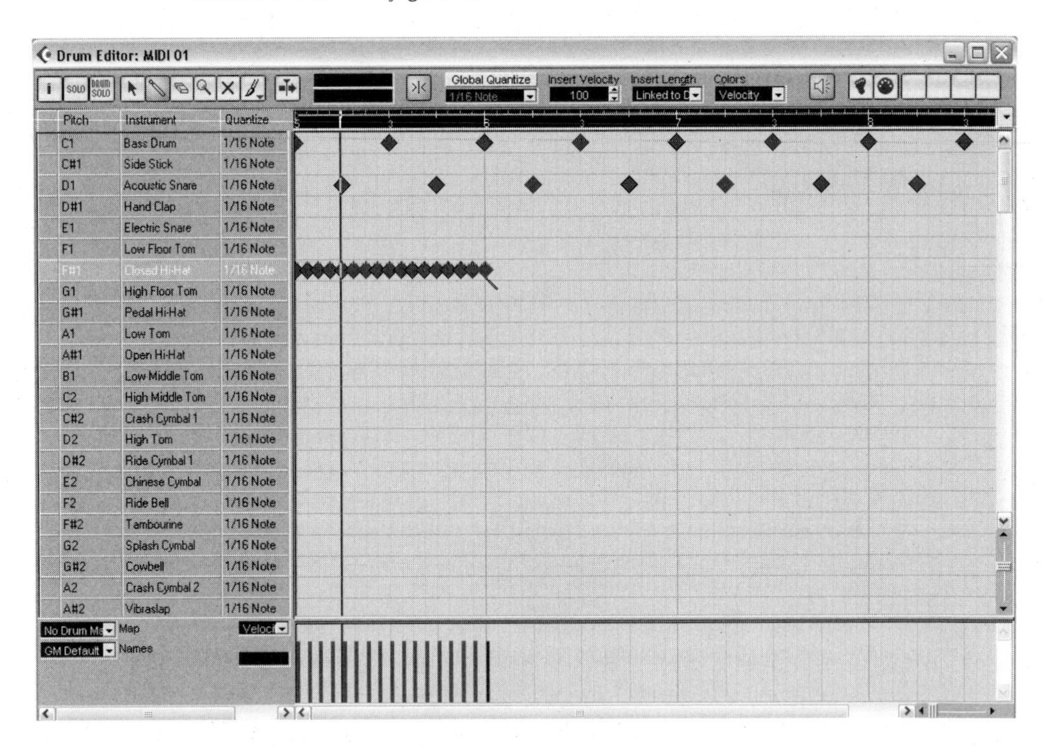

Figure 6.38
Adding many more hits to the Drum Editor.

The grid acts as quantization so that you always put a diamond in time. This of course can be turned off or you can change it for each individual drum sound. To see what I mean, turn off the 'Global Quantize' at the top and if you can't see the quantize column drag the divider between the drum sounds and the grid to the right to reveal it. So, for instance, if you wanted to paint in a load of hi-hats, then select the quantize you want, maybe 1/8 note, then click and drag all the way across the grid.

At the bottom of the grid is the 'controller' pane. This is where you can apply different MIDI controllers over the notes. By default it shows Velocity and you'll notice the lines that appear for each diamond you add. If you take your drum stick and click in the controller pane you can change the velocity values for those notes. The pane shows the values of the notes for whatever drum sound you have selected (Figure 6.39).

The color of the lines, and the corresponding diamond, give an indication of the velocity, with blue being very low and red being very high. Varying the velocity of hits within the pattern is a good way of reintroducing a human feel to the pattern.

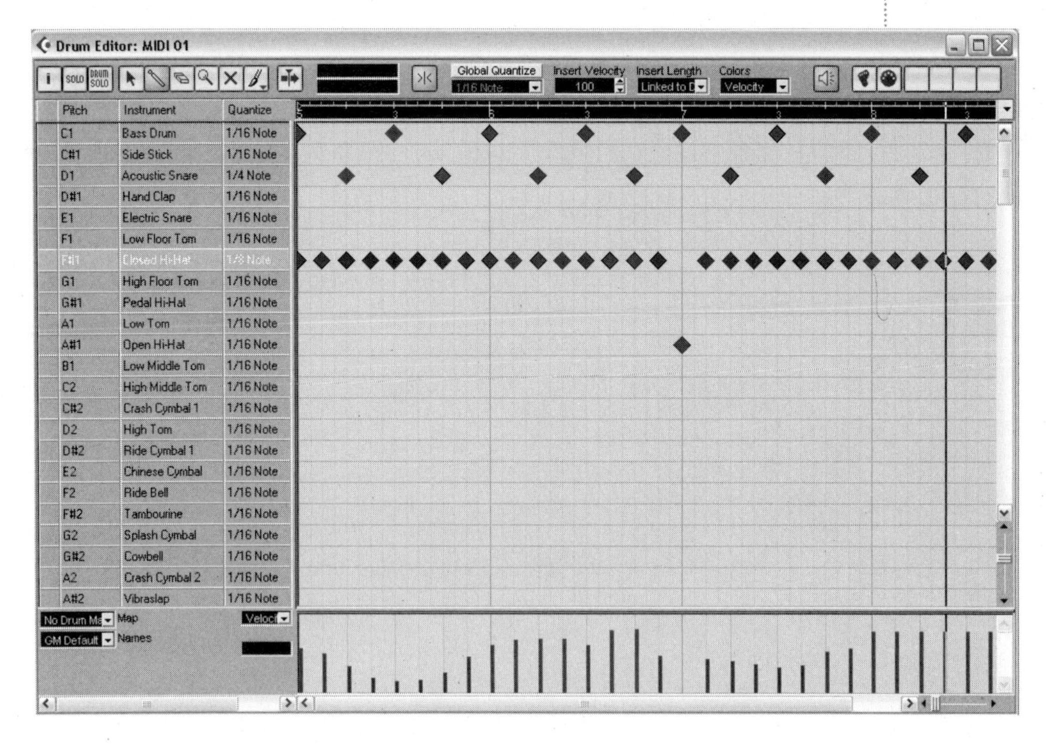

Figure 6.39
Velocity control in the bottom pane of the Drum Editor.

A real drummer rarely hits a drum with the same velocity every time. This also allows you to use the different samples contained within a velocity layer – if it has one.

Close the Drum Editor and you'll see that your empty event is now full of little black lines that represent the data you've just entered.

So, that's one four-bar pattern created. How do we go about creating more patterns and stringing them together in a song?

Arranging patterns

To create another pattern, we can do exactly as we did before, by either playing in live or creating a event and using the Drum Editor. However, one much quicker way of adding another pattern is to take our existing one, copy it, and edit it. If you select the event, you can use the Edit menu to copy it and then paste it wherever the song position line is. An easier way is to hold the Alt key and click and drag the event to wherever we want to put the copy. This creates a copy of the original event.

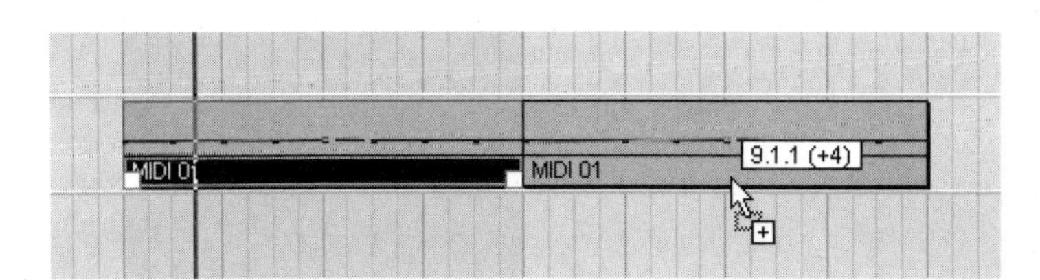

Figure 6.40
Duplicating MIDI events.

We now have two identical four-bar events. Right-click the new copy and select 'MIDI – Open Drum Editor'. You can now edit the copy to make a new pattern.

To change the right marker to include the new event for looped playback, click on the little arrow on the right end of the blue line in the timeline and drag it to the right.

You can add further events this way, making copies of the original or any of the copies. When it comes to putting them in the correct order to construct your song, all you have to do is click and drag the events around. You can even drop them onto different MIDI tracks if you like, that way you could use a different drum kit for events you've put on that track. You could load up the DR-008 and have it doing alternate patterns by placing every other event onto a second MIDI track.

> **Info**
>
> Selecting the 'Split' tool, which looks like a pair of scissors, and clicking in the middle of an event splits it in two and now each part can be treated as an individual event.

One more useful bit of editing for this section. So far we've dealt with four-bar patterns. I'm sure you can see that you can make patterns of other lengths just as easily. What you can also do is chop up these events into whatever size you choose, allowing you to make, for instance, four one-bar patterns out of one four-bar pattern.

Naming the events so you can tell them apart would probably be a good idea at this point. In the top-left corner of Cubase is a button which reveals the 'Event InfoLine'.

Reveal Event InfoLine

Name selected event here

Figure 6.41
The Event InfoLine.

Now you can re-arrange your patterns or events as you like.

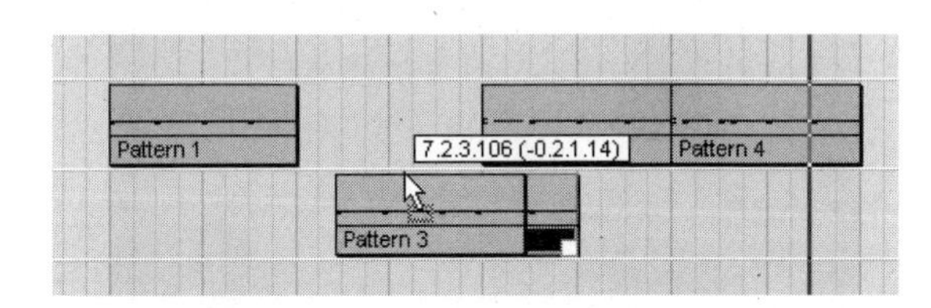

Figure 6.42
Arranging patterns.

Preset patterns

You may be thinking at this point, after all the playing and editing and re-arranging, which is all cool stuff, that it seems to take a lot of trouble to get to a point where Cubase can play back a half-decent drum pattern. With the SR-16 you just select 'Rock 1' and off it goes. You may want to create your own patterns in the end, but often you just want something instant to play along to in order to get the creative juices flowing. Cubase is essentially a blank canvas. It doesn't like to dictate the sort of music you do and so comes devoid of things like preset patterns.

We did see in the DR-008 that it had the ability to allocate patterns to a single pad using its DD Sequence module, and this comes with some presets, however that's only available in the DR-008.

During my research for this book, I looked all over the place for some sort of preset pattern plug-in for Cubase. Cakewalk's flagship studio software 'Sonar', Cubase's main rival, has a plug-in called 'Session Drummer', which does exactly what we are after, but unfortunately works only with Sonar.

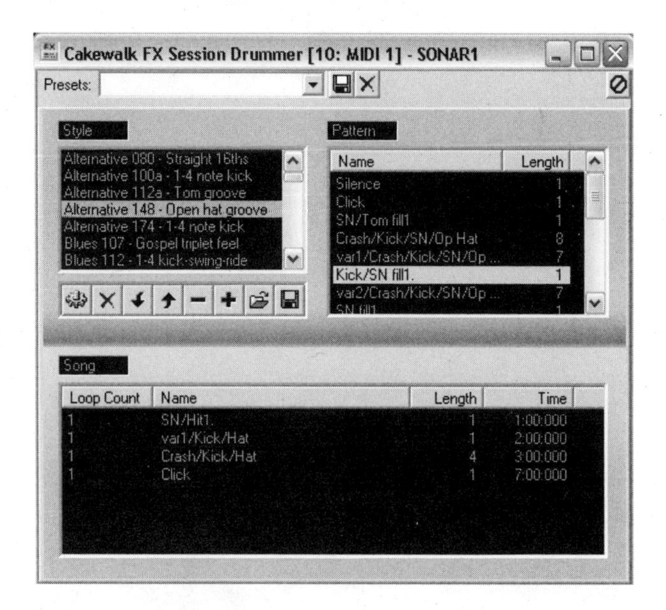

Figure 6.43
Cakewalk Sonar's Session Drummer.

I asked plug-in manufacturers and even my friends at Steinberg and everyone agreed it was a good idea, but no one knew of such a product, until I asked Angus at Fxpansion, the creator of the DR-008. He pointed me in the direction of a company called MusicLab who produce a product called SlicyDrummer which just might do the trick. I have of course, included a trial version of SlicyDrummer on the CD-ROM. You'll find it in the 'Software/MusicLab' folder. Double click the 'slicydrummer_trial.exe' file to install it.

SlicyDrummer is an 'MFX' MIDI plug-in that can act on a MIDI track. Cubase doesn't support these by default but you can persuade it to do so by adding the 'mfxwrapper.dll' that you'll find in the MusicLab folder, to the 'Components' folder that can be found in the 'Cubase SX Demo' folder. Its usual location is:

C:\program files\steinberg\Cubase sx demo\components

Once SlicyDrummer is installed, copy that file to the 'Components' folder, restart Cubase, and it'll be able to use it.

The 'Fill-inDrummer', which you'll also find in the MusicLab folder, is another plug-in that allows you to create 'fills' quickly and easily. It works in a very similar way to SlicyDrummer, but I won't talk about it here. Feel free to install it and try it out as well if you like.

Info

Sometimes I tire of all these names made up of two words pushed together and yet retain the capital letters – teaches our children TerribleGrammar!

MusicLab's SlicyDrummer

MIDI plug-ins are accessed in a similar way to VST effects plug-ins for audio tracks. Select the first MIDI track (remove any existing events from our pattern making), and click on the 'Inserts' bar on the left in the track info column. Click in the first insert slot and you'll find a very different list to the audio plug-ins. All sorts of interesting MIDI stuff can be done with these plug-ins, like creating instant chords from a single note, or adding an arpeggio, but for the moment we're interested in the SlicyDrummer, so select it.

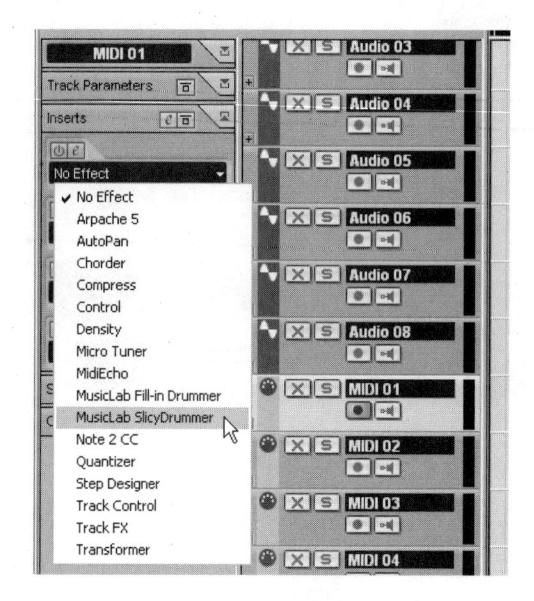

Figure 6.44
The SlicyDrummer can be found in the inserts on a MIDI track.

As soon as you select the plug-in, the registration screen will pop up urging you to buy the product, and maybe you will, but not just now. Click the 'Register Later' button to continue – you have 14 days to try it out.

Just for a change we'll use Angus' DR-008 as the drum sounds this time. He did suggest we try this software in the first place and we can use up a few minutes of the 4-hour time limit. At least it won't keep going silent on us!

Load up the DR-008 VSTi and set it as the output of the MIDI track we've selected. To bring back up the usual track info column, so you can select the output, click the button in the right corner next to the track name box. Don't forget to load up the acoustic kit.

The SlicyDrummer editor should already be open; if not, bring up the inserts and click the little 'e' button next to the plug-in (Figure 6.45).

Hit the play button on Cubase's transport bar and you'll hear a ready-made pattern. Now that's exactly what we were after! SlicyDrummer will continue to play the current pattern as long as Cubase is in play.

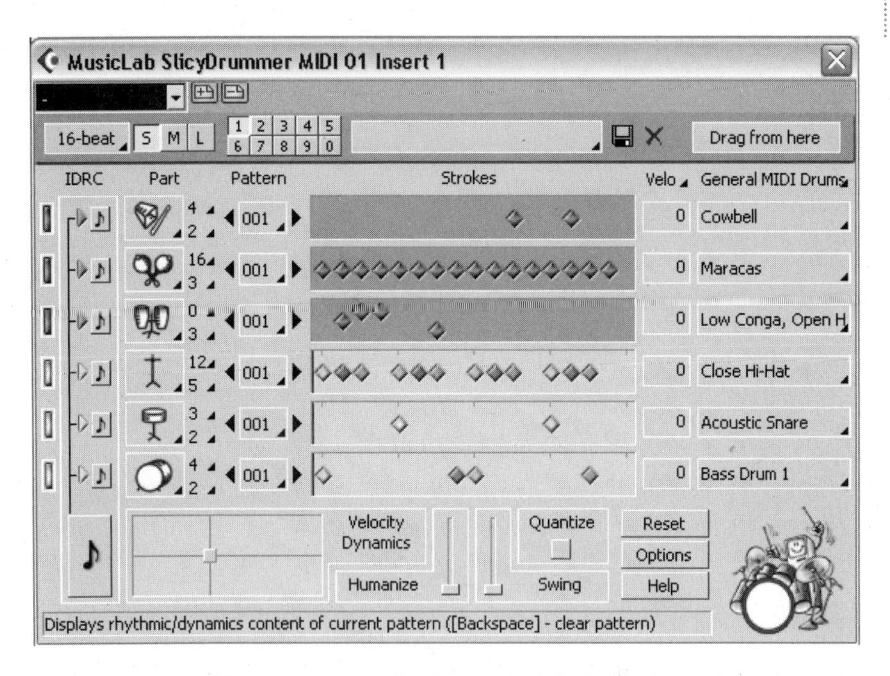

Figure 6.45
MusicLab SlicyDrummer.

To choose a different pattern, click in the initially blank bar at the top and a menu full of all sorts of patterns will emerge. The full version comes with over 2000.

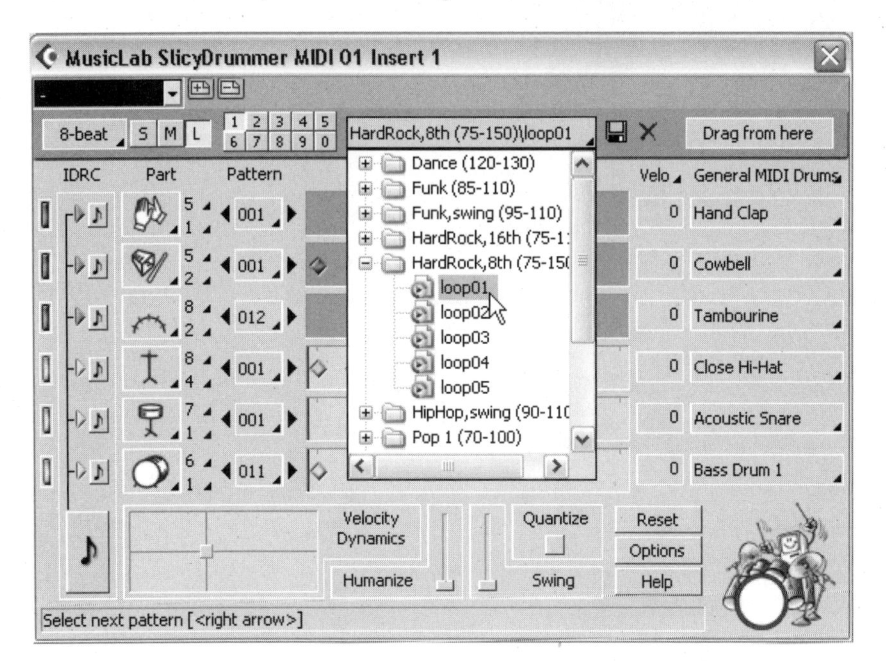

Figure 6.46
Selecting a pattern in SlicyDrummer.

Any new pattern you select jumps in at the next bar. Now, you can't really create your own patterns from scratch with this program, no amount of clicking in the grid area will change a note. However, it does have something rather clever. It has the ability to randomly generate patterns using a clever algorithm that somehow manages to make them sound right.

See the column of notes on the left under 'IDRC', well this is the Intelligent Drum Rhythm Compose section. You can choose whether you want to intelligently compose one part – click the little note next to the part, or intelligently compose the entire pattern – click the big note. The green light for each part has to be on for it to participate in the composition. It can certainly create some interesting ideas.

You can change the note, and so the pad in the DR-008, that each part is pointing to and you have sliders to 'Humanize' (vary velocity) and add 'Swing' (quantize). Each pattern for each part has variations under 'Pattern' and you can save any patterns that you're happy with.

The question then comes down to how we integrate these patterns into Cubase. We can't keep manually changing patterns while we're trying to play guitar alongside. Here we have something else rather clever. You can take the pattern you've created in SlicyDrummer and slap it onto a MIDI track as an event, and it couldn't be simpler to do.

Select the second MIDI track and set its output to the DR-008. Set the left and right markers around as many bars as you want the length of the pattern event to be. Right-click on the second track in the arrange window and select 'MIDI - Merge MIDI in Loop'. A little 'MIDI Merge Options' window pops up, just have 'Include Inserts' ticked and click 'OK'.

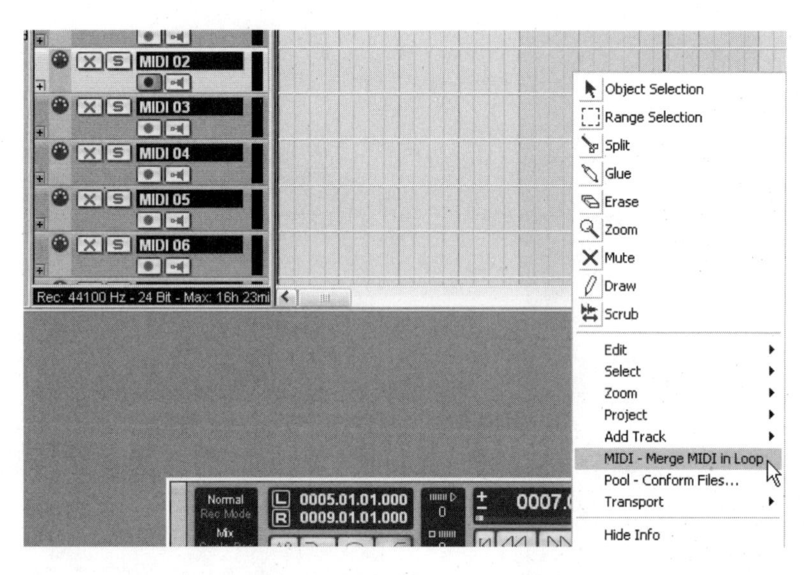

Figure 6.47
Sending a SlicyDrummer pattern to a MIDI track.

As if by magic, the pattern from SlicyDrummer appears as an event between the markers.

Figure 6.48
The SlicyDrummer pattern appears as a MIDI event.

Before you press play to hear it, turn off the SlicyDrummer using the bypass button next to the insert, otherwise it'll start playing again. You can now move the left and right markers, choose or create another pattern in SlicyDrummer and do the same thing again.

One final feature is that you can actually run SlicyDrummer as a plug-in inside the DR-008, just like you did with the DD Sequencer. Right-click a pad, select SlicyDrummer, open the editor and choose a pattern. Then you can trigger the pattern by playing that pad. You could have a whole number of patterns set up on pads, set Cubase into record and press the note that's assigned to that pad to trigger whichever pattern you choose. It's a great way of working on the drum track.

I predict that more products of this nature are going to arrive before too long. Both Steinberg and Angus hinted at it in a 'you never know what's around the corner' kind of way. Steinberg produced the very successful 'Virtual Guitarist', which is a stunningly realistic rhythm guitarist plug-in – not something we'd be interested in at all as we already play guitar, but you've already heard it and been fooled by it. It was used to create the acoustic 'DualStrum' part of the Cubase demo song. Anyway, allegedly there are more products to come in this 'Virtual' line and you can be sure that one of them will be the 'Virtual Drummer'.

News just in

Wouldn't you know it, just as I get towards finishing the book, both Fxpansion and Steinberg manage to bring out the answer to the whole drum pattern thing, just as I predicted not a week ago in the above paragraph.

Fxpansion BFD

Information is a bit sketchy at the moment, but it's billed as a 'Premium Acoustic Drum Library Module' featuring six vintage acoustic drum kits, and a 'Groove Librarian' containing over 500 patterns and beats covering every style imaginable. Lots of talk about the quality of the kits and the interaction between user and grooves. This looks very promising indeed, well, on paper at least.

Steinberg Groove Agent

I was lucky enough to play with a beta version, and it's fabulous.

It has an interesting interface with a timeline slider that can select between drum kits and drum styles from the 1950s to the present day. You can then choose whatever style you want to play with whatever kit. You can swap drum sounds between kits and change various attributes. The styles all have many variations and you can alter the complexity of the patterns and you have a fill button, and a random fill button which plays a fill whenever it feels like it. You can keep the timing tight or let it humanize all over the place. It sounds amazing and was a lot of fun to play with. It should be available by the time this book is released and try as I might I can't seem to persuade anyone at Steinberg to let me get an early copy – ho hum.

Both these products could really be the answer for pattern-based drums in Cubase. Keep an eye out for them.

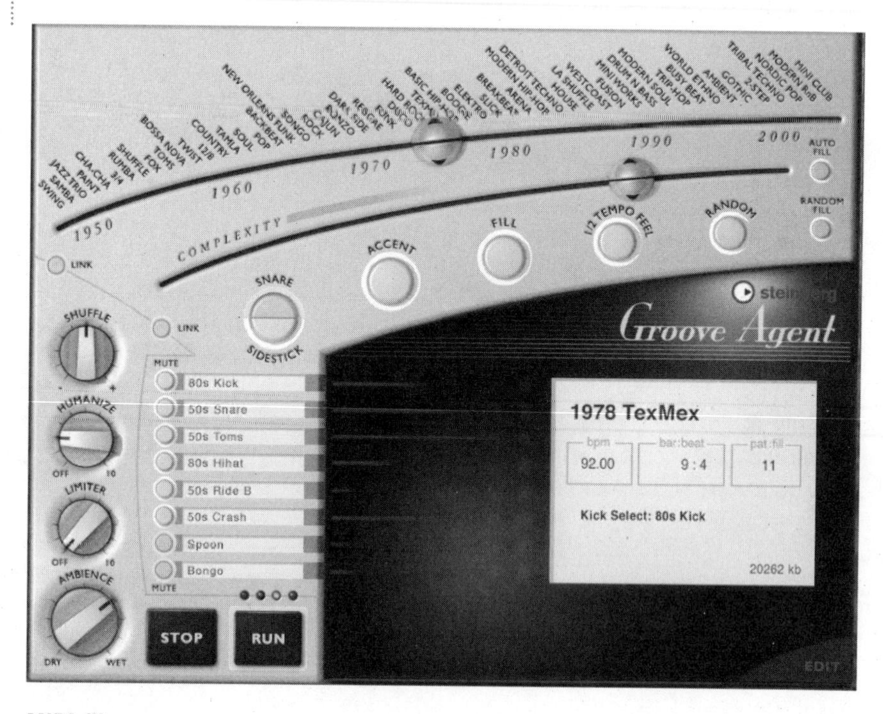

Figure 6.49
Groove Agent – a software drum machine in the traditional sense.

MIDI files

Figure 6.50
Twiddly Bits - MIDI file patterns for every occasion.

Before the existence of SlicyDrummer, or the Session Drummer in Sonar, there have been companies who produce professionally recorded drum patterns that you can use within your sequencer. These are not housed in any kind of interesting user interface, they are essentially patterns of a few bars that you can import as events onto a MIDI track. One of the biggest range is 'Twiddly Bits' from a company called Keyfax. So, rather than create your own patterns, you can import someone else's and use them or tailor them to your own songs. Each MIDI file contains a number of variations on a theme and imports onto difference tracks so you can easily audition them.

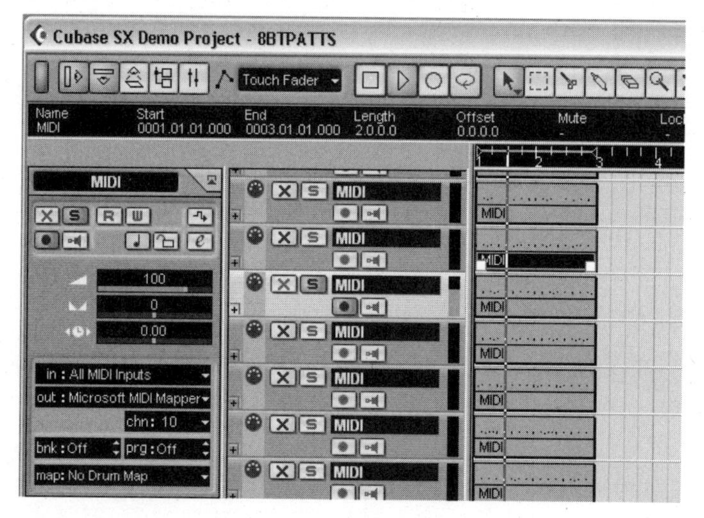

Figure 6.51
Twiddly Bits imported into Cubase.

Then it's just a matter of copying and pasting them about the place. The advantage of these MIDI files is that they've been created by professional drummers using MIDI drum kits, so the 'feel' of them is about as realistic as you are going to get.

This brings this mammoth section on programming drums to an end. I know I sometimes spend hours working on drum tracks to get them just how I want them, so I thought that going into some detail on the subject would be a good idea. Besides, many of the things I've gone over are applicable to using other software synths, not just drum machines, so it'll come in handy later on. However, we're not done with drums just yet. Now we need to get into using real drum loops.

Using drum loops

Since the advent of samplers, musicians have been using drum loops to form the rhythm section of their music. Instead of trying to program drums, why not just record someone playing real drums, and then chop it up into samples of a few bars. Realistically a lot of drum loops get sampled off existing recordings and used on new tracks. The main advantage of sampled drums loops is that they can sound fabulous. The main disadvantage is that you don't have quite so much creative control over them as you do with programming patterns.

Info

A 'loop', in case you're wondering, is usually a short recording of percussion that when looped on playback sounds continuous and in sync with itself.

Computers give us more power than ever to manipulate drum loops and there are stacks of software out there that deal purely with loops and samples. Many of these sorts of programs don't allow you to record actual audio tracks, so they are not entirely useful to us guitarists. However, for creating backing, accompaniment, working on ideas or creating your own loops, they can be helpful and a lot of fun.

We're going to take a quick look a one loop-based program before we deal with using loops in Cubase.

ACID

Sonic Foundry are the makers of one of the most respected, professional audio editors available on the PC; it's called Sound Forge. A few years ago they came up with a revolutionary technology that allowed them to take a drum loop and alter its pitch without changing the tempo, and change its tempo without altering the pitch. It may not sound very exciting, but this is something that is very difficult to do. If you consider some recorded sound on tape or vinyl, if you wanted to raise the pitch of the sound you would have to speed it up. Similarly if you wanted to speed up or slow down the playback, the pitch would change. For instance if you play a vinyl album at 45rpm, the music would be speeded up and at a higher pitch. The rules are the same with digital recordings. If you consider a sampler, a piece of software or hardware that plays back samples, then in order to play a sample of, say, a flute, across the range of a keyboard that sample is speeded up or slowed down to reach the various pitches. Now, with technology contained in programs like ACID, it is possible to alter pitch and tempo independently. However, it's not perfect and there's only so far you can go either way before the sample starts to sound 'wrong'.

Let's take a look. I've included a copy of ACID on the CD-ROM and a number of loops and demo songs to give you an idea of what it can do. I won't go into any great depth, but I hope you find it a useful bit of software. You'll find it in

Info

Sonic Foundry and ACID XPress are registered trademarks of Sonic Foundry, Inc. Other products mentioned are the trademarks of their respective manufacturers. Copyright ©2003 Sonic Foundry, Inc. All rights reserved.

'Software/Sonic Foundry ACID'. Double-click the 'acidxpress30g_bld365.exe' file to install it.

When you start up 'ACID XPress', it asks if you would like to run a demo, or start ACID XPress, or enter a serial number. ACID XPress is a completely free, fully functional version of ACID that gives you 10 tracks to play with and everything you need to mess about with loops; however, in order to use it you have to register it with Sonic Foundry. So, just for the purposes of this example, choose to run a demo version and select 'ACID Style' as it's the simplest version and closest to XPress.

ACID has two main windows. At the top you have your tracks and arrange window, not unlike Cubase, and at the bottom you have an explorer window. If you 'explore' to the 'Loops' folder on the CD-ROM you'll find an 'ACID Loops' folder in which there are some loops and ACID demo songs. Double click the 'Acid Slow Jazz.acd' file to load up the demo.

Figure 6.52
Sonic Foundry's ACID.

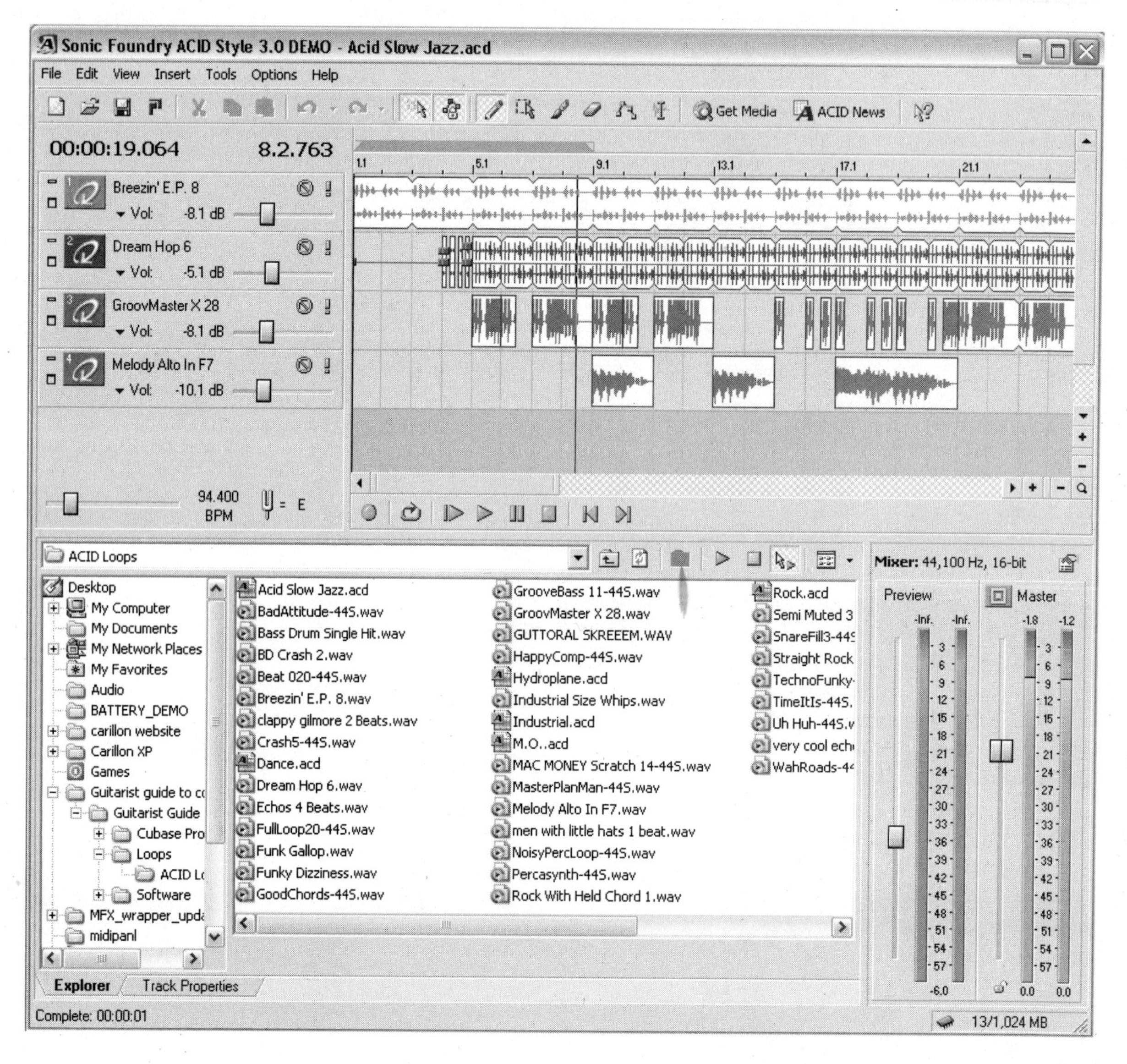

Beneath the tracks to the left, there's a BPM slider which shows the tempo, and also a tuning fork showing the current pitch of the song. While the demo is playing back, try moving the BPM slider to the right and left to hear the way ACID copes with 'time stretching' the samples. Pretty good eh? Try also changing the pitch by clicking on the tuning fork.

The song is made up from a number of loops, not all drum loops obviously. The wonderful thing about ACID is that it takes loops of any tempo and puts them together in sync. You can then use the pitch shift to change key through the song.

Let's look at how you add the loops to make a song. Start with a blank song – 'New' under the 'File' menu. As you click on loops in the explorer window, they will automatically audition for you. To add a loop to a track, double-click it. Let's start with the 'Straight Rock 1' drum loop. A track will appear called 'Straight Rock 1' and when you put your mouse onto the track it turns into a pencil, and now we can literally draw the loop in wherever we want it to be. The indentations show where the loop begins and ends.

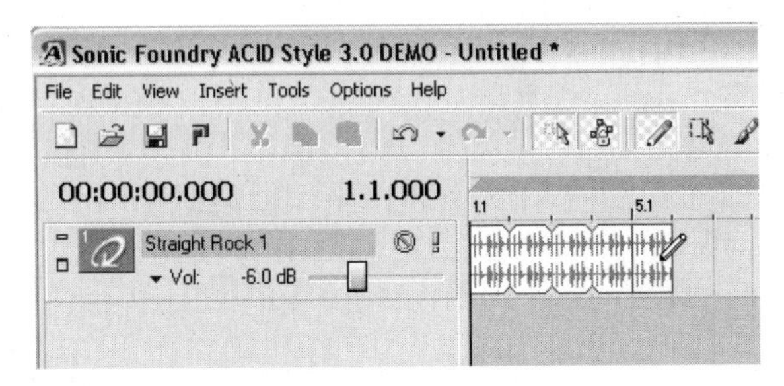

Figure 6.53
Drawing loops into ACID.

Press the 'Loop Playback' button and press play to get the drums playing. Now try auditioning some other loops until you find, perhaps a bassline that you like. Notice how whatever loop you audition it will play back in sync with the drums. I probably don't need to tell you anything else as ACID is so simple to use. You can add more loops and paint them wherever you like. You've also got pan and volume controls and, with the full version, plug-in effects as well.

Once you're happy with your song, you can export it as an audio file and then import that into Cubase so you can add your guitar alongside. It's a great way of putting together drum tracks as well as other accompaniments. There's a huge library of loops available on CD and downloadable from the Internet, specially created for ACID. 'ACIDized Loops', as they're called, contain extra information on the tempo and pitch of the song that a regular loop doesn't. This enables ACID to incorporate the loops straight away without having to detect the pitch or work out the tempo for which it may need your help. With regular loops you may have to instruct ACID to alter its pitch or length a little so that it's perfectly in tune and sync. If you select the contents of a track and click on the 'Track Properties' tab under the explorer window, you'll see where this is done.

Don't forget that you can use all the features of ACID XPress as soon as you register it with Sonic Foundry.

Info

Cakewalk's Sonar supports ACIDized loops directly within the program, which is a nice feature.

Loops in Cubase

Cubase SX has some great drum looping features of its own, however, as Cubase is a more 'open' recording program, where it also deals with non tempo based audio and straight audio tracks it doesn't have some the features you'd find in a specialized program like ACID.

For the purposes of this example, I've included a few drum loops in the 'Loops' folder on the CD-ROM. These loops were recorded with a live drummer in a very expensive studio and come from the 'Loopstation' library of thousands of loops that are included with Carillon Audio System's computers.

Cubase supports the 'drag and drop' of audio files, which means you can drag audio files from a folder and drop them directly onto an audio track. So, open the 'Loops' folder and drag the first loop, 'dry_ride_breakbeat_1.wav', onto the first audio track.

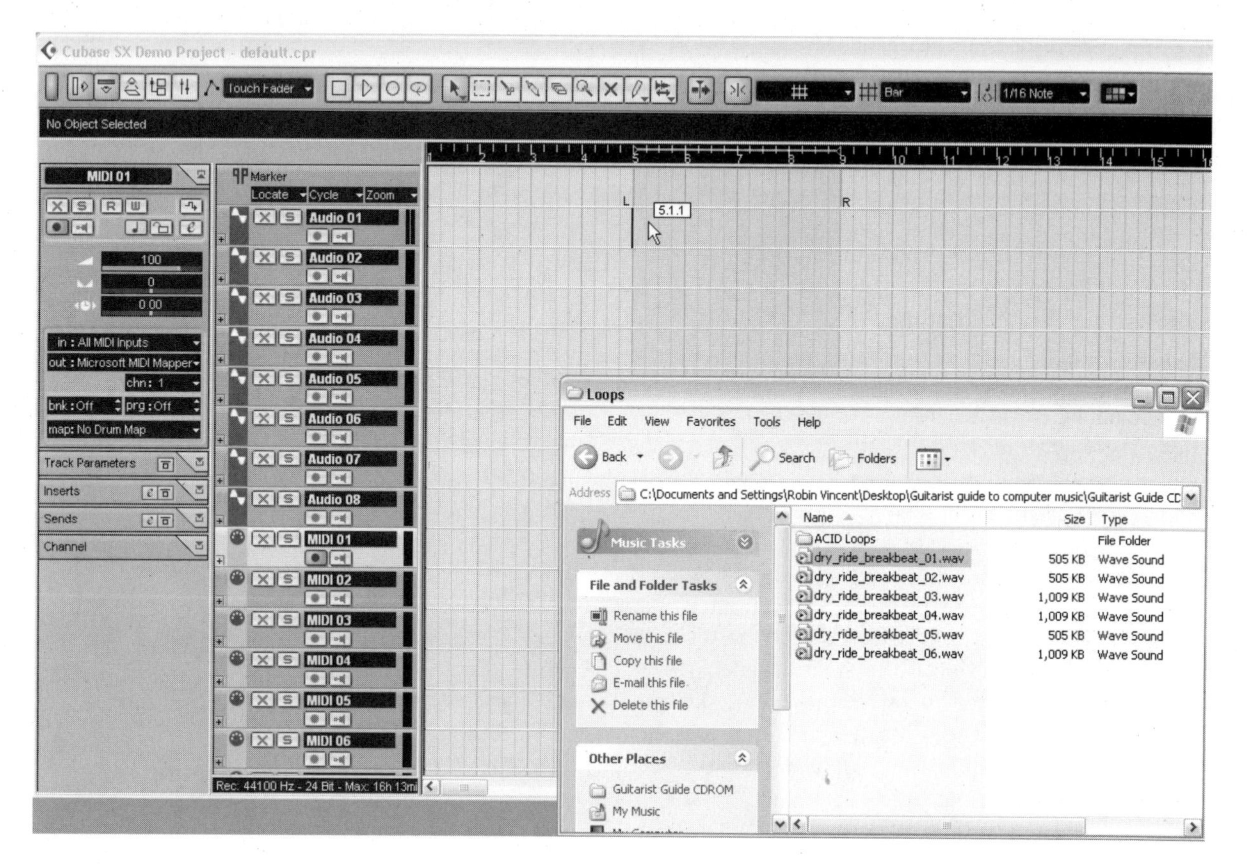

Figure 6.54
Drag and dropping drum loops into Cubase.

When the 'Import Options' window appears, tick the box next to 'Copy to working directory'. This will take the loop off the CD and copy it to the hard drive, which is the best place for it.

Select the loop and press 'P' to set the markers around it. If you put Cubase into looped playback you'll hear that it loops perfectly.

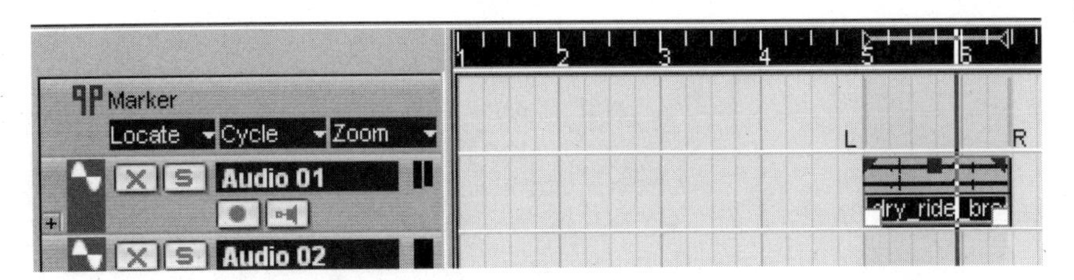

Figure 6.55
Looping a drum loop between markers.

However, if you turn on the metronome, you'll hear that it's terribly out of sync with the tempo of the project. What we need to do is match the tempo in Cubase to the tempo of the loop. You could do this by first moving the left and right markers so that they are around a single bar, the loop now loops back before it's reached the end, and then change the tempo on the transport bar until the loop sits between the markers and plays back perfectly.

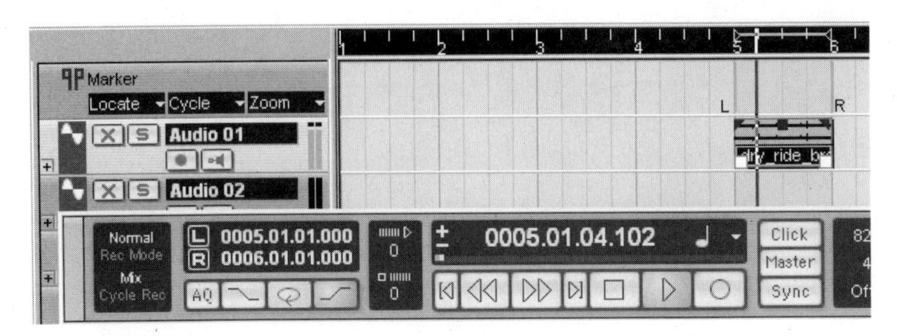

Figure 6.56
Set the tempo to match the loop on the transport bar.

Now, I happen to know that the tempo of this loop is 82 bpm, so if you want a shortcut, just set 82 as the tempo and it'll loop perfectly.

Let's add another loop. Drag and drop the 'Hall_acoustic_breakbeat_46.wav' sample onto the second audio track.

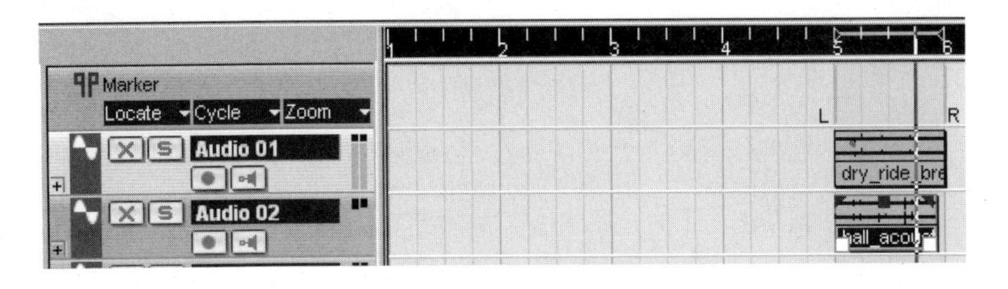

Figure 6.57
Adding another loop of a different tempo.

On playback you'll notice that the two do not match up, in fact you can see it on the screen, the 'Hall_acoustic' loop is shorter, which means that it's got a different tempo.

We'd like to use both loops in our song, so how do we match them up? Well Cubase has a feature called 'audio slicing' where it chops up the loop into slices so you can move the beats about in order to stretch or squash the loop so it matches the tempo. This is much easier to show than it is to describe.

Double-click the 'Hall_acoustic' event to open the sample editor window. You can do all sorts of things here, but at the moment we're interested in beat slicing. Click on the last button on the toolbar, the 'Hitpoints mode' button that looks like an upside-down triangle on a stick, and a few vertical lines will appear on the loop.

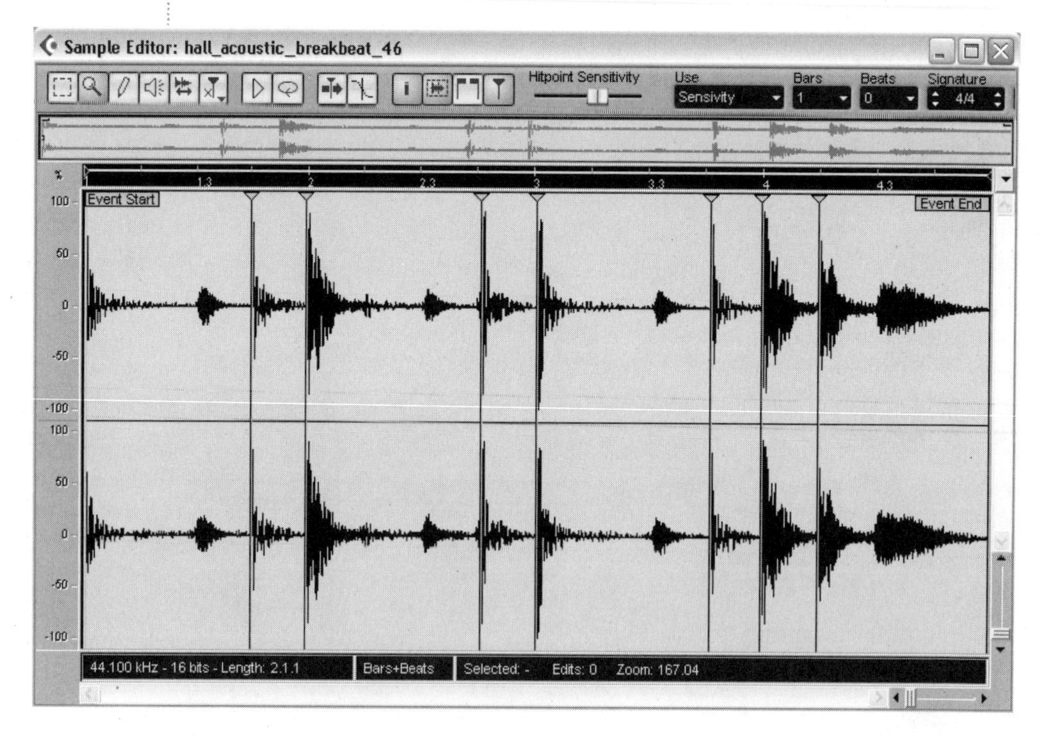

Figure 6.58
Detecting hitpoints in the sample editor.

Cubase has detected where the main beats, or hits, are in the loop and put in 'hitpoints' which will be where the slices are made. At the top is a 'Hitpoint Sensitivity' slider. If you move it to the right, Cubase will pick out more hitpoints from some of the quieter sounds in the loop. We don't need too many though, so the default hitpoints will do fine. You can adjust these hitpoints manually and add or remove them as you see fit. It takes a bit of experimentation before you know exactly where to and where not to put hitpoints, and you don't even know what the effect will be yet. One more important setting is the bar length. Make sure you set the correct bar length of the loop in the fields at the top right. This loop is just one bar long.

From the 'Audio' menu in Cubase, select 'Hitpoints – Create Audio Slices'. The sample editor window will close and you notice that the 'Hall_acoustic' event now fits perfectly in the bar.

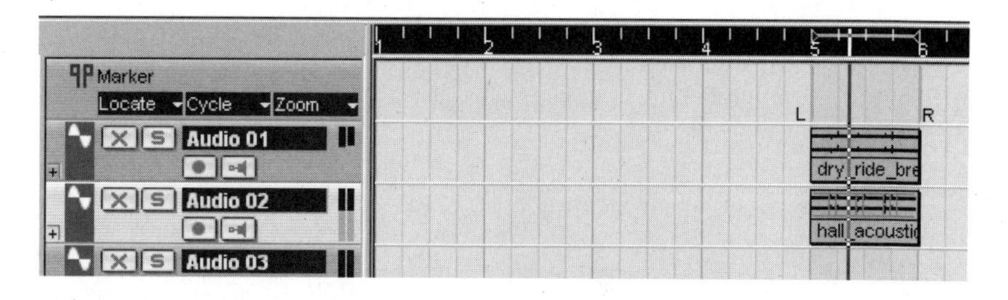

Figure 6.59
Both loops now have the same tempo.

Press play and they'll be in sync. Quite marvelous. If you zoom into the events to have a closer look (you can use the sliders at the bottom right of the arrange window, or right click – zoom – zoom selection) you'll see that the loop has been

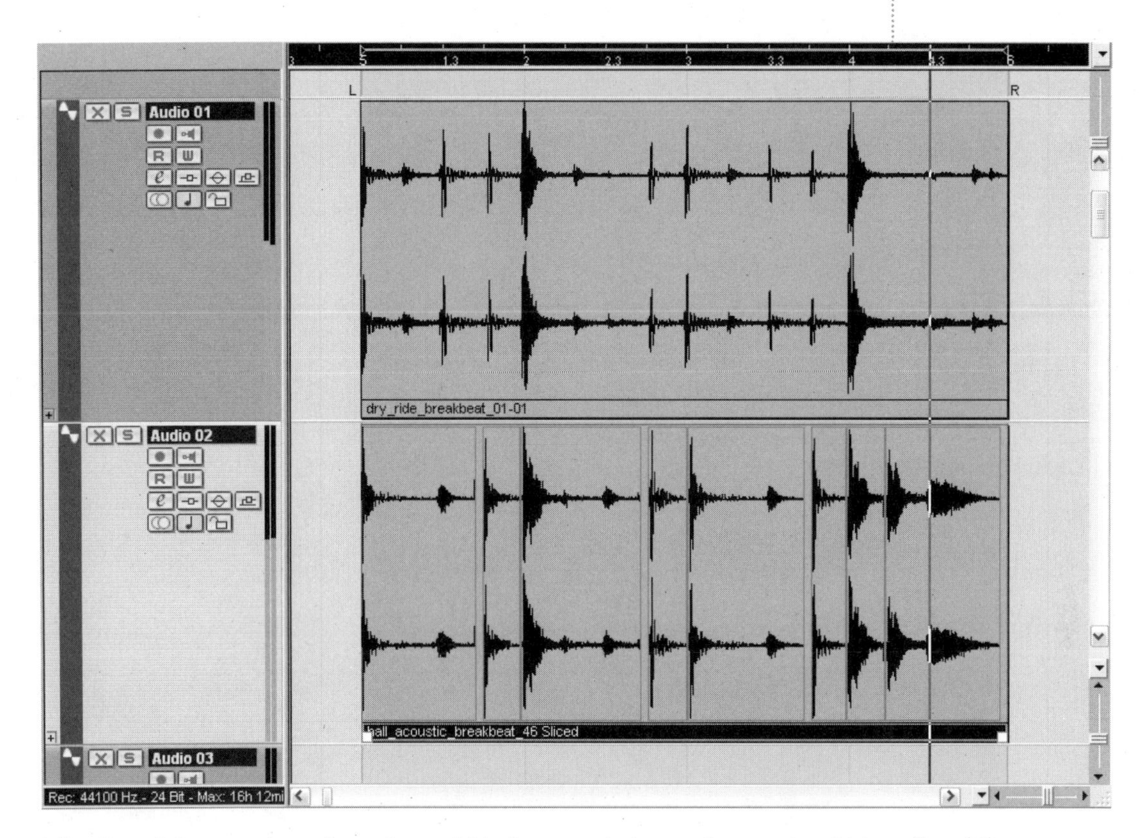

Figure 6.60
A closer view of the sliced loop.

'sliced' up into a number of events, and it's the gaps between the events which have enabled the loop to fill the whole bar.

Now that the loop has been sliced, we can do some quite interesting things with it, such as delete individual events or move or rearrange the events to create a completely different loop.

If you solo the second track so you are only listening to the 'Hall_acoustic' loop, you'll notice a little glitch in the middle, something that doesn't sound quite right. Let's see if we can sort that out. Double-click the event and it'll open in the 'Audio Part Editor' – leave Cubase playing. What you see is the sliced events within the audio event. Zoom in on our trouble spot in the middle. You might need to turn off the 'Autoscroll' which is the button like the 'hitpoint mode' one but with an arrow going through it. Take the 'Object Selection' arrow tool and click on the left event of the two troublemakers. Turn off the 'Snap' button, the last one on the toolbar, so that we can make some fine adjustments. On the bottom right of the event is a small white square, or tag. Click and drag that tag to the left and you can move the end point of the event so that it doesn't include the little glitch at the end (Figure 6.61). Problem solved. Well it might not be completely perfect, but it's certainly better.

So if this audio slicing can let you adjust the tempo of loops, then we should be able to change the tempo of the project and have all the loops follow along. Yes indeed, but only if they are sliced, so first you need to slice up the first loop.

Just as you did before – double-click the event, turn on 'Hitpoint Mode', go to the 'Audio' menu and select 'Hitpoints – Create Audio Slices'.

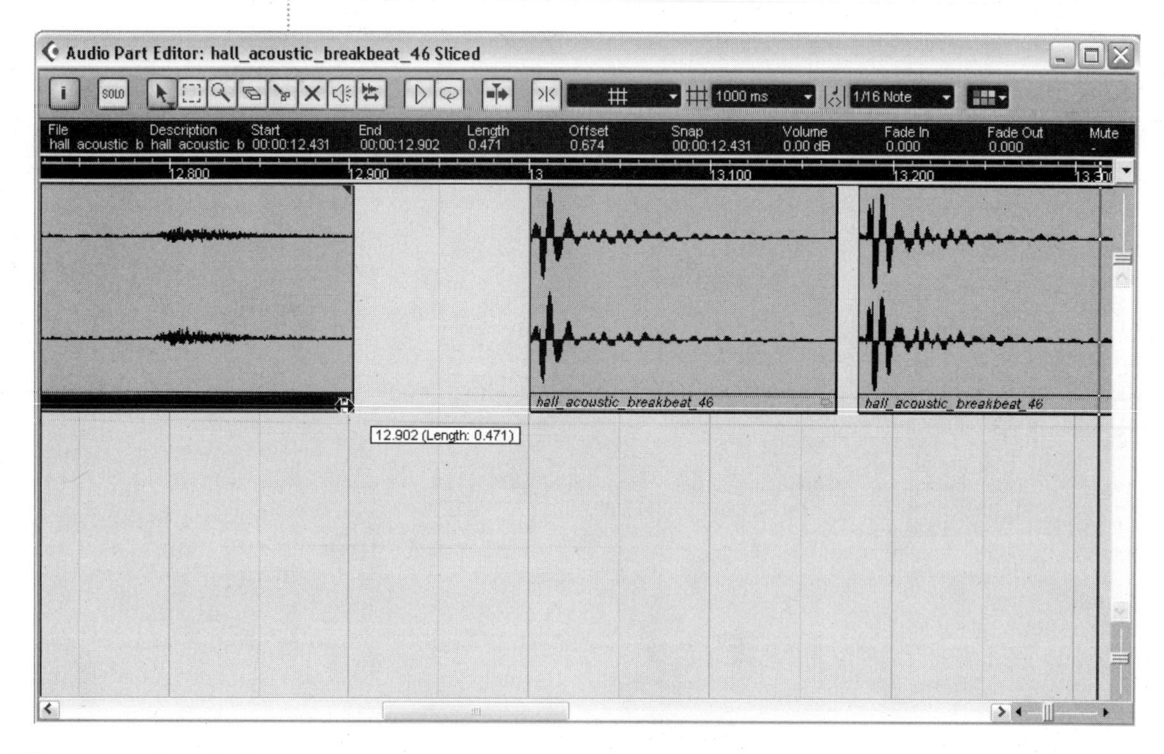

Figure 6.61
Editing the individual slices.

Change the tempo on the transport bar to 100 bpm. Sounds all right, doesn't it? Now try changing it down to 70 bpm. It's not quite keeping it together as well. This is because of the placement and number of hitpoints. At the moment, some of the events contain more than one beat. With a bit of practice and some adjustment to the events you can get it sounding as good as you want.

There are other programs that are specialized in doing this kind of loop editing. 'Recycle' from Propellerhead is probably the most common. It does pretty much exactly what we've been doing except it's more accurate and adjustable. Recycle then outputs the loop as a 'REX' file, which is essentially the loop with the slices built in. Cubase can import REX files directly so it's a good way of improving your looping results.

The rest of the loops in the folder are all at 82 bpm and are variations on our original loop. You can drag them all at once into Cubase and then rearrange them to turn them into a complete drum track – just as we did with the MIDI events earlier on. To copy and paste one of the loops just hold the Alt key and click and drag.

To make your events easier to distinguish in the arrange window, you can add colors to them. Select the event and then select a color from the menu at the top and to the right of the quantize options (Figure 6.62).

That'll do on drums I think. We've gone through a great deal of stuff in Cubase that'll stand you in good stead for the following chapters. Hopefully by now you'll be getting into this computer music lark, finding it easier and more interesting with every page. If you're feeling a bit like your brain is going to explode with information overload, then I'd recommend heading down to the pub. You can always come back to the rest of the book tomorrow. In fact, why don't we all go? Mine's a pint of John Smiths and a packet of peanuts.

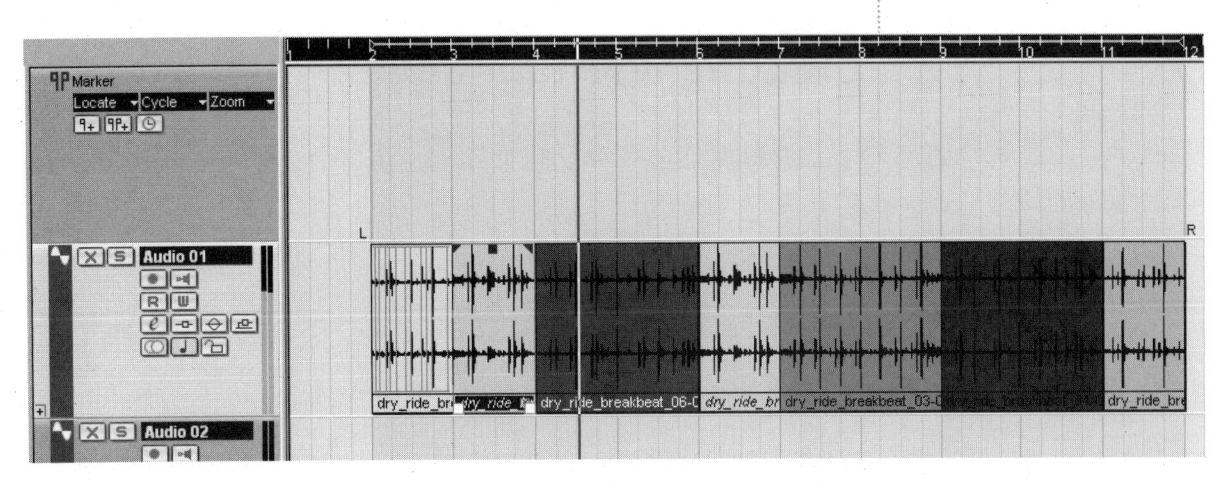

Figure 6.62
For those of you watching in black and white, the blue is behind the pink.

Creating a virtual band

With the drums well and truly sorted out, we could also do with some other instruments to make our virtual band complete. A bass guitar would be a good start, then maybe some nice Rhodes electric piano. Why stop there? Have you ever wanted to add strings to your music? How about a nice string quartet, or maybe go the whole hog with an orchestra? Perhaps you could simply infect your music with some weird electronic noises and filtered bleeps. All these things are possible with your computer.

Talking about software synths

This is the real cutting edge of computer music. It's developing, evolving, and improving all the time and holds, in its sweaty palm, the last nail in the coffin of the hardware-based studio. Traditionally, if you want new sounds, you go out and buy a new synth or sound module, wire it up, plug it in and off you go. How about if instead you could have the same sounds, at the same quality, but fully integrated into your studio software? Doesn't require any setting up or plugging in, doesn't come in a clunky box that gets in the way, you don't have to deal with a tiny display to tell you what's going on, and you could even download a demo version before you buy (at a fraction of the cost of hardware) so you can try it out in your own home. The advantages are obvious, but can they really replace 'real' hardware synths? Yes, I really think they can.

Development

In the beginning, 'soft synths' were very simple and designed as playback only devices, which meant that you couldn't play them from a keyboard in real time – the latency was just enormous, so they didn't even try. Some you could send MIDI files to and they would play back. Others were completely self-sufficient and able to create their own sequences. Probably the best known and most successful was Rebirth RB-338 from a Swedish company called Propellerhead. They took the Roland TB-303 'bassline' and TR-808 drum machine and 'modeled' them in software. These were the staple bits of gear for electronic and dance music, producing fat filtered bass lines and hypnotic drum patterns that, often chemically enhanced, ravers would dance to for hours on end. Rebirth is completely self-contained and allowed enthusiasts, who had little chance of getting hold of the very rare hardware,

Figure 7.1
Propellerhead's Rebirth RB-338

to create their own music with just a mouse – no keyboard or musical training required. It was an instant hit. Later they added the TR-909 and some effects, and it's still very popular today.

When Steinberg came along with their ASIO technology and VST plug-in engine, they made the possibility of playing in real time a reality, and soft synths exploded.

Most soft synths were based upon pure analog synthesis, partly because the programmers were into that kind of scene, and also because creating computer models of things like oscillators, filters, and envelopes was relatively easy in comparison to the wavetables, samples, layering, and higher polyphony of digital synths.

Native Instruments, from Germany, had been creating incredibly complex soft synths with their 'Generator' software, allowing the user to patch together as many of the building blocks of analog synthesis they desired, later evolving into their award winning 'Reaktor' software. They stunned everyone by releasing an incredibly lifelike model of the Sequential Circuits Prophet 5 synthesiser (Figure 7.2).

The electronic music community started to take a serious interest in soft synths. Not long after they stunned everyone again with a model of the Hammond B3 organ (Figure 7.3), and suddenly the rest of the world was interested in soft synths.

As the power of computers grew, so did the complexity and quality of the soft synths and along with models of other classic synths, such as the Waldorf PPG and Yamaha DX7, came completely new forms of sound generation and synthesis. The arsenal of synths available now to the computer-based musician is astounding.

Figure 7.2 (top)
Native Instruments Pro 53, modeled on the Sequential Circuits Prophet 5.

Figure 7.3
Native Instruments B4, modeled on the Hammond B3.

Software samplers

While the Europeans were messing around with electronic noises, a company in Texas was working on a way to harness the power of the computer for use as a sampler. Hardware samplers, an essential piece of studio gear, typically could handle 32MB of samples loaded at one time. They worked by taking a sample of an instrument, such as a saxophone, playing a single note and then playing it via MIDI.

Figure 7.4
Tascam (Nemesys Music) GigaStudio 160.

The sampler would speed up or slow down the sample to reach the various pitches. However, if you used a single sampled note, you wouldn't have to go far in pitch before it lost its reality and sounded very unlike a saxophone. So you would sample more notes so that each sample had to cover only a few keys. This used up a chunk of the 32MB very quickly. Then there's velocity layers, because the sax would sound different depending of how hard it was blown, and it wasn't long before the sampler's memory was full.

To make a sampled instrument sound lifelike, you ideally need samples for every note, and for every velocity and also for a long time. Looping a sample to make it sustain never really sounded right. A computer could typically hold much more memory than a sampler and also they had the immense space of hard disks, and Nemesys Music (now a part of Tascam) set out to exploit it.

The result was the groundbreaking software 'GigaSampler' which used new driver technology to enable samples to be streamed directly off hard disk, in real time, in response to a keyboard or MIDI. The first sampled instrument they included with the software was a 1GB (GigaByte) multi-sample of a Yamaha grand piano. Every note sampled at multiple velocities with completely natural decay. The realism was astonishing. Now with their GigaStudio software they support up to 64 loaded instruments, 160 note polyphony, and sample sizes as large as your computer can handle.

A single computer running GigaStudio is now rapidly replacing whole racks of samplers in studios. Some studios even have a number of computers dedicated to GigaStudio to give them access to a huge library of samples. You can now get samples of entire orchestras of incredible quality that come on multiple DVDs. The Vienna Symphonic Library set, as an example, is over 95GB in size and sounds truly fantastic.

This is probably more than we need at the moment, but they certainly led the way in soft sampler technology. Now there are many different choices of soft sampler. The DR-008 and Battery plug-ins we've played with are essentially soft samplers, as they use samples as their sound source.

Besides GigaStudio, the two other samplers of note are 'Halion' from Steinberg and 'Kontakt' from Native Instruments. Both come with libraries of great sounding samples and have all the tools you need to make your own sample instruments. They also support more traditional sample formats like Akai, so you can still use the library you built up on a hardware sampler, as well as GigaStudio format instruments. GigaStudio's strength is its performance with huge samples, but lacks any real time editing, whereas Kontakt and Halion excel at the instant messing around and tweaking of samples while you're playing. Kontakt and Halion are also VSTis and so run inside of Cubase, whereas GigaStudio runs as a stand-alone piece of software, so it's not quite as integrated as the other two.

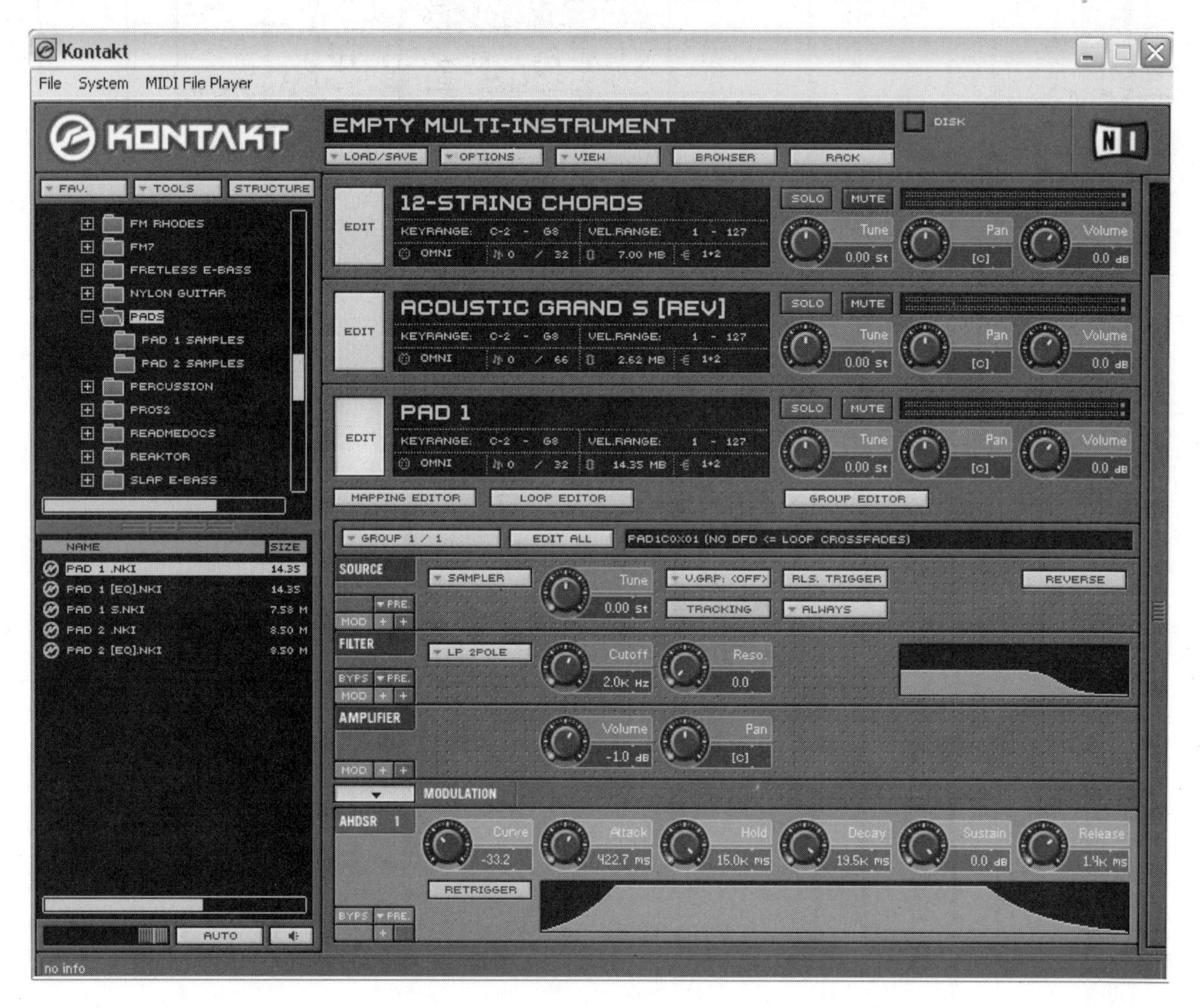

Figure 7.5
Native Instruments Kontakt Software Sampler.

Creating a VSTi bass line in Cubase

Let's start making some more music and add a bass to our drums. So far I've made you do everything yourself, recording audio, making patterns, slicing drums, this time I've prepared a little project to get you started. In the 'Cubase Projects' folder, you'll find a project called 'bassline'. That's the one we want, open it in Cubase.

OK, so I haven't done much, but what I have done is to create a 12-bar drum track using the drum loops we were playing with in the last chapter. What I intend to do now is show you how to add a bass line to it.

Info

You need to copy the folder to the hard drive before the file can be opened in Cubase.

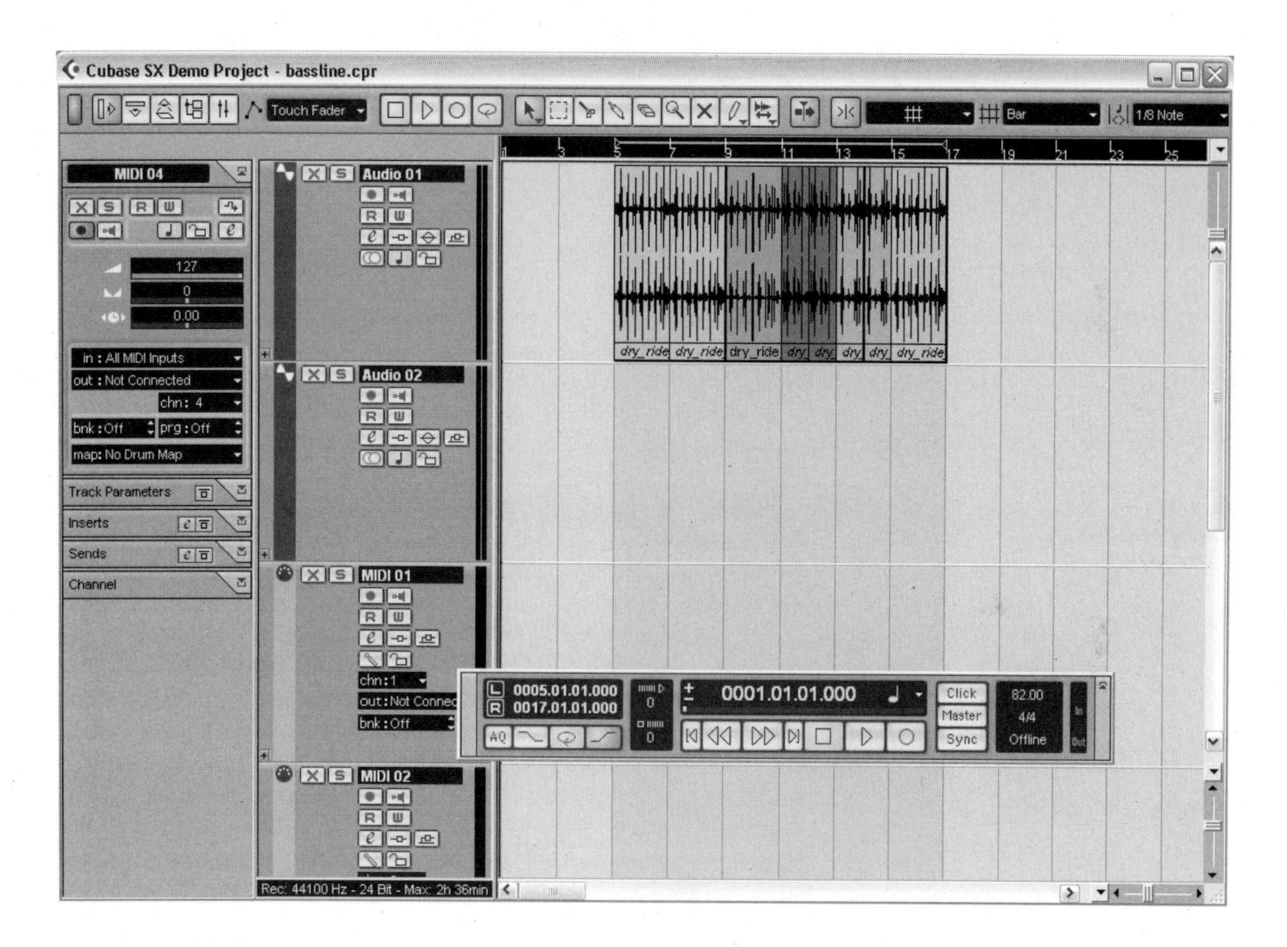

Figure 7.6
The Bassline project with drums ready to go.

Cubase has a VSTi called the 'Virtual Bass Unit VB1' and that's what we're going to use as our MIDI sound source. Press F11 to bring up the VSTi window and you'll find the vb-1 under 'Synths'. Select the first MIDI track and set the vb-1 as the output (Figure 7.7).

If you have a MIDI keyboard attached, then you can start playing the bass straight away. The latency situation is exactly the same as with the drums. If you don't have a keyboard then this time there aren't any pads to click, so you'll have to use the 'Piano Roll' editor which we'll come onto shortly. The VB1 has a number of controls on its editor. You can move the pickup and plectrum position; alter the shape of the sound, how much dampening being used and the volume. You'll

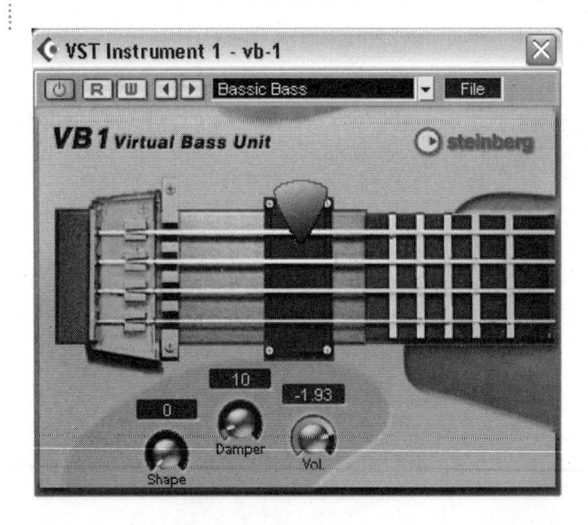

Figure 7.7
The VB1 Virtual Bass Unit.

also find some presets under the drop-down menu at the top. The 'Bassic Bass' though is the best one for now. It's probably not the most realistic-sounding bass guitar in the world, but it will certainly do and I'll show you how to improve on it later.

Recording this bass track is exactly the same as recording those drum patterns. Just select the MIDI track, hit record, and off you go. What we want to aim for is a nice 12-bar blues riff, shall we say in 'A'.

Have a go (remember the metronome setup if you want a count-in click) and at the end you should have a nice new MIDI event full of notes.

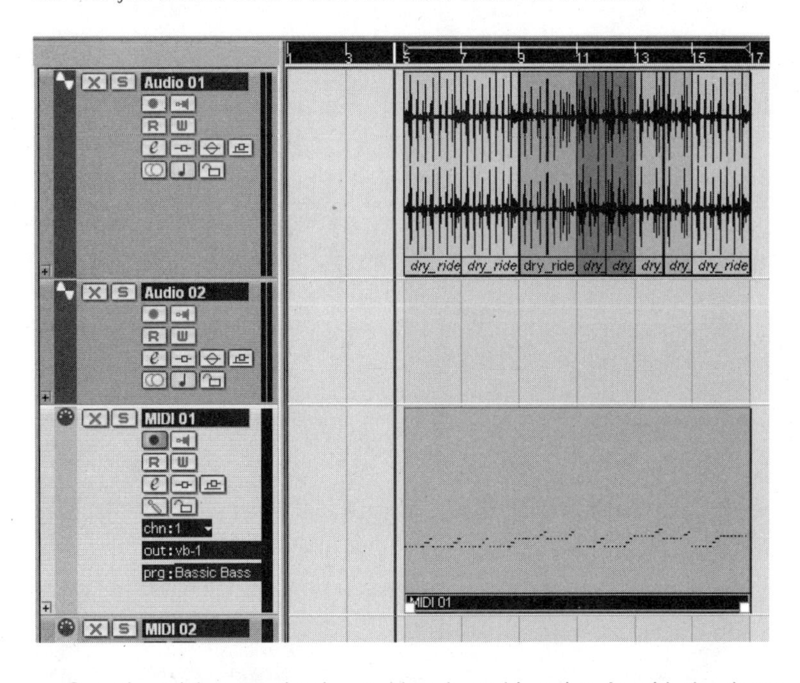

Figure 7.8
The recorded bassline track.

Quantize might come in nice and handy at this point. As with the drums, pressing 'Q' will quantize the notes to the grid as specified in the quantize selector, to tighten up your sloppy playing. You may find that some of the notes have been quantized in the wrong direction. Well, we can sort that out in the 'Key Editor' win-

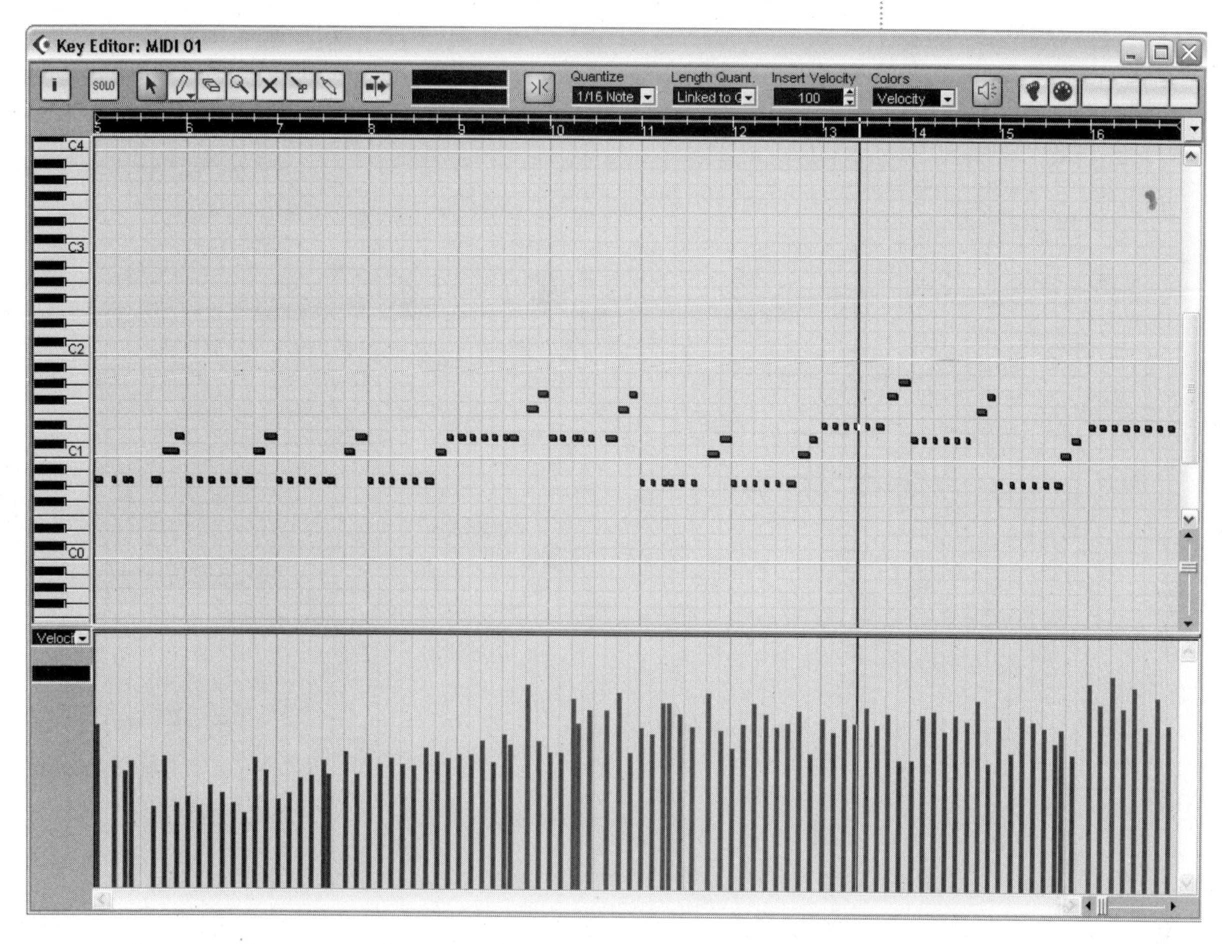

Figure 7.9
The bass line in the Key Editor.

dow, also known as the 'Piano Roll' window for reasons that will become abundantly clear as soon as it opens. Double click the MIDI event to open the 'Key Editor' window (Figure 7.9).

This looks a bit similar to the drum editor and, in fact, it's exactly the same except that rather than having drum names down the left, we now have a piano keyboard, and rather than diamonds, we have little rectangles representing the notes. If you click on a note, you can drag it to wherever you want, in time or pitch. So if there are any notes which are not on the beat where you want them, you can move them. Also if you have any bum notes or accidental notes you can remove them here. For those of you who don't have a MIDI keyboard, this is where you can create your music as you can write in notes with your mouse.

So, let's try creating the bass line with a mouse rather than a keyboard.

Info

For those of you who don't have a MIDI keyboard, this is where you can create your music as you can write in notes with your mouse.

Using the Key Editor to create notes

Back to the project window and delete the MIDI event we recorded a moment ago. Using the 'Draw' pencil tool, draw a new event on the MIDI track of just a bar in length. Press 'P' to move the markers around it and double-click the event to open the 'Key Editor'.

Start Cubase playing around our new event and we'll start writing in our bassline. Blues in 'A' I think we said, so we want a simple thudding A followed by a couple of other notes to make it interesting. So, find the A beneath C1, take the draw tool and click in the very first beat, next to the keyboard. Leave a grid space and click in the third grid, labeled at the top '1.3'. Do this all the way across so that you have the bass playing on the first and third part of every beat.

Figure 7.10
Adding some notes to the bar.

Select the arrow tool, and move the last two notes up to D and E, respectively. Now it should sound like a very simple blues bassline.

The width of the rectangle denotes the length of the note, or how long the note was held. If we increase the length of the D and E notes to twice their size it makes it sound a bit more realistic. Use the arrow tool and move the mouse to the end of the note until a sideways arrow appears – then click and drag.

Back in the Project window, we can copy this bassline across all 12 bars by copying the event. Alternatively we can use the 'Repeat' command to do this automatically. Right-click on the region and select 'Edit – Repeat'. Stick in '11' as the count and click 'OK'. Release the loop on the transport bar and the bass will play for the whole 12 bars.

Great! But now we want to add some chord changes. At the fifth bar we want to change to 'D' for two bars. At the moment both bars have separate events, but it would be easier to edit the two bars together, so we can glue the two events together using the 'Glue' tool. If you click the Glue tool onto the event in the fifth bar, it will automatically combine itself with the next event, making a single event (Figure 7.11).

Select the arrow tool and double-click our 2-bar event to open the Key Editor. Select all the notes, either by dragging a box around them with the arrow/selection tool or by pressing Ctrl+A on your keyboard. Then click on the first note and drag it up to D; the rest will follow.

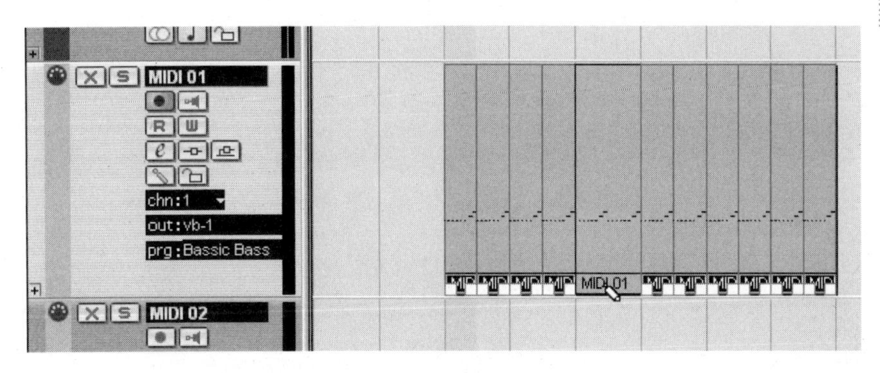

Figure 7.11
Gluing two events together.

Bar 9 should be E, so double-click the ninth event, select the notes, and move them up to E. The tenth should be D again so do the same, and finally the last bar should be E. Instead of editing the last bar, you could delete it and 'Alt drag' the other E bar to copy it to the last bar.

Super, that's our 12-bar blues sorted out nicely. Let's see if we can sort out that bass sound.

Using effects with VSTis

The output of a VSTi is audio, the same as the output of a hardware sound module. It's not an audio track, it's being triggered by MIDI, and we can't apply an audio effect to a MIDI track - because it doesn't contain any sound (I can hear your brain cells clicking). However, as the output of the VSTi is audio, and that audio is being generated within Cubase, we can apply audio effects to its output.

Let me show you. We can't add an effect to the track so we have to do this somewhere else. The output of the VSTi appears as a channel on the Cubase mixer, which is where we can use the plug-ins. Press F3 to bring up the Cubase mixer.

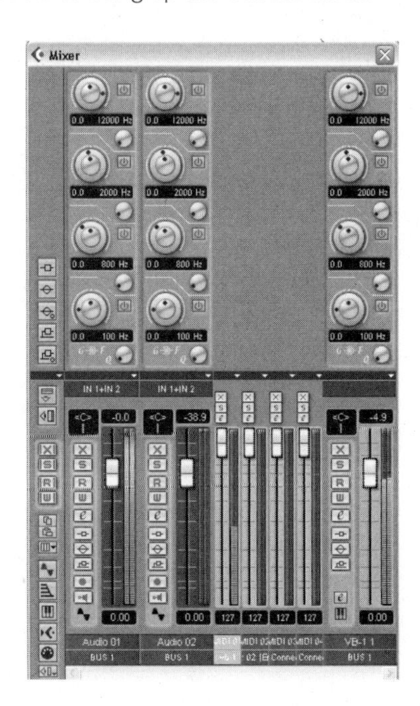

Figure 7.12
The Cubase Track Mixer.

In the default project, the mixer would show a great deal more channels than this, but our bassline project has only a couple of tracks and so that's what you get. The first channel is the drums, in fact you can label it as such by double-clicking on where it says 'Audio 01'. Second channel is not used as yet. Then we have the MIDI tracks. This just shows the activity for the MIDI tracks. The level it shows is velocity, it's not audio and we can't add any effects to it. Finally on the right we have the output channel of the VB1. Now this is audio, so we can treat it like any other audio channel. The top half of the mixer is currently showing EQ or Equalization. The top half can also show Inserts and Sends. Click the little white down arrow between the faders and the EQ for the VB1 and select 'Inserts' from the menu.

In the first slot, insert the Amplitube plug-in. In Amplitube you'll find some bass guitar presets. Click on 'Load' and select 'Bass – Rock Solid'. Suddenly you'll find that the VB1 is sounding much beefier than it was before. Nice one. I'd strongly recommend getting your guitar out and jamming alongside, You could even record a rhythm guitar track and then play lead over the top. In fact, why don't you try that right now while I go off and make a cup of tea.

Adding other instruments

The bassline is just the start of what you could add to your music. You could get the 'Halion Strings Edition' and add a few cellos, or the 'Lounge Lizard' electric piano from Applied Acoustics to add a bit of 'Rhodes', to mention just a couple of the hundreds of software synths available.

Cubase comes with another VSTi called the 'A1', which is an analog style synth capable of lots of different sounds and textures. Load it up onto MIDI track 2 (it's under 'Synths' on the VSTi menu) as I've just had a great idea for another track.

Figure 7.13
The A1 Analog Synth Unit.

There's an awful lot of presets available from the drop-down menu, so many in fact that it's too big for your screen and you have to drag the mouse down to see them all. This is terribly annoying. There's a better place to select the patches and that's over on the left in the track info column. If you click where it says 'prg', all the preset patches appear with a much easier way of scrolling through them. Play a few patches to get an idea of what sort of sounds it can make, and if you don't have a MIDI keyboard then you can click on the keyboard on the A1 itself.

The A1 has lots of knobs and stuff for editing the sounds. Just click on them and drag to move the knobs and you'll soon get the hang of it. There are two controls always being overused on analog synths, but they get used a lot because they make great sounds, and that's the 'Cut-off' and 'Resonance' knobs in the 'Filter' section. If you put the resonance to maximum and then vary the cut-off as you play. you'll hear the full effect. I've just discovered that you can use the wheel on your mouse to move the knobs - just rest the cursor on the knob and move the wheel. How cool is that? A filter is usually a 'low pass' filter, which means it allows all frequencies through below the cut-off setting. So as you raise the cut-off, you'll hear higher frequencies coming in, or as you lower it you'll be left with just the bass. The A1 also has 'high pass', 'band pass', and 'notch' filters.

Anyway, back to our 12-bar blues, I thought we could add a touch of 'dub' to it by sticking in an organ chord on the off beat. Select the 'Cheapo Organ JH' patch on the A1 and I'll show you what I mean.

As with the bassline, let's create a single bar event in the arrange window with the draw tool, in line with the first bar of the song. Press 'P' and start Cubase playing around it, and double-click the event to go into the Key Editor.

We want a simple A minor chord on the off beat. So draw in notes A2, C3, and E3 on beat 1.3. Do the same on every beat, so 2.3, 3.3, and 4.3.

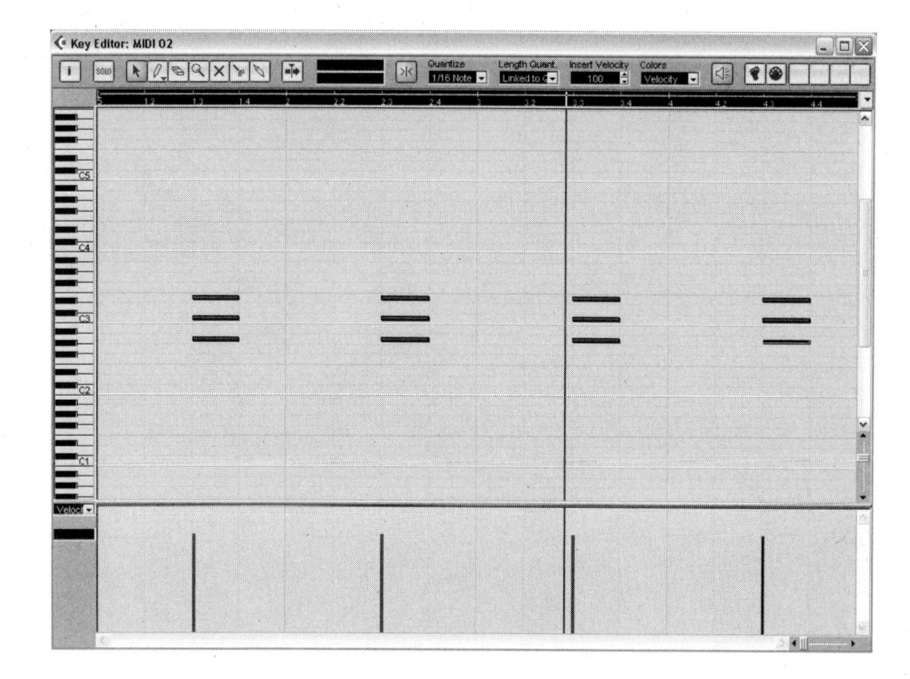

Figure 7.14
Adding chords in the Key Editor.

That 'rules'. Now, back to the arrange window, right-click, and select 'Edit – Repeat' and enter a count of 11. Exactly the same as with the bassline, glue together bars 5 and 6 and move all the notes together so that the bottom note is D3, bar 9 up to E3, 10 to D3 and the last bar to E3. That sounds so good my tea's gone cold while I've been jamming along. Well it sounds good to me in any case.

If you've managed to make a complete pig's ear out of creating these two tracks and want to know what it's supposed to sound like, load up the 'all_done_for_you.cpr' project in the 'Bassline' project folder. If you then go back a page or two and look at the two tracks, I'm sure you'll see where you went wrong.

CPU performance

It's probably important to mention at this point that your computer has a finite supply of processing power. Each time you load up a VSTi or add an effect, you use up more of the computer's power. There comes a point where you can't add anything else without Cubase grinding to a complete halt.

You can see the current load on the CPU in the 'VST Performance' meter. Press F12 to bring it up.

Figure 7.15
Measuring VST Performance of the CPU and hard disk.

The top line shows the load on the CPU, the second shows the strain on the hard disk. If you were playing back lots and lots of tracks of audio then the disk meter would begin to register until, again, it grinds to a halt. The performance meter in my all_done_for_you.cpr project shows about 30% on my computer – Intel Pentium 4/2GHz, so there's still plenty of room. If you have a lower powered computer, then you may have already run into problems. If that's the case, the first thing to remove is the Amplitube plug-in. This is quite a CPU-hungry beast and it's also the demo version, which isn't quite as tuned as the latest full version.

As all plug-ins are run by the CPU, it follows that the more powerful your computer, the more plug-ins and VSTis you're going to be able to run. It's impossible to say exactly how much power you need for what, as plug-ins vary in the amount of CPU power they use. Also, with soft samplers it depends on the number of instruments loaded, and the size of the samples, and also the polyphony. It can be quite a balance at times. There are ways around these problems, which we'll look at in a later chapter, and always remember that your computer is doing some fabulous things for you.

Adding and editing a guitar track

It would be good, I think, to demonstrate what it was that impressed me about digital recording on a computer all that time ago. It was all that stuff about copying and pasting guitar riffs, and this song we've been working on is ripe for guitar fudging, as it were.

Close the current project and go to 'open' and select the 'Guitar fudge' project that's in the same 'Bassline' project folder.

What I've done is to set our 12-bar dub blues playing and recorded some random guitar alongside. I let it loop record so I ended up with seven takes of the 12 bars. Each take I attempted to play something different in the hope that I'd hit on something less than terrible, although that seems unlikely. I then took each take, applied the Warp VST plug-in and put each one on a separate audio track. If you've opened the project then scroll down to the bottom and you'll see the seven new audio tracks. What we will try to do is salvage a single, half-decent guitar track from the rubbish that emanated from my fingers over the seven takes.

All the tracks are muted out, so set the project into looped playback around the 12 bars and click the mute button on the first take so that you can hear it. Then, on each loop, mute that track and un-mute the next one until you've heard all the amazing (stop laughing) material we have to work with.

In the second take, I went for a good old-fashioned blues riff, which was all right for the first two bars and then I mucked it up in bar 3. So, as an easy start, let's take the first two bars of the second take and paste them into the first two bars of our guitar track (under the drum track). Take the Split (scissors) tool and cut the 'guitar take 2' track at the second bar.

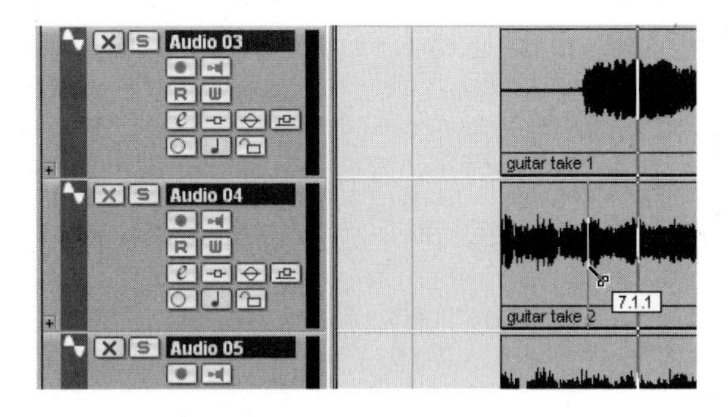

Figure 7.16
Splitting off our first riff.

Select the Object (arrow) tool, hold the Alt key, and drag the two bars up to the 'Guitar Track'. Use the Alt key again to copy and drag the two bars to the next two bars.

Figure 7.17
Copy and drag to the next two bars.

If you mute out the guitar takes and set the song playing, you'll hear the same riff played over all four bars, and it doesn't sound too bad. That's the first 'A' section taken care of. Let's look for something interesting for the 'D' section. Loop bars 9–11 in the timeline (bars 5 and 6 of the actual song), so that you are just listening to the 2-bar 'D' section, and go through the guitar takes in search of something interesting. Obviously you can wander off and do your own thing at this point, but if you're interested in my choices for a decent guitar track out of the rubbish I recorded, then I'd use take 7 as the first bar and take 6 as the second. Snip out two bars and Alt drag them up to the guitar track. Bar 5 is now a kind of reverse blues riff of the first four bars, and bar 6 is a little lead riff. Cool, halfway through and I imagine that you've got the hang of it. It's easy and really good fun, messing it about, moving things around, coming up with new ideas. You can finish the track off on your own now, and if you want to hear what I came up with then open the 'guitar fudge finished' project and take a listen.

Isn't this all just cheating? Using the computer to make up for our inadequacies as a musician? Maybe, but we're not playing at Wembley - we're mucking around with musical ideas, using Cubase as a sketch-pad if you like. This is, though, a common criticism of using a computer for music. Somehow, critics feel, if you're not using tape then you're being 'dishonest'.

Jack White, from The White Stripes, who I think are simply genius, was recently quoted in the *Guardian Weekend* supplement saying that he thought (to paraphrase) using software to correct your singing or playing is not an honest way to create music, and how could you be proud of something you didn't actually play? For a moment I thought it was a wise and reasoned statement, but then I realized it was so full of holes that you could drive a bus through it. What is 'honest' when it comes to playing and recording music? Take a delay pedal: how honest is it to use technology to repeat something you are playing? What about overdrive and distortion – are you being dishonest if you use an effect rather than overdriving an actual tube amplifier? How honest is an electric guitar? Surely the sound of fingers against catgut is real honesty? What about multi-track recording? If you record yourself twice playing different parts, can you honestly recreate that on stage?

Although I understand where Mr. White is coming from, I feel it's a bit naïve to believe that only old technology is honest. When the Beatles and George Martin began experimenting with sound in the '60's, I'm sure they would have taken advantage of computer technology, had it been available, as Sir Martin does today. It's not a question of honesty, it's a question of realizing the music you want to make.

Recording in a studio has never been purely about capturing a live performance. It's about experimentation and creativity, producing music and putting down ideas that wouldn't necessarily be possible to reproduce live. Computers are not destroying music, they are allowing more people to experiment. This may well produce a lot of computerized rubbish, but it will also produce some works of complete genius – as all recording equipment has always done. The tools for making music haven't really changed, they've simply become more interesting.

Hands- and feet-on control

As we began fiddling with the A1 synth, it probably became apparent that using a mouse to move a knob is not at all the same thing as moving a real knob, on a real synth, with your fingers. All too true. For many of us for whom the mouse is a seamless extension of the hand, the lack of tactile control has probably not occurred to us. For those of us used to hardware mixers, this has probably been the greatest concern of moving to a computer for recording. It needn't be.

It's a bit like an evolution of technology. Years ago when everything was analog, synths were covered with knobs and sliders all instantly accessible to the user, like the Prophet 5 I mentioned in the last chapter. Then along came digital synths, which were black, sleek, and slab-like with nothing on them except a tiny screen and a couple of buttons. For all their great sounds and advantages like MIDI, they were a pig to program. Just to tweak a single parameter meant searching through pages of data, on that little screen. Nowadays we find that the latest generation of synths come bristling in knobs and sliders again, so you get the great sounds and the tactile instant control. Software synths have gone through a similar evolutionary stage and now, using MIDI, we are reintroducing hardware back into our virtual studio as 'controllers', banks of knobs and dummy mixers that control everything on screen. The great thing about it is that you can use the same control 'surface' to control whatever software synth or software mixer you like.

Talking about MIDI control

Our old friend MIDI has everything we need to perform the function of a controller. In addition to sending out note information, it can also transmit volume, panning, cut-off, resonance, in fact it has 128 different control messages allowing us to assign them to whatever parameter our software permits.

If you take something simple like volume, then you could build a hardware controller with eight faders and assign each one to control the level of eight channels in the Cubase mixer. So, we have real tactile mixing on a computer. MIDI can also be sent back to our hardware controller, so if you move a fader with the mouse, that movement will be sent back to the controller. With the addition of motorized faders (yes, honestly) the hardware faders would move spookily in response. A practical use would be to be able to recall various mixes and have the hardware reflect exactly what's going on in the software.

To integrate things further, many software companies have teamed up with hardware manufacturers to produce control surfaces that have direct software control, as well as MIDI, and are already setup for the user, so they can just plug it in and go.

Mixer control surfaces

Steinberg, on their own, have produced the 'Houston', a nine-fader (motorized) controller with knobs and transport controls that give you instant access to all sorts of areas in Cubase at the touch of a button.

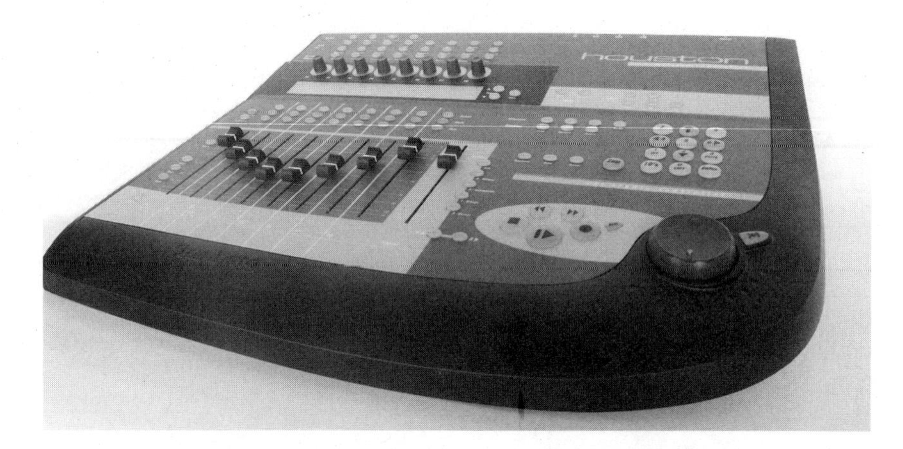

Figure 8.1
Steinberg Houston Surface Controller.

Mackie, the famous makers of professional analog mixers, have produced the 'Mackie Control', nine motorized faders plus a few knobs and transport controls. This has the advantage of being able to work with all sorts of software and is expandable, so you can add extra banks of eight faders up to as many as you like.

Figure 8.2
Mackie's expandable control surface.

Knobs

If you think that a full-on control surface is a bit much for you, then you can get simple banks of knobs that'll control anything.

The first MIDI knob controller was probably the Phatboy from Keyfax, and was used massively with Propellerhead's Rebirth software.

Figure 8.3
Keyfax Phatboy MIDI controller.

Figure 8.4
Midiman Radium controller keyboard.

More recently, knobs have begun to turn up on dummy MIDI keyboard controllers. MAudio/Midiman have a range of 'keystation' keyboards that feature both knobs and sliders for tons of hands-on control.

Another keyboard controller company called Evolution has also got in on the act with their keyboards and also a cool little knob and slider controller called the UC-33. It can also attach to the computer via USB so you wouldn't need an extra MIDI port.

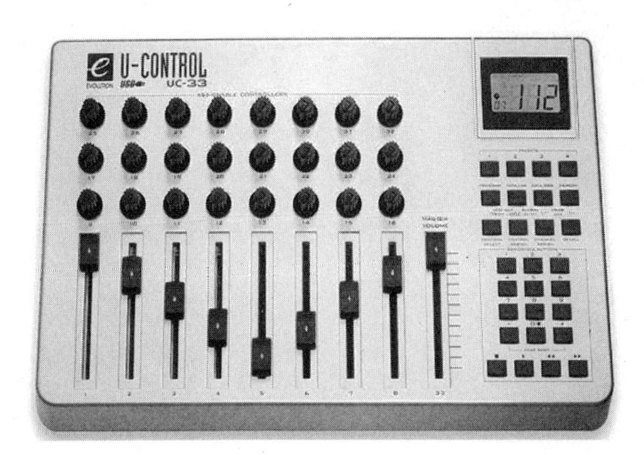

Figure 8.5
Evolution UC-33 MIDI controller – lots of knobs and sliders for controlling everything.

Drum control

MIDI drum kits have been around for a fair while for those who want to get the feel of their drum patterns completely human. Most of us just bash keys on our keyboards and it works fine. However, there are a couple of MIDI pad controllers worth looking at if you need to do your drums more justice.

The first is the descendant of the original Octopad from Roland, the SPD20. Sporting eight velocity sensitive pads and stacks of built-in sounds, it's a great bit of kit for banging out beats on. You can use drum sticks on it and everything.

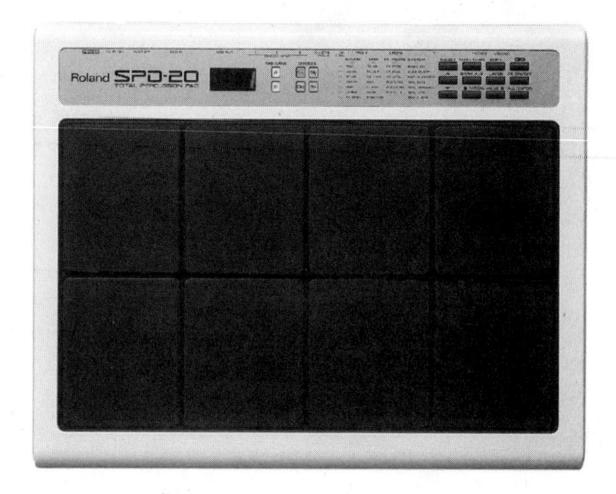

Figure 8.6
Roland SPD-20 8 pad drum controller.

It has a little brother called the SPD-6, which has six smaller pads and a few sounds, but would probably fit on your desk easier than the SPD-20. They also have the HPD-15 'HandSonic' percussion controller, which looks a lot like an electronic bongo. Which is good, as that's exactly what it's supposed to be.

Figure 8.7
Roland HandSonic percussion controller.

Figure 8.8
Akai MPD16 drum pad controller – fantastic with Battery or the DR-008.

And finally from Akai, the makers of hardware samplers, we have the MPD16, which is based upon the front end of their extremely successful MPC range of samplers. The pads are all fully assignable and if you were missing the feel of the pads on your SR-16 then this might be the ideal replacement.

Having said that, you could of course use the SR-16 pads to play drums on the computer as well. You could bash the pads and record the hits into Cubase, or use it to play Battery or whatever.

MIDI floorboards

As a guitarist, what you really want to be able to do is turn effects on and off with your feet, and so you can. MIDI floorboards have been around for a while, designed to control MIDI compatible effects boxes, and are finding a new lease of life attached to the computer.

Figure 8.9
Behringer FCB1010 MIDI Foot Controller.

The nicest looking one is from Behringer, the FCB1010, with 10 patch footswitches, two bank up/down footswitches, and two expression pedals. Now, the footswitches just select patches, so you can change effects patches within an effects box, so they are not as versatile as a continuous controller like a knob or slider, and in fact very few things on the computer respond to patch change commands. However, with a clever bit of fiddling we can get the footswitches to act as controller messages with values of either zero or 127, meaning that we can turn things like software effects on and off. The expression pedals work just as knobs would and so are very useful.

At the end of this chapter, I'll go into some detail about getting a MIDI floorboard to work more usefully with Cubase.

Controlling stuff in Cubase

Many bits of software, stand-alone soft synths in particular, have a MIDI 'learn' feature. This is extremely cool and allows you to select a virtual knob, or whatever you want to control. Move the hardware knob on your controller and the knob on screen will 'learn' whatever MIDI data that knob is sending out and move accordingly. So with a mouse click and a twist, you can get all your hardware knobs controlling stuff on screen.

Some software comes with 'maps' for certain controllers, so that all the knobs or faders on your hardware controller are already 'mapped' to control things on screen.

Cubase does have some MIDI learn features, but it's not quite as straightforward as it is on a soft synth. In a stand-alone soft synth, all the knobs and parameters are all in the same place. In Cubase you can insert VSTis in any of 32 slots, on different channels, with more than one of the same, so a little bit more work is required to specify exactly what's controlling what in Cubase.

To demonstrate how you go about setting up controllers in Cubase, we'll use the one MIDI controller you're likely to find on nearly every MIDI keyboard – the 'mod' (modulation) wheel. The mod wheel is a just a MIDI controller which has been set to send out data on controller number 1, which is traditionally the modulation effect. We can 'map' this controller to control pretty much any parameter in Cubase. If you have a Roland or Edirol keyboard, then you won't have a mod 'wheel' as such, you'll have a sideways pitch bend wheel/joystick where if you push it forward it sends out modulation – it won't be quite as accurate as a wheel, but it'll do. If you don't have modulation at all, then you could use the pitch-bend wheel, but it doesn't work quite as well as the data is slightly different. You may have some other slider on your keyboard, like 'volume' or 'data', these can work also, the main thing to check is whether you get a MIDI In indication in Cubase's transport bar when you move. If you do then it'll work.

Controlling the mixer

Our first mission is to get our mod wheel to control the fader of the first audio channel in the mixer. Press F3 to bring up the mixer and move it to one side making sure that you can see the first channel. Next, go to the 'Devices' menu and select 'Device Setup'. Click on the 'Add/Remove' tab. You'll see a list of various pre-mapped controllers. I'm assuming you don't have any of those, so we set up up our own 'Generic Remote' to control mixer elements. Select 'Generic Remote' and click 'Add' (Figure 8.10).

Then, 'Generic Remote' appears in the list of devices on the left, select it and click the 'Setup' tab (Figure 8.11).

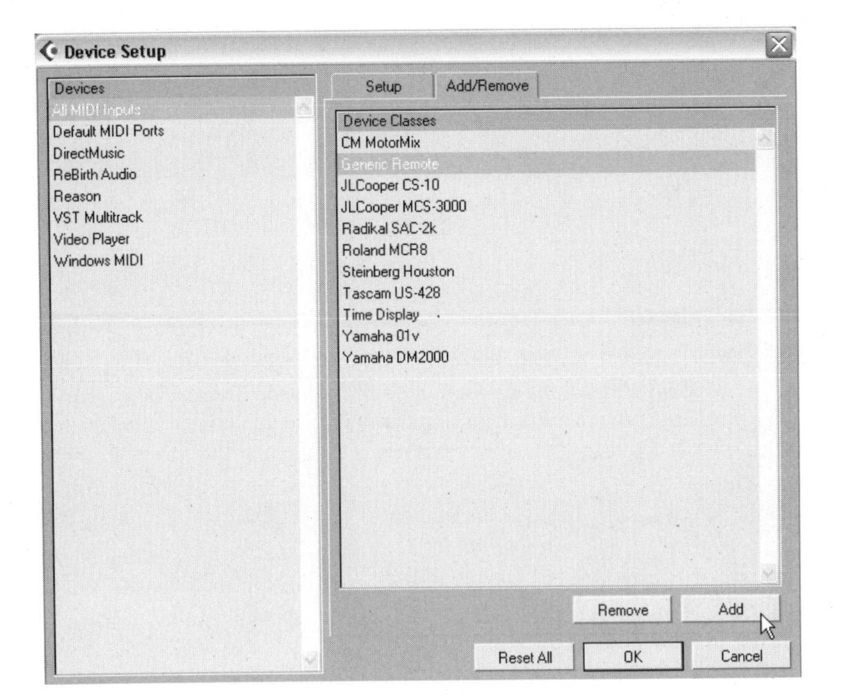

Figure 8.10
Adding a Generic Remote in the Device Setup window.

Figure 8.11
Generic Remote Setup window showing the default settings.

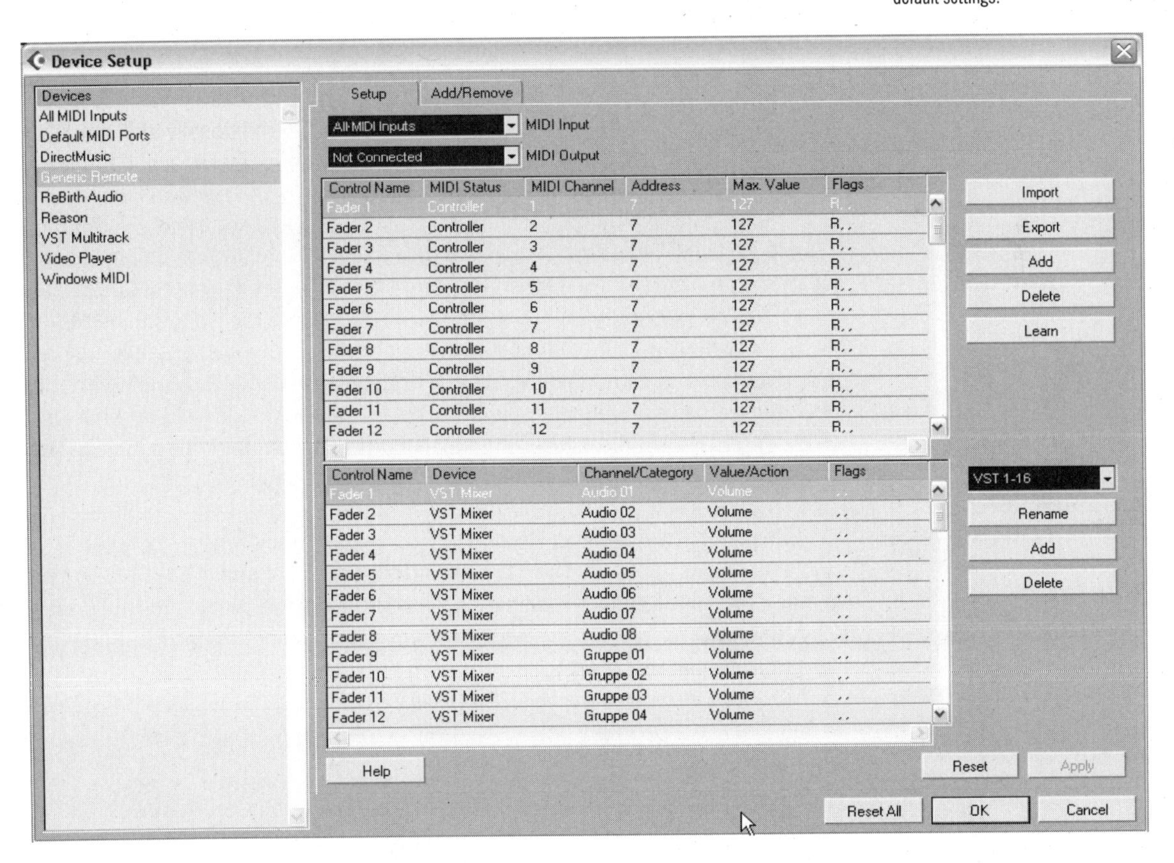

Cubase automatically loads up a default bunch of settings which may well work with your controller. In the top half of the screen, we have information about the controllers, and in the bottom half we have what parameter those controllers are mapped to. At the top, where it says 'Control Name', double-click 'Fader 1' and rename it 'Mod Wheel'. In the bottom half, click 'Fader 1' and it'll change to 'Mod Wheel'. You need to specify the MIDI input that your MIDI controller is connected to. Select 'All MIDI Inputs', or your specific input, from the 'MIDI Input' menu. At the bottom right of the window, click the 'Apply' button.

Now, position the Device Setup window in such a way that you can see the mixer channel 1 behind it. With 'Mod Wheel' selected at the top, move the mod wheel on your keyboard a couple of times, doesn't matter how much, and click the 'Learn' button. The 'Address' on the Mod Wheel line will change to 1; it's 'learnt' the address of that data coming in from your mod wheel. You should immediately see, if you move your mod wheel, that the fader on channel 1 in the mixer moves in response to it.

If you look at the bottom half, where the controllers are mapped, you'll find that you can select tons of different parameters to control. Click on 'Volume' under 'Value/Action' and a massive list will appear all applying to functions of the first audio channel – as specified by the 'Channel/Category' selection. Good ones to try that you'll be able to see instantly on the mixer would be 'Pan Left-Right', 'EQ 1 Gain', and 'EQ 1 Freq'. So far this is all restricted to the first audio channel. We can make it a bit more versatile by choosing 'Selected' under the 'Channel/Category' menu. Click 'OK' to close the Device Setup window. Now your mod wheel will control the fader of whatever mixer channel you click on (select).

If you had a bank of MIDI controller knobs or sliders, you could map each one to specific faders, so that you could control lots of channels at once. Or you could map them to different controls on a single channel, and then using the 'Selected' option control whatever channel you wanted. Once you've created your map you can save the settings by 'Exporting' them for recall later. You can also set up the controls in 'banks' enabling you to use the same knob to control different things depending on the bank selected. In the Generic Remote setup window, you can see on the right a drop-down menu currently displaying 'VST 1-16'. These are your banks. You can rename them and add as many as you like. As an example, set your mod wheel back to controlling volume and rename the bank 'Volume'. Next click the 'Add' button to add another bank. This is a new bank, so no mapping has been set up as yet, so we need to do this by hand. Under 'Device' select 'VST Mixer', 'Channel/Category' select 'Selected', and 'Value/Action' select 'Pan Left-Right'. Rename the bank 'Pan' and click 'OK' to close the window.

Figure 8.12
The Generic Remote window has a drop-down menu where you can select different remote banks.

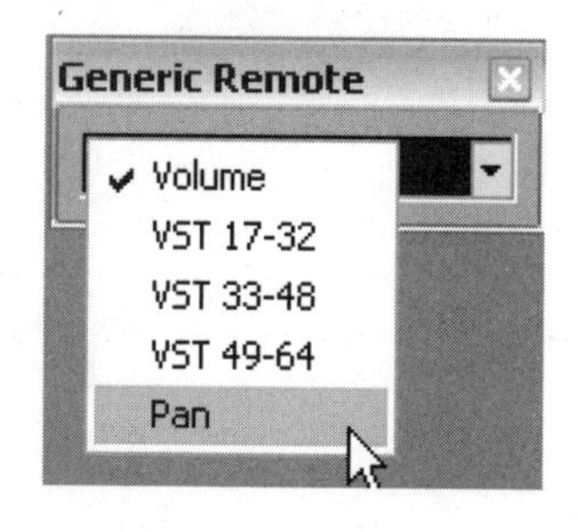

To change between banks we need to bring up the 'Generic Remote' window, you'll find this at the top of the 'Devices' menu. Select a channel on the mixer and your mod wheel will control volume. From the drop down menu on the little Generic Remote window (Figure 8.12) select the 'Pan' bank, and now the same mod wheel is controlling pan.

The other banks from the default settings are still there, you can always delete them in the Device Setup window.

These banks give you a great deal of versatility when using just a handful of MIDI controller knobs. For instance, you could have one bank set up to control the faders, then another bank set up for EQ and another controlling a specific effect.

Controlling effects

Effect parameters can be controlled in the same way, using the Generic Remote. Being able to control Amplitube with a bank of knobs rather than a mouse would be a wonderful thing. Let's try that using our mod wheel.

On the first audio track, insert the Amplitube effect into slot 1. Open the Generic Remote Setup window (Devices – Device Setup). To save any confusion with the last bit of controlling we did, click the 'reset' button at the bottom to return the Generic remote to its defaults. Then, as before, select 'Fader 1' at the top, move the mod wheel, and click 'learn'.

The effects are part of the VST mixer and so when you insert one the parameters appear in the Value/Action menu. You won't see them straight away, you have to click to bring up the list of parameters, and then click at the bottom to scroll through piles of them until you reach the Amplitube controls at the very bottom. This is something I hope Steinberg will improve upon at some point as it's really annoying. From the list of Amplitube controls select 'INS1 Amplitube Preamp Model'.

Control Name	MIDI Status	MIDI Channel	Address	Max. Value	Flags
Fader 1	Controller	1	1	127	R,,
Fader 2	Controller	2	7	127	R,,
Fader 3	Controller	3	7	127	R,,
Fader 4	Controller	4	7	127	R,,
Fader 5	Controller	5	7	127	R,,
Fader 6	Controller	6	7	127	R,,
Fader 7	Controller	7	7	127	R,,
Fader 8	Controller	8	7	127	R,,
Fader 9	Controller	9	7	127	R,,
Fader 10	Controller	10	7	127	R,,
Fader 11	Controller	11	7	127	R,,
Fader 12	Controller	12	7	127	R,,

Control Name	Device	Channel/Category	Value/Action	Flags
Fader 1	VST Mixer	Selected	INS1 Amplitube Pree	,,
Fader 2	VST Mixer	Audio 02	Volume	,,
Fader 3	VST Mixer	Audio 03	Volume	,,
Fader 4	VST Mixer	Audio 04	Volume	,,
Fader 5	VST Mixer	Audio 05	Volume	,,
Fader 6	VST Mixer	Audio 06	Volume	,,
Fader 7	VST Mixer	Audio 07	Volume	,,
Fader 8	VST Mixer	Audio 08	Volume	,,
Fader 9	VST Mixer	A1 L	Volume	,,
Fader 10	VST Mixer	Gruppe 01	Volume	,,
Fader 11	VST Mixer	Gruppe 02	Volume	,,
Fader 12	VST Mixer	Gruppe 03	Volume	,,

Figure 8.13
The Generic Remote settings for controlling the pre-amp model in Amplitube with the mod wheel.

Figure 8.14
Amplitube under control. Your mod wheel will now be controlling the pre-amp model.

Click 'OK' to close the window and you'll now be able to choose the Preamp model in Amplitube by using your mod wheel (Figure 8.14).

That's much more like it. I hope your concerns about hands-on control are beginning to fade a little.

> **Info**
>
> With a bank of knobs, you'd be able to control the whole thing just as if it was a Line6 Pod.

Controlling VSTis

The editing controls on a VSTi are not a part of the VST Mixer and so we can't use the Generic Remote to assign controllers to them. Most VSTis have MIDI commands already assigned to their knobs and other parameters. So if you have a MIDI controller where the controller numbers can be allocated to the knobs in the hardware, then you could control things directly without having to do anything in software.

To prevent any confusion, we should release the mod wheel from its burden of the Generic Remote. If you open the Device Setup window again, click the 'Add/Remove' tab, select 'Generic Remote' on the left and click 'Remove'.

Load up the A1 VSTi and set it as the output of the first MIDI track. Check to see if you can play it from the keyboard.

If you move your mod wheel, you'll see the little mod wheel next to the keyboard on the A1 move as well. This has already been mapped for you. But what if we'd like to use our mod wheel to control something else, or what if we can't change the controller numbers on the knobs we have?

Well, Cubase has a very useful tool called the 'Transformer' which can do many interesting and odd things with MIDI, but more importantly it will transform any incoming MIDI command into any other command. This means we can take our mod wheel and transform it to control any of the A1's parameters that has a MIDI controller number assigned to it.

Let's try it out. With the MIDI track selected, click on 'Inserts' in the track info column. The Transformer is accessible as a MIDI plug-in, so insert into the first slot.

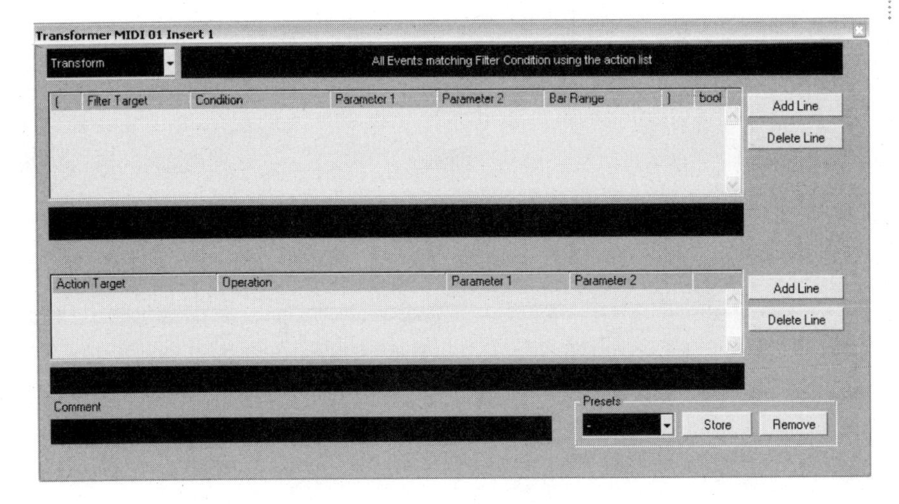

Figure 8.15
The MIDI Transformer plug-in.

OK, so it's not the most inspiring or intuitive thing you've ever looked at, but if you follow my instructions you'll do fine. What we are trying to achieve is to convert the mod wheel controller number '1' into a different controller number that controls something interesting on the A1, like the filter cut-off. Take a look at the A1 (close the Transformer window for a moment) and put your mouse cursor over the Cut-off knob in the filter section. In the little display in the middle of the A1 you'll see that the controller number for the Cut-off is '74'. So, we are looking to change controller number 1 from the mod wheel into controller number 74 so we can control the filter cut-off.

Back in the Transformer, click 'Add Line' for the top half. This is going to describe our mod wheel. For 'Filter Target' set 'Value1', for 'Condition' set 'Equal', and for 'Parameter 1 set '1'. So the Transformer is expecting a value, which is equal to 1, that's our mod wheel. See? It's easier than you thought.

Click 'Add Line' in the bottom half. This will describe what we want to do to the data coming through the top line. For 'Action Target', set 'Value1', for operation set 'Set to fixed value' and for 'Parameter 1' set '74'.

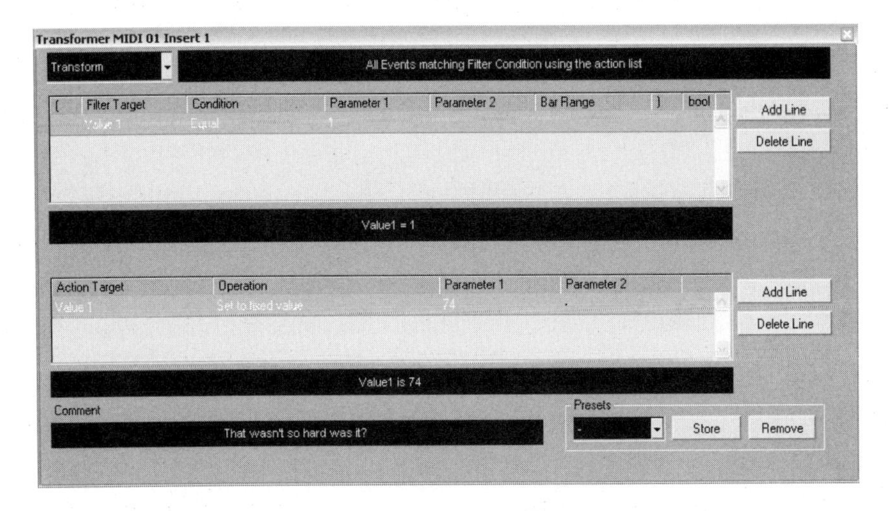

Figure 8.16
The Transformer with a transform. Changing controller number 1 into number 74.

So, what the Transformer is now doing is when it receives a controller number equal to 1, it will change it to a fixed value of 74.

Close the Transformer and check out the A1. Your mod wheel will now be fiddling with the filter cut-off. You can store any transforms that you create, so you could set up a Transformer for each VSTi you have and simply call them up when you want to use them.

I'm now going to go into some depth about setting up a MIDI floorboard for use with Cubase. It's a bit tricky and involves a combination of transforming outside Cubase, using virtual drivers and the Generic Remote. The expression pedal side of things is no problem; treat them exactly as you did the mod wheel. It's those foot switches that cause all the trouble. If you're interested, then read on. If not, then I'd suggest jumping to the next chapter, which has lots of cool stuff about mixing.

Using a MIDI floorboard with Cubase

Info

Patch and program are exchangeable terms that mean the same thing.

MIDI floorboards are designed to be used with MIDI effects processors, and so they provide you with all the functions you need to control those effects. Primarily this means patch or program changes.

Each foot switch on the board will select a different effects patch so you can change the effects you are using while you play.

You might have a lovely effects box like the TC Electronics G-Force, and using a MIDI floorboard you can have complete control over it. You'd use the pedals to select a certain effects patch, with probably a combination of effects, and then use your expression pedal to alter a parameter or two.

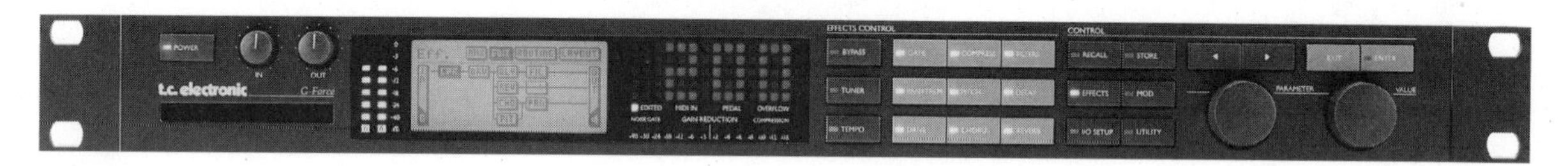

Figure 8.17
TC Electronics G-Force guitar effects processor.

We've already seen how programs like Cubase can have every aspect controlled via MIDI, so it seems logical that a MIDI floorboard could do a good job. Effects in Cubase do have a number of user definable programs that can be selected using a floorboard, however, each effect in Cubase is an individual so you don't have any way to create a couple of multiple effects patches that can be switched between via a MIDI patch change message. There is software available that will let you chain together effects, save them as patches, and recall them. However, as far as I can work out, there is no way of switching between patches via MIDI. TC Works SparkFX Machine is a great way of patching a load of effects together in Cubase. You can load whatever effects you like into the matrix and also choose the routing between the effects – great for experimental guitar players, but the ability to switch between patches with a foot switch does not seem to exist (Figure 8.18).

Maybe it's something to do with the MIDI control implementation in Cubase, or maybe it's the plug-in interface that causes the problem. Either way it's an awful nuisance.

What it all really boils down to is that Cubase uses MIDI 'Controller' messages to control parameters, knobs, and stuff, whereas our floorboard is kicking out program change messages. Using an expression pedal is really easy, as this is sending

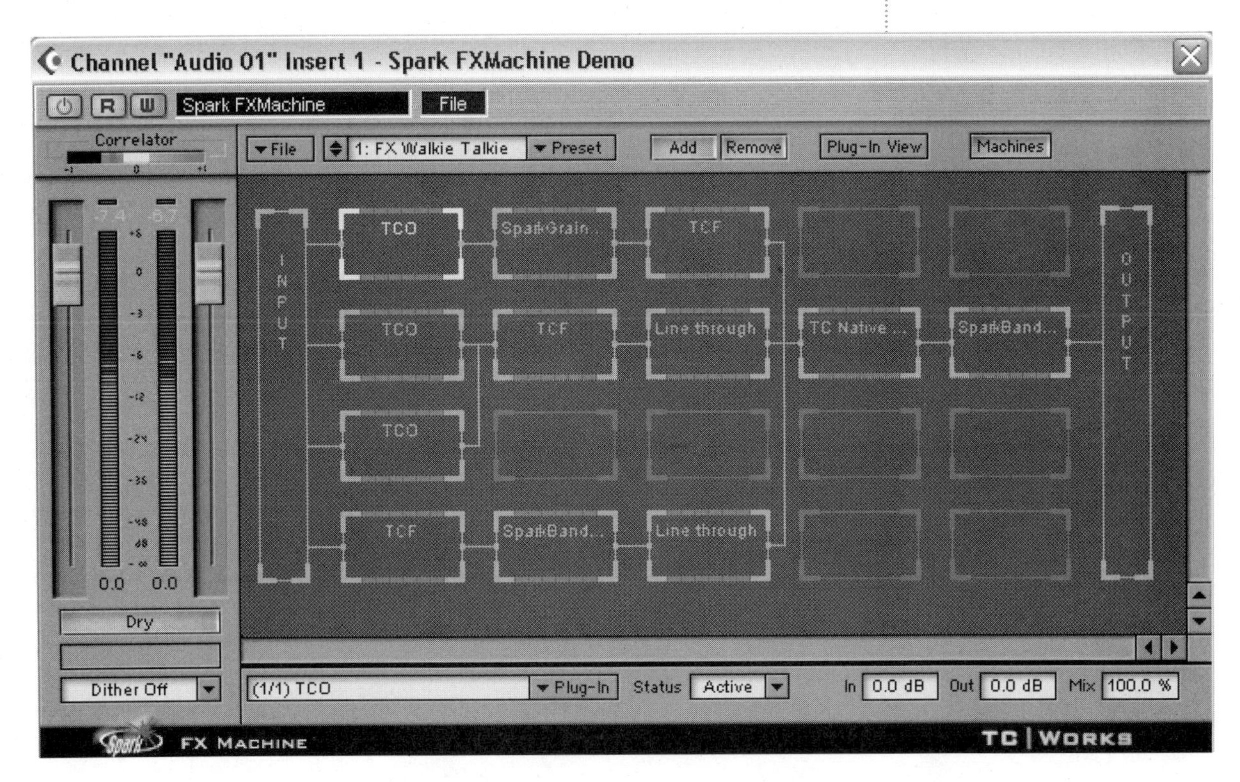

Figure 8.18
TC Works Spark FX Machine can chain effects together in a grid or matrix.

out controller information and you can use it to control anything you like, as we did with the mod wheel earlier, but it's these frustratingly useful foot switches that we need to get working for us.

The purpose of all this is to get performance control over an effect and the Amplitube plug-in is the ideal candidate. It's got lots of knobs and stomp boxes and wah pedals, all of which could be beautifully controlled from our floorboard. Now, full control is a bit tricky and we'll come onto that in a moment. First I want to look at getting some basic program changes working using the user definable programs found on each plug-in.

Basic floorboard control in Cubase

This is very similar to when we assigned the mod wheel to control the pre-amp model in Amplitube. Again we are going to use the Generic Remote device but this time to map our floorboard to the program change of an effect.

Let's have something simple to start with, like Chorus. Select the first audio track and insert the Chorus effect (Figure 8.19).

The Chorus has a number of different preset programs accessible from where it currently says 'Default'. What would be good would be to be able to select those programs with our floorboard. This is no trouble at all.

Open the Generic Remote setup window - you may still have it installed from the last time we fiddled with it. Go to Devices – Device Setup, then if it's not already there, click on 'Add/Remove', select 'Generic Remote', and click 'Add'. Then select the Generic Remote Device in the left column and click the 'Setup' tab.

I'm assuming if you have a MIDI floorboard controller that you've got it connected with a MIDI cable to your computer.

Figure 8.19
Cubase chorus effect – selecting a preset.

Make sure that you've selected the MIDI input that the floorboard is attached to, and if you needed to change this, always click 'Apply' at the bottom.

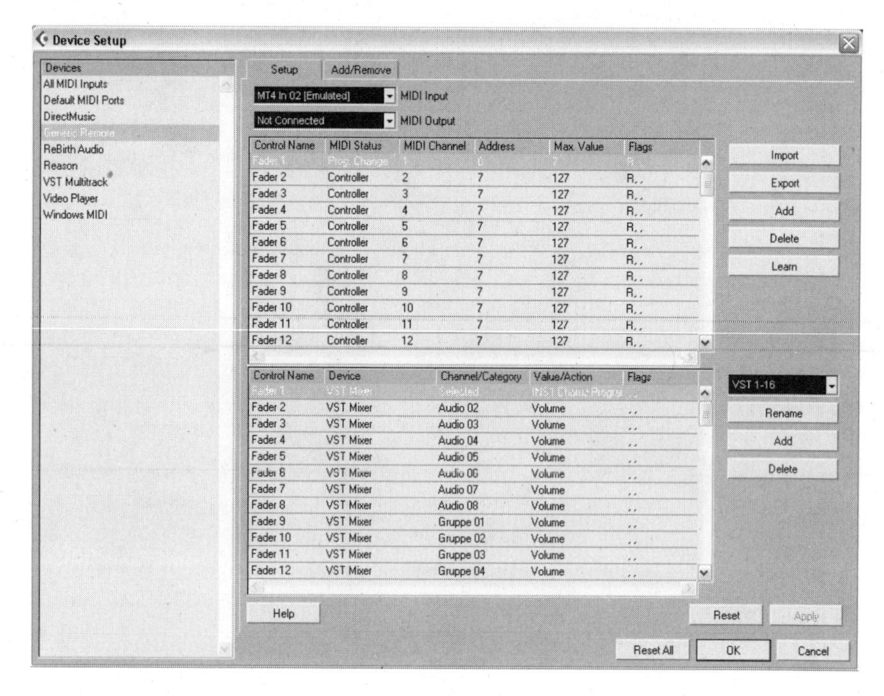

Figure 8.20
The Generic Remote setup window.

Select 'Fader 1' at the top, stomp on the first foot switch on your floorboard, and press the 'Learn' button. The MIDI Status of the Fader 1 line should have changed to 'Prog. Change'. Now the problem with program change messages in this instance is that they send out a single fixed value. A controller, like the mod wheel or expression pedal, sends out a whole range of values between 0 and 127. Cubase is expecting the Chorus presets to be selected using controller data, so each of the presets is spread equally between 0 and 127. So if there were 10 presets then the first one would be selected by sending any controller message of values roughly between 0 and 12, the second preset would be 13 to 24 and so on. Our foot switches send out single values of 0 to 9, or however many pedals you have, and then you have to go up a bank to reach 10 to 19 and so on. So selecting the presets in this way would be rather tedious, as we would have to use a different bank for each one. We just want it nice and simple, a different preset on each pedal. To accomplish this we need to restrict the number of values the effect can use for its presets. We do this in the 'Max. Value' column. The Chorus has 8 presets including the default and so if we restrict it to values between 0 and 7 then each value will have a different preset on it. Enter '7' as the maximum value.

In the bottom half of the screen, we need to direct our program changes to the Chorus effect. So, for Fader 1, which you could rename 'Chorus Program' or something, in the 'Value/Action' column you need to click and scroll down all the way until you find 'INS1 Chorus Program'.

While we're here, we could map the expression pedal to something like the Chorus mix amount. Select 'Fader 2' at the top, move your expression pedal, click 'learn'. Select 'Fader 2' at the bottom, put 'Channel/Category' to 'Selected' and select 'INS1 Chorus Mix' as the 'Value/Action'.

Click 'OK' and go back to the Chorus effect. You should now be able to select the presets using your first eight pedals and move the mix slider with your expression pedal. That's pretty good then, isn't it? You can create banks in the Generic Remote setup window so you can set up control over lots of different loaded effects and then switch between them. Unfortunately you can't seem to be able to switch between the Generic Remote banks with a foot switch – I'll definitely have a few suggestions for Steinberg once I've finished this book!

Floorboard control of Amplitube in Cubase

Of course, we can use the same control over Amplitube, but if you open it up (insert it in the first slot, in place of the Chorus we had open a moment ago) I'll point out the limitations.

Figure 8.21
Amplitube.

If you look at the preset programs, we have Programs 1–4. Load up a preset from the 'load' menu and then select Program 2 and load another preset until all four have different presets loaded. Go back to the Generic Remote setup and you'll notice that the Amplitube program select has been automatically entered as the Value/Action in place of the Chorus. However, this doesn't seem to work, and Amplitube ignores your pedals until you physically select the 'INS1 Amplitube Program' from the list – that's a nice bug they could iron out. This time we have only four programs, so we need to enter '3' as the maximum value in the top line. Select the 'Wah Position' for the expression pedal and click 'OK'.

Now you can change between the four programs with the first four pedals on your floorboard. And if you go to the Stomp window, you can see the wah position moving in response to your expression pedal. Now, wouldn't it also be pretty nice to be able to turn the wah and the other stomps on and off with our pedals? Yes it would indeed, but this is where we seem to hit some problems. It appears as if it's impossible to allocate separate pedals to separate parameters. They can all control the same parameter, as with the program selection, but program change messages cannot be separated out to control different things. Unlike a controller message, which has an identity and a value, so for instance volume is controller number 7 and pan is controller number 10, you could use two expression pedals, one assigned to each controller and each can act independently with values from 0 – 127, program change messages can only have values and share the same identity and so cannot act independently.

Now, one solution should be to use the preset programs to load up whatever number of combinations of amps and effects we like. Unfortunately there are only four presets and I can't for the life of me find out how, or if, you can add more. You can save and load effects banks, but that doesn't really help when we want to select in real time from a floorboard. Amplitube, like some other plug-ins, uses its own preset menu in the plug-in, bypassing the Cubase one, which effectively prevents us from using MIDI control on it.

What I've shown you so far is pretty cool, and you do get good control over the effects. But I want more. With a Line6 Pod, you can twiddle knobs and connect up a floorboard and control everything, and I want to be able to do exactly the same with Amplitube. So, in our ideal world we want to be able to use our floorboard not only to select the four programs but also to turn on and off the stomp boxes, and on top of that, if we had a MIDI controller with knobs on, then we want those to move the knobs in Amplitube. This is a really tall order, and it's going to require going outside of Cubase to mess with the MIDI before it reaches the plug-in.

If you're up for it, then I can show you what I've come up with. If you think that you've got all you need, then skip on to the next chapter, as this is not for the faint-hearted.

All-singing and all-dancing control of Amplitube in Cubase

This is the dark art of bending MIDI control to your own will. I've not seen or heard of anyone using a MIDI floorboard in this way. At a recent NAMM trade fair in California (music manufacturers and retail show – kind of like the Ideal Home exhibition but for music products) I was there showing Carillon Audio Systems computers and I had a system setup as a guitarist's package running Amplitube and Warp VST. Both the demonstrator from IK Multimedia and the actual writer of Warp VST were amazed at the control I'd setup with a floorboard and an eight-knob MIDI controller. So, you see, I am the master, and you, my friend, are about to learn my secrets (Figure 8.22).

The floorboard kicks out patch change commands and Cubase likes to receive controller messages to control parameters in effects. So, what we should do is somehow force the floorboard to send out control data. We've already seen how we can 'Transform' our mod wheel to a different controller number to control the A1, so surely there must be something we can do to transform the floorboard from patch change to controller. Unfortunately the 'Transformer' in Cubase acts only on MIDI tracks otherwise it would be a cool tool for this. So we need to look outside the box as it were and find a MIDI utility that might do the job for us.

By far the most comprehensive MIDI utility program is 'MIDI-OX'. It's a magical shareware program that you only need to purchase if you are using it for commercial ends. MIDI-OX can do a whole myriad of scary things to MIDI but the two we're interested in are:

Figure 8.22
The Carillon Guitar System on display at NAMM in Anaheim, Ca.

Data Mapping – this allows us to convert the patch change message into a controller message.
MIDI Merge – allows us to combine two controllers, our floorboard and our keyboard, or something with knobs on, to work together in the same Generic Remote.

It would be good to formulate some kind of plan to get a clear idea of exactly what it is we want to do. I'm assuming that you have a 10-pedal controller, like the Behringer FCB1010, if not then you can always use bank up/down to get to the other pedals (see Figure 8.9).

- The first four pedals should select the four programs
- The five pedals on the top row (6–10) should turn on/off the stomp boxes
- The first expression pedal should control wah
- The second expression pedal should control volume
- Using a second controller, whether that's a bank of knobs or just a keyboards mod wheel, to control the amp knobs

First we need to install the software. MIDI-OX comes in two parts, or at least there are two MIDI-OX products that we need to use together to achieve all this. You'll find them in the Software folder on the CD-ROM, in the MIDI-OX folder. The first file 'midioxse.exe' is the main program; double-click to install. The next part is not quite so straightforward. In order to steal MIDI from the floorboard, mess with it and then send it back to Cubase we need to install a virtual MIDI driver. So MIDI-OX will send the result to a virtual MIDI output which will act as a virtual MIDI input in Cubase. This driver is called the MIDI Yoke (I think there's some farmyard referencing going on with Oxes and Yokes – funny people). We have to manually install this driver as if we were adding new hardware to our computer:

Open the Windows Control Panel, choose 'Add Hardware', and click 'Next'. Windows will now make a vain attempt to locate this mystery hardware that you are trying to install and will fail. It will then ask if you have connected to the hardware, to which you reply 'Yes'. From the list that appears, scroll to the bottom and select 'Add a new hardware device'. Windows will persist in trying to help you, but on the next screen, select 'Install the hardware that I manually select from the list'. Scroll down to the bottom and select 'Sound, video and game controllers'. Click on 'Have Disk' and browse to the 'MIDI Yoke' folder on the CD-ROM where upon Windows will discover the 'MIDI Yoke NT' driver and promptly install it.

MIDI Yoke actually creates eight virtual drivers which will all appear in Cubase. We only need the one. Open up MIDI-OX and let's get on with it.

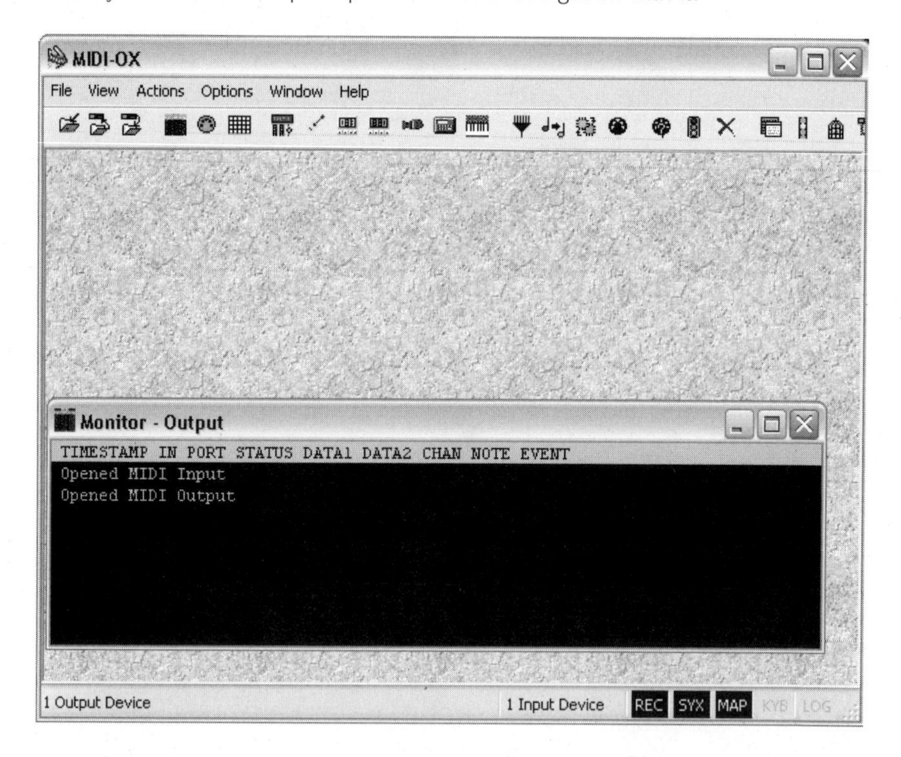

Figure 8.23
MIDI-OX for all your MIDI needs.

First thing we need to do is make sure the right MIDI inputs are selected. Under the 'Options' menu you'll find 'MIDI Devices' (Figure 8.24).

For MIDI inputs, select the MIDI ports you have your floorboard and other controller (if you have one) connected to. In my case, I've got the FCB1010 connected to the second MT4 port and my keyboard connected to the first. For MIDI output, select the first virtual MIDI driver 'MIDI Yoke NT 1'. Click 'OK'.

Back in MIDI-OX, it's quite interesting to see what's going on. The output monitor should already be open, but there's also an input monitor, under the 'View' menu which will let us see the difference between the input and output messages going through MIDI-OX from our controllers (Figure 8.25).

As you stomp on pedals, you'll see that MIDI-OX is displaying exactly which MIDI message is being sent, and you'll see that it's all program change messages which appear to select various piano sounds – not something we should worry about.

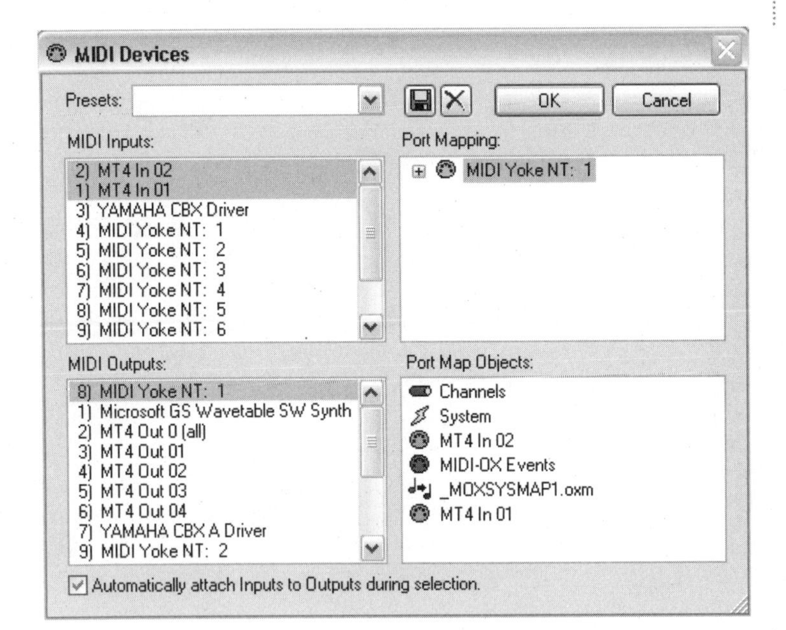

Figure 8.24
MIDI-OX MIDI device options. Select the MIDI inputs that you have your floorboard or keyboard attached to.

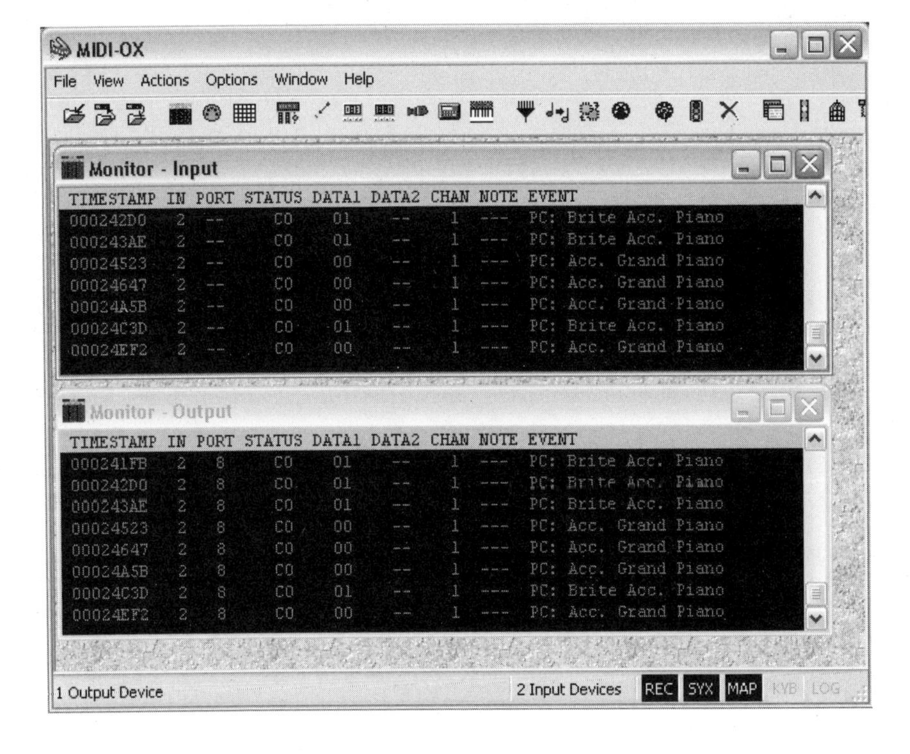

Figure 8.25
MIDI-OX monitoring the MIDI going through. The piano programs that appear in response to your pedals are just the General MIDI names for that program number. If you plugged your floorboard into a GM sound module, your pedals would select those exact sounds.

To convert the program change messages into controllers, we need to open the Data Mapping window – click on the button on the toolbar that looks like a red note pointing to a gray note with an arrow. If you put your mouse over it, it comes up as 'MIDI Data Mapping Transforms'.

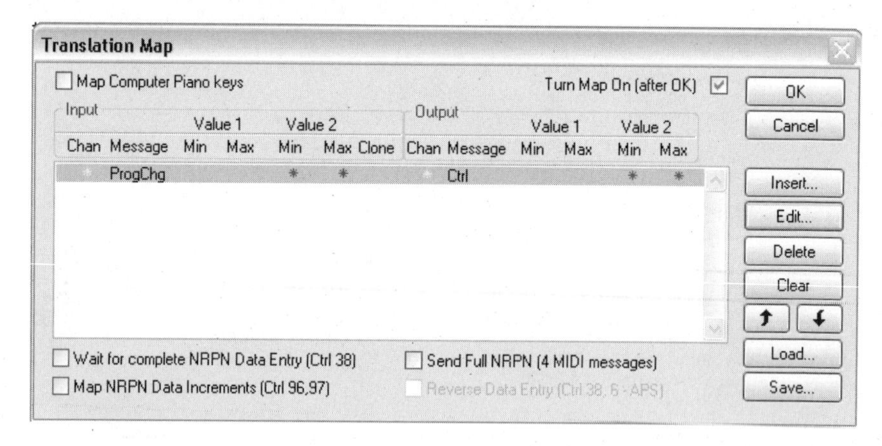

Figure 8.26
MIDI-OX setting up a transform.

Click the 'Insert' button and another window pops up where we can enter what we want to transform and what we want to transform into. Top row, 'When the input matches', we want 'ProgChange' under 'Event Type'. All the rest just mean 'Any' which is fine. On the Output row, we want the 'Event Type' to say 'Ctrl'. Click 'OK' on both windows and look at the monitors in MIDI-OX. You should now see as you stomp pedals that the input shows a program change and the output shows a controller – nice one. However, we are forgetting one thing. We want the first four pedals to send program change messages to change the programs in Amplitube. No problem. Open the Data Mapping window again, click 'Edit', and stick a number 4 in the minimum 'Patch #' value. Now it will ignore your first four pedals, check the monitors to see (Figure 8.27).

Now I think we're ready to do some serious Generic Remote mapping in Cubase. You must leave the MIDI-OX open and running for this to work.

Open Cubase, insert Amplitube onto the first audio track, and open the Generic Remote setup window. Let's do this properly this time and create a whole bank devoted to Amplitube. So, add a new bank and rename it 'Amplitube' and delete all the existing entries and the other banks so we have a nice clean slate. For the MIDI input, we need to set it to 'MIDI Yoke NT 1' so that it uses the output of MIDI-OX with our data mapping. Click 'Apply'.

Add a new a new line and call it 'Program'. Stomp on your first pedal and click 'Learn'. Set the maximum value to '3' and under 'Flags' select 'Receive', this means that it will act on any MIDI message it receives. Now in the bottom half, set 'Device' to 'VST Mixer', and 'Channel/Category' to 'Selected' - this means it will work on any audio channel we have selected. Then for 'Value/Action', select 'INS1 Amplitube Program'. This is where we were before; we can now select the four programs using our first four pedals.

Now let's tackle the stomp boxes. If you have a large enough screen then you can have Amplitube open on the 'Stomp' window behind the Generic Remote setup window so you can see the control working straight away.

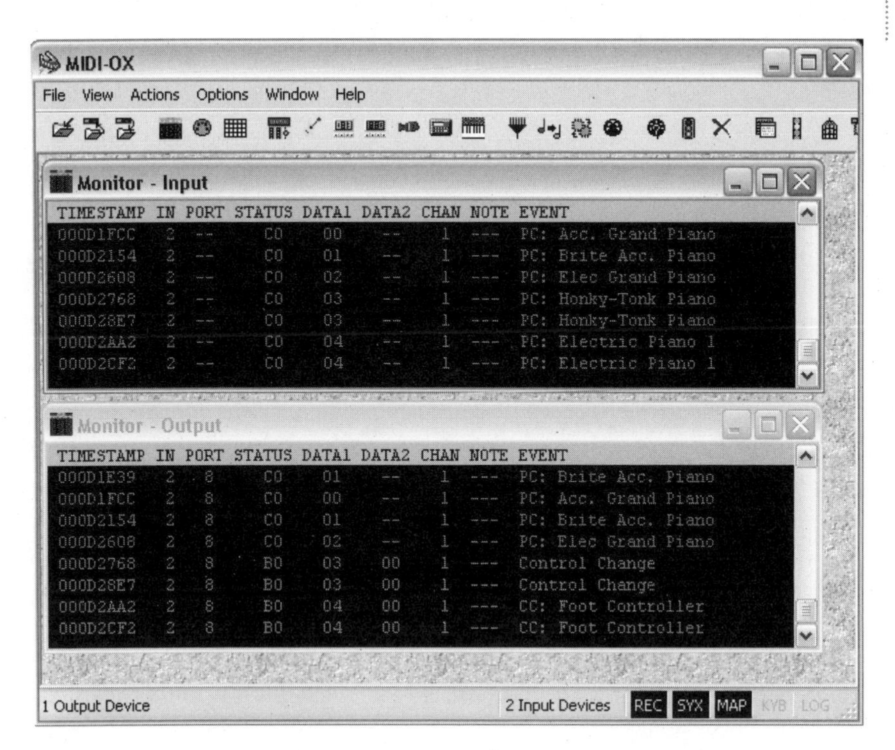

Figure 8.27
MIDI-OX showing the transform at work.

Add a new line; this will mirror the first line for some reason, but make sure you select the second line or you'll muck up the first line we've set up. Stomp on the first pedal on the top row, in my case, pedal 6, and click 'Learn'. You'll see the work that MIDI-OX is doing as the pedal is seen as a controller and not a program change – set the maximum value back to 127. Name the line 'Pedal 6' or whatever and in the bottom half set it to 'VST Mixer', 'Selected' and 'INS1 Amplitube Wah on/off' for the Value/Action. If you can see the Amplitube stomp boxes behind the setup window you'll notice that pedal 6 still doesn't do a damn thing. Click 'OK' and exit the setup window and look at the stomp boxes. If you click on the Wah stomp and turn it on, you can then stomp on pedal 6 and turn it off; however, it won't then turn it back on again. This is because the pedal is sending out a single controller number of 5. The wah has two states, on or off, controlled by a possible 128 values (0–127), so anything up to 63 will turn it off, and anything from 64 upwards would turn it on. Fortunately Cubase has a handy solution. Open the Generic Remote setup window again and look at the 'Flags' for the pedal 6 entry in the bottom half. Select the 'Toggle' option. This now switches between the minimum and maximum value for every press of the pedal, which results in us being able to turn the wah on and off with pedal 6. If you've got that then the rest is easy.

Add a new line, make sure you select it, call it 'Pedal 7', stomp on your pedal, click 'Learn', make sure the maximum value is set to 127. In the bottom half, set it to 'VST Mixer' and 'Selected', choose the 'INS1 Amplitube Sto Del on/off' for the Value/Action and turn on the Toggle flag. Make sure you select the right Delay, as there's also a stereo delay in the effects section of Amplitube. I'm sure you can now do the rest yourself until you have a pedal assigned to each stomp.

Now we want to assign the first expression pedal to the wah amount. Same as before, add a line, move the expression pedal and click 'Learn'. Bottom half, set 'VST Mixer', 'Selected' and choose 'INS Amplitube Wah Amount' as the Value/Action, and no flags required. Hang on a second - that didn't seem to work at all. In fact, moving my expression pedal seems to make the Chorus pedal flash on and off. We've hit a slight problem. An expression pedal is usually set up to control volume, which is controller number 7, but our pedal number 8 is already kicking out controller number 7, and so the two are clashing. The way out of this is to assign the expression pedal a new controller number. This is something you'd have to do on the floorboard itself. With the Behringer FCB1010 I'm using, you can set the controller number for each expression pedal for each preset. Each pedal represents a preset, so for each pedal, I have to set up the expression pedal to send out a different number, let's say '11'. At the same time I'll set my second expression pedal to 12 to avoid any other confusion. With a bit of luck, we've now ironed out all the problems, and with our extraordinary persistence we might actually get there. So, re-learn the expression pedal with its new number and it controls the wah amount perfectly. The second expression pedal I'm going to set up to control the output level. I have one pedal left, number 5, so I might as well set that up for something. How about 'Amp Bypass'?

Now we've got the floorboard running like a good'un, and now we need to get to work on those knobs. Ideally for this you need a load of MIDI controller knobs. I'm really liking the look of the Evolution UC-33 - lots of great knobs and a blue LCD display.

Figure 8.28
Evolution UC-33 MIDI controller.

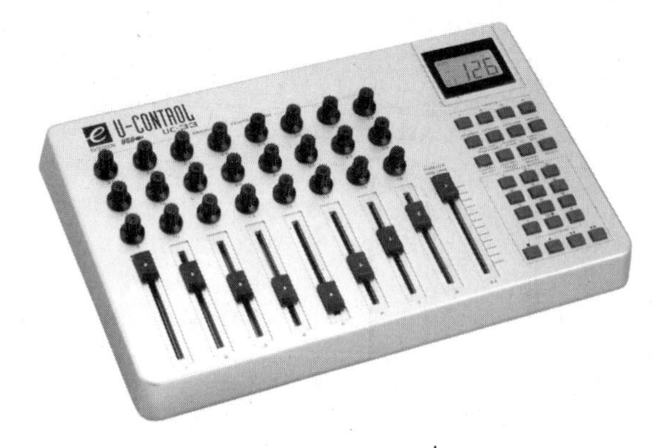

Failing that, then let's use the mod wheel on our keyboard just to demonstrate the point. Back in the Generic Remote setup, you'll notice that you can only have one MIDI input. This is why we used the MIDI-OX to merge the MIDI from our floorboard and the MIDI from our keyboard to the same virtual MIDI Yoke port.

So, one last time as you know this by now, add a new line, move the mod wheel, click 'Learn' and set it to control perhaps the preamp model. If you have more MIDI knobs, then you can get them to control all the other knobs in Amplitube. One problem you may come across is that your knobs might conflict with the controller numbers of the pedals. The easiest way around this is to change the MIDI channel of your keyboard, that way there's no chance of clashing.

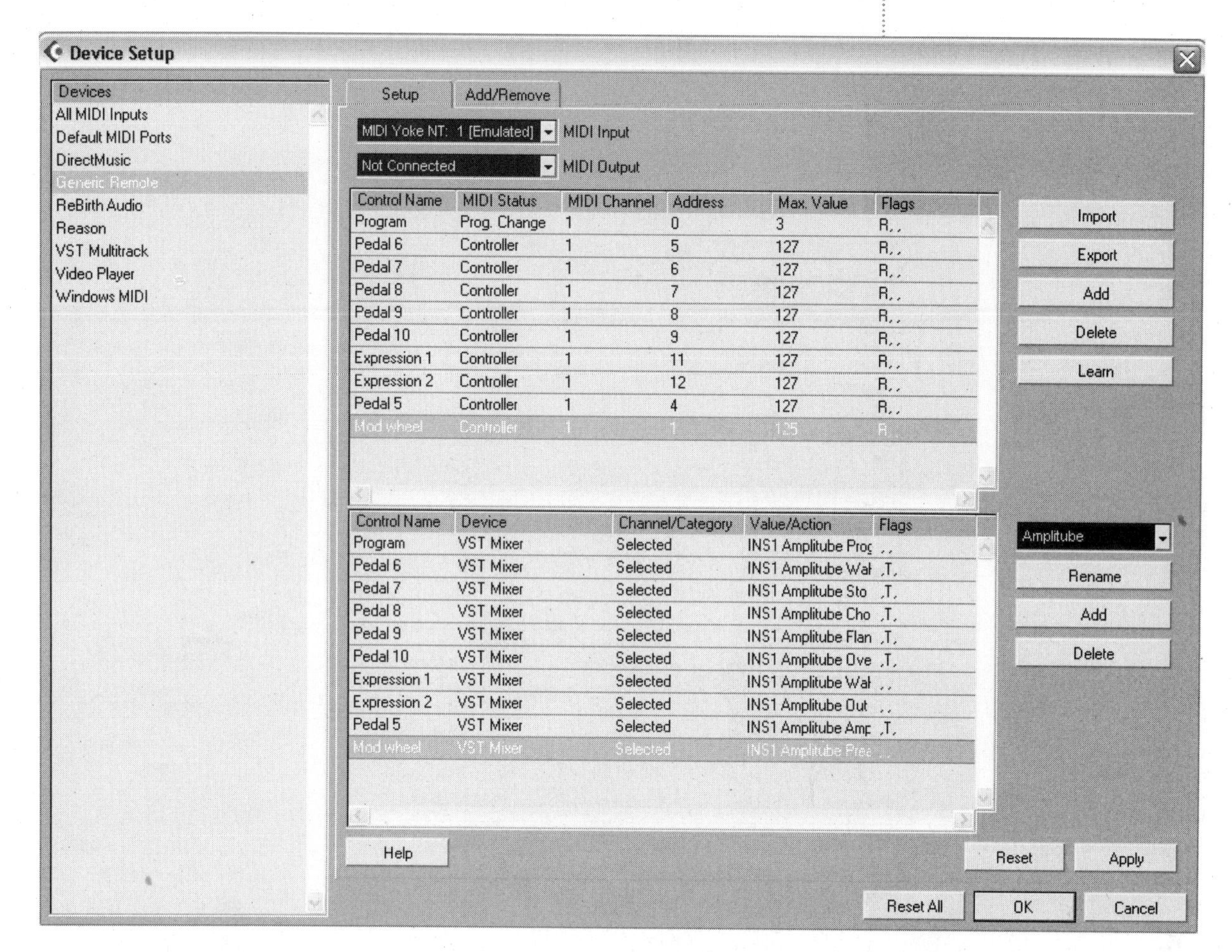

Figure 8.29
Generic Remote setup page with Amplitube well and truly controlled.

After all the hard work, you can now save this Generic Remote by clicking the 'Export' button, and this even works in the demo version.

Amplitube is now as controllable and useful in performance as a Line6 Pod would be. This sort of control, although a bit of struggle to set up, is what finally bridges the gap between hardware and software. I imagine that the controlling options in Cubase will improve to incorporate the sorts of things we want to do in time. Certainly I reckon it won't be long before a USB floorboard arrives designed to be used expressly with the computer – once this sort of thing catches on.

Info

Remember that you and I are the only people in the world who know how to do this.

Transport control

One more thing while we're at it. Why use a mouse to click on play or record when you can do it from your floorboard?

Using the same Generic Remote that we are using for Amplitube, we can simply add the transport controls. Add five new fields to the top list and name them Rewind, Forward, Stop, Play, and Record. Now, to avoid any clashes between controller numbers already set up, use a higher bank number on your floorboard, and then use the 'Learn' function to assign five pedals to each of the transport controls.

In the bottom half under 'Device', choose 'Transport', 'Channel – Device' and under 'Value' choose the relevant transport control. Turn 'Toggle' on and you're ready to go.

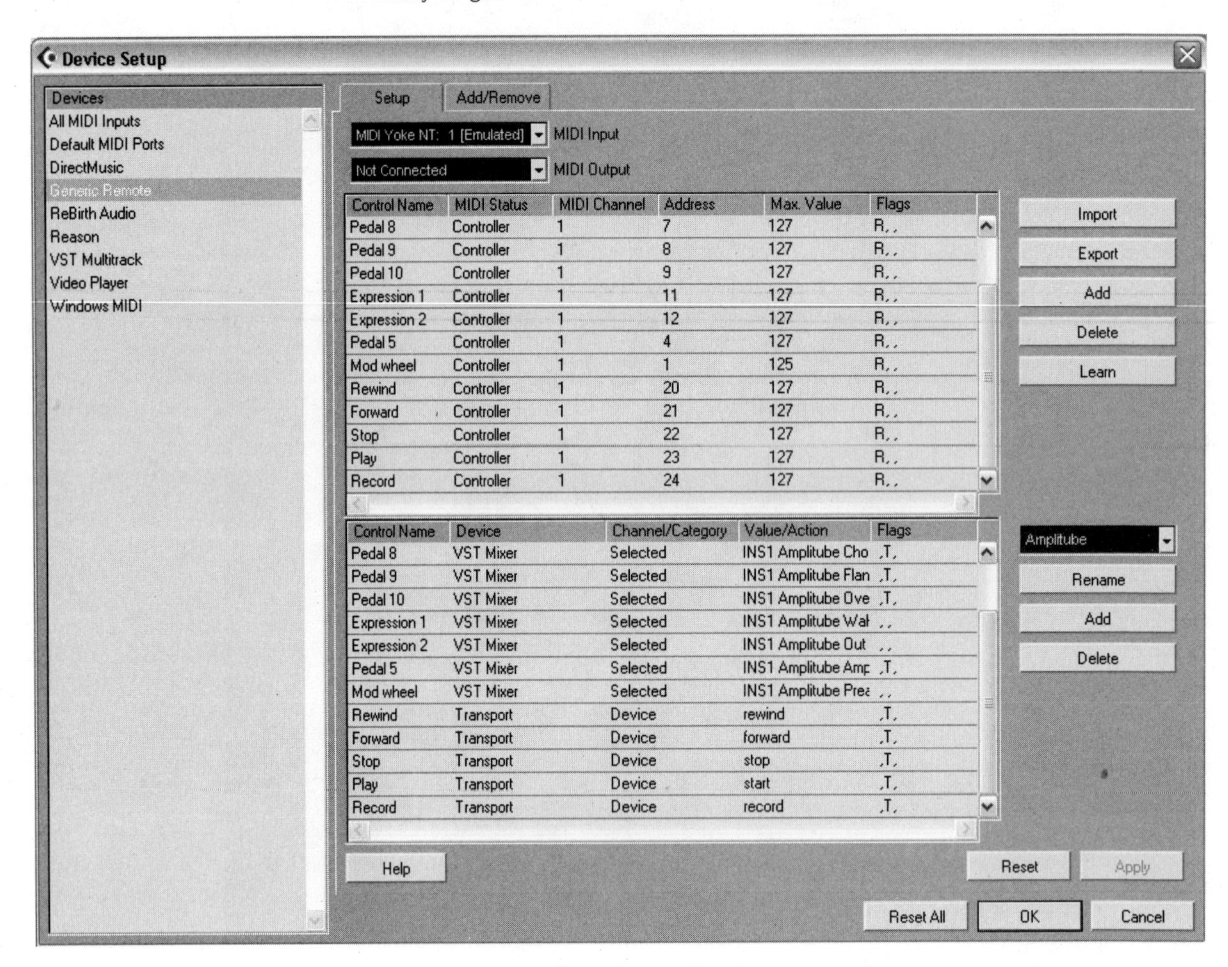

Figure 8.30
Adding Transport Control to the Generic Remote.

So, now not only do you have complete effects control, but you can also drop Cubase into record with the touch of a footswitch, leaving your hands free to do more important things like playing the guitar.

Mixing and automating

Mixing is all about getting the overall sound of your project together. You've got audio tracks of perhaps guitars and vocals, and you've got MIDI tracks of VSTis, drums, bass, maybe some synths, and now you need to create the right 'mix' so that your song sounds fantastic. At a basic level, we're talking about levels, or volume, and getting the right level of all the tracks relative to each other. Then there's 'pan', which is the track's position between left and right in the stereo field – or how much of each speaker it comes out of. You might want to add effects to tracks, or compress them or alter the EQ to get the tracks to 'sit right' with each other.

All these things are exactly the same sort of things you'd be doing with a hardware mixer and tape-based recording in a studio. You have the same tools like compression and EQ, you have the same faders and routing controls, there's nothing at all mysterious about mixing on the computer. With the MIDI controllers we looked at, you can even have the same tactile feel of mixing using a control surface.

The computer has some added bonuses, though, that you won't find in an analog studio. Stuff like automation, being able to record fader movements, and other parameters. Even with a control surface you have only two hands, so trying to alter the pan of one track slowly over time as well as moving multiple faders up and down simultaneously would stretch even the most ambidextrous of us. With our recording software, we can have all the mixer features of each track in constant motion if we wish. Fading stuff in and out, moving it about in the stereo field, changing EQ, taking effects in and out, all of this can be going on in our mix. If you then want to try another way of mixing it, you can save the old mix and come back to it later, so you never lose any of those great ideas.

If, like me, you've ever been in a situation where your band has booked some studio time to get a demo together, then you'll know how it goes. After the competitions on who can get the tape machine to stop closest to zero on rewind, you all start 'contributing' to the mixing process. This is where those 'musical differences' start coming into play as you fight to get your track to be louder and fatter than anyone else's. The guitar's got to be at the front after all. Just when you think you've got some kind of compromise mix going, the drummer just has to twiddle with a few more knobs and before you know it, the mix is all over the place and the studio time is ticking away. With a computer, once all the recording is done, you can all make alternative mixes and have them saved separately for instant recall. Even better, you can burn copies of all the tracks as data onto CDs and each of you take one home to play with on your own computer, in your own time. You can then come back together and compare your mixes and create a whole new thing to argue about.

Mixing in Cubase

Let's take a look at the mixing facilities in Cubase. You've probably already had a bit of a play with the mixer, and I'll show you where all the usual mixer bits hang out. It's not my intention to teach you how to get a great mix, as that's an artform in itself, but rather to give you a few pointers and give you access to the tools you need to begin mixing yourself. There are some generally accepted rules concerning mixing, but ultimately it comes down to what you think sounds good.

For this section, I've created a whole song for you, unmixed and raw, so we can see how the mixing affects the overall sound. Now, I don't want any snide remarks about my guitar playing or the choice of style, I just wanted something simple, a bit groovy, and hopefully inoffensive to the majority of my readers. So you'll find a project in the Cubase Projects folder called 'Mixing Demo.cpr'. Open it up and let's have a look (Figure 9.1).

The song is made up of two audio tracks of recorded clean guitar, one rhythm, one lead, although I get a bit confused which is doing what during the song, and ten MIDI tracks playing the A1, VB-1, and LM-7 VSTis. It's a whole band's worth of stuff (Figure 9.2).

Figure 9.1
The Mixing Demo project.

Figure 8.1
The Generic Remote setup window.

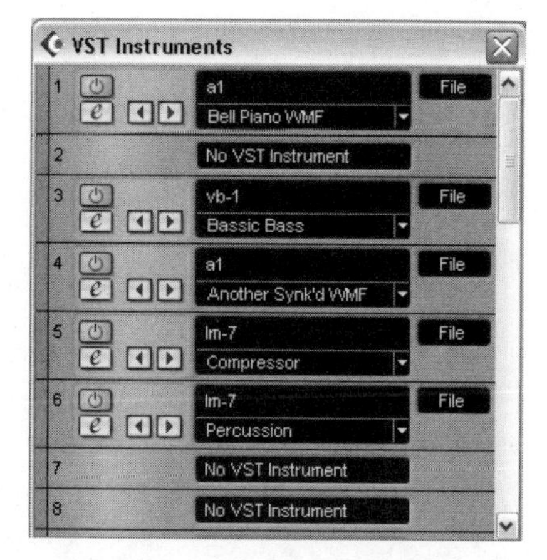

Figure 9.2
Instruments used in the Mixing Demo.

I've got two A1s loaded, one using a 'Bell Piano' sound which is running my 'Rhodes' track and it was as close as I could get, the other one has 'Another Synk'd' sound loaded which sounds a bit like a funky clavichord and so is running my 'Clav' track. The VB-1 is on the standard 'Bassic Bass' sound and then I have two LM-7s loaded, one with the 'Compressor' kit for the usual kick, snare, and cymbals, the other with the 'Percussion' kit for the errr... percussion.

You'll notice that most of the MIDI tracks are made up of one or two bar events copied throughout the song. It was only the Rhodes MIDI track that was played live all the way through. The song has been arranged to create a bit of a build up at the beginning and then basically repeats ad nauseum, with the odd break. I created the song by first coming up with a percussion loop and a bass line, and then recorded the guitar alongside for as long as I felt like. This was before I'd arranged the events around, which is why the guitar runs for the whole length of the song. Along with the mixing, we'll also edit the guitar tracks a bit to make them fit better with the general flow of the song.

If you play the song back you'll hear, amongst other things, that the two guitar tracks, although beautifully crafted, are far too loud in comparison to everything else. They also sound very 'dry' and a bit muddled together. The bass guitar is very quiet and so are the kick and snare sounds. There's plenty we can do to remedy that.

If you have any trouble playing back the song, if it sounds crackly or seems to pop, then check the buffer settings for the soundcard. You may have lowered the buffer to get better response when playing the VSTis, you may now have to increase it again to get smooth playback of this many VSTi tracks. Go to the control panel in Devices – Device Setup – VST Multitrack – ASIO Control Panel.

Before we start moving faders around, let's find out where the mixing facilities are. There are two ways of looking at the mixing facilities in Cubase. First of all, there's the 'Track Mixer' which shows all tracks like a mixing desk, and then there's the 'VST Channel' editor that shows the mixer settings for a single channel or track. We'll be mostly looking at the Track Mixer, so let's have a quick look at the VST Channel editor first.

VST Channel Editor

Select the Rhythm guitar track, and make sure the monitor button is off or it will mute the track while waiting for an input signal. In the Track Info column click the 'e' button (Edit VST Channel).

This shows all the mixer settings for this audio track in one window. From left to right you have the level fader and pan controls, then the Insert Effects section just as you saw in the Track Info column, then the EQ section with four bands and a graphic display of what's going on, and finally the effect sends section.

Figure 9.3
VST Channel Editor.

Track Mixer

The Track Mixer can be found under the 'Devices' menu or by pressing the F3 key on your keyboard. It shows all the tracks in order and also the master outputs.

The layout is just as you'd find on a traditional mixer and the interface mimics the knobs and sliders of the real thing. To show all the settings for each channel, like with the VST Channel Editor, would make the mixer unusably large on the screen, so instead you can switch between the various elements such as inserts, EQ and sends using the 'Show' buttons on the side. You can also view the EQ and Sends as either 'dials' or just lines and numbers, whatever you find easier to work with. Alternatively you can do the same for an individual channel by clicking on the little white triangle in the space between the top and bottom halves of the mixer, and selecting from the list. You can also choose what types of channel you want to show in the mixer, so for instance at the moment we've hidden the MIDI channels, so the MIDI tracks are not represented here but the output of the VSTis are, which is what we actually want to mix. With a click of the 'Extended/Normal Mixer' button you can also hide the top half of the mixer so your screen is not as cluttered when dealing purely with the level mixing.

Figure 9.4
The Track Mixer with a 4-band parametric EQ above each channel.

Taking a closer look at a single channel, we can see a whole array of buttons alongside. At the top it shows the input used on the channel for recording, then we have panning control for placing the track in the stereo field. Mute and Solo we've come across before. The Read and Write Automation buttons turn on and off the automation features for this channel – we'll come onto this later. The 'e' button brings up the VST Channel Editor so we can see all the settings together. Next there are buttons to bypass the inserts and EQ and to disable the send effect. Then we have the record enable and monitor buttons as we find on the track itself. Finally at the bottom we have the output routing. If your soundcard has multiple outputs then they will appear here as buses, just like if you had an analog mixer with multiple bus outputs.

Finally, on the right of the mixer, assuming you have the 'Show Master' button pressed, we have the Master outputs. These control the level of the overall stereo output to your soundcard. You can also insert effects here that will affect the whole mix. You might find while we're mixing that you encounter a bit of digital distortion because the levels are too high. Use the Master fader to reduce the level slightly so that the peak lights above the fader do not go red.

Let's try sorting this mix out, then.

Figure 9.5
A single VST Channel strip.

Applying effects

The first thing we should do is get the guitar sound right, and I imagine that Amplitube would be a good plug-in to use. For that matter we could also use it to beef up the bass as we did in Chapter 7. As I mentioned before, Amplitube is quite a hefty plug-in and so having three instances of it running, one for bass, and one for each guitar, might be more than your computer can handle at this time. What we would normally do in this situation is to get the sound right on the first track and then 'apply' the effect to that track. This means that Cubase re-records the track with the plug-in giving us the sound we want without having to leave the plug-in open, using up our valuable CPU resources. The downside is that we can't then go back and change the guitar sound, but this would be completely normal if you recorded the guitar with effects on it in the first place.

We do this differently to how we normally insert an effect. This time we want to apply an effect directly to the track and get Cubase to process up the result.

Select the Rhythm Guitar event in the arrange window and right-click. From the menu select 'Plug-ins' and then the 'IK Multimedia - Amplitube' plug-in.

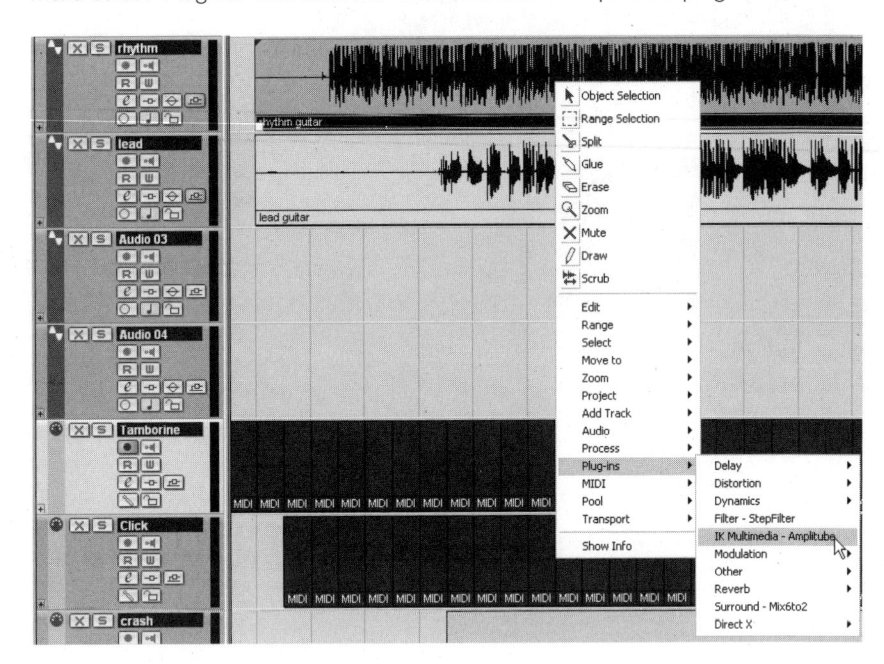

Figure 9.6
Applying Amplitube to an audio event.

Instead of pressing play, we use the 'Preview' button on the Amplitube window. This will begin playback of the rhythm guitar track and allow us to find the right sound in Amplitube (Figure 9.7).

Once you're happy with the sound, press the 'Process' button and Cubase will apply the effect directly on the track. Cubase does have a handy 'undo' history so if you decide later that the sound you chose is awful, you can always go back and undo the process. You might also find that you can choose an appropriate sound more easily if the rest of the song is playing back as well. You can do this by first of all using Amplitube just as an insert, get the sound right and remember what it was, or save if as a preset, then take out the effect and apply it with the remembered settings. Don't apply Amplitube to the Lead Guitar track, as we'll want to look at automating Amplitube on that track later on, so we'll keep the track dry but by all means stick Amplitube in as an insert.

With the bass it's a different kettle of fish. This is not an audio track, it's a MIDI track being played through a VSTi, so there isn't any audio as such to process an effect onto. We can insert an effect onto the output of the VB1, as we did before, but we can't process the plug-in onto it. Instead what you can do is mix down the track with the effect on it. A 'mixdown' is a recording made at the master outputs,

Figure 9.7
Amplitube as an offline plug-in.

and it records the entire song as a single audio file. This is what you would put onto a CD to play the song to your friends. If you were to solo the bass track, you could create a mixdown of just that track with any inserted effects recorded as well. We'll deal with this much more in the next chapter, but it's important to see this as a possibility when creating and mixing your music. If you were to mix down a VSTi track, then it could appear as an audio track, meaning that you could turn off the VSTi, saving yourself more CPU processing power. This is how you would get around the limitations of your computer's power when you want to use more VSTis than your computer can safely handle.

Unfortunately, the demo version of Cubase does not allow for mixdowns or the exporting of audio, so you won't be able to try it. Instead, what I've done is to create a new version of this project with the bass track already mixed down with Amplitube for you. On top of that, I've applied the Warp VST guitar plug-in to the Rhythm guitar track so you can hear what that sounds like, and it also avoids those annoying clicks that the demo of Amplitube creates. So, close the existing project and open the one in the same folder called 'Mixing Demo bass and guitar mixed.cpr'.

With this new project, you'll see the bass as an audio track at the top. I've deleted the bass MIDI track and unloaded the VB1 VSTi. Now the bass sounds much meatier. The rhythm guitar is now way too loud but sounding nice (or nasty depending on your point of view) and crunchy, which is what Warp VST excels at.

Let's move some faders to balance the song out a bit. Insert Amplitube onto the lead guitar track, and I'd recommend the 'jimi and the wind' VIP preset for instant gratification. It might be useful to loop part of the song while we're doing this so we don't have to keep rewinding and playing again. We should choose a bit where everything is playing. If you select the event in the middle of the song on the 'Clav' track, it goes from bar 34 to 64, and press 'P' to set the markers.

Set Cubase playing back with the Loop button on between the markers. Press F3 to bring up the mixer.

Level adjustment

Starting from the left, bring down the level of the rhythm guitar so it's not dominating the whole song. The lead guitar could also do with dropping a bit but maybe not quite as much as the rhythm. The bass is sounding pretty good now, so we can leave that thumping. The Rhodes is tinkering away in the background, so that's fine for now. The Clav on the other hand is very loud and a bit annoying, so let's drop that a little. The drums are a bit lost, so we should bring them up a bit, but the percussion kit sounds pretty good, so we'll leave that alone. Already you should be hearing the difference.

Panning

Positioning the tracks in stereo creates instant 'space' in the mix, or as many people put it, creates 'separation' between the tracks. A good way of thinking about it is to imagine the instruments on stage and where they would normally be. Drums and bass would probably be in the centre of the stage, one guitarist on either side and the keyboard player wherever you can fit him so he's not in the way while the rest of you rock about. So, let's split the guitars, rhythm left, lead right – not all the way but between 35 and 40. Bass stays central, but we could separate the two keyboards. Put the Rhodes about 20 left and the Clav 20 right. Leave the drums central. I reckon that'll sound much better.

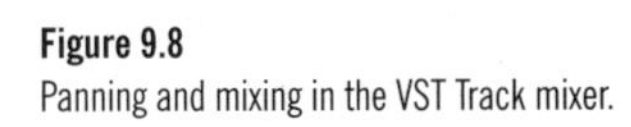

Figure 9.8
Panning and mixing in the VST Track mixer.

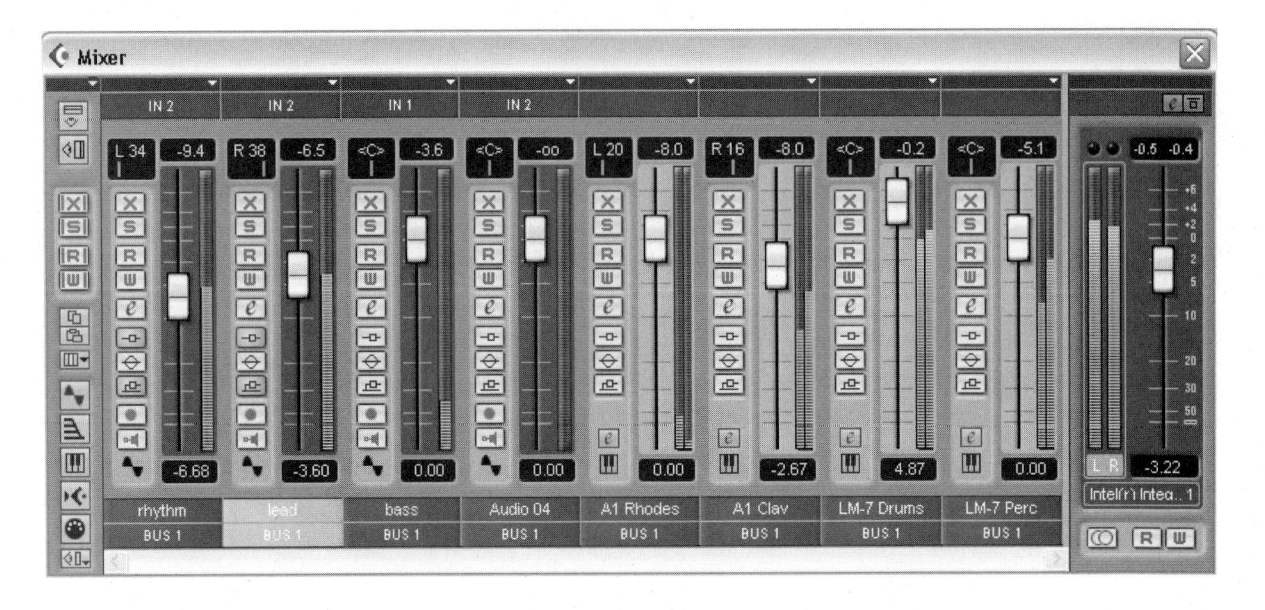

Effects

We've dealt with this before, but it would be nice to do it in the context of a song. An effect which is often used to give the impression of depth and positioning forwards and backwards, as opposed to side to side with panning, is reverb. Let's set up a reverb as a send effect and then send some of each track to it. Press F6 to bring up the send effects window and load the 'Reverb A' into the first slot. Choose the 'Large' reverb preset so we can create a lot of space. In the mixer click the 'Show All Sends' button and you'll see at the top of the mixer the Reverb A is already in place. Turn on the send for each channel (standby/bypass button) and adjust the amount for each track. This might require some experimentation, and it's very easy to add too much and end up with everything muddled – 'muddied' is perhaps the better term. Try about a third on the guitars, none on the bass, more on the Rhodes and Clav and just a touch on the drums. You might also want to try soloing each track as you do it to give yourself a better idea of how it's affecting the sound.

If you bring up the sends window (F6), you can turn the effect on and off so you can hear exactly the difference it's making.

Figure 9.9
The Sends in the Track mixer.

Let's now attack the annoying Clav track and see if we can make it sound a tad more interesting. Click the 'Show All Inserts' button and in the first insert for the Clav track, load up the 'DoubleDelay'. The default preset is perfect. Into the second slot load up the 'StepFilter' and again the default preset is perfect. That's more like it - we've now got an interesting filtered delay thing going on that was completely unexpected.

EQ

Equalization is about boosting or cutting various frequencies or frequency bands to change the tone of the sound. This is like a fancy version of the treble and bass tone controls or graphic EQ you might find on your hi-fi. It's a simple sort of filtering. There are all sorts of rules associated with EQ but, as with all mixing, it all comes down to what sounds good to you. A good example of use is to pick out and boost the kick drum. Click the 'Show All EQ As Dials' button and go to the LM7 – Drums channel. Personally I find it quite hard to visualize EQ settings, so it's much easier to see what's going on in the VST Channel Editor. Press the little 'e' button on the LM7 – drums channel to bring it up. Solo the track so we can just hear the drums playing. Turn on the first EQ section called 'lo' as this deals with the low frequencies which is also where we'll find our bass drum. You'll see a little '1' appear in the graphic display above the knobs. If you grab hold of the '1' with your mouse and move it up, you'll see what's called a 'low shelf' appear. This is boosting all the low frequencies with the shape of the curve. You should hear the kick drum start to boom a bit. If you drag to the right, you'll hear the whole kit being boosted to distortion. Bring the '1' back and settle it over the 100Hz mark, which is about the frequency of the kit drum, and set it to 6dB.

> **Info**
>
> Decibel (dB) is a measurement of 'loudness' which is actually a ratio, and 6dB is essentially a doubling of loudness. It's not important to understand, and a short explanation is always a clumsy one. Suffice it to say that more is more and less is less.

The bottom knob of the EQ is called resonance or 'Q' and it dictates the steepness of the EQ filter, or how wide the band is around the peak. If you increase this, you'll see the difference on the display. If you now drag the '1' to the left and right again, you'll hear a familiar filtering effect as narrow frequency bands are being boosted. Return it again to our 100Hz mark and set the 'Q' to about 1.5. This should be boosting our kick drum nicely.

Figure 9.10
Using EQ in the VST Channel Editor.

EQ is probably the most commonly used of all processors, and a skilful engineer would use it to separate out frequency bands to give more separation to the various instruments in the mix.

Dynamics

The difference between the loudest and softest sounds is known as the 'dynamic range'. Or you could say that a piece of music that moves between loud and soft passages is very 'dynamic'. Dynamic processing is used primarily to squash the dynamic range of tracks so that the quiet sounds don't get lost in the mix and the loud ones are reduced from being too over the top. A good example would be with a vocalist. They may want to scream in some parts of the song and whisper in others. With dynamic compression, you can squash (compress) the dynamic range of the performance so that despite the tone of the voice, the track remains at the same volume. It also has the effect of bringing things forward in the mix.

Cubase, of course, has dynamics processing built in and has a couple of plug-ins that we can use. The drums will give us the most obvious result of the use of dynamics, so insert the 'Dynamics' plug-in onto the 'LM7 – Drums' channel.

If you start with the 'Full Dynamics' preset, you'll instantly hear the effect it has. The Compressor reduces the gain of any sounds over the threshold setting by the amount set by the ratio. The drop in gain is then countered by the 'make-up gain' setting, which boosts the compressed signal. The Autogate is essentially a noise gate that silences the audio as soon as it drops below a certain threshold. This plug-in also allows you to set the frequency range that will trigger the gate. This can give you some interesting effects like the gate being opened (so audio comes through) only when a high frequency sound, like a hi-hat, occurs. The Limiter ensures that the output level never exceeds a set level - very handy to avoid distortion.

If you choose the 'Compressor' preset, you'll hear that the drums are much beefier and solid, and you can hear all parts of the kit really well in the mix.

I think you'll agree that the song is sounding much better than it did when we were first introduced to each other, and all we've done is messed with a few mixer settings. This is all very well for this looped section of the song, but what about if you want to change things in different parts? Well, you can always do that live on playback, and while you're at it, you can record all the movements and edit them afterwards, or improve upon them. Let's enter the spooky world of automation.

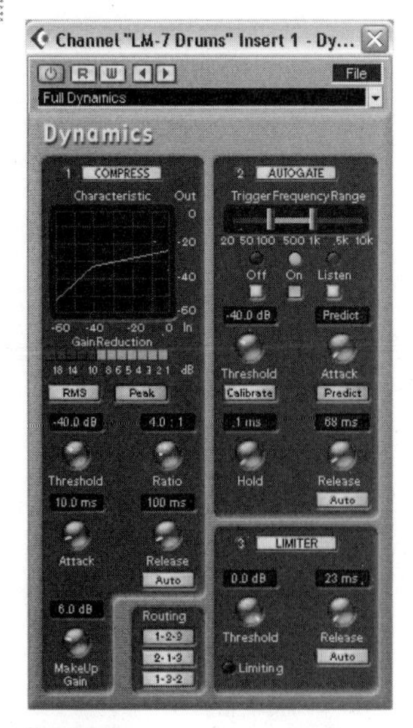

Figure 9.11
The Dynamics plug-in that comprises compression, limiting, and a noise gate.

Automation

Automation is a simply fabulous tool for mixing and many other functions. It allows us to take our hands off the mouse and make Cubase do the work for us. It couldn't be any simpler either, which is nice, so let's try it.

Loop a smaller section in the arrange window, maybe a bar or two, and set it playing. Back in the mixer, on the first channel, our rhythm guitar, click the 'R' and 'W' buttons that turn on read and write automation. Cubase is now ready to write automation for this track and as it loops, it will read it back. You'll see what I mean any second now. As Cubase begins the loop again, move the fader around with your mouse until it repeats. The fader will now move about on its own following the movements you made on the first loop. It's that easy. With the 'Write Automation' button on for any track, Cubase will record the movements of anything you touch, whether that's EQ or effects parameters or anything to do with the mixer. If you grab the moving fader with your mouse, you can overwrite the existing automation. If you turn off 'write' and just leave 'read' on, you can move the fader as you wish with the mouse but as soon as you release, it will jump back to the automation.

There are three automation modes – Touch Fader, Autolatch, and X-Over – and these are selectable from a drop-down list next to the toolbar in the project window.

- Touch Fader – writing begins when a control is touched and ends when the mouse is released. This is what we've done so far and is the most common way of automating.
- Autolatch – writing begins when a control is touched but not stopped until you turn off the Write button. So when you release the mouse, the same value will be continuously written.
- X-Over – same as Autolatch, but as soon as you cross any existing automation curve, the writing is stopped.

I suggest you keep it as 'Touch Fader' for now. We've seen how automation can be edited and changed just by grabbing the fader, but we can also do it in a far more elegant fashion in the project window. Any automation for each track can be viewed and edited alongside the track. Zoom in on the Rhythm guitar track, at the bar where you were looping and adding automation. On the bottom left of the track is a little '+' button, press it and out should pop the volume automation subtrack.

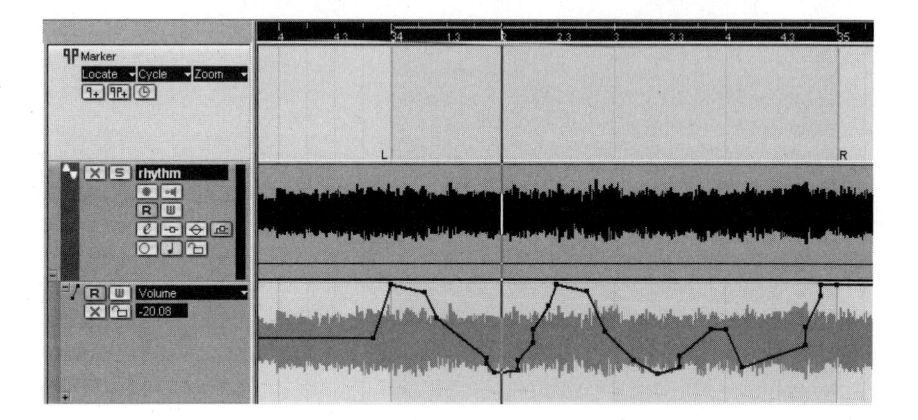

Figure 9.12
The automation subtrack showing volume fader movements for the rhythm guitar track.

The volume automation subtrack shows a blue line, representing the written automation, on top of a dimmer copy of the audio event, so you can see exactly where you are. If you select the Rhythm track and look at the Track Info column, click on the 'Channel' bar so you can see the volume fader. With read and write on, hit play and move the fader. You'll now see the automation being written to the volume subtrack.

The blue line can of course be edited with the mouse. Just take the draw/pencil tool and give it a try. Drawing freehand is fine, but Cubase can offer a bit more than that. If you click and hold on the Draw button on the toolbar, you get a couple of other options:

- Line – draws a straight line – great for moving parameters smoothly
- Parabola – draws a curve – great for fade in/out
- Sine – draws a sine wave – great for modulation
- Triangle – draws a row of triangles – great for ups and downs
- Square – draws a square wave shaped line – great for switching between two values

The width of these lines is set by the grid and quantize resolution. You very soon get the hang of it. You can also move the little black 'handles' around with the normal arrow tool if you want to edit rather than draw in new stuff.

Fiddling with the volume automation will of course mess up our original mixer settings, but you can always turn off the Read button and restore the fader to where it was.

Automating effects

What would be interesting would be to automate the wah effect in Amplitube on the Lead guitar track. You can add whatever parameter you like as an automation subtrack. If you open the first subtrack for the lead track, volume, you can click on where it says 'Volume' and select from the available parameters or choose 'More..' to pick from a larger list of parameters than are currently available for that track – you'll see all the Amplitube parameters available to you. However, an easier way of doing it is to set the track into 'Write' and move the parameter you want to use. The automation subtrack for that parameter will automatically appear in the first list.

So, go back to the beginning of the song, take Cubase out of Loop playback, as we want the effect to be over the whole track, and turn on write automation for the lead track. Open the Amplitube window and go to the Stomp section. Turn on the Wah stomp pedal and set the mode knob to 'on'. Press play and use your mouse on the wah knob for all you're worth so that Jimi would be proud. If you're feeling really adventurous then you could always map your mod wheel to the wah knob like we did in the last chapter.

If you prefer, of course, you could use something like the sine wave drawing tool to simulate the waggling of your foot on a wah pedal.

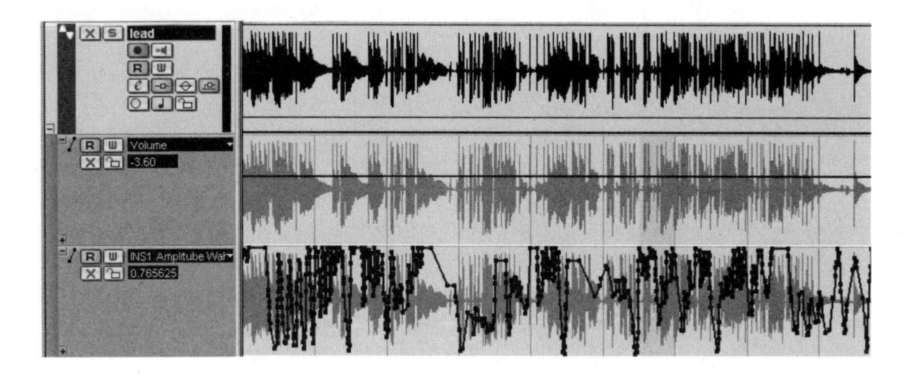

Figure 9.13
Wah automation over the lead track.

Automating VSTis

This is slightly different, as they don't have an actual track in the project window. They have a MIDI track that is playing them, but that track could be playing any VSTi or external synth for that matter, and so separate automation tracks are created when you try to automate a VSTi.

Let's see if we can destroy the nice inoffensive Rhodes track with a bit of filter twiddling in the A1 window. Open up the A1 with the Bell Piano patch loaded, the one that's running the Rhodes track and click the Write Automation button. Put Cubase into playback, and in the filter section put the Resonance knob to maximum and then start fiddling with the Cut-off knob. You should hear the effect right away, and keep going for as long as you like. Take the A1 out of Write and turn on Read. Rewind the track to where you started fiddling and you'll see the knobs move by themselves. Super, but where's the automation subtrack so I can edit it? Well, if you scroll down to the bottom of the project window, you'll see that a new track has been created with a little folder icon called the 'VST Instrument Automation' track. If you click the little '+' button to reveal the A1 subtracks, you'll see the automation. If the subtrack is labeled 'unknown', just click on it and select 'Cut-off' and on another select 'Resonance' and you'll see the automation of both knobs.

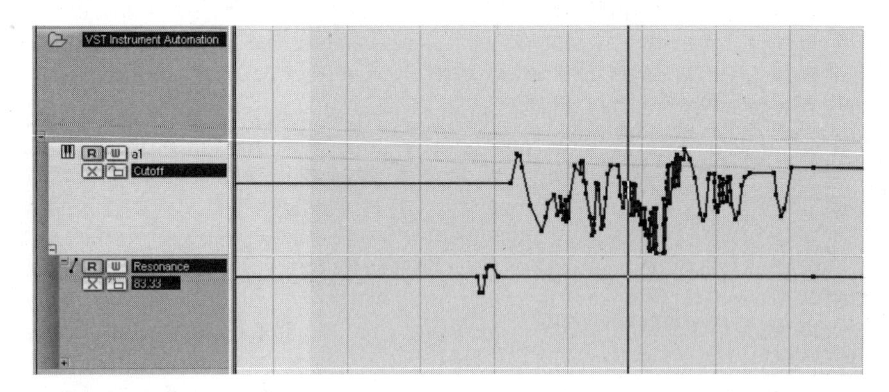

Figure 9.14
Cutoff and Resonance automation tracks for the A1 Rhodes track.

It's probably a good idea to move this track up alongside the relevant MIDI track so you can see how they match up. You can edit the data in exactly the same way as you did with the mixer and effects – everything works the same way.

You can also copy and paste automation in a similar way to events. You can use the 'Range Selection' tool from the toolbar to select some of the automation and then drag it elsewhere, or copy/drag using the Alt key.

Tidying up

Before we finish with this song, let's tidy up those audio tracks so they fit better. For a start, they come in too soon and then it would good if they disappeared in the breaks. I have touched on this before, but I thought another example in a song context would be useful.

You might want to undo some of the automation you did before, especially on our poor Rhodes track. You may also want to reload the A1 to remove any edits you made. You'll find undo under the Edit menu.

I would suggest that the Rhythm guitar does not need to come in until bar 34, when the main section arrives in full force. We can remove the guitar up until then in a couple of ways. One way would be to use automation with the Mute button, but this isn't very visual in the arrange page. You could take the scissors tool and split the rhythm event at bar 34 and delete the first half. Or, you could select the event and click and drag on the little white square at the bottom-left. If you drag to the right, you can hide all of the audio up to bar 34.

For the break at bar 64, we can use the scissors tool to split the event at bar 64 and then bar 66. The middle section could be deleted, or you could use the Mute tool (the big cross) to mute out that section, leaving it visible, which might be handy.

For the Lead guitar track, I reckon it sounds cool all the way through. At the beginning, though, there's a bit before the guitar actually plays which is incidental noise and fret stroking, so we could move the front of the event up to where the action actually starts. The break at bar 64 should be muted out as with the rhythm guitar – gives a really good dynamic effect that way.

So, with the guitars fitted to the rest of the song, the overall mix is sounding pretty damn good. I hope that's given you a good idea of what mixing is all about and how you achieve it within Cubase, and I promise that you won't have to listen to that song ever again.

Figure 9.15
The last time you have to see this one.

Creating a finished product

Back in the old days (the days before you bought this book) the finished product was something other people had to worry about. It was something that record companies, producers, publishers, and promoters dealt with. We're just interested in making music, cutting a decent demo, and waiting for that elusive contract to sign so someone actually pays us to get drunk in studios rather than having to fork out for it ourselves. That was before you had a studio on your computer, before you had access to the same sorts of tools that they use, before you became the master of your own mastering. Well, maybe. There's no substitute for someone pumping a truckload of hard currency into your music and development, and there's certainly no substitute for a good engineer and a experienced producer who knows how to work magic into the recording and mastering process. However, there's no reason why you can't produce stuff of releasable quality on your home PC, as you could with your 4-track for that matter.

When it comes down to it, I think we all know, deep down, that it's the music and creative ideas that matter, not the technology that allowed them to flourish. If that's the case, then why are we here? We're here, using our computer, because I'm convinced that it gives you the best chance of turning your ideas into reality, and at a sound quality you'll feel proud of. We can all get a bit 'precious' about the quality of our production, and with the tools available on the computer we can produce professional sounding music that you wouldn't feel embarrassed to sell. A computer won't teach you to become a mastering engineer any more than it'll teach you how to mix. These things still require time and practice, which is why people make a living out of it. What I'll show you primarily is how to put your music onto CD and onto the Internet, so you don't have to wait for the holy grail of a record contract before people get to listen to your work.

'Mastering' is a creative process that does the final work on your music. It adds polish and energy to the final product, and if you're creating a whole album, it'll ensure that the individual songs sound 'right' together. It's an art form that requires its own expertise. However, with some software and a few cool plug-ins, we can do a pretty good job of finishing off our music and it'll sound good enough, which is what this is all about.

Before we can get anywhere, we need to 'mix down' our music to a format where we can stick it onto a CD or the Internet. Previously you might have mixed down to cassette, or, if you're a bit more pro, to DAT. With a software studio, the mix never has to leave the computer; we can do everything right here.

Mixing down in Cubase SX

Unfortunately, the demo version of Cubase SX does not allow you to export any mixdowns of your music, and so it shouldn't - it's a demo. So, I'll go through the motions on your behalf in a real copy of Cubase so you know what the process is.

It's very simple. Once you're happy with your mix, click on the File menu and select 'Export – Audio Mixdown'.

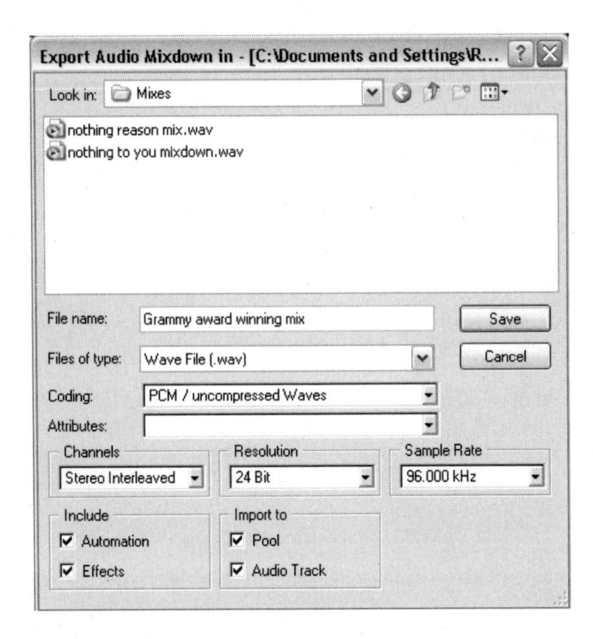

Figure 10.1
The mixdown window.

There are some very important settings here that you need to be aware of:

- *Files of Type* – lists the type of file formats that your mixdown can be saved as. The standard for CD and normal Windows audio is 'Wave File (.wav)'. You can also select 'AIFF', which is the Apple Mac format equivalent. There are a number of Internet-related options such as RealAudio and more importantly MP3, that we'll come onto later.
- *Coding/Attributes* – these are specific to the file type and should only concern us when using MP3 or other internet formats, as it defines the compression and so the quality. More on this later.
- *Channels* – Mono, Stereo, or Stereo Interleaved. Mono is a single channel, useful when mixing down a single track with an effect for use back in Cubase. Stereo in this instance means two separate channels of audio, effectively two mono channels and produces two separate files. Stereo Interleaved is the same as Stereo but this time creates a single file containing both channels – this is the one we want.
- *Resolution/Sample Rate* – defines the quality of the audio, as we discussed way back at the beginning of the book. If we wanted to put our mixdown straight onto CD, then it needs to be 16-bit and 44.1kHz. However, if we want to do some mastering style editing after the mixdown, then it's best to export the audio at the highest quality we can.

Finally at the bottom we need to make sure that both 'Automation' and 'Effects' are ticked so that they are included in the mixdown.

Click on 'Save' and Cubase will process the whole mix for you in a couple of seconds or a couple of minutes depending on the complexity of the mix. What you are left with is a file, a 'wave' file which is your mix. Make sure you name it something useful and put it somewhere where you can easily find it again. That's it, all done. You could now double-click the file and play it in media player, if you like.

Before we get too excited and whack it straight onto CD, let's check out some other software tools that give us a bit of mastering power.

Mastering software

There are three pieces of software generally regarded to be the best audio editors and mastering tools around. These are Sound Forge from Sonic Foundry, Cool Edit from Syntrillium, and Wavelab from Steinberg. All three can do essentially the same things, although each has its own unique features. Wavelab is probably the prettiest one with all sorts of lovely-looking meters and displays giving you an idea of exactly what's going on with your audio.

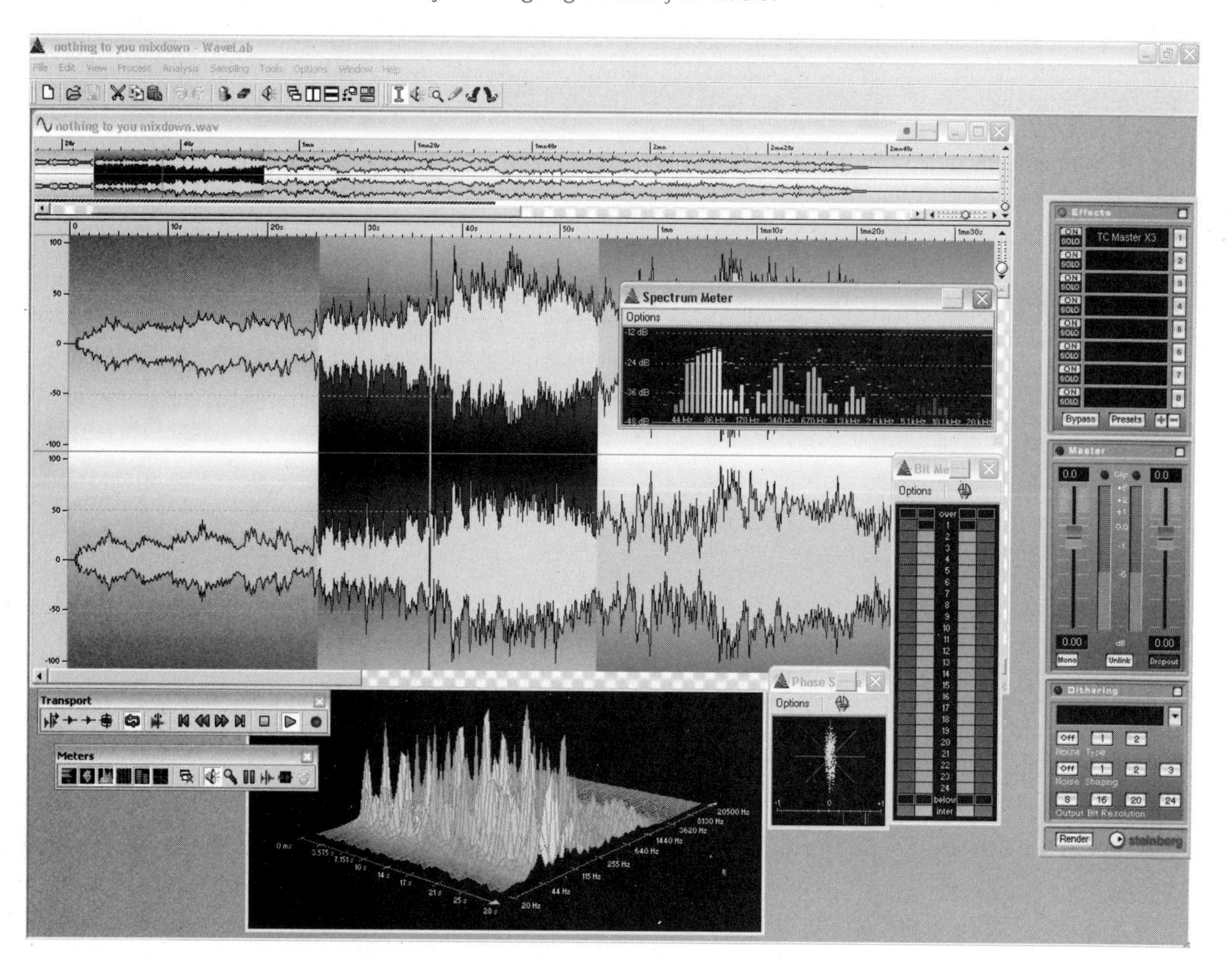

Figure 10.2
Wavelab, mastering in full color.

Something gets lost in the grayscale image in this book, but I can assure it that it's an orgy of color.

So what is it you actually do in mastering software? Well there are simple things such as trimming the audio. When you've done your export from Cubase, you might have left too much silence at the beginning or end, or there may be incidental sounds you need to get rid of. Noise reduction is certainly a useful tool, and programs like Sound Forge's Noise Reduction plug-in can take a noise print of a quiet section of the audio and then remove that noise from an entire track. This may be more useful for editing individual tracks after recording than during the mastering process. Analysis tools help you look at the frequency spectrum of the audio so you can see how well different frequencies are represented. Maybe the audio is too 'bassy'; then a spectrum analysis will show this and also tell you what frequencies should be boosted or cut with EQ to even it out.

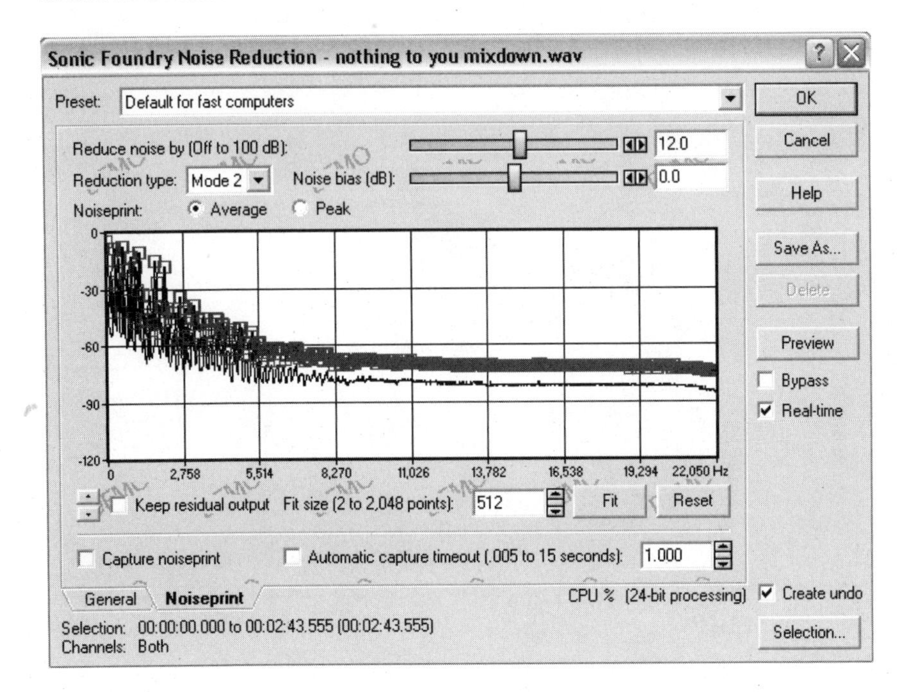

Figure 10.3
Noise printing in Sound Forge.

Overall though, the main tool has to be a combination of compression, expansion, and limiting, and these are the things you find being used in mastering houses and studios. The TC Electronics Finalizer is a particularly popular hardware mastering tool for its stunning array of mastering facilities and sound quality.

Figure 10.4
TC Electronics Finalizer, for finalizing a mix.

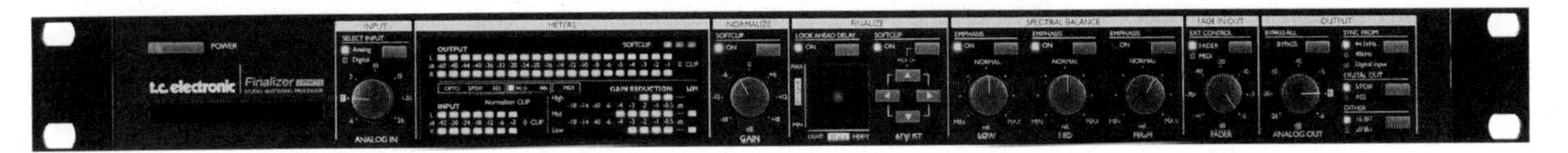

And guess what? There's a plug-in version available - hurray for the computer. This plug-in is a bit different though – it can run only on a hardware DSP card called the Powercore from TC Electronic subsidiary TC Works. The card fits inside your computer and runs an impressive bunch of very high quality effect plug-ins inside your software. The plug-in, called the Master X, uses the same algorithms and programming found in the Finalizer and sounds superb.

I've done a comparison for you to listen to. On the CD-ROM is a folder called 'Mixes'. Inside you'll find a number of files but we're interested in two of them:

'nothing clip unprocessed.wav'
'nothing clip mastered.wav'

They are a verse and chorus from the same song that I wrote and recorded with a friend of mine called Michelle, whose voice you hear on the track. It uses the first vocal take we did, and I haven't been able to get her back to finish it off, so please allow some leeway. Anyway, the first clip is straight out of Cubase, the second is with the Master X plug-in using a 'CD Master' preset. Double-click to play.

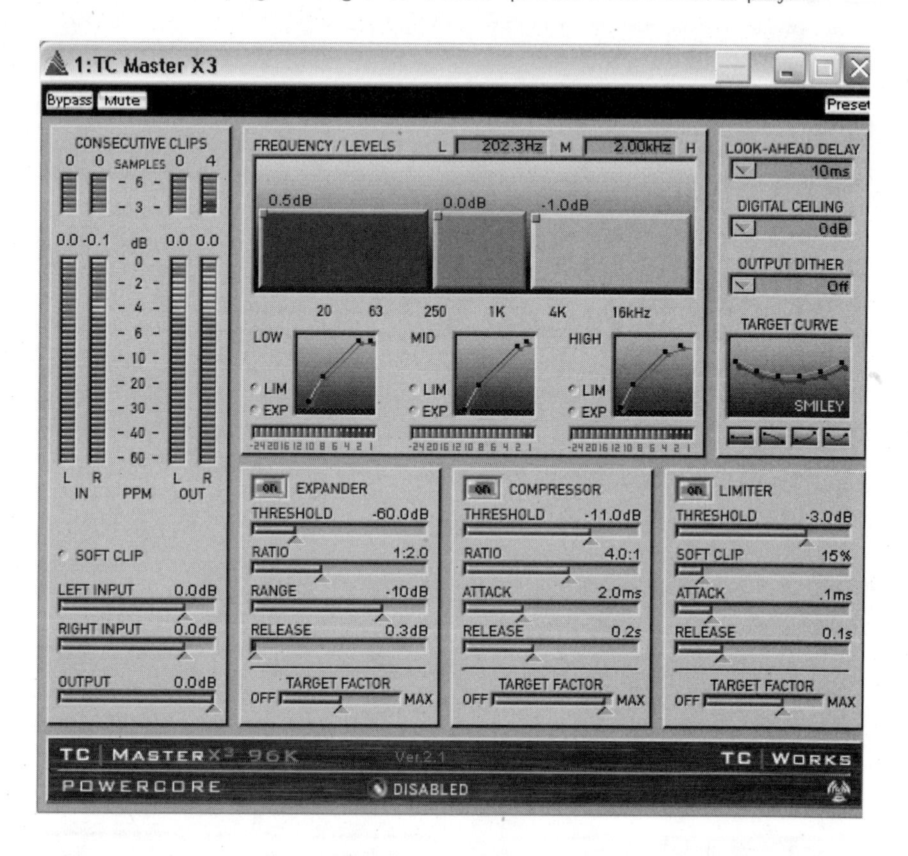

Figure 10.5
The TC Powercore's Master X3 mastering plug-in.

The most striking difference that I hope you can hear is the level of loudness and energy in the 'mastered' version. The next difference is the increase in higher frequencies; it just sounds 'brighter' than the unprocessed version. Now, I confess that I am not a mastering engineer, but simply using the presets on this plug-in has improved my final mix no end. Sound Forge has a similar plug-in called the 'Wavehammer' and also a multi-band compressor which is ideal for creating this kind of effect.

One other reason why I like to use mastering software is because it takes you away from your normal recording and mixing environment. Once I've finished and exported a mix from Cubase, I'd tend to come back to it on another day, open it up in Sound Forge or whatever, and approach it with fresh ears. There's no temptation to tweak the mix a bit as you're not in Cubase anymore, so instead you concentrate on using the mastering tools to get your mix sounding fantastic.

Putting your mix onto CD

Windows XP is a bit of a dream for this as it already includes the ability to burn audio CDs from wave files. Remember that your wave files have to be saved as 16-bit 44.1kHz stereo interleaved files or they will not be able to be played on a normal CD player. You also need to have a CD-R (CD Writer) drive installed in your computer.

To create an audio CD from your mixdown file, right-click it and select 'Send to – CD Drive'. You can try this with the files in the 'Mixes' folder if you like, but copy them off the CD onto your computer first.

Figure 10.6
Sending audio files to CD in Windows XP.

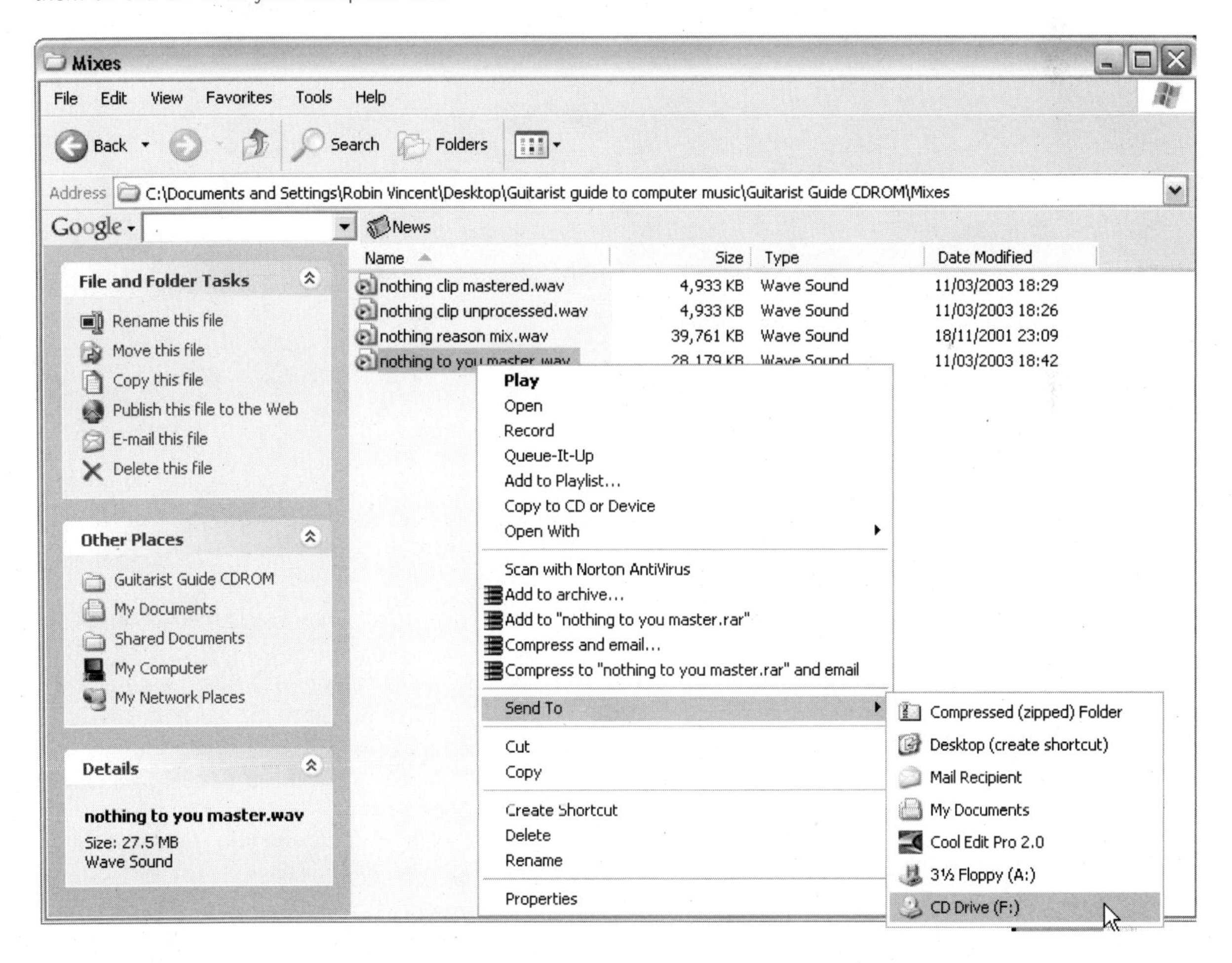

Alternatively you can drag files onto the CD drive icon in 'My Computer'. A help bubble will appear in the bottom right of your screen telling you that you have files ready to be written to CD. If you click the bubble, it'll take you straight to the CD Drive. The top option in the left hand taskbar says 'Write these files to CD', or you'll find it under the 'File' menu, so select it. This launches the CD writing wizard. You can call the CD anything under 16 characters and click 'Next' to continue. Now Windows has detected that you are using audio files and so asks if you want to create an audio CD or a data CD. We want 'Audio CD'.

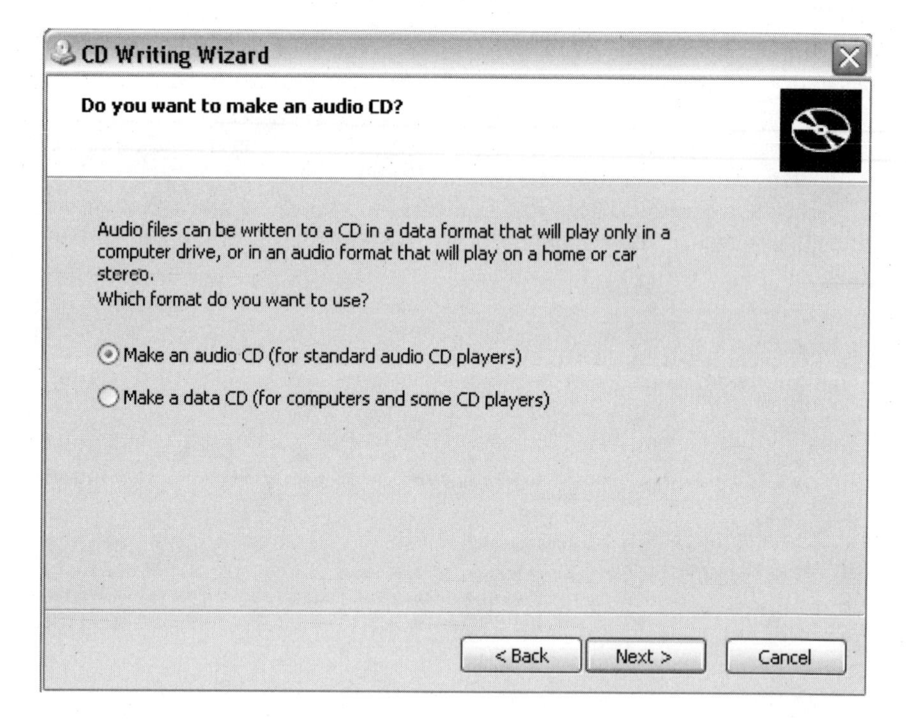

Figure 10.7
CD writing wizard.

Next, something unexpected happens. Windows opens the Media Player software and inserts our tracks into a playlist under 'Copy to CD'. Hit the 'Copy' button and in a few minutes, the CD will be written and ejected out of your PC. Run over to your CD player, pop it in, and if you've used your own mixes, then you'll be listening to yourself on CD!

If you like, you can do it all from Media Player rather than bothering with all this right-click, send-to business, but that's up to you.

There are plenty of other bits of CD writing software out there which give you more features than Media Player. Ahead Nero is a good one for both audio and data, as is Roxio's Easy CD Creator. Steinberg and Cakewalk both produce more music-oriented burning software called 'Get it on CD' and 'Pyro' respectively, either will do the job well.

Lastly you can also get software that will print CD labels for the CD and the jewel case. Well, for that matter you can get printers that will print directly onto CD, but they are a bit pricey. You can create your own designs, your own inlay cards and a cover with your smiling face on it (time to get a digital camera) – how fabulous is that?

Info

There's really something to be said for having your music on a physical 'thing' like a CD - there's just something very cool about it.

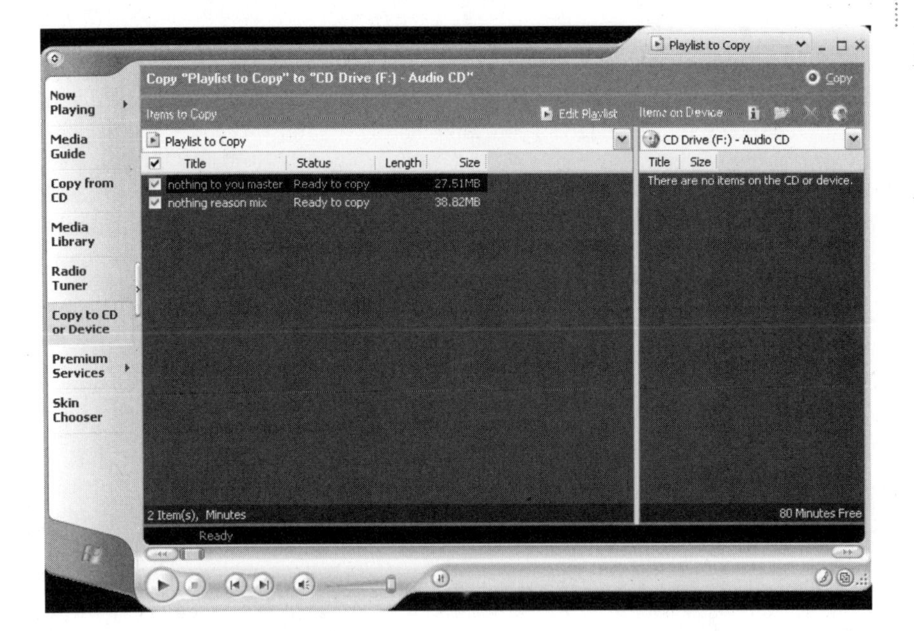

Figure 10.8
Writing CDs with Media Player.

Creating MP3s of your music

'So what's this MP3 business all about, then?' my dad asked the other week. 'It's something to do with music and there seems to be a lot of it about'. Getting back up off the floor and gathering myself after the shock that he actually asked me something I know about, I was able to relate the wonders of MP3 to my not-such-a-luddite-after-all father. It's true that everyone has at least heard of it, even if you're not entirely sure what or where it is. Now I can reveal all.

What is MP3?

MP3 is a type of audio file, very similar to wave files, except they have a much smaller file size due to the fact that they have been very cleverly compressed. This has nothing to do with dynamics compression used on audio in mixing and recording - this is about data compression, like using a 'zip' file. The compression is clever because it reduces the file size without reducing the quality of the audio (arguably, oh and people do like to argue). The file you end up with has the extension '.mp3' the same as a wave file has the extension '.wav'. That's mostly where the name comes from.

MP3 stands for 'MPEG audio layer 3', MPEG being the 'Moving Pictures Expert Group' who are a bunch of people who go around trying to compress things, like video and audio, in order to make them more manageable for computers and the Internet. We talked about sampling and digital quality at the beginning of the book and I mentioned that the higher the resolution of the digital audio (larger bit depth, greater sample rate), the more information is generated and so more space is needed to store it. This gives you very large files. CD quality audio, 16-bit 44.1kHz in stereo uses up 10MB per minute, so a three-minute song would be 30MB. A whole album would be funnily enough a whole CD's worth, which is about 640MB. It follows that to make the audio files smaller, you could use a lower resolution like 8-bit or 22kHz, but this you must realize (remembering the joining the dots to make a curve analogy) would reduce the quality of the sound.

But why would you want to reduce the size of your audio files? Well, the Internet is a global publishing house. Started off with text, your text for the world to read, then images, pictures of stuff, and then it became sophisticated enough to hold sound, video, and other media, so you can publish your music on the 'Net for people around the world to download and listen to. Now, your 3-minute, 30MB song is huge in Internet terms. If you were using a standard 56k modem, it could download probably half a MB per minute (with the wind behind you), so it could take easily an hour to download a single 3-minute song of CD quality. That would have to be one very devoted fan to wait that long. To make publishing audio on the Internet a reality, we had to find a way of reducing the file size, but without reducing the quality.

It was the Fraunhofer Institute who concentrated their efforts on purely audio encoding (all other MPEG standards have involved video) and came up with MP3, 'CD quality' at one-twelfth of the size of the original. So rather than an hour, it might take just 6 minutes. With a Broadband or ISDN connection, it might take half a minute, or even better it would just play back, in realtime, straight off the webpage, so suddenly people have instant access to your music.

So how do they do that then? The MP3 format uses perceptual audio coding and psychoacoustic compression to remove all superfluous information. What this means is that it removes all the stuff in the file that you don't really hear anyway, high and low frequencies that your ears can't detect and other clever bits of psychoacoustic skulduggery. The result is astounding and, to the untrained ear, sounds the same as the original. It's more accurately referred to as 'near CD quality'. This is of course where all the fuss about copyright and the death of the music industry comes in. People could take commercial CDs and convert them to MP3 and then email them to their friends who would, near as damn it, have a perfectly good-sounding copy. Not only that, but the use of file sharing programs, brought into being by the likes of 'Napster', allowed complete strangers to share their entire CD collections online for anyone to download. So, theoretically one person could buy the CD and within a few minutes everyone in the world could have a copy. Outrageous and, of course, completely illegal.

As a bit of a test for your own ears, I've put three versions of the same song called 'youletmeknow' in the mixes folder. It's a song penned by the lovely Michelle, who again sings on the track, and it was recorded about three years on my old PC. It's a rough mix that actually ended up being re-recorded for a compilation CD, which is nice. Anyway, listen to the original, CD quality version 'youletmeknow_mastered.wav' (double click to play in Media Player), and then listen to the MP3 version 'youletmeknow_128kps.mp3' and I challenge anyone to tell the two apart.

If you look at the file sizes, the original is 26,338kB, and the MP3 is only 2,390kB. Amazing, isn't it? MP3 'encoding', as it's called, has various levels of compression and quality and 128kps (kilo-bits-per-second) is the MP3 equivalent to CD quality. For even smaller file sizes, you can use a lower quality of encoding. As an example I've created an MP3 at half the quality of the first one called 'youletmeknow_64kps.mp3'. This is only 1,196kB in size, half that of the other one. If you play it, you'll immediately hear the difference and it becomes more obvious what the MP3 encoding actually does to the audio. Sounds a bit like it was recorded in a bucket with a bad tape machine. MP3 encoding at 128kps is the perfect compromise of quality and file size for today's Internet speeds.

Making your own MP3s

Most recording software nowadays contains an MP3 encoder. The Fraunhofer Institute were very shrewd and patented their technology so that in order to use their MP3 encoder, you have to buy a license. It's not very expensive and you can get MP3 encoding software for a few dollars. Cubase has one included in the price, and all you have to do is export your mixdown and select 'MP3' as your file type – which of course you can't do with the demo version.

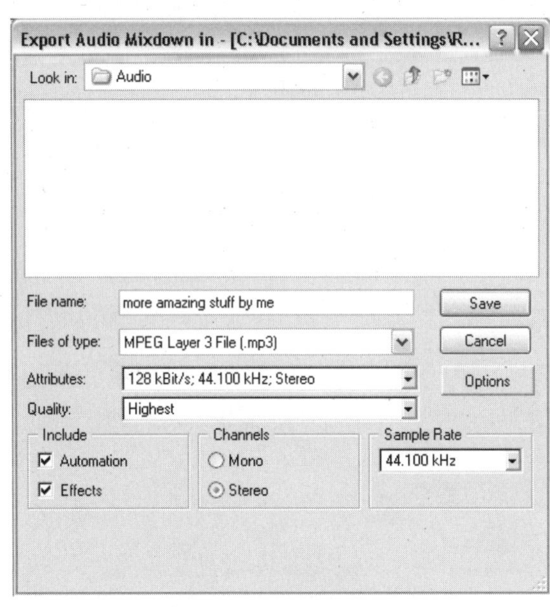

Figure 10.9
Exporting a mix as an MP3 from Cubase.

Figure 10.10
Winamp MP3 player.

There's stacks of other software out there that does it though, many of which will turn a whole CD into MP3s for you in a matter of minutes. I'm gradually archiving my record collection to MP3. Got nearly 1000 tunes taking up only 3GB of space. If I'd left them as waves, this would be nearer 35GB. The great thing is that if I fancied listening to some music, I can load them all up in Media Player or another player like WinAmp, hit shuffle and I can get any one of 1000 songs come up – great for parties. Similarly I can transfer them to my hardware MP3 player which accepts CDs. A CD will hold about 200 or so songs, which is fabulous for long journeys. It has revolutionized the way I listen to music.

Publishing your music on the Internet

You've got your perfect mix, you've encoded it as an MP3, and you're ready for the world to get a taste of your talents. What do you do now? You need three things:

- An Internet connection
- Your MP3 file
- Some web space to upload it to (transfer onto the Internet, as opposed to 'download' which is taking files off the Internet to your computer)

If you have an Internet connection then it'll be with an ISP (Internet Service Provider) who provide you with the connection, access to the World Wide Web (www), and email via your phone or cable socket. Usually, as part of your connection package, you'll get a few megabytes of web space where you can publish your own web pages (html) and upload files of any type up to the limit of the space you have. You could see it as a little 'online' hard drive if you like. The ISP will also be able to provide you with the information you need to enable you to upload web pages and other files like MP3s to your web space. Usually it involves a file transfer utility called an 'ftp' (file transfer protocol) program. One side of the program looks at your files on your computer, the other side connects to your web space and allows you to transfer files between the two. This is all a bit archaic really nowadays and many ISPs, like AOL, provide much more user-friendly ways of doing the same thing.

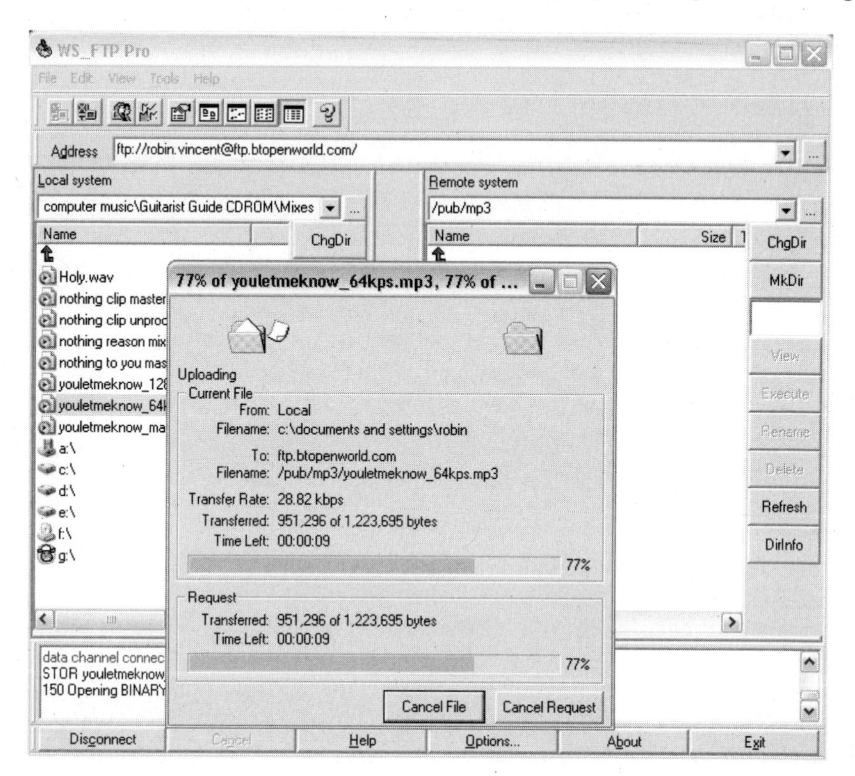

Figure 10.11
Uploading MP3s onto the Internet

Once your MP3 is uploaded, how do other people get listen to it? Well they need to have the web address of your file; this is referred to as a URL (Uniform Resource Locator). Stick that URL in the address bar at the top of their web browser (Internet Explorer, Netscape etc) and they'll start downloading the file.

As an example, here's the URL of an MP3 of mine that you've heard already, that's hanging about in some web space I haven't used for years:

http://freespace.virgin.net/robin.vincent/youletmeknow.mp3

It may take a few moments to think about it and then it'll either start playing back, or a window will pop up asking you if you wish to save it to your computer. If you get the save option, then you'll have to wait a couple of minutes until it's downloaded and then double-click the downloaded file, which is now on your computer, to play.

This kind of direct download works fine but we're missing a trick here. The wonder of the internet is its ability to link file and pages together using html (Hypertext Markup Language). Html is the format in which web pages are coded and few people have to worry about the actual code, as such, nowadays as we have plenty of programs that do all that for us. Text and pictures in Word can be saved as an html document, which instantly becomes a web page once uploaded. So, instead of having just the MP3 file, why not have a web page that tells the listener all about you, your music, your family, and your dog. Stick some pictures and graphics on the page and it all becomes far more interesting. Then, on the web page you put a 'link' to your MP3 file. The link is the URL address of the file again, but this time they just have to click on the link on the web page to download or listen to the music. Here's the URL for the web page that features the above MP3:

http://freespace.virgin.net/robin.vincent/crumble.htm

It's a terrible, gaudy old page (Figure 10.12) that has some old and sometimes terrible music linked from it, but it's a useful demonstration. I'm not going to tell you how to create actual pages and stuff, as there's thousands of books out there on the subject, not to mention websites that'll tell you much better than I can.

Oh no, Madonna just randomized out of Winamp singing American Pie while I'm

Info

For more on this subject, check out the book 'Creating a Music Website' by PC Publishing.

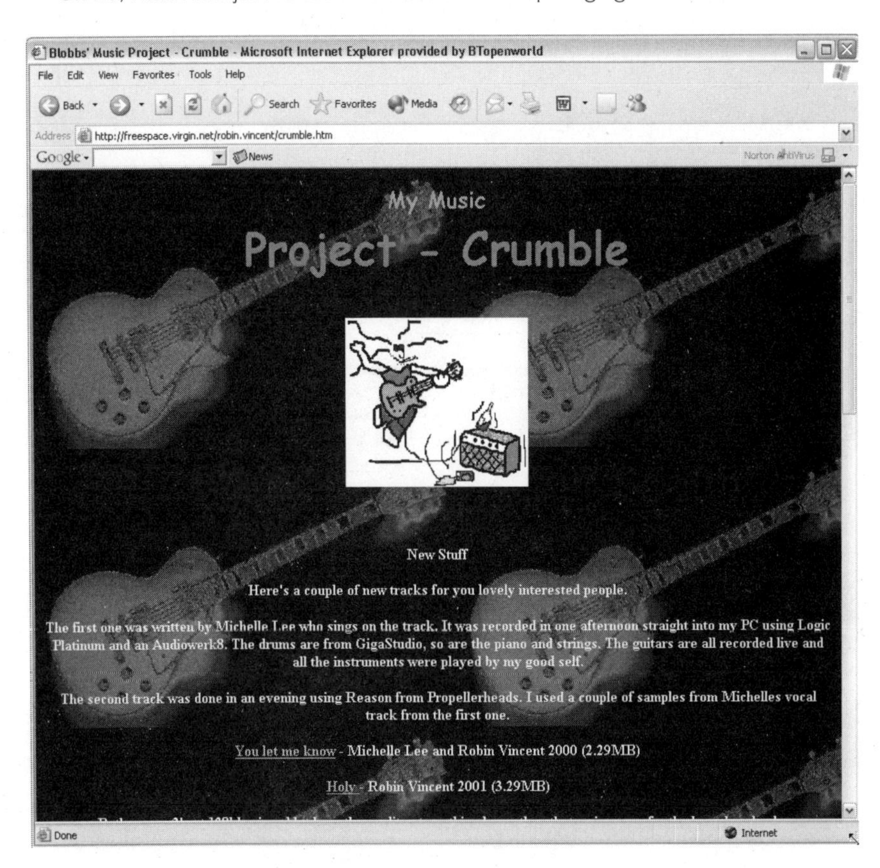

Figure 10.12
Get to your MP3 with a click on a webpage.

writing! What are the odds of that out of a thousand? Where's the skip button? ... Audioslave, that's more like it.

With your MP3 uploaded and your web page sitting pretty on the Internet, congratulations, you're a published artist! Theoretically anyone in the world with an Internet connection can get to your page and listen to your music.

How is anyone actually going to find the page? Well that's the thing, there are trillions of pages out there and the likelihood of someone stumbling upon your page inadvertently is extremely slim. In fact the chances are so small you could call it no chance at all. This calls for a bit of self promotion. You can go to search engines, like Yahoo, and register your web page/site so that if anyone searches for your name, the page might well pop up. All a bit unlikely though, unless the content of your site actually has something people would search for. No, it probably serves better as an extension to what you would normally do to promote your music. Maybe you've got a gig, you could put the URL on the flyers and advertising so people could listen to the music before or after the gig. Maybe you rent out your studio or your services as a musician and you could include it in your advertising. Or, maybe, you could just email the URL to your friends and family and go 'look mum, I'm on the Internet'. It's entirely up to you.

If you are serious about your music and want to get noticed, then there are websites that'll host your MP3s for you and categorize them as part of an MP3 community. So rather than using your own web space, which will fill up quite quickly once you've uploaded a couple of songs, you use their web space. Usually they give you a little web page where you put information about yourself and list your music ready for listening. You can often do this for free and find yourself on a website amongst

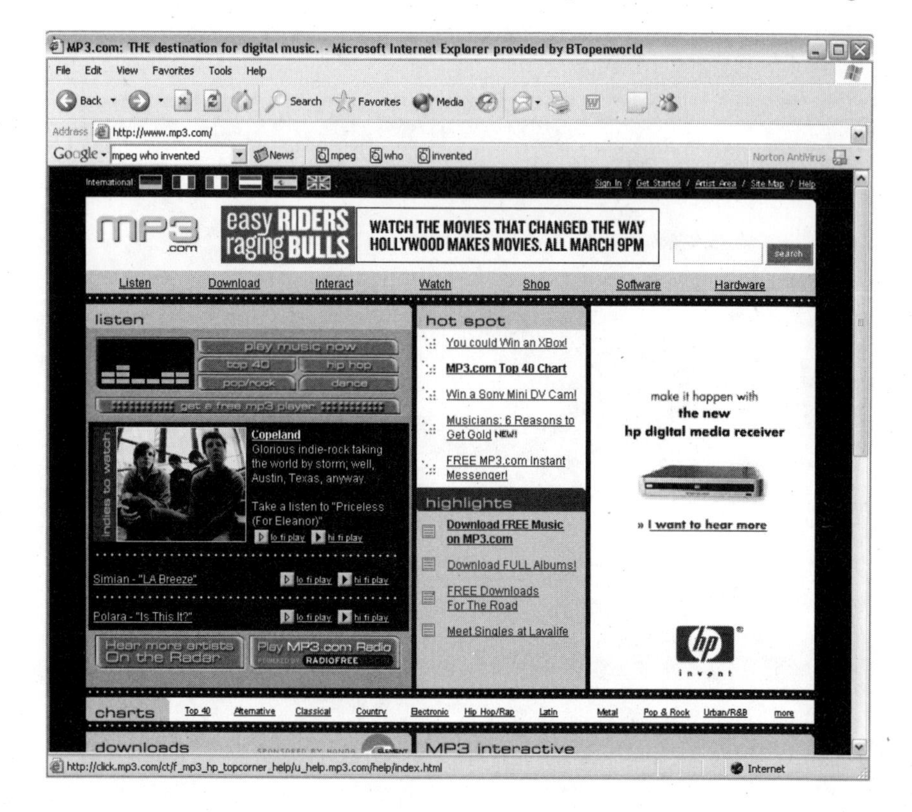

Figure 10.13
MP3.com, the biggest library of MP3 music on the 'Net.

perhaps thousands of other people's music. People can then come to the site, search for the type of music they want to listen to and then, maybe, stumble upon yours. Well there's a much better chance than if you were out there on your own.

The most popular site for this is MP3.com, which is now so huge, thousands and thousands of artists, that they have to restrict non paying users to three songs each. You can subscribe to their Gold member scheme and upload more MP3s and also get included in promotions and maybe even compilations. MP3.com has got pages of information on MP3 software and hardware, and tips and all sorts of help, so it's a good general MP3 resource (Figure 10.13).

A smaller, more localized site is 'Vitaminic'. They have sites by country, so it's vitaminic.co.uk for the UK and .com for the States, .it for Italy and so on. You can upload as many MP3s as you like (I think) and, ironically, they even have a service where they can produce real packaged CDs for you to sell off your web page. You can also charge people for listening to your music if you want, priced per download. It is possible to make money doing this I guess, but I've never tried. I like the idea of putting up, say, three tracks for people to freely download and then offer a CD of 10 more tracks or something for people to buy. It could work, and ultimately this is the point of it all - making money from your music while bypassing all the record company nonsense and their 80% cut.

Here's my Vitaminic site as an example, but don't worry, I don't charge for anything, yet.

http://stage.vitaminic.co.uk/crumble/

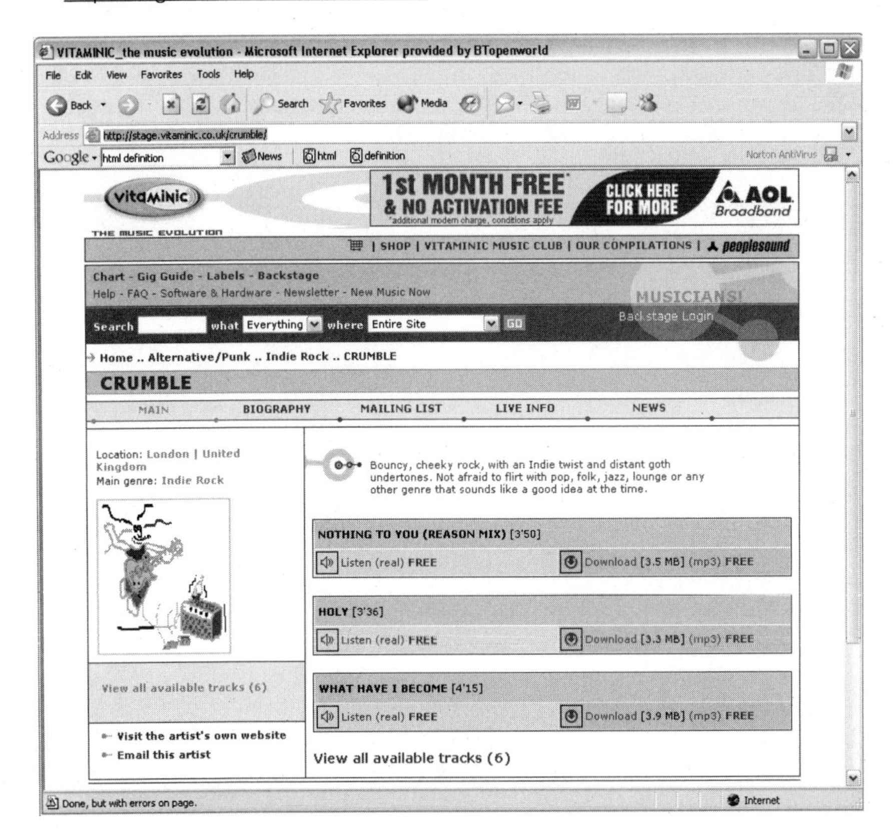

Figure 10.14
My page on the MP3 website Vitaminic.

Copyright

So how can you prevent other people downloading your music and selling it as their own? Scary thought, but exactly the same rules apply as they do in the real world, and it's up to you what you do. The old methods of posting your music to yourself recorded delivery, and then leaving it unopened on a shelf somewhere, still works when you open it in court to prove predated ownership. Even better, send it to your solicitor or bank to put in the safe. Also the MP3 site will log when you uploaded it which may or may not help, the law gets bit hazy where the Internet is concerned. If you put your music up for free downloads, then essentially you want as many people as possible to hear it, so people copying it shouldn't be considered a problem but a good thing. If you're selling CDs then it's a different matter.

If you want to properly copyright your work, then you need to get in touch with the MCPS – Mechanical Copyright Protection Society (www.mcps.co.uk), who collect royalties on behalf of members for any broadcast or sale of their music. However this only covers physical product, CDs, vinyl, mini-disks, etc., not MP3 or Internet-distributed music.

The whole record industry is frantically trying to find ways to copy-protect music so they can sell on the Internet without giving the world the ability to simply copy it to everyone else. It's a difficult problem and I'm yet to see a workable answer. I feel that although CD sales have fallen in recent years there are a large chunk of people, myself included, who want physical product in their hands, and actually get some small sense of satisfaction from leaving the house and visiting a record store to buy a CD or three. Without the record companies 'filtering' the music we listen to we are left with an overwhelming number of tunes where actually finding anything that's any good gets increasingly hard. If everyone's music is free, and no one is investing money into artists so that they can spend time working on their craft, we will gain an awful lot of rubbish at the expense of the fabulous music that comes from professional recording artists. Record companies, love them or hate them, do invest in music and that can only be a good thing. On the other hand, music free for everyone? Viva la revolution.

Other Internet music formats

MP3 is not the only audio format knocking around on the Internet. RealNetworks (http://www.real.com) have been around for ages and were the first to develop the idea of 'streaming' audio and video off a webpage for instant playback, rather than having to download it first. They have technologies such as RealAudio and RealVideo that people can use to broadcast music, video, presentations, radio stations all off a web page. One interesting function is that it will vary the quality of the stream depending on your connection speed, so it'll always give you the best quality sound it can while maintaining the stream. This can also be very annoying as you're listening to music and suddenly it drops down to a lower quality.

Quicktime (http://www.apple.com) from Apple is another streaming technology that's become very popular with film studios as a way of putting high-quality film trailers on the 'Net. Now up to version 6, it has very clever encoding technology that can retain quality while making the file sizes impressively small, similar to MP3. But it's Quicktime's ability to stream high-quality media off the 'Net in more or less real

Figure 10.15
Movie trailers with Quicktime. You'll find lots of cool ones on the Apple.com website.

time that's really impressive. If you buy Quicktime Pro, rather than just getting the freeware player, you can create and upload your own Quicktime movies and audio.

Windows Media Player (http://www.microsoft.com) nowadays has all the ability to stream audio, video, MP3, and its own WMA files off the Internet, and with increasing connecti,on speeds live TV over the Internet is completely possible. In fact Microsoft has recently released a Media Centre package that turns your PC into an entertainment center with TV, music, films, and DVD playback from both Internet and your own disks, and comes complete with a remote control.

A slightly more bizarre format, well, in name anyway, is 'Ogg Vorbis' (http://www.vobis.com) which claims to be better quality that MP3 although it essentially does the same thing. The one thing it does have going for it is that it's completely free and open source so you don't have to pay anyone for the privilege.

'MP3 Pro' is an advanced next generation of MP3 (http://www.mp3prozone.com) which reports to retain much more sound quality at lower bit rates. This means that you can have smaller files sizes than MP3 but with the same quality. It does this by using 'Spectral Band Replication' (SBR) which is a very efficient method of capturing the high frequency components of an audio signal.

Anyway, getting off the point a bit here. The thing that MP3 has got going for it is that it's an open format that practically everything supports. The files can be downloaded and played in other players, they don't rely on streaming, although they can do that, too. It's very simple, easily understood and sounds fantastic, so for Internet music and beyond, it's definitely the best choice.

Studio setups

Earlier in the book, I've shown how to connect a guitar and a keyboard to the computer in a very simple way. Now we want to look at how to integrate the computer with all your gear, allowing it to be the nerve center of your studio. You may have racks of equipment, mixers, synths, microphones, effects, and recording hardware, or you might just have a guitar. It doesn't matter - the computer can be everything or just another tool in your toolbox.

What I'll show you is a number of example ways to set it all up. Hopefully I'll hit on something similar to what you have, culminating in the complete integration of software and hardware and a completely virtual studio.

Basic setup

This first one is to consolidate what we've already covered. Basic connections between a computer with a soundcard, a guitar, MIDI keyboard, and speakers. Let's try to follow what's going on by numbers.

Figure 11.1
A basic setup with a simple soundcard.

1. Plug a guitar cable into your guitar.
2. The standard soundcard has mini-jack inputs, so you need to use an adapter to take your guitar cables jack down to a mini-jack.
3. Plug the adapted cable into the microphone socket on the soundcard.
4. MIDI keyboards often now come with a USB socket. If yours does, go to number 6. If not, then take a MIDI cable and plug it into the MIDI OUT on the keyboard.
5. Using a MIDI/Joystick adapter, plug the other end of the MIDI cable into the joystick port.
6. A MIDI keyboard with a USB socket is providing its own MIDI interface to the computer. Just plug the USB cable from the keyboard into the USB port on the computer, install the driver, and the keyboard's connected to the computer.
7. Line output on the soundcard is also a mini-jack, so you'll need a stereo mini-jack cable.
8. The Line output goes to your powered speakers: one left, one right. If you have passive speakers, then plug the Line Output into the amp that's powering the speakers.

Your recording software will be able to record the guitar, and the keyboard will be able to play software synths. All the sound from the guitar and the soft synths will come out of the Line Output into your speakers.

Enhanced basic setup

Let's improve on what we have a bit and ditch the old standard soundcard and replace it with soundcard of much higher quality, like the M Audio Audiophile 2496. It's a 24-bit recording card with Line Input and Output on RCA phono connections, plus a built-in MIDI interface. We can't plug the guitar straight in this time, so we'll

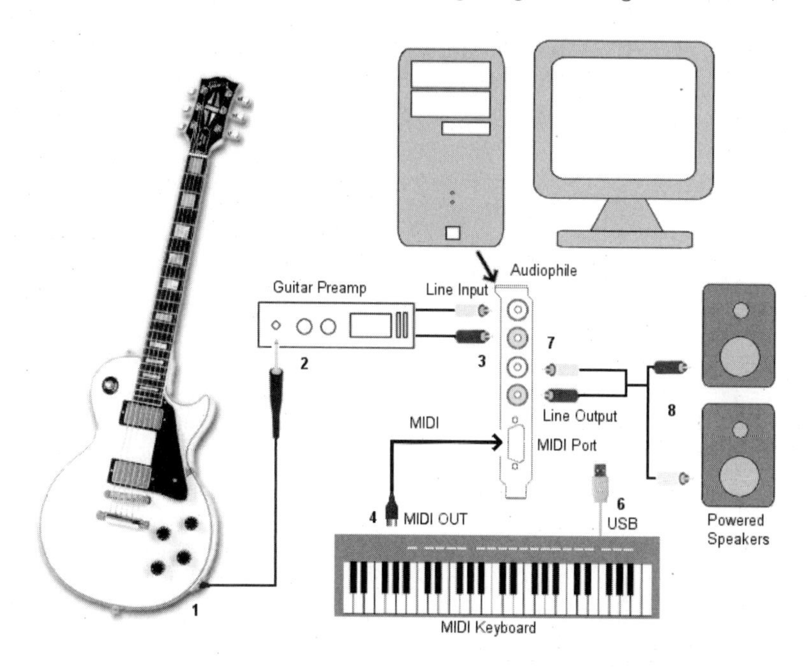

Figure 11.2
Enhanced basic setup using a more 'pro' soundcard.

use a preamp to get the signal up to line level. This is the same setup you would use if you wanted to use a guitar preamp with your standard soundcard.

1. Plug a guitar cable into your guitar.
2. Plug the other end of the guitar cable into your guitar preamp and get yourself a suitable level.
3. The stereo line output of the preamp goes into the Line Input on the Audiophile (soundcard).
4. MIDI keyboards often now come with a USB socket. If yours does, go to number 6. If not, then take a MIDI cable and plug it into the MIDI OUT on the keyboard.
5. Plug the other end of the MIDI cable into the MIDI IN on the Audiophile's MIDI interface adapter cable (MIDI/joystick adapter if using standard soundcard).
6. A MIDI keyboard with a USB socket is providing its own MIDI interface to the computer. Just plug the USB cable from the keyboard into the USB port on the computer, install the driver, and the keyboard's connected to the computer.
7. Plug RCA phono cables into the Line Output of the Audiophile.
8. The line output goes to your powered speakers: one left, one right. If you have passive speakers, then plug the Line Output into the amp that's powering the speakers.

As before, the recording software will be able to record the preamped guitar (at lovely high quality), and you'll be able to properly use the software effects in real time because of the Audiophile's low latency ASIO drivers. The MIDI keyboard can happily play software synths with no delay, and all the sound, guitar, and soft synths emerges at the Line Output to your speakers.

Basic mixer setup

We're going to add three new bits of gear to our setup (Figure 11.3). First, the MIDI keyboard has become a synth of some kind, like a Roland XP-50 or Korg Triton, and we want to use the sounds in it. Second, we've added a microphone to record some nice vocals. Finally, we've added a mixer. This could also be your old 4-track, which will allow us to hear the output of the recorded guitar and the hardware synth at the same time, as well as give us some pre-amplification for the microphone. We're still only using a soundcard with a stereo input, and this setup highlights the limitations.

1. Plug a guitar cable into your guitar (getting good at this bit).
2. Plug a suitable cable into your microphone.
3. Plug the mic and guitar into separate channels on the mixer. You could use a separate preamp for the guitar and the microphone, if you like.
4. The keyboard has both a MIDI OUT and IN; this is so we can send MIDI OUT to the computer for recording, and then receive the MIDI back IN from the sequencer so the synth plays the sounds (drums and instrument backing).
5. The Audiophile's MIDI interface provides the MIDI IN and OUT sockets. Remember that the OUT from the keyboard goes to the IN on the interface and vice versa.
6. We want to be able to hear the synth, so we plug the audio output into the mixer.

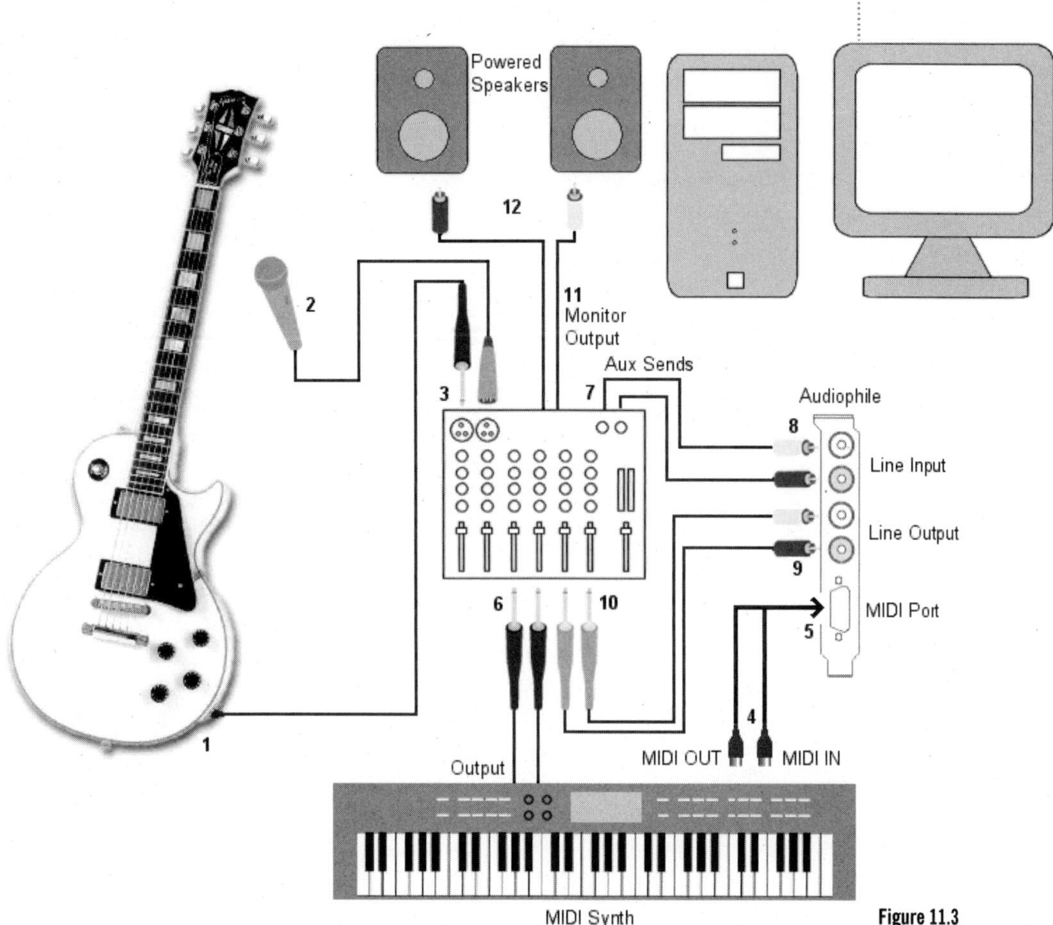

Figure 11.3
Basic setup using a mixer with a 'pro' soundcard.

7. This is the bit people usually have trouble with. We want to be able to record the mic and guitar onto the computer. If we used the mixer's master outputs, then while we are recording the guitar we would record the backing from the synth at the same time onto the same track. We don't want to do this, we want to record everything onto different tracks, and we don't want to record the synth until we're completely sure of the MIDI arrangement in the software (you still with me?). So, we need to SEND the guitar and the mic to the soundcard on its own. How do we do this? We use SENDS. All mixers have an auxiliary send or two, sometimes called 'FX Sends', as that's what they are normally used for – sending out to effects. However, this time we are going to use them like an output, and send the guitar/mic channel out of the send and to the soundcard. So, turn up the send knob on the guitar and mic channels, and make sure the sends on the other channels are at zero. Now we'll be able to hear the synth, but it won't get recorded with the guitar. Super, got that? Good.
8. The output from the aux send, ideally two for stereo, is plugged into the Line Input on the Audiophile (soundcard).

9. Now, we want to be able to hear the recorded guitar at the same time as the output of the hardware synth, so the Line Output of the Audiophile needs to be plugged into the mixer.
10. Make sure the aux send on the channels for the soundcard's output are at zero or you might get feedback through the computer.
11. The monitor output of the mixer carries the recorded tracks from the computer and the output of the synth and should be plugged into your speakers.
12. All the sound comes out of your powered speakers, or amp and speaker arrangement.

A good note to make at this point is that although you're using a mixer, you're not actually using it to mix anything. All you've got is a stereo output from the synth, possibly carrying multiple tracks of different instruments and the stereo output from the computer, which could carry a couple of guitars, vocals, and harmony. So, all the mixing needs to be done on the computer, in Cubase or whatever you're using.

If you want to do a mixdown in Cubase, you must first record the output of your synth onto the computer. At the moment, the synth is playing sounds in response to the MIDI tracks in Cubase. The 'sound' of those synths is not in Cubase, it's just a bunch of MIDI instructions which is sent out of the computer's MIDI OUT to the hardware synth, which then creates the sound. Ideally, what you want to do is record each MIDI instrument as a separate audio track. You do this by soloing a MIDI track in Cubase (so no other tracks play), turn up the aux sends on the synth mixer channels (the real mixer, not the one in Cubase), enable a stereo audio track in Cubase, and hit record. The output of the synth, for that track, will go through the mixer and get recorded in Cubase as audio. Take the next MIDI track, solo it, and do the process again onto another audio track. Once all the synth tracks are recorded as audio, you can turn off the MIDI tracks and concentrate on audio mixing in Cubase. Now you can do the mixdown because all the sound is recorded in Cubase. This is different from using VST Instruments, as their 'sound' is already inside Cubase; the hardware synth's is not. Got that? I hope so, I really do. There's an article in one of the appendices at the back of the book describing the different between MIDI and audio. I've included it just to reinforce the issue and give you a fresh angle on it.

8-bus mixer setup

The traditional modest studio consists of an 8-track open reel tape recorder and a large mixing desk with eight buses and tape returns. The mixer is the center of the studio, it's familiar, and you know your way around it and it just looks great. It would be a shame to replace it with a beige box and a mouse. Of course it would, so don't do it. The computer can work just like a tape machine, and do a lot more besides, but for this setup let's just show how you would connect it up for 8-bus multitrack recording (Figure 11.4).

This time, the soundcard is not just a card, it's a 1U rack box containing eight analog inputs and eight analog outputs. The box connects to the computer via a PCI card – just like a soundcard, but where all the in and outs are on the rack box, not the card. A good example of a soundcard of this type is the M Audio Delta

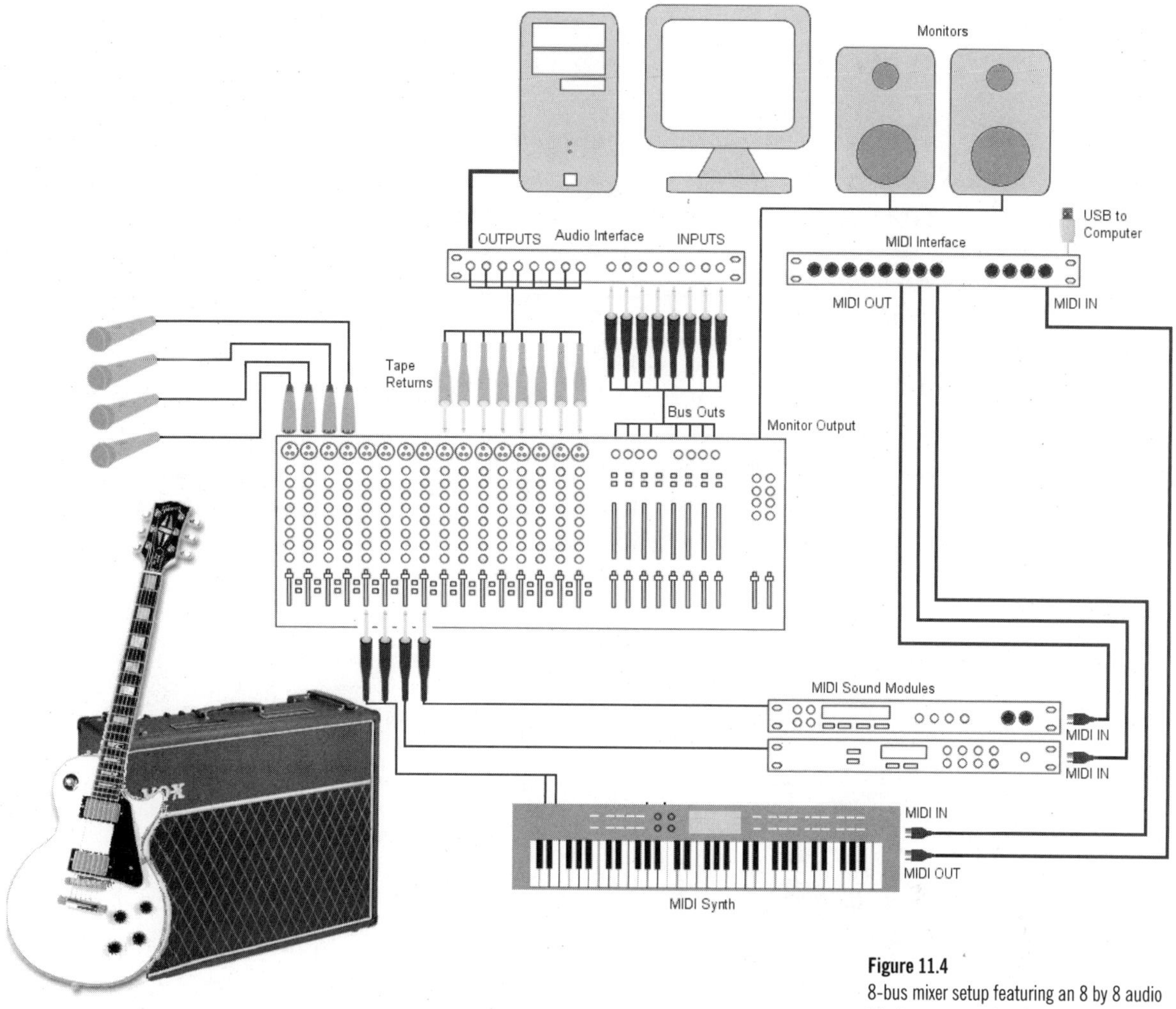

Figure 11.4
8-bus mixer setup featuring an 8 by 8 audio interface connected to the computer.

1010, it has eight analog in/out and stereo digital S/PDIF in/out (hence the '1010' name). If you've got a large mixer, then you might well have a few hardware synths, sound modules, and the like. I'll add a larger MIDI interface to the computer so you can use all of these independently with Cubase (Figure 11.4).

No need for numbers on this one, as it works in exactly the same way as your open reel does. The Audio Interface gives you the eight recording inputs and the eight tape returns to and from the desk. The MIDI interface provides ports for all the synths and sound modules and connects to the PC via USB.

With this setup, you can treat the computer as a sequencer for the MIDI gear and a tape machine. You don't have to do any mixing or editing on the computer if you don't want to, just use it as the recording medium. If you have other sound processors, like compressors or effects boxes, then you can use them in the same way you always have – nothing has changed, all you've done is added a computer.

Now once the computer is in place, I hope that you'll find it much more useful than just a recorder – but that's entirely up to you.

Digital mixer setup

Let's take a high-tech twist with the 8-bus desk and replace it with a digital mixer, such as the Yamaha 01V, 03D or 02R (Figure 11.5).

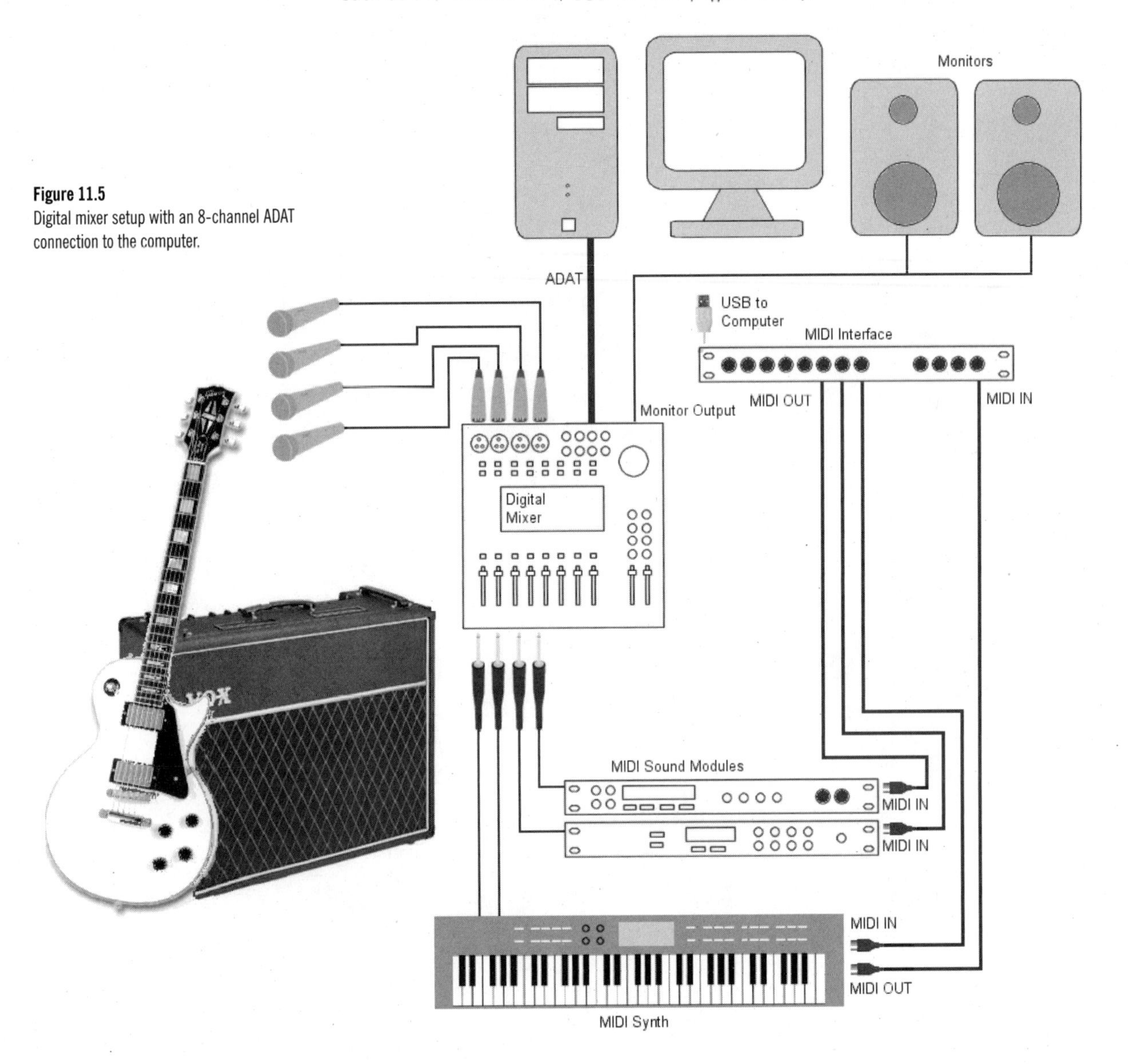

Figure 11.5
Digital mixer setup with an 8-channel ADAT connection to the computer.

The digital mixer takes the place of the audio interface in the last setup. It's the digital mixer that does the analog to digital conversion, usually at much higher quality than the usual soundcard, and then routes it to the computer for recording via a digital ADAT interface. ADAT used to be an 8-track digital tape format created by Alesis. Nowadays it's become a standard for transfer of eight-channel digital audio into and out of computers. The computer has, in place of the soundcard, an ADAT card with one or more ADAT ports, each capable of eight channels. So it's the same as the 8-bus analog setup but without all the cabling. The digital mixer also has the advantage of things like motorized faders, digital effects, and EQ. The mixer can also be used to control the mixer in the software, so you've got more mixing going on than you could probably cope with.

A setup with a digital mixer is extremely versatile, professional, and high quality.

The virtual studio

Right, let's ditch all the hardware, the sound modules, the mixer, and let's concentrate on a simple, but professional, virtual setup. Some sort of hardware will always be required if you're recording instruments, but this doesn't have to be as clunky as a mixer or as restrictive as in our first basic setups. The key is to get hold of the right soundcard, or audio interface, for what you want to do. It's not hard to do. You want to record a guitar and some vocals, then get yourself a soundcard that has guitar and microphone inputs. A good example would be the Edirol DA2496. It's a hig- quality, 24-bit audio interface with two phantom-powered microphone inputs, two guitar inputs, MIDI IN/OUT, and a headphone socket, amongst other things. It's got everything you need to record directly into the computer, at fabulous quality, without all this mucking around with preamps, mixers and routing, and sends and buses.

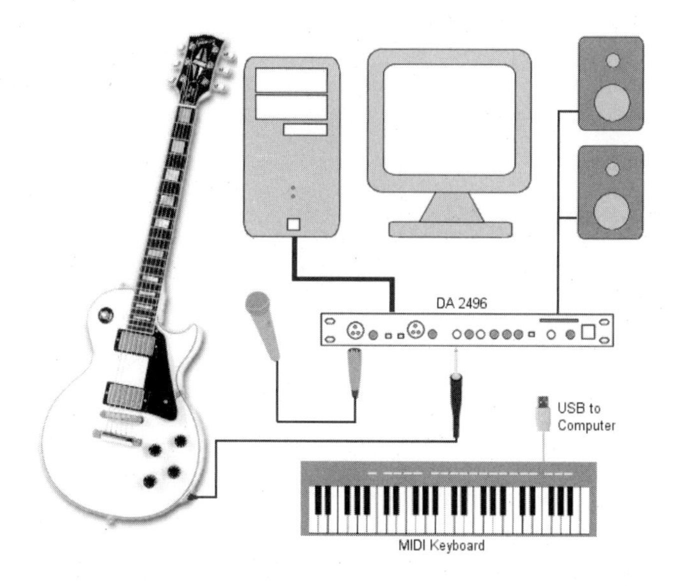

Figure 11.6
The virtual studio – moving all the hardware into software.

See how simple and clean this setup is (Figure 11.6)? It's like a breath of fresh air. We've turned all the MIDI synths into software ones that take up a lot less room. The mixer is now in Cubase, all automated and animated. The Edirol DA2496 is taking care of the inputs and outputs. The mic sockets have gain and trim knobs, as does the guitar input, so you haven't lost complete control to software. With two mics, two guitars, and a load of line inputs as well, you've got plenty of room to jam a whole band in there. The connection to the computer is via a PCI card, just like with the Delta 1010, that connects to the audio interface (DA2496 in this instance).

For the guitar, the high impedance input on the DA2496 is perfect for a direct input. You don't need an amp or preamp or effects box. Running software effects like Amplitube can give you all the tone you need. Similarly, you've got tons of software dynamics for the microphone inputs. The simple USB MIDI keyboard gives you access to a world of software sounds. The fast ASIO drivers of the DA2496 ensure that you don't experience any latency.

This is such a great little setup, and I can heartily recommend it. The only downside is the lack of real tactile control, but we can easily sort that out with our final example.

Virtual studio with real control

In this example (Figure 11.7), I'll bring in a number of control devices that act upon the software. None of these devices has any sound or audio circuitry - they are purely there to control various aspects of the software on the computer. In this example, I'll use the Aardvark Direct Pro Q10 audio interface. It's got eight microphone inputs on the front for recording directly into the computer. The first two inputs also have insert points so you can, if you want, use a hardware compressor – best of both worlds. The other nice thing with the Q10 is that you can stack up to four of them connected to a single computer, giving you 32 analog inputs.

Now we're talking. We've taken the software realm and placed it firmly back in your hands. Not only have you got professional quality recording of a whole band through the Q10, but you've got fingertip, thumb, palm and foot control over every faculty of the software. I've even added a second monitor screen so you can have the tracks and editing on one and the synths and effects on another. Let's remind ourselves of what's going on.

- *Guitar* – plugged into the Q10 for recording. Using guitar effects in Cubase to shape the sound.
- *Microphone* – plugged into the Q10 for recording, along with seven others if you like.
- *Behringer FCB1010* – our MIDI controller is all set up to control Amplitube and other effects.
- *Steinberg Houston* – complete control of the Cubase mixer and transport functions.
- *Midiman Radium Keyboard* – for playing all those fabulous VSTis. It's even got built-in knobs and sliders for instant editing of whatever VSTi you're playing.
- *Evolution UC-33* – a controller for all occasions, you could make the knobs control the amp models in Amplitube as well as stacks of other effects and synths.
- *Akai MPD16* – instant finger-slapping control over Battery or some other drum-based VSTi.

Connecting it all is so simple with almost everything just needing a USB socket; install a driver and it's done. You might need a USB hub to handle all these bits of gear, but they're just a couple of bucks.

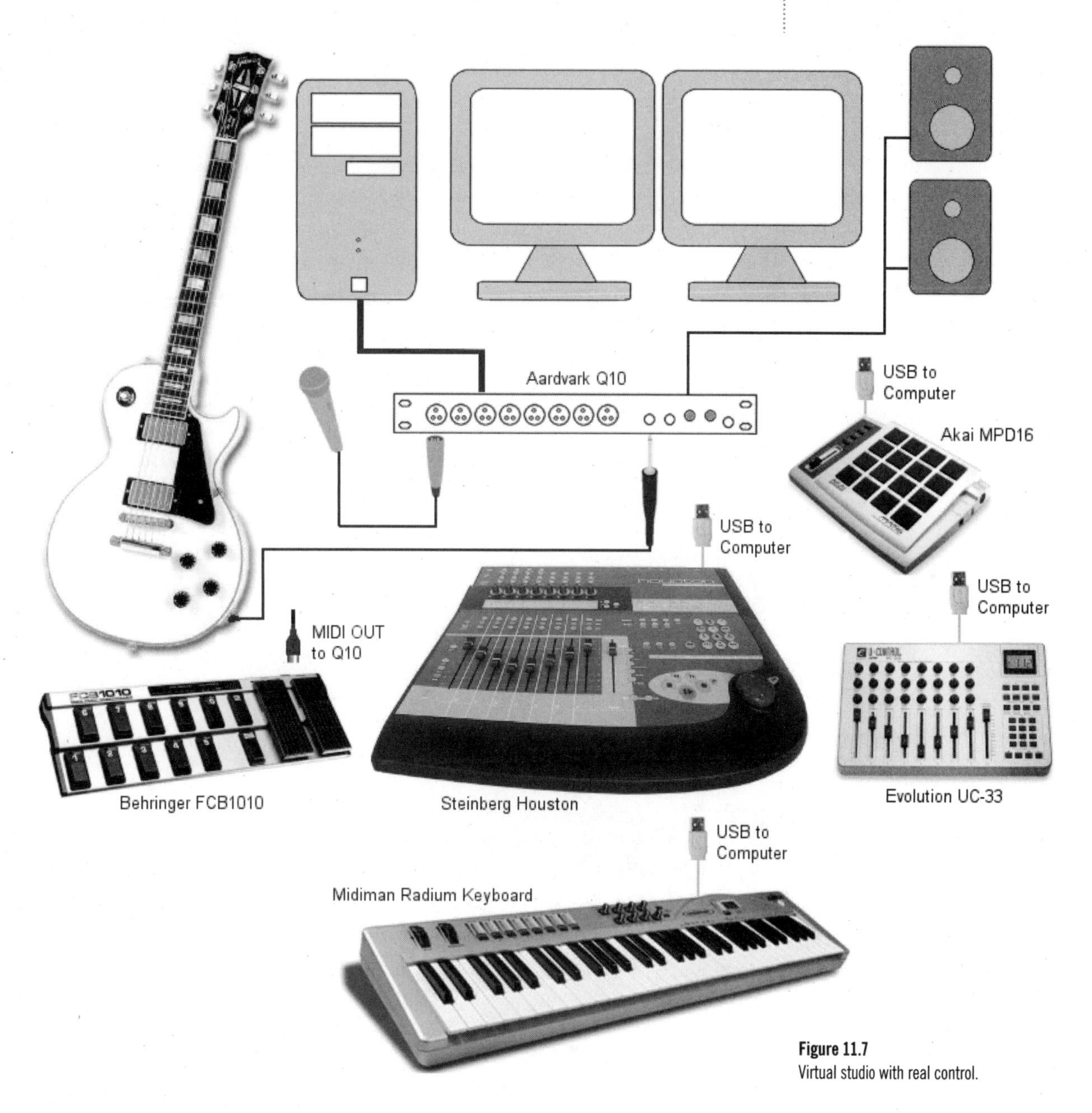

Figure 11.7
Virtual studio with real control.

If you really must have everything, then combine this last example with the 8-bus one. Although you can replace all your hardware with software versions and hardware controllers, you still don't have to. You can use it all, combine whatever you want, replace some, keep some, and you can integrate it however you want. The whole argument between software and hardware is nonsense if you ask me – use both, or whatever turns you on.

Taking it on the road

Let's take a quick diversion for a few minutes and talk about the possibilities of gigging with a computer. Now I know what you're thinking: how on earth do I expect you to take a desktop computer, the screen, mouse, keyboard, and all the other peripherals and controllers along to a seedy dive of a pub gig? Well, you can do that. I've done that. Taking a desktop computer to a gig is completely possible, and many modern artists now travel with more than one computer running parts of their show. But they tend to have people employed to take care of all that sort of stuff. For the regular, gigging guitarist, we're really talking about smaller gigs in pubs and clubs, where you really don't want to be lugging around an expensive and fragile desktop computer. This is where the laptop or 'notebook' computer comes in.

Figure 12.1
Your own portable studio.

The laptop has been adopted as a musical instrument by many electronic music artists. Running software like Propellerhead's Reason and Ableton Live, they can create loop- and synth-based music on the fly and twist and edit it to their heart's content. I have two friends who do gigs using two Apple Powerbooks running Reason and other soft synths, synced together, and the noise they make is just fantastic. However, if you're talking about live performance with a guitar, then it's a slightly different thing from what our electronic cousins are doing.

Assuming, for the moment, that you're a single performer gigging with your guitar, up to now you've had a couple of choices when it comes to simulating the rest of the band. You might use a backing tape that you play and sing along to, or you might be a bit more savvy and use MIDI files playing from the floppy drive of an

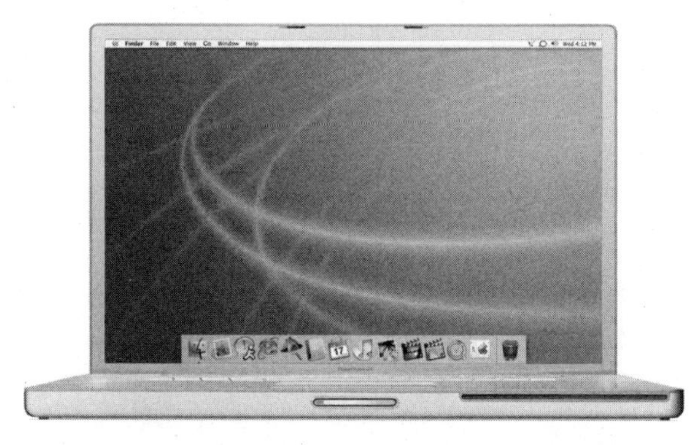

Figure 12.2
Big picture luxury on Apple's 17-inch monitor Powerbook.

electronic keyboard, or you might use something like the Yamaha MDF3 MIDI data filter to play MIDI files through a sound module. Playing MIDI files is a very easy thing for a computer to do - we've been essentially doing this already in Cubase.

Get yourself a laptop and you can store thousands upon thousands of MIDI files, all cataloged, so it's easy to find even the most bizarre request. Of course, you can also store and catalog your backing tapes as MP3s. If you start creating your backing with the computer, you can mix it all down to MP3 and have them ready for instant access. You could have them all loaded up in Media Player and select whichever you want for instant playback. Already the laptop computer is looking like a useful piece of equipment. Not only could it play back the MIDI files, but it could also show you the score, guitar chords, tab, and lyrics at the same time, which is fabulous if, like me, you can't hold more than two songs in your head.

There's another advantage in being able to see your backing as well as hear it – visual cues. I did a gig about four years ago using a big desktop computer to run the backing while I played guitar and a friend sang. Being musically ambitious, the songs were quite complex and dotted with interesting bits and sections. Watching the tracks on the screen move as they played, I was always completely sure where I was and what was going to happen next. There was one song where it began with just my guitar until toward the end of the song, a load of nice strings came in. I had to play to a click track on headphones, and I could see the string tracks coming along so I knew exactly when they would come in. Difficult to do with a backing tape.

Info

It's hard to find a simple MIDI file player nowadays, as the technology seems to have been stolen by the karaoke crew who have plugged all sorts of unnecessary things into it.

Using software effects live

Effect plug-ins are great when you're recording and creating music in the comfort of your own home or studio. Once you start using plug-ins, and your hardware begins to fade into redundancy, you may wonder how you are going to recreate your new virtual guitar sound on stage. So far, I've talked about using a laptop as an elaborate MIDI file and backing database, but it can also be your performance effects processor. You can probably see that you could take Cubase along and use your effects and your MIDI controllers as you did in the studio. In fact, using a laptop means that you are taking your whole studio with you wherever you go, which is pretty cool. However, in Cubase loading effects, setting up patch changes and chains of multi-effects is not, perhaps, as instant as turning a dial on a hardware effect processor. Along with that, you have to make sure that you've got the track set up for monitoring, and there are loads of other things going on that you don't really need when you just want to play guitar. So, what would be nice would be a simple way of loading up effects patches for instant playback with the minimum of fuss. Enter the 'VST Host' program. These are programs designed to load effects and VSTis for real-time live playing. There's no sequencing or recording facilities, just instant access to your library of effects and instruments.

The undoubted king of VST Host programs comes from a company called DSound, who have been working on turning the computer into a live effects processor for a few years now. The results are simply fabulous.

GT Player

Their guitar effects processor comes with a dozen or so stomp box effects ready to go and allows you to load up whatever VST effects you like. You can then store them as multi-effect patches and the hardware style interface lets you dial up and load them at will.

Figure 12.3
GT Player with Stomp FX and Amplitube loaded.

Breathtaking, isn't it? I know I should have told you about this before, but I wanted to keep something back for later in the book, just when you thought all the cool stuff was over.

The top rack unit controls the effects, patches, and parameters, while the bottom 'Track Player' is an audio playback device. The Track Player lets you load up wave files into a playlist, so any backing tracks you have can be loaded here for instant playback. So, not only do you have a fabulous effects processor, you also have a built-in backing track player, perfect for those one-man and guitar (and now a laptop) gigs. You'll of course want to try this out, and being the conscientious writer that I am, I've included it on the CD-ROM. It's in the 'Software/Dsound GT Player' folder - just double-click to install. There are actually two programs included in the demo: GT Player – the guitar effects processor, and RT Player – a VSTi and effects player. We'll come onto the RT Player in a moment. If you start up the GT Player, you'll first be faced with setting up the audio driver. This is exactly the same as with Cubase. Click 'No' if it asks you to test the drivers, and then select either your soundcard's ASIO driver or the 'ASIO Direct X Full Duplex' driver. If this fails for any reason, then choose the 'ASIO Multimedia' driver and let it run the test. If that fails, well, you'll just have to look rather than listen, as the driver implementation is not as finely tuned as it is in Cubase.

The first thing to do is turn on the power button on the left. The demo has three programs already set up, which you can access using the dial or the arrow buttons. Once selected, you have to press the 'Load' button to load up the effects. To see what effects are loaded, press the 'Edit' button to get to the Program Editor.

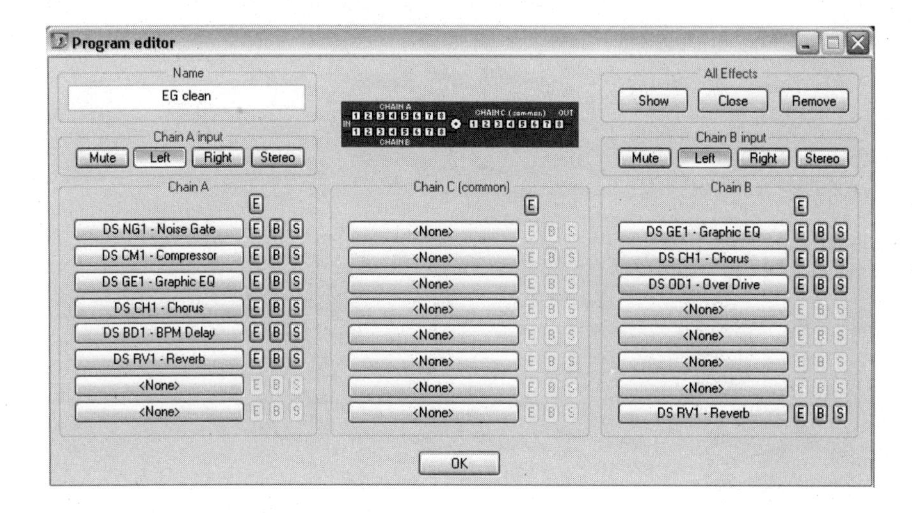

Figure 12.4
GT Player Program Editor where you can chain effects.

You have two effect chains, A and B, and a master effects chain C. Into each slot you can load whatever effect you like. Pressing the 'E' button next to a loaded effect brings up its editor window. Click 'OK' to close the program editor. You can also view all the loaded effects at once by changing the GT Player's 'Mode' from 'Program' to 'Effects'. Click the 'Mode' button once and then click the 'Edit' button, and all the Stomp FX boxes will dramatically appear.

This is great, but stomp boxes are for stomping, and so some MIDI control could be on order. This can be set up very much like we did in Cubase. This time, though, the GT Player is an effects processor that responds completely to program/patch change messages exactly as a hardware one would. So, using your MIDI floorboard, you can simply select programs by treading on the relevant foot switches. All the individual effects parameters can be assigned MIDI controllers, so again you can use the expression pedal to control wah amount or something like that. To get stomp control over the stomp boxes, we need to revisit our MIDI-OX experience and convert the footswitch program change messages into MIDI controller messages. What I would recommend is that you leave the first couple of banks on the floorboard to control program change and then, using MIDI-OX, transform the next bank into controller messages and assign them to the stomp boxes. It's exactly as we set it up for Cubase. The MIDI mapping window can be found under the 'Options' button, and the MIDI input can be specified under 'Options – Preferences'.

RT Player

The RT Player is very similar to the GT Player but supports VST Instruments making it a live software synth player. Just like the GT Player, you can load up effects, but this time you can chain together VSTis to create a terribly powerful sound source. You can layer them up or have them on separate MIDI channels so you can play them individually. This is a great piece of performance software.

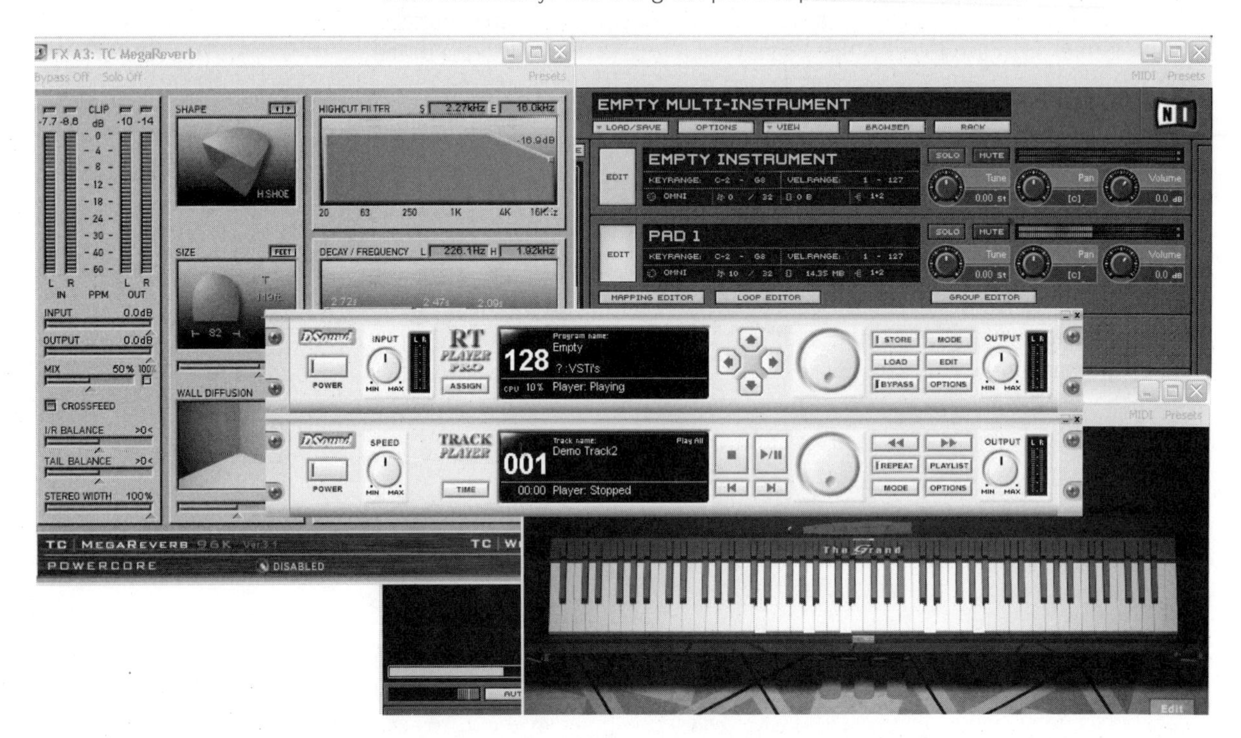

Figure 12.5
RT Player with Native Instruments Kontakt, Steinberg's The Grand, and the TC MegaReverb loaded.

I think you'll agree that these are powerful bits of software for live performance. Imagine how much easier it is to travel to a gig on the bus, guitar over one shoulder, laptop over the other, rather than lugging all that hardware around.

Getting sound into and out of a laptop

Soundcards built into laptops don't tend to be very good as far as recording sound is concerned. They are of the same sort of quality that you find with basic soundcards or those built onto motherboards. All the soundcards we've looked at so far have involved a PCI card of some sort installed inside the computer. Laptops are not big enough to accommodate such things. Instead, over the last couple of years, USB and Firewire technologies have developed a whole stack of external 'soundcards' that simply plug into the USB or Firewire ports on the computer. I've mentioned USB MIDI controllers, but there are also now USB audio boxes that can give you very high quality audio into and out of your computer. Firewire is the same, although less common on PCs. Apple adopted this technology for all their computers.

USB and Firewire audio

There is one small problem with USB and that's to do with its bandwidth, or the amount of data it can actually get into and out of the computer at one time. High-quality audio does involve a great deal of data, and so at the moment, USB can handle up to about four channels of 24-bit audio. USB 2.0, the latest version of the technology, is much improved, and larger 8-channel audio interfaces are starting to come onto the market.

Figure 12.6
Edirol UA-1000 USB 2.0 audio interface capable of eight in/eight out.

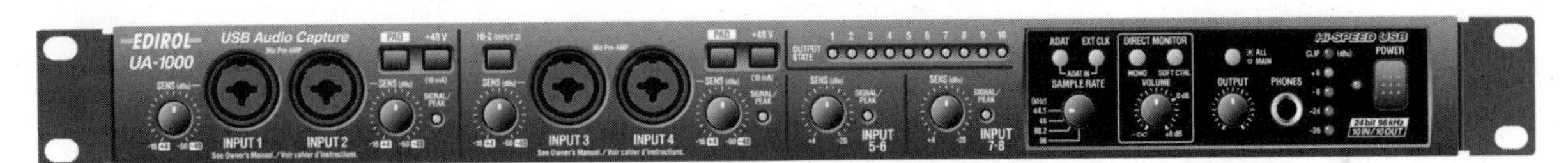

The UA-1000 from Edirol is the first serious USB2.0 contender, and it's a fabulous bit of gear for the guitarist.

Although regular USB can't handle many channels of audio, it's certainly enough for running your guitar through your laptop and getting a great sound along with your backing music. Most USB boxes can also take their power from the USB port and so don't need plugging into the mains, making for a completely portable solution.

Firewire has a greater bandwidth than USB and so can handle far more channels, although USB2.0 has certainly caught up. It's all the same idea really; just plug it in and off you go. MOTU (Mark of the Unicorn) is a remarkably named manufacturer of audio interfaces who was an early adopter of Firewire technology. Their 828 interface has been a great success.

Figure 12.7
MOTU 828 Firewire audio interface.

Both the Edirol and the MOTU are probably overkill for simply wanting to get some quality audio out of a laptop. Companies like Edirol and M Audio provide some simple portable solutions that would easily fit inside your laptop's carry case. The UA-20 from Edirol is a good example.

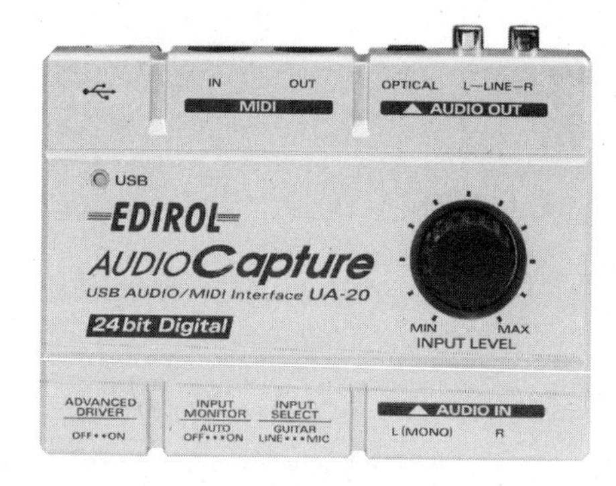

Figure 12.8
Edirol UA-20 USB audio interface. Simple stereo in/out.

I'll list more cool products in the next chapter.

Getting the right laptop

This is always going to be a bit tricky, as there are so many around. The important thing to realize is that they are not going to be as powerful or versatile as a desktop computer in terms of what audio hardware is available for them. However, the portability can make up for an awful lot. Laptops nowadays are very fast and quite capable of handling dozens of tracks of audio, synths, and effects. With the USB/Firewire connectivity, there's no real installation required either, so it's a very simple way of getting into computer music.

The biggest problem you'll have when playing live is the potential for tipping your beer into it, or, in a moment of guitar solo passion, pulling it off the table. So

Figure 12.9
The Toughbook from Panasonic is resistant to spillage.

it would be worthwhile looking into the toughness of the laptop you want to buy. There are number of companies who specialize in making military-type portable computers; you know, the kind of thing that would be happily running communications in a war zone. I'm not saying that it automatically qualifies to survive a Nu Metal gig, but it would certainly stand up to the odd thrown pint or two. Panasonic make some of the more stylish ones called Toughbooks.

The Toughbook 28 turns into a rather nice aluminium briefcase and is water-resistant and shock-resistant, etc. The nicer-looking R1 doesn't claim to be indestructible, but it's thin, lightweight, and water-resistant.

Of course you'll pay extra for the toughness, but I guess it's down to the sort of gigs you have.

A round-up of computer hardware and software

This is a comprehensive selection of currently available products that I feel have some direct use for a guitarist. There's probably loads more stuff out there, but this will give you a good idea what to look for. Obviously these things may date rather quickly, but successful technology does tend to stick around, and software, albeit in different versions, seems to retain the same name forever. It's not an exhaustive list, and I'm bound to miss things, for which I apologize, but if I'm not aware of it then they haven't done a good job of telling anyone about it.

Deciding what's right for you

The all-important question - the one I get asked every day, to which you already know the answer, if you think about it a little. You've got to ask yourself what it is you want to do and base your decision on it. Not helping much, am I? Well, it's like buying a car. Any car will get you where you want to go, the same as any soundcard will be able to record. But if you want to get five people in the back and go off trundling through forests then that might steer you away from a Mini toward something more like a Range Rover. It's not so different with soundcards. If you have an 8-bus desk, then you'll want a soundcard with eight line inputs. If it's just you, a guitar, and a microphone, then you might want something with a guitar and mic socket. Software can be a little trickier, but the best thing is that they can all do very similar things, so it's hard to go wrong, really. There's no mystery to it and you should find what you're looking for in the following list.

Soundcards

I don't want to bore you with all the dull specifications and technical details - these are readily available from the manufacturers and their websites, which I'll also list - so let's assume that they all have fabulous-quality 24-bit converters and fast ASIO drivers. So instead I'll give you a few lines on their key features and what I think is cool about them, plus a rough guide to price. I'm aware that in the time between me writing this and you reading it, there may be some changes in what's available. New and exciting stuff comes out all the time, but you can bet that the companies I mention here will be responsible for any of the cool new stuff. So once you've had a look, check out their webpage for the latest and greatest. I will be including both traditional PCI soundcards and USB/Firewire external boxes. As a rule of thumb,

PCI cards will perform better in terms of the number of audio channels in/out and the speed of drivers, but these external boxes are excellent nowadays and could work just as well for what you want to do. So, in no particular order:

M Audio

Also known as Midiman, this is one of the most consistent manufacturers of quality soundcards. It's the security in knowing that their stuff 'just works'. It's easy to install, good value, and sounds great.

Website

http://www.m-audio.com

Audiophile 2496

I'll start with this card, as I use it as a benchmark by which all other cards are measured. It doesn't have any features that are particularly interesting to a guitarist, but if you want good quality stereo recording, this should be the first card you look at. If money is an issue, I recommend not going any lower than this little beauty. Simply stereo in/out, digital S/PDIF, and a MIDI interface. $245.00

Interestingly M Audio have recently brought out a USB version of the Audiophile, offering the same quality but in a little external box that plugs straight into your USB port. It has the added bonus of a headphone socket. $325.00.

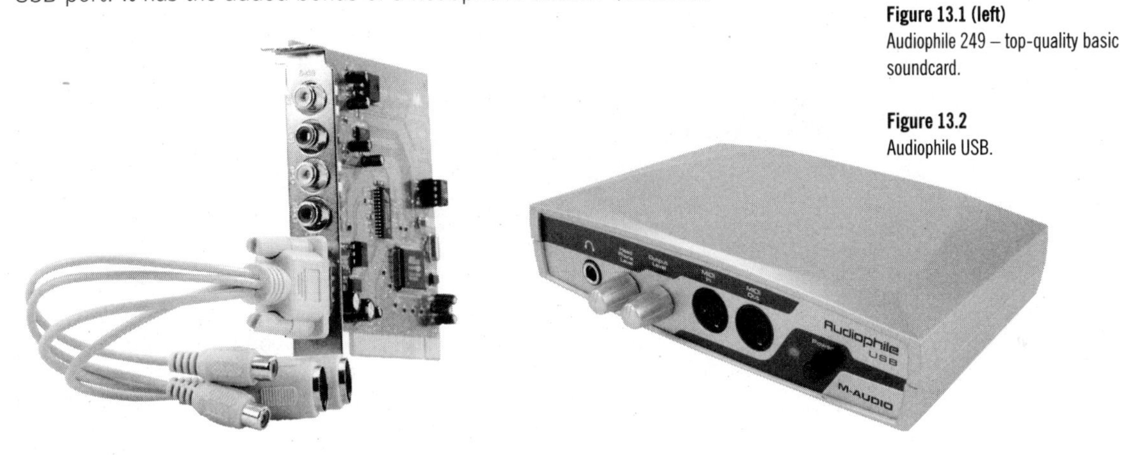

Figure 13.1 (left)
Audiophile 249 – top-quality basic soundcard.

Figure 13.2
Audiophile USB.

Omni Studio

One of the best home studio solutions available in my opinion - so good in fact that I use one myself. Essentially it's an 8-channel mixer in a box. You have four record-

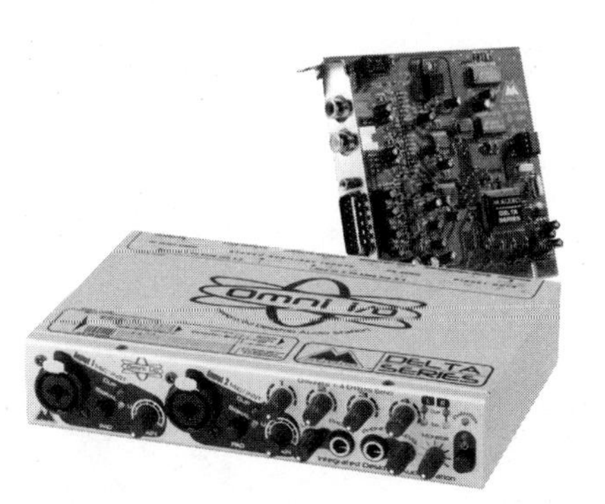

Figure 13.3
The Omni Studio. An 8-channel mixer in a box.

ing inputs and four aux inputs, so you can also plug in the output of external synths without using up recording channels. Two nice phantom-powered mic preamps, with gain controls to turn them into guitar inputs, with inserts so you can use a hardware compressor, which is very useful. Each recording input also has an aux send for external effects.

If you have a few bits of external hardware you want to use with your computer, then this is a perfect box. The real clincher for me is the two independent headphone sockets, meaning that if you're working with someone, both of you can hear what's going on when using microphones. It attaches to the computer via a Delta 66 card included in the 'Studio' version, which uses the same conversion technology as the Audiophile. My only criticism is that it's a little small, so the knobs are a bit close together. Oh, and the fact that it doesn't have a built-in MIDI interface. $730.00.

MobilePre USB

A nice little USB box featuring the mic preamps from the Omni and also two guitar inputs. It only handles stereo in/out at one time and can only do 16-bit recording, which is a shame, and no MIDI. However, it's good value, with some useful inputs and doesn't require external power, so it's perfect for laptops. $210.00.

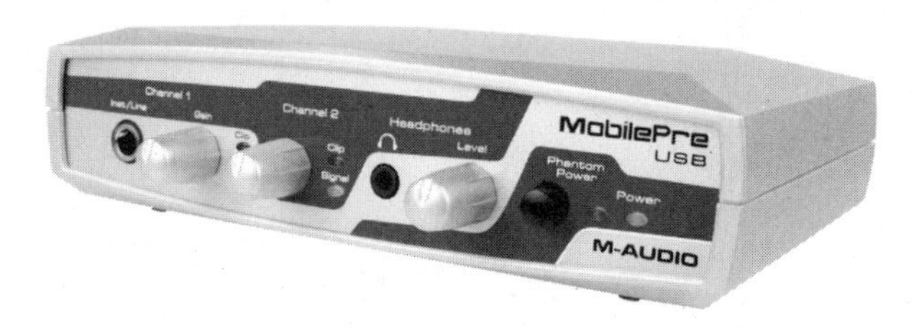

Figure 13.4
MobilePre USB.

Delta 1010

This is M Audio's flagship product. It's a high-quality 8 in/out analog audio interface with balanced connections, S/PDIF, and MIDI, all in a nice 1U rack. Ideal for the 8-bus mixer setup I talked about. It's not flash or pretty, just good quality. $800.00 - $975.00.

Figure 13.5
Delta 1010. Hardworking analog I/O in a rack.

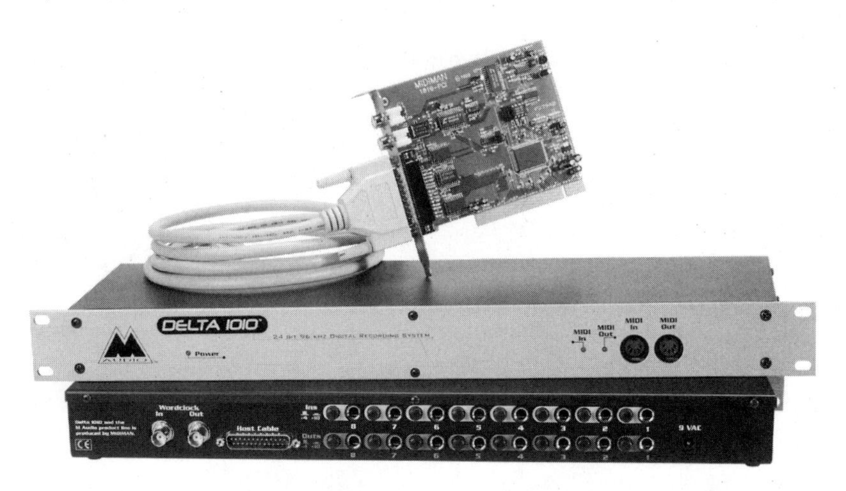

Edirol

Once a small part of the Roland empire, now they are a blossoming company in their own right, producing increasingly good quality stuff.

Website

http://www.edirol.com

DA2496

My current favorite of their product line. It's very like the Delta1010 but with twin mic preamps, high impedance guitar inputs, and a headphone socket. Well laid-out controls, an output level meter, rugged construction, and an internal power supply (no wall wart!) make this a cool piece of gear. $730.00.

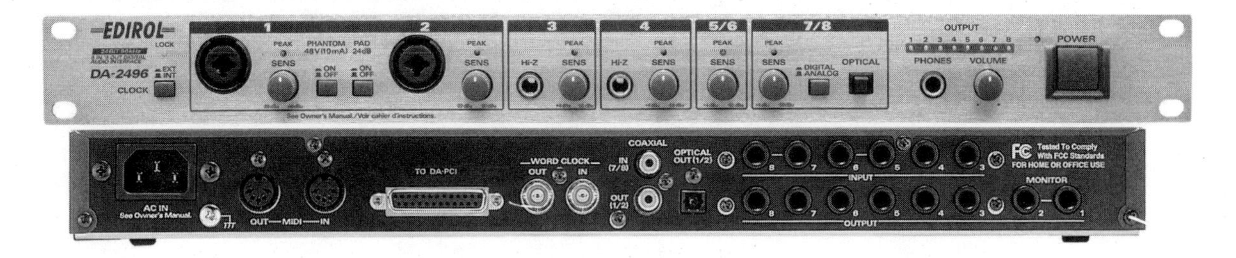

Figure 13.6
Edirol DA-2496 digital audio interface.

UA-1000

Hot off the production line is the first audio interface to take advantage of the increased bandwidth of USB2.0, and it's a nice looking bit of equipment.

The feature list is very impressive, as is the blue metallic finish. eight analog in/out in total, including four mic preamps, each with inserts for effects and compressors, and a high impedance guitar input. Unexpectedly, it also has an ADAT port for 8-channel digital connection, plus S/PDIF. Good monitoring on the front and a headphone socket and finally a MIDI interface make for one packed package. $TBA.

Figure 13.7
Edirol UA-1000 – the next generation of USB audio interface.

UA-5

USB 'Audio Capture' box with stereo in/out featuring two mic preamps and a guitar input. Headphone socket and S/PDIF digital round it off, however, no MIDI. $400.00

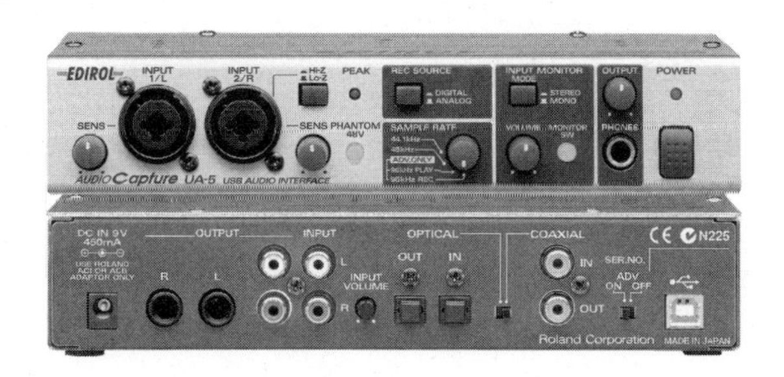

Figure 13.8
Edirol UA-5 audio capture box.

UA-700

Another stereo in/out USB box but quite unlike anything you've seen before. This is Edirol's take on the Line6 Pod, and they've produced a fabulous-sounding amp modeler and effects unit that has the one thing the Pod lacks direct connection to the computer. $650.00.

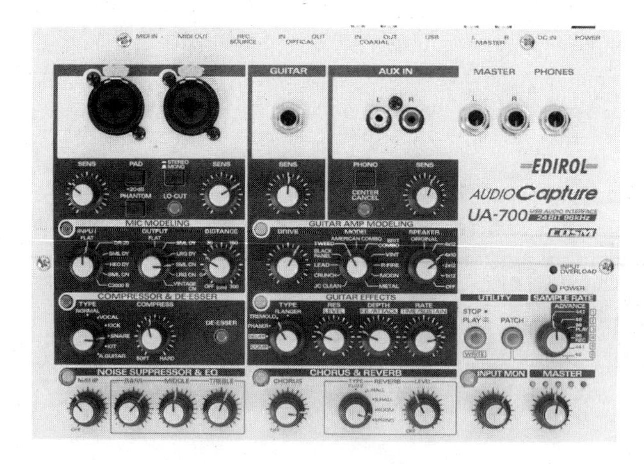

Figure 13.9
Edirol UA-700 amp modeler and effects unit.

It's a cool desktop box, with two mic preamps and, of course, a guitar input. You have complete control over all the amp models and effects on the box itself, and you can use it without the computer if you like. It uses COSM (Composite Object Sound Modeling) technology to model 11 guitar amps and five microphones. The effects section includes Flanger, Phaser, Tremolo, Delay, and you EQ and reverb on the master effects. It's a comprehensive guitar solution and even comes with a software editor, giving you access to even more controls.

UA-20

Simple stereo in/out USB box with mic and guitar inputs, MIDI, and a nice, big knob on the top. Small enough to fit in a pocket and powered via the USB connection, it's perfect for laptops. $245.00.

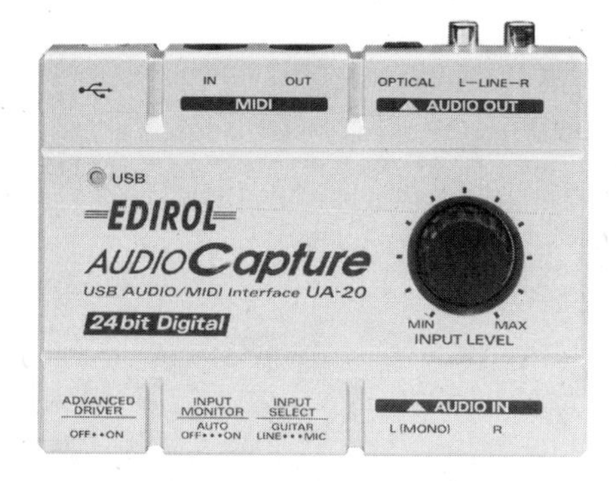

Figure 13.10
Edirol UA-20 USB audio/MIDI interface.

UR-80

The complete, all-in-one, mixer, controller, USB audio, and MIDI interface box is starting to make a name for itself as people find out what it can do. Edirol released the first one, the U-8, a couple of years ago, and the UR-80 is its evolution into a fabulous bit of gear.

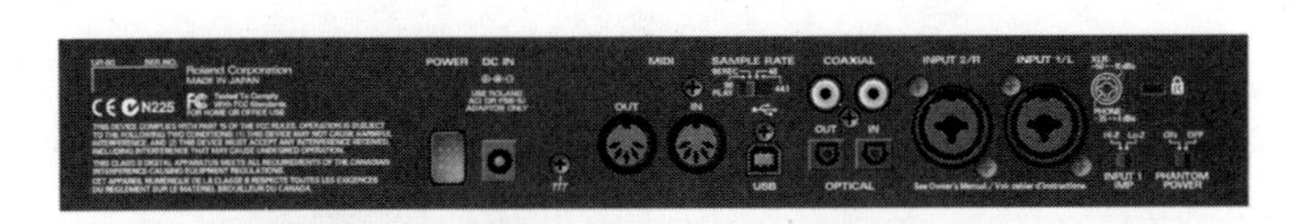

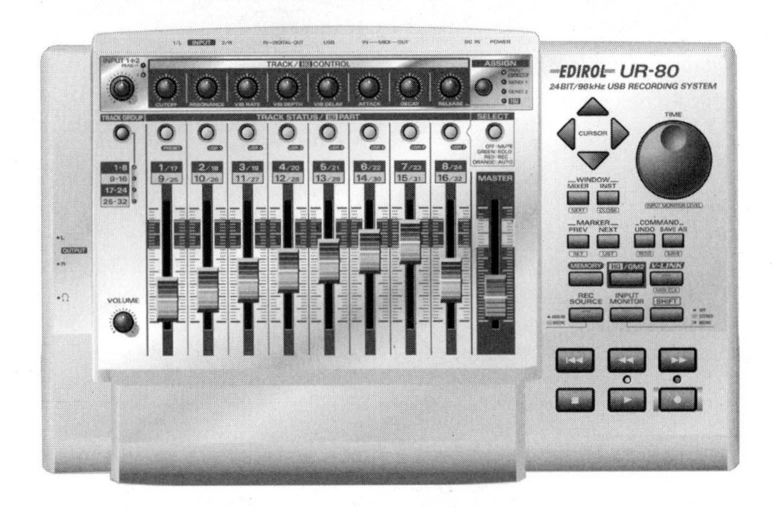

Figure 13.11
Edirol UR-80 USB recording system. It gives recording into the computer and MIDI control at the same time.

So what does it do? (which is always the first question people ask when they see it.) Well, first of all it's a stereo in/out USB box (including mic and guitar and headphones), which might be initially deceptive, and it also has the usual S/PDIF and MIDI ports. But then it gets really interesting. It's a MIDI control surface with 43 assignable buttons, knobs, and sliders, so it'll control any software you want. In something like Cubase, it has preset functions, like controlling up to 24 faders in the mixer (three banks of eight), pan controls, send amounts, and then has patches for the controls of many VSTis. It has a jog wheel for moving around in the arrange page and transport controls. It's all good hands-on stuff. It also comes with a high-quality General MIDI VST Instrument called the Hyper Canvas.

Simple in/out, but excellent control possibilities. $TBA.

Aardvark

Aardvark have been making very professional audio boxes for years - always very solid and functional, but never very pretty. This has changed dramatically over the last year or two when someone decided it was time for a makeover.

Website
http://www.aardvarkaudio.com

DirectPro Q10

Stunning audio interface, with eight mic inputs on the front (four phantom-powered), two guitar inputs, MIDI, and S/PDIF. Unfortunately, you can't see it with the black and white picture (Figure 13.12), but it's simply gorgeous in its silver and purple col-

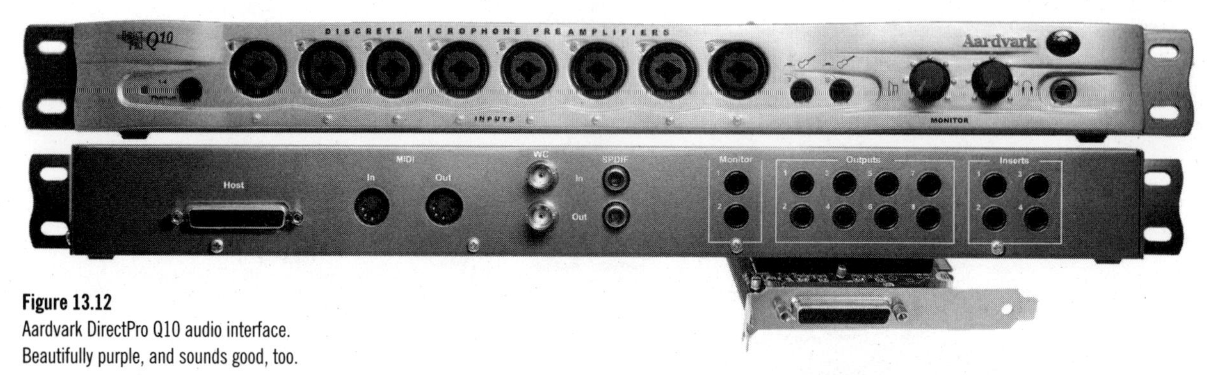

Figure 13.12
Aardvark DirectPro Q10 audio interface. Beautifully purple, and sounds good, too.

oring. It comes with a DSP-driven software mixer with comprehensive routing and monitoring options. The best thing is that you can stack up to four of these beauties, giving you 32 inputs, more than enough for even the most elaborate band.

USB3

They managed to squeeze three in and out of this USB box, giving mic and guitar inputs, a cool level slider, output meter, and a headphone output. Good quality, simple, and very portable. $245.00.

Figure 13.13
Aardvark USB3

Website

http://www.rme-audio.com

RME

Serious German company that produce serious bits of gear that work seriously well.

HDSP 9652

Probably the best-selling ADAT interface card in the world, and the least interesting to the humble guitarist as it's all ADAT, 24 channels of it. However, it's the perfect solution if you have a digital mixing desk or other ADAT enabled gear to interface to the computer. Faultless and simple. This new version comes with a DSP-powered mixer program, which is cool, and two MIDI ports. $650.00.

Presonus Audio Electronics

They make lots of nice tube preamps and dynamic processors, good-looking professional audio boxes.

Website

http://www.presonus.com

FIREstation

One of the first audio interfaces to sport Yamaha's 'mLan' interface, which is essentially a Firewire port, but Yamaha did something clever to make it run even better. It's a beautiful 8 in/out box with ADAT, MIDI, and S/PDIF. The two mic preamps are excellent quality, and the controls on the front turn it into an 8-channel mixer. It can also be used on its own as an ADAT converter box. $1,130.00.

Figure 13.14 Presonus FIREstation audio interface featuring mLAN.

Digidesign

Website

http://www.digidesign.com

The leaders of professional studio systems with their Pro Tools HD software and accompanying hardware. Pro Tools systems can be found in professional studios around the world. It's all very good and very expensive. However, a few years ago they turned some of their attention to the home and project studio markets and have released three exceptional products which feature a cut-down version of their professional audio software called Pro Tools LE. It is similar in many ways to Cubase but concentrates firmly on the audio side of music production. It does have some MIDI facilities and some software instrument support, but it does not support the open formats of VST, so it can only run plug-ins specially written for it. However, as a solid, no-nonsense, 32-track studio, it's hard to beat.

Digidesign has been a dedicated Apple Mac-oriented company for many years, so its move into the Windows platform has been quite slow and taken some time to perfect. Things have really come together for them with Windows XP, and now their products are every bit as good on the PC as they are on the Mac. They have also recently released ASIO drivers, which they previously considered to be an inferior technology. So this means that the quality of Digidesign hardware can now be used with other programs. I'll talk more about Pro Tools LE in the software section.

Digi001

Their first foray into the project studio market was the nicely featured Digi001. It was one of the first audio interfaces to feature mic preamps, of which it has two,

Figure 13.15 Digidesign's Digi001 audio interface.

with gain knobs and phantom power. It has a total of 18 in/out with eight analog, eight on ADAT and S/PDIF. By today's standards, it lacks things like inserts and aux sends, but it still remains a very capable product. $975.00.

Digi002

Now this is a great piece of gear. Similar in type to the Edirol UR-80, but it goes to another level of quality and functionality when used with the Pro Tools LE software.

Figure 13.16
Digi002 digital mixer, controller and audio interface.

It has the feel of a professional digital mixer, and that's what it is. Eight motorized faders, transport controls, knobs, and a display telling you what the knob is currently doing. It connects to the PC via Firewire and offers four mic inputs, eight line in/out, ADAT, and S/PDIF. It's completely integrated with Pro Tools LE, giving full control over everything. Although there now is an ASIO driver, the control functions of the Digi002 with something like Cubase would be quite limited. A bit pricey at $3,250.00, but then that's Digidesign.

Figure 13.17
The Digidesign Mbox.

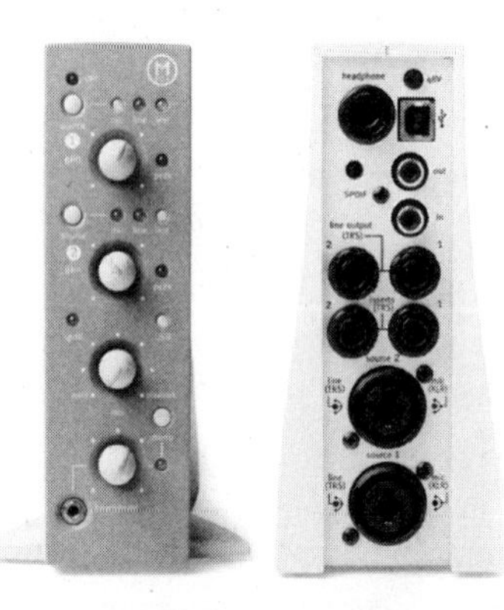

Mbox

A cool addition to the range angled at laptop users, the Mbox is another Firewire box with good home studio features.

It's simply stereo in/out but with two mic preamps made by the professional hardware company Focusrite, so they sound magnificent. Handy knobs on the front controlling gain and output level, and a headphone socket rounds it off nicely. No power supply required, so it really is portable. $610.00.

Tascam

The inventers of the 4-track PortaStudio have made a fair attempt at keeping up with the move to computer by producing two, PortaStudio-esque USB boxes. They look and feel like Portastudios but connect to the computer for recording via USB.

http://www.tascam.com

US-224

It has mic, line, and guitar inputs, and four faders that control the software mixer in either the included recording software or other programs. Transport controls and a jog wheel make for a neat little package. $375.00. It's simple and familiar and good value.

Figure 13.18
The Tascam US-224. It's not a PortaStudio, but it behaves like one.

US-428

The bigger brother of the US-224, this has four inputs, mic, line, guitar, and eight faders giving far more control over the software. $520.00. It has more knobs and more functionality and is a great solution for the money.

Figure 13.19
The Tascam US-428.

Line6 Guitar Port

What an odd little box this is. No one is entirely sure what it does, but it certainly looks kind of cool. Nice big knob and stuff, but it's not entirely what it seems. Essentially, it's a USB audio box with a guitar input and one big knob, designed to work with the included effects and tutorial software. The effects are really good, as you'd expect from Line6, and the tutorial software is interesting but relies heavily on online content, which is a drag if you don't have a fast connection. As a 'Play More Learn More' box of tricks, it's very good, but its main fault is that it lacks any other recording input, so you can't record microphones or line level sources. Most recording software only works reliably with one soundcard at a time, so it would be a hassle to use it alongside another recording card. It's a shame that Line6 didn't go that little bit further with it – perhaps they will. $210.00.

Website

http://www.line6.com

Website

http://www.yamaha.com

Yamaha

Yamaha made one of the most popular soundcards of the last century, the SW1000XG. It was great because it had a huge XG synth on board with loads of great sounds, and a good bunch of effects. At the same time, they had the over-complicated DSP Factory card, which had fabulous effects on board and powerful routing if anyone could figure out how to use it. However, as recording cards, their ASIO drivers lacked the speed of their contemporaries. A successor to the SW1000XG and DSP factory has been long overdue.

Last summer a friend from the Yamaha UK R&D department came to see me to pick my brains for ideas on a new computer recording product that Yamaha should consider to bring them back into the market. What I suggested was that they take one of their excellent digital mixers, like the 01V, wire it into the computer and make it control everything, and that's exactly what they did. Now I'm not saying that Yamaha have me to thank for their spanking new 01X, but I like to think, in some small way, I had a hand in it somewhere – true story.

01X

Essentially it's their 01V digital mixer, which plugs directly into the computer and controls everything.

As a digital mixer, it has 28 channels, each with 4-band EQ and two 32-bit effects processors, so on its own it's a nice bit of equipment. Using their 'mLan' version of Firewire, it can connect directly into a PC for recording to hard disk. It's got mic preamps, line inputs, ADAT, all the usual stuff. With their studio manager software, you can store and recall any mixer settings at any time. Everything is automated and motorized and brings direct control over the software you are using (Cubase, etc). It also has MIDI built in just for fun. But that's not all. It will also ship with a stack of top-quality VST effect plug-ins.

At the time of writing, it's still about four months away, but I saw one at the Musikmesse show in Frankfurt recently and it was definitely the talk of the show. It's a digital mixer, a multi-channel audio interface, MIDI interface, effects processor, and control surface all in one and should retail for about $1,950.00.

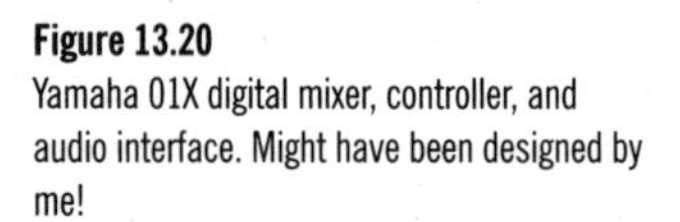

Figure 13.20
Yamaha 01X digital mixer, controller, and audio interface. Might have been designed by me!

Creative

Website

http://www.creative.com

Wasn't sure whether to include this or not, but I have to face the fact that there are thousands of them out there and you are likely to have one already, or if not, you have probably considered it. Creative makes the SoundBlaster range of cards, the leaders in soundcards for games and multimedia. With the SoundBlaster Live! Card a few years back, they attempted to enter the home studio market. It was a great success, because at the time many people didn't know any better. By the time they released the 'Audigy', many people did know better, and they came under fire by many users who felt more than a bit cheated that it didn't really do what they implied it would. Fabulous features, lots of connections, great price, but they talked about it being 24-bit, which it wasn't. Well, it was on playback but not on recording – a bit of a vital mistake really.

They did have ASIO drivers this time, unlike the SBLive, but they were stuck at the 48kHz sampling rate, which is great for recording but really annoying when it comes down to importing samples recorded at the standard 44.1kHz, as they were speeded up by the increase in sample rate. Also annoying when it came to writing CDs of your music, as you had to convert down to 44.1kHz. So, the Audigy was close to a good music product but certainly no cigars. Enter the Audigy 2.

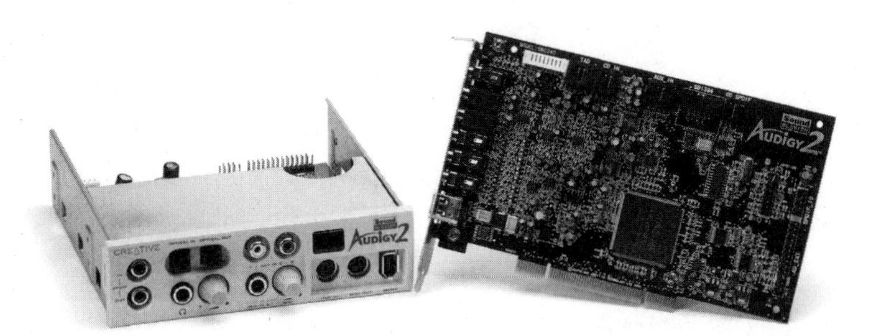

Figure 13.21
Audigy 2 Platinum.

This time it's a true 24-bit card and up to 192kHz for DVD playback. It's got proper jack socket inputs for mic and guitar on the front, as well as MIDI, S/PDIF and a headphone socket. On the card itself, you have the surround-sound outputs and usual multimedia mic and line inputs. A Firewire socket on both the card and drive unit complete the hardware. The ASIO drivers they have now are excellent and you can vary the sample rate, which is a bonus.

The Audigy 2 comes with lots of built-in audio effects for games and other applications, but these don't work in ASIO mode. It also comes with a decent hardware synth and a software one that uses SoundFonts, which are a bit like samples. So, it's a very capable card, with loads of features and a great price. However, I still have my reservations. The main drive of Creative has always been toward multimedia rather than serious music-making, and the card comes packed with tons and tons of 'bloatware', that's largely unnecessary software to do everything. So it's running special games-related software, music library software, surround-sound effects software, DVD enhanced this, that, and the other, and all of it gets in the way of your computer performing at its best for music production. For the gamer (of which I'm a fully paid up member), it has fabulous sound facilities, for home theater, as well, it's excellent, and for mucking around with music, it's not a bad bit of equipment. There are just more dedicated soundcards that I feel would work much better for serious recording. $290.00.

Website

http://www.terratec.com

Terratec

Terratec mainly produce very capable multimedia soundcards but have also made some good cards for the home studio market, like the EWS88MT, a good quality 8 in/out audio soundcard. Their most popular card to date has been a marriage between their multimedia technology and more serious audio considerations.

DMX 6 Fire 24/96

This was aimed squarely at the territory of the SoundBlaster Audigy, and they did a really good job. Rather than pack it full of multimedia functions, Terratec leaned firmly toward the music market by concentrating on what really mattered – recording quality.

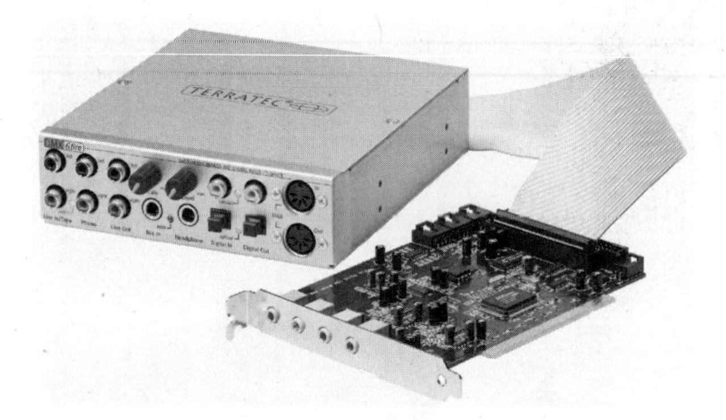

Figure 13.22
Terratec DMX 6 Fire 24/96.

The similarities are immediately apparent. It has the same drive bay unit with lots of lovely connections on it. Mic and line inputs, S/PDIF, and MIDI, all very accessible. It also has a phono level input so you can plug a turntable straight in, which is a nice touch. It comes with excellent ASIO drivers and was capable of 24-bit right from the start. It has the same surround-sound and DVD playback facilities as the Audigy and also has excellent sound for games; however, it does it without all the unnecessary software running in the background, taking up all your precious resources. The sound quality for recording was far better than the original Audigy and probably on a par with the new version. If you're looking for this kind of all-in-one games and music card, then I would definitely recommend it over the Creative option. $275.00.

That'll do for soundcards, I think. Overwhelming it may be, but just concentrate on what you want to connect to the PC, and you can't go too wrong.

Recording software

The all-important choice of recording software. This is where you actually make your music, so I guess it's pretty important, really. We've already looked at Cubase SX in some depth, and you may already be convinced that it's the one for you; however, there are other choices and one of them may fit your purposes better. There are tons of music programs out there, but the vast majority tend to concentrate on electronic, loop-based, or dance music, which is a great shame. So, the products I've chosen all include real-time effects, audio recording, and mixing, which is what we're about. Again, I won't go into massive detail, just point out the cool stuff and slap in the occasional opinion.

Steinberg

Getting pretty familiar with Cubase SX already, but they do have a range of products to suit your needs and budget.

Cubasis VST 4.0

Entry-level home studio software that is packed full of features. It supports up to 48 audio tracks of wave or MP3, and 64 MIDI tracks. Comes with a load of effects and VSTis and is completely compatible with any other VST effects or instruments. It has a plug-in called the 'Voice Detective', the idea being that you could sing into Cubasis and the plug-in will detect the pitch and produce the corresponding MIDI note. You could use this to play single notes on your guitar and get them to play back synths – a bit like a primitive MIDI guitar.

Figure 13.23
Cubasis VST 4.0. 48 tracks of recording on a tight budget.

It's a very comprehensive package and even features surround-sound mixing. However, it does not have the MIDI control over effects or automation facilities found in its bigger brother Cubase and only has a single insert per track which may be restricting, but at just $115.00, you get an awful lot for your money.

Cubase SL and SX

As you've seen, Cubase SX is a pretty serious piece of recording software. Cubase has maintained its mantle of 'Industry Standard' since its earlier versions on the

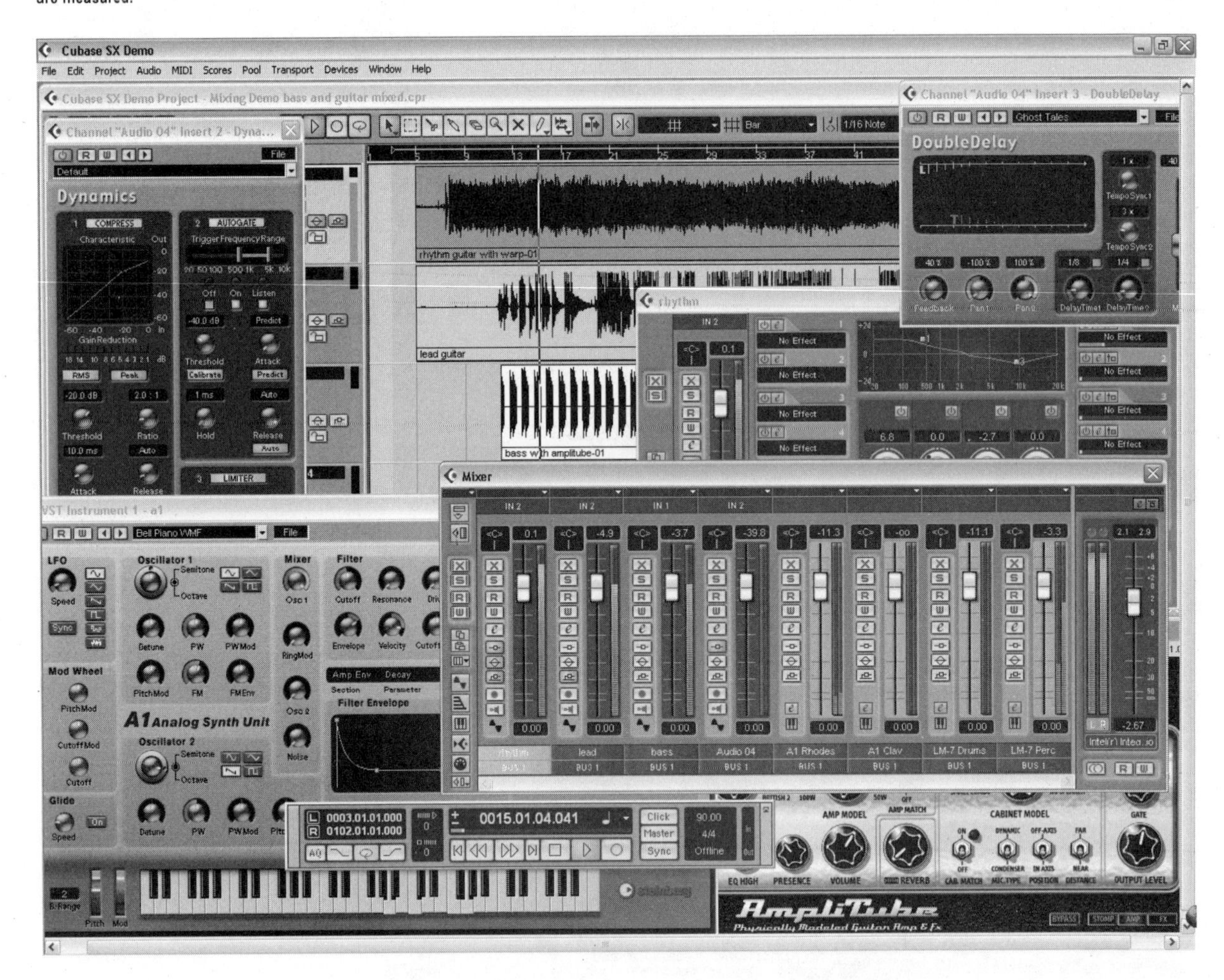

Figure 13.24
Cubase SX - the standard by which all others are measured.

Atari ST many years ago. Now it offers as many audio and MIDI tracks as your computer can handle, VST effects and VSTis, mixing, automation, MIDI control, scoring, and surround mixing. It sets a very high standard and, combined with the right hardware, can be a complete professional studio. The two versions, SL and SX, are very similar. SL doesn't have the advanced score editing, the surround-sound mixing, or some of the more professional plug-ins, and SX supports more VSTis loaded at one time. Unless there's something specific that SX does that you need, then I'd recommend SL as the best buy. SL $400.00, SX $900.00.

Nuendo 2.0

Steinberg designed this product as a 'Media Production Studio' aimed squarely at the Pro Tools market of professional producers. It has a streamlined interface that's fast, stable, and intuitive to use.

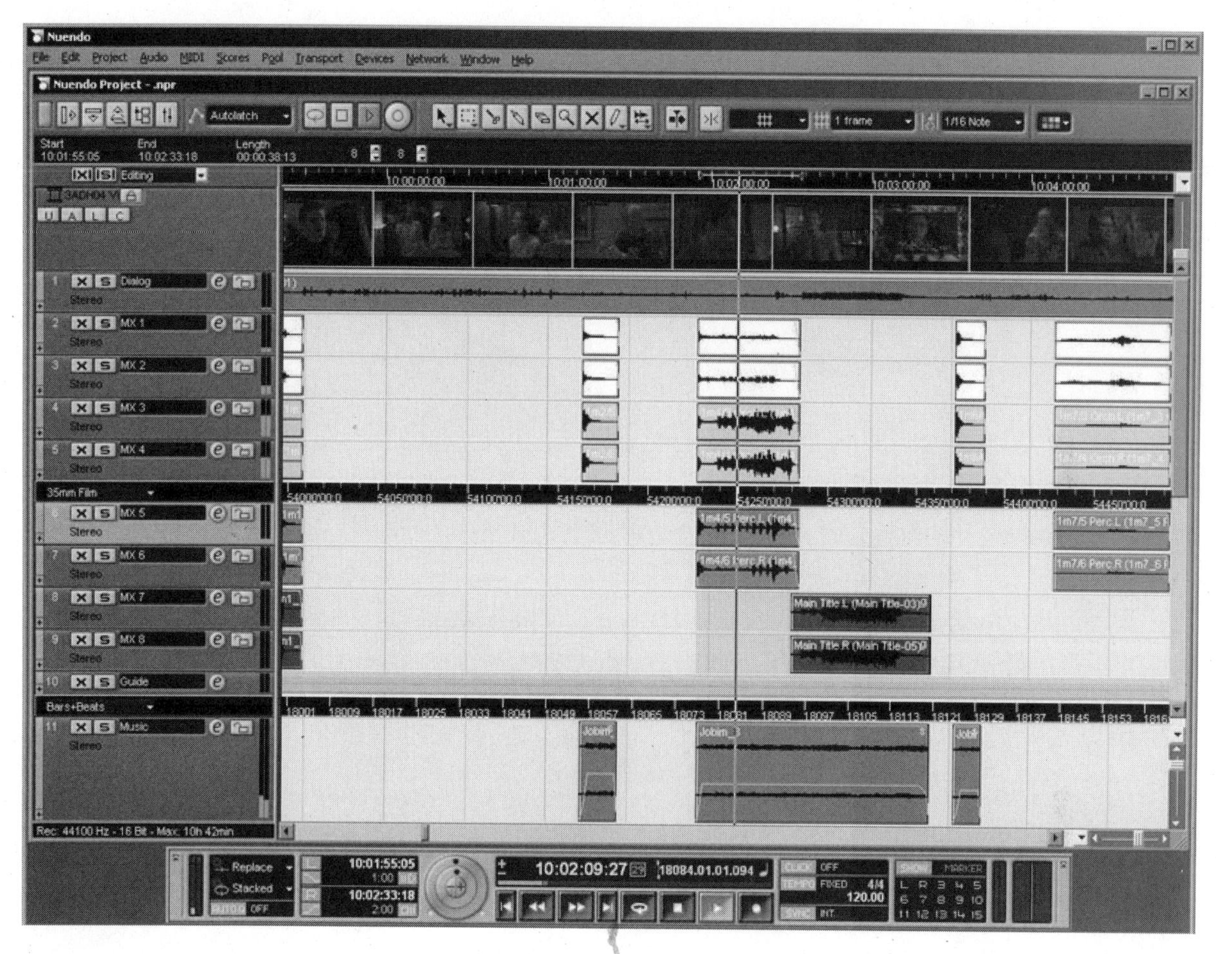

Other pro features include audio over networks, batch processing, surround-sound processing and mixing, full-screen video, high-quality plug-ins, and splitting recordings across different drives. It's an audio recording and editing powerhouse. $1,450.00.

Figure 13.25
Nuendo 2.0. It's a bit pro.

Cakewalk

Cakewalk products were born and bred on the PC, unlike many other programs that were originally from the Atari or the Apple Mac. So, stability and familiarity to anyone who's used Windows programs before made it a very popular program. In fact, Cakewalk in one version or another is the world's best-selling music program. One advantage they have over Cubase is that all Cakewalk products support the 'WDM' Windows Driver Model standard for soundcard drivers. This means that any Windows soundcards can work with very low latency with Cakewalk taking away the necessity of more expensive soundcards with ASIO drivers. However, I have found that ASIO drivers seem to be more stable and perform better under pressure than WDM, and as it happens Cakewalk are about to release an update to support ASIO as well. That said, you will get better performance out of Cakewalk products using a normal, non-ASIO soundcard than you will with Steinberg products.

They have a large range of products, here are a few of them.

Guitar Tracks Pro

Cakewalk have some products specifically written for the guitarist, which is cool. This is their best one. Guitar Tracks Pro is a 32-track studio featuring a guitar amp simulator, called 'Revalver', tuner, effects, and a loop-based drum generator. It also supports ACID loops. Guitar Tracks Pro doesn't have any MIDI facilities or support of software synths, but it's a simple and effective replacement for a 4-track style recorder. $165.00.

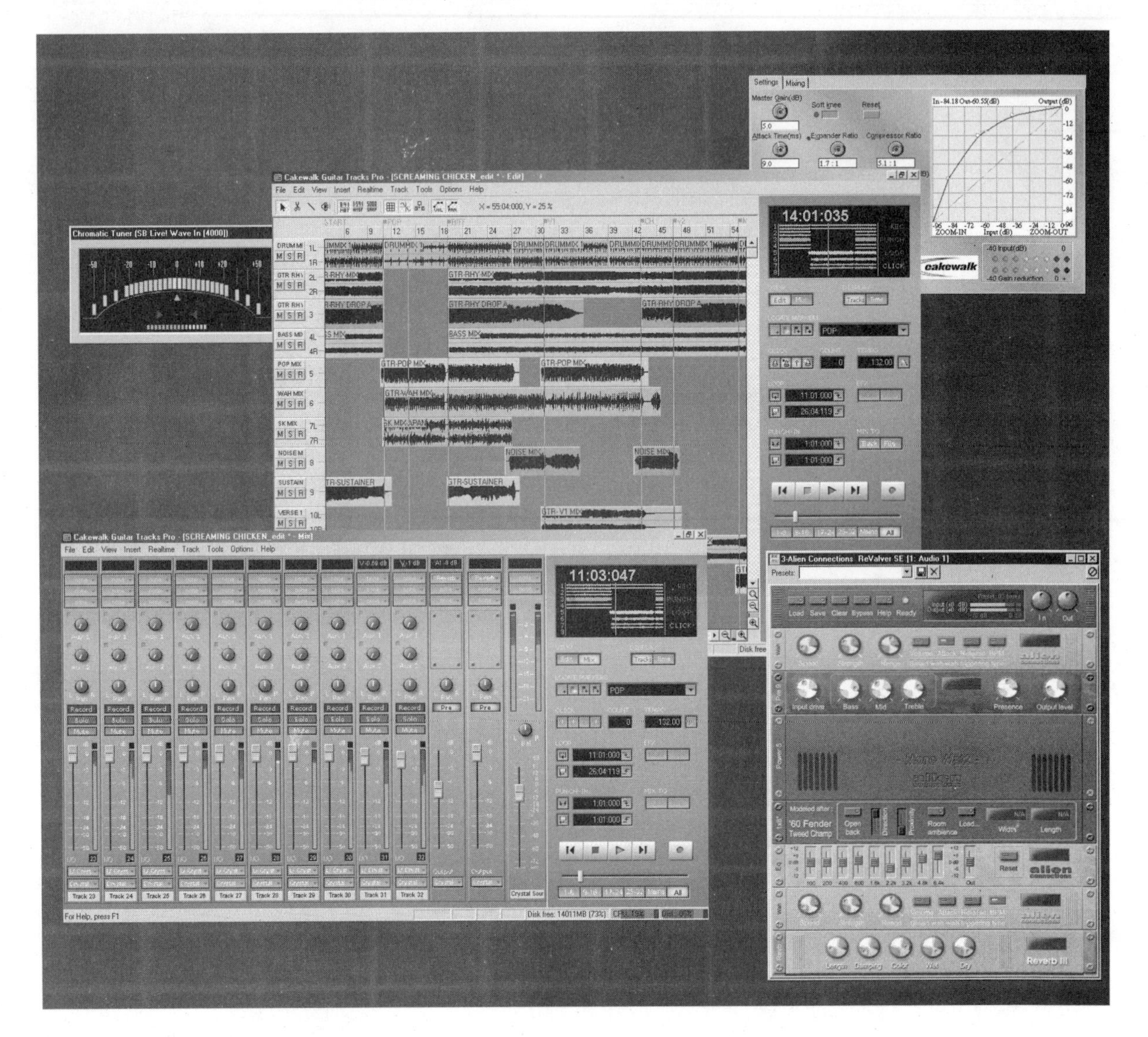

Figure 13.26
Guitar Tracks Pro. Great for just audio recording.

Cakewalk Home Studio

No limit on audio this time, and it has MIDI in abundance. Packed full of effects and also support for DXis (DirectX Instruments), which are an alternative format to the Steinberg VSTi protocol. You have some simple scoring and layout functions, with guitar chords and lyrics. Easy to use and with a lot of power, it does indeed make a great little home studio. $130.00.

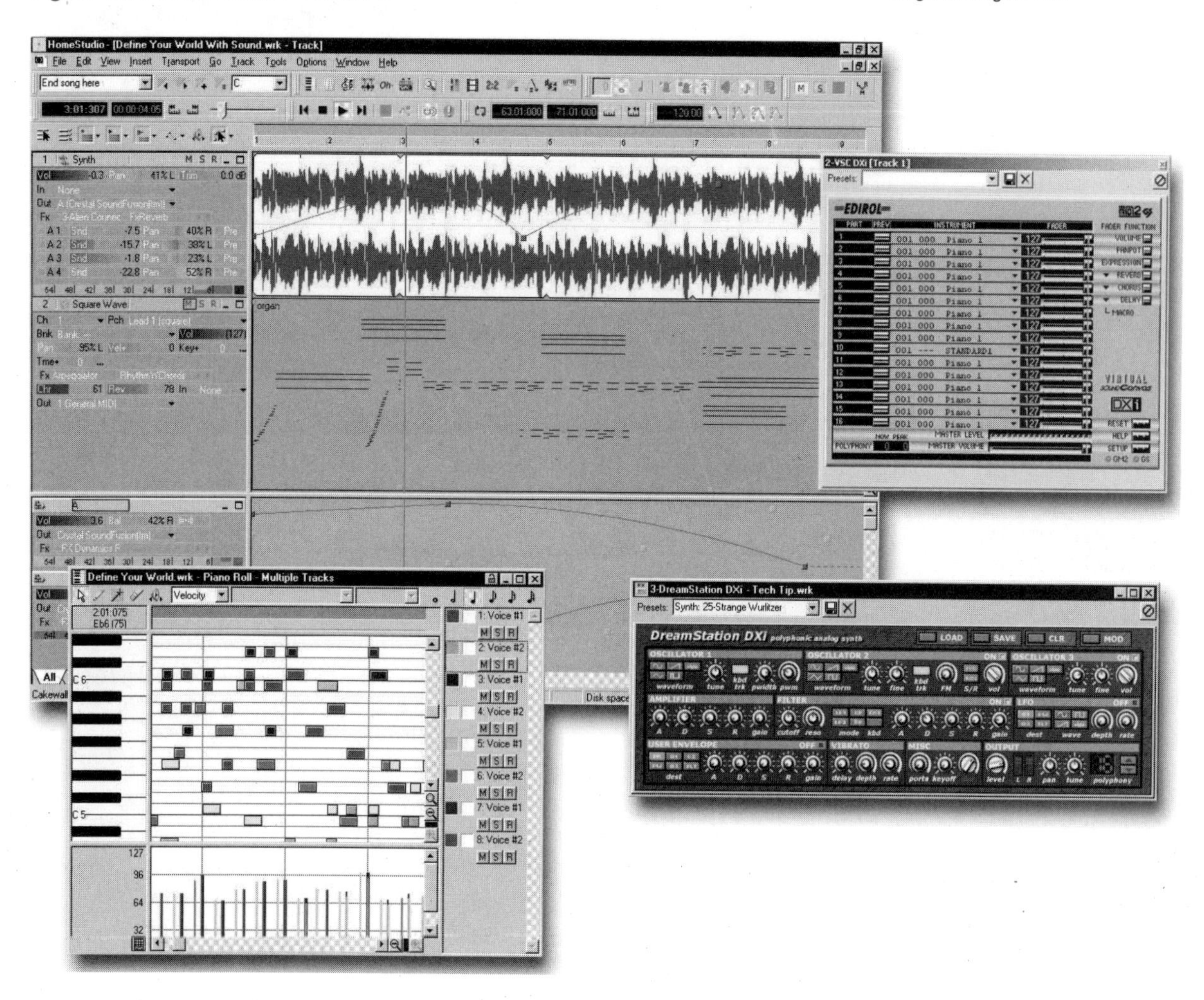

Figure 13.27
Cakewalk Home Studio. Good all-around budget recording software.

Sonar

Cakewalk's flagship product is a fully professional recording environment with effects, mixing, automation, softsynths, and some things you wouldn't expect, like loop construction, scoring, tabulature, and the Session drummer. Cakewalk have recently included ASIO support in this program and have just added a built-in 'VST Wrapper', written by our friends at Fxpansion, that allows Sonar to run VST effects and VSTis, so now it's fully compatible with all Steinberg's products.

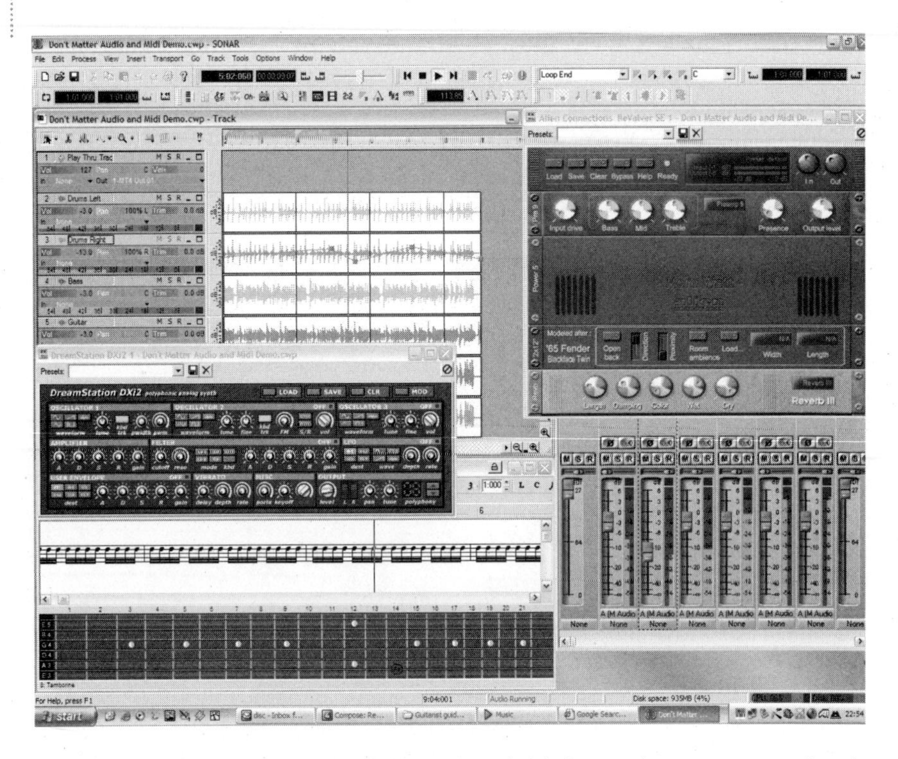

Figure 13.28
Sonar. Excellent software studio.

This is the best alternative to Cubase around. It's fast and easy to use and really can be an entire studio. $405.00.

Website

http://www.digidesign.com

Digidesign

You can't talk about recording software without mentioning Pro Tools. It's the software the 'proper' pro studios use, or so we're led to believe. There's no doubt that studios around the world use Digidesign software and hardware in their recording process, but it no longer holds the crown it once did.

The strength of Digidesign and Pro Tools is that the software and hardware are written specifically for each other; you can't run Pro Tools with anything but Digidesign hardware. This makes it very stable, and Digidesign have complete control over how it will perform and can state exactly what you need to fill your requirements.

Everything about it is of extremely high quality and also very expensive. The Digi001, 002, and Mbox options are great recording solutions and good value compared to the higher-end Pro Tools systems.

Pro Tools LE

What's good about Pro Tools is that it's very plain and streamlined and works in exactly the same way an open reel multitrack tape recorder works, with the same terms used and everything laid out like you'd find on a real mixer. It assumes you know what you're talking about and so is not that intuitive for someone who's not from a recording background. Excellent automation, editing, and mixing make this a competent recording program. However, it does lack a bit on the MIDI side and, as it doesn't support either VST or DirectX, the choice of effects and instruments

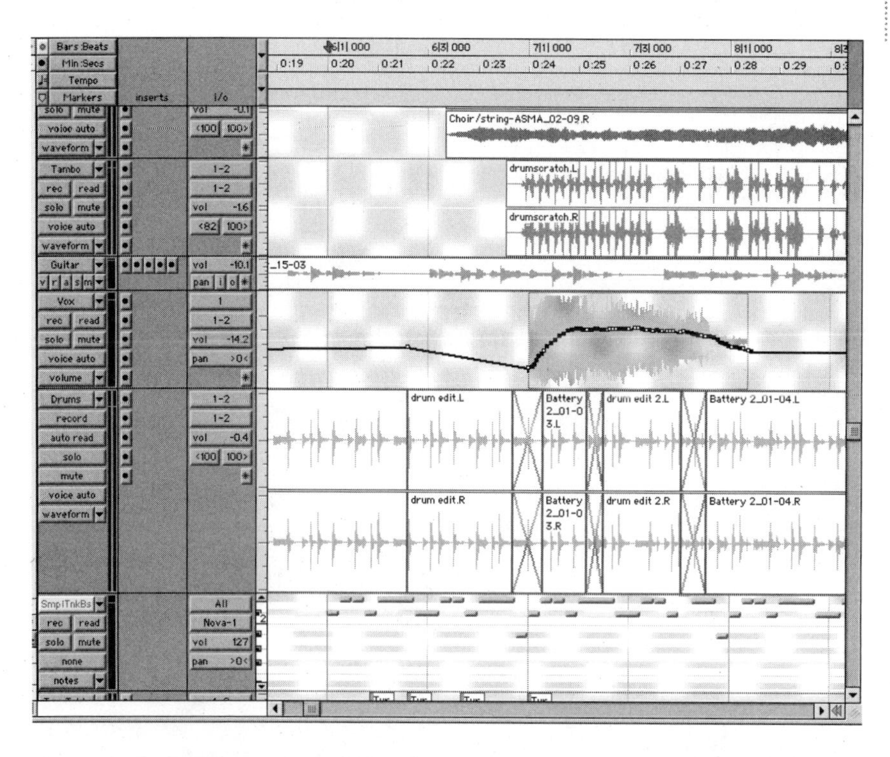

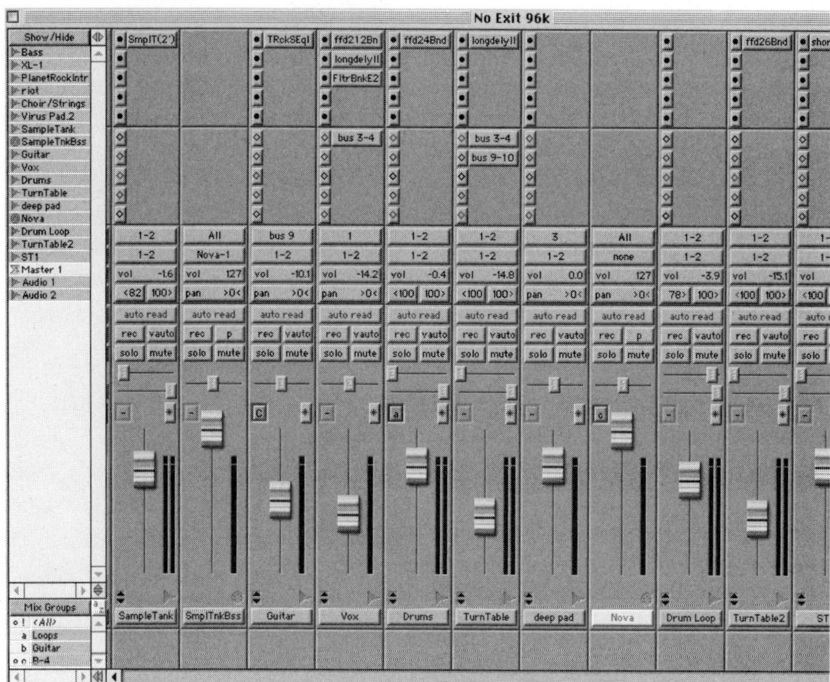

Figure 13.29
Pro Tools LE – Edit and Mix Windows. A slightly cut-down version of what pro studios use.

(using the RTAS [Real Time Audio Suite] format) is a bit thin on the ground. Only 32 audio tracks allowed in this version, but that's usually enough.

A bit dull-looking, isn't it? One fabulous plug-in only available for Pro Tools is the SansAmp PSA-1 from BombFactory. It's an exact model of the hardware version and sounds fantastic. Line6 also has a plug-in called the 'Amp Farm' available for the TDM version of Pro Tools. TDM is the high-end version of Pro Tools that runs with DSP cards and will set you back several thousand dollars.

Figure 13.30
SansAmp PSA-1 and the Line6 AmpFarm.

Pro Tools cannot be bought separately, as it can only run with Digidesign hardware, so the price will vary depending on whether you go for the Digi001, 002, Mbox, or some serious Pro Tools HD (TDM) monster system.

Effects plug-ins

We've looked at a few of these already, but they are just the tip of the iceberg. There are hundreds of VST and DirectX plug-ins around, some good, some bad, some free, some very expensive. I'll restrict my choice to the ones written specifically for guitar, although, of course, you can use whatever effects you like.

Website

http://www.amplitube.com

IK Multimedia - Amplitube

Can't really say anything more about this as you've experienced it firsthand in Chapter 5. Suffice to say that it's generally considered to be the best-sounding amp modeler available. It can create thousands of different tones and has lots of great presets to keep you going for hours. Comes in VST and RTAS versions for about $370.00.

Website

http://www.steinberg.net

Steinberg WarpVST

Simple and gorgeous-sounding model of three amps and three cabinets, using technology from Hughes and Kettner, the German makers of the blackest, and metalist guitar amps around (Figure 5.18). Clean Jazz Chorus, Plexi Tube Head, and Warp Rectified channels of increasing nastiness (in a good way), each with the usual gain, tone, and presence controls, and three different cabinets. It's my favorite. $245.00.

DSound – GT Player and Stomp'n FX

You can no longer buy the Stomp'n FX plug-ins on their own, as they now come with the GT Player – which is no bad thing at all. As we've seen, it's a powerful piece of performance software. The Stomp boxes will also appear in Cubase or Cakewalk as plug-ins, so you can use them in your recordings. It's an absolute bargain at $65.00.

Website
http://www.dsound1.com

BombFactory SansAmp PSA-1

BombFactory make some of the most interesting plug-ins for Pro Tools, and the SansAmp PSA-1 is no exception (Figure 13.30). A brilliant recreation of a great bit of hardware. $275.00 for the RTAS version for Pro Tools LE only.

Website
http://www.bombfactory.com

Alien Connections – ReValver

Comprehensive amp and effects modeler that gives you a rack of simulated hardware to play with. A 'Lite' version comes with the Cakewalk products. It can also be run standalone, so you can just load it up and play. Only available as a DirectX plug-in, and there's a demo available for download from the website. $115.00.

Website
http://www.alienconnections.com

Figure 13.31
Alien-Connections ReValver amp and effects modeler.

Mackie/Universal Audio – Nigel

This is a bit different because it's a plug-in that only works on its own DSP card. Demand for more and better quality plug-ins is very high, but we do tend to keep running out of processing power on the poor, old overworked computer. So, a couple of companies, realizing that the complexity of their plug-ins would fry most computers' circuitry, produced cards with DSP (digital signal processing) chips on them to take all the processing away from the computer. It's essentially putting a hardware effects unit inside the computer. Universal Audio, now owned by Mackie, have

Website
http://www.mackie.com

one of the best ranges of effects available for their DSP card, the UAD-1, and this includes the fabulous 'Nigel' guitar amp modeler and effects processor. It comes with the card and a whole bunch of other pro-quality effects for about $965.00.

Figure 13.32
Nigel – guitar amp modeler.

Drum software

Decent drums and percussion are always important to the guitarist, and so I've put together this little selection of drum-related plug-in instruments, most of which we've covered, but here's a summary.

Native Instruments Battery

Website
http://www.native-instruments.com

We've seen it in action in Chapter 6, Figure 6.6. It's a great piece of drum software that's simple to use and comes with tons and tons of drum samples and dozens of kits. You can create your own kits and edit them all over the place. $145.00.

Fxpansion

Website
http://www.fxpansion.com

DR-008

We've seen this as well (Figure 6.10), and it's also a great piece of drum software but with many more features and odd sequence and pattern possibilities. Load of kits, and you can make your own. $160.00.

BFD

Premium Acoustic Drum Library Module. No screenshot, no demo, just a small description on the website about it having five fabulous kits and lots of groovy patterns. Too late for this roundup, but I'm sure it'll be available by the time you read this. $320.00.

Steinberg

Website
http://www.steinberg.net

LM4 MK2

Steinberg already includes their LM7 drum module with Cubase. The LM4 is a more comprehensive version featuring some fabulous kits. Mk2 brought along editing and layering and other such things missing from the first version. $165.00.

Figure 13.33
Steinberg's LM4 Mk2 drum sample kit.

Waldorf Attack

Written by synth manufacturer Waldorf, the Attack drum synth is a VSTi that synthesizes drum sounds. This is not the place you'll find pristine acoustic drum samples, but rather the fierce bleeps and thuds of electronic percussion.

Figure 13.34
Waldorf Attack drum synth, for more electronic-sounding drums.

Groove Agent

Not-quite-released drum machine in the true sense with different kits and styles covering 50 years of music. Alter complexity of the patterns, instant fills, tailor the drum kits to your heart's desire (Figure 6.49). One to look out for. $290.00.

Musiclab

Website

http://www.musiclab.com

SlicyDrummer (Figure 6.45) and FillinDrummer are excellent MIDI plug-ins that can create instant drum patterns for you to feed to your drum sound module. They are each around $85.00.

Spectrasonics – Stylus

Website

http://www.spectrasonics.com

Spectrasonics were originally a sample company selling CDs packed with samples of instruments and everything else for use with hardware or software samplers. Recently, they have made a foray into the virtual instrument market by combining their sample library with a front-end player. Stylus is known as the Vinyl Groove Module and contains stacks of drum and percussion loops. The great thing about these loops is that they can be cut up and each part of the loop played separately, meaning that you can create your own loops with the individual parts. The original loop can be imported as a MIDI file and then edited. Although targeted at the dance and DJ markets, it's a very useful drum tool for everyone. $260.00.

Figure 13.35
Spectrasonics Stylus – a ton of loops and grooves.

Reel Drums

Website

http://www.reeldrums.com

One answer to getting the right drum sound and the right patterns is to get a real drummer in and record it properly. This is not always very convenient for most of us, as it requires a lot of room, a lot of gear, and understanding neighbors. This is where Reel Drums comes in. What they've done (Gil and Chris, a couple of good friends of mine in the US) is professionally recorded a real drummer playing a real kit, and not in stereo, but in multitrack. What you get is various styles of drumming, patterns, fills, etc., in a multitrack format so you have complete mixing control over the whole drum kit. You can chop the patterns up, move it around, edit them in any way you like. They are available on lots of CDs already in Pro Tools Session or Nuendo/Cubase Project format, so you just load them up. Steinberg used to do something similar called the 'VST Drum Sessions', but these seem to have vanished in recent times. Starts from around $325.00.

Software synths and samplers

Alongside the software drum machines, there are many other software instruments available. You can get any sound you want in software, whether that's complex synthesis or something simple like a good piano sound. Here's a small selection of some of the good ones that I feel might be appropriate in a traditional guitarist-type way.

Steinberg

Halion 2

Steinberg's own software sampler opens up whole libraries of sounds. It comes with half a dozen disks of sample instruments including an excellent Rhodes piano and some great drum kits. The new version includes tons of editing, filtering, and modulation options, making this a very versatile and powerful sampler. $285.00 for version 1, new version $TBA.

Website

http://www.steinberg.net

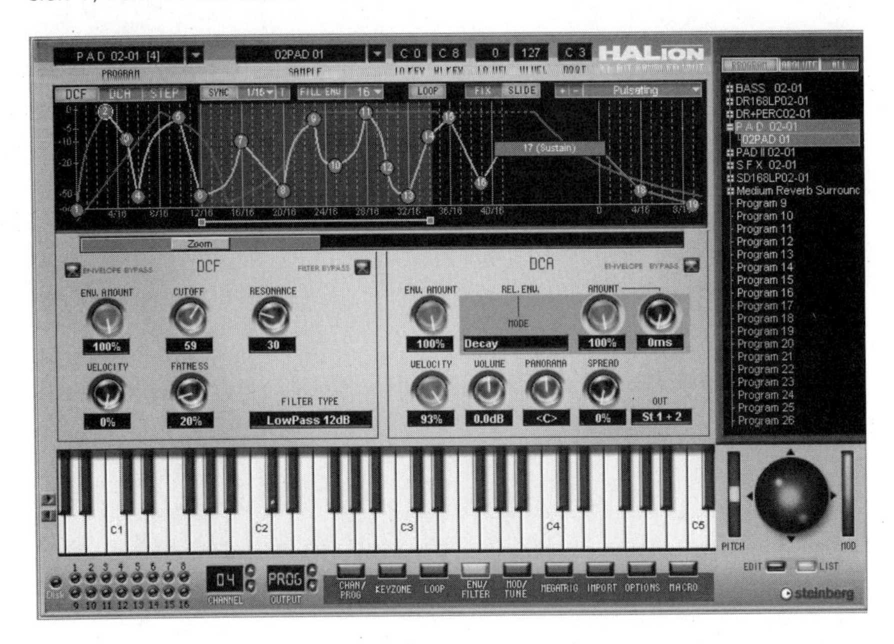

Figure 13.36
Halion 2 software sampler.

Halion Strings Edition

The demand for quality string sounds is such that Steinberg decided to create a special version of Halion and combine it with a fabulous string library. Full of rich and warm strings covering the whole string family. $325.00.

Figure 13.37
Halion Strings edition.

The Grand

It's just a piano, but it sounds fantastic. If you are after a realistic piano sound, then this has got to be top of your list. $225.00.

Figure 13.38
The Grand. Simply piano.

Native Instruments

Creators of some of the best software instruments available, here are two:

Website

http://www.native-instruments.com

Kontakt

A very powerful sampler that can load up pretty much any sample format. Its power is in its editing, modulation, and filtering abilities using those excellent Native Instrument filters that appear in all their products. Comes with a fair few sounds to

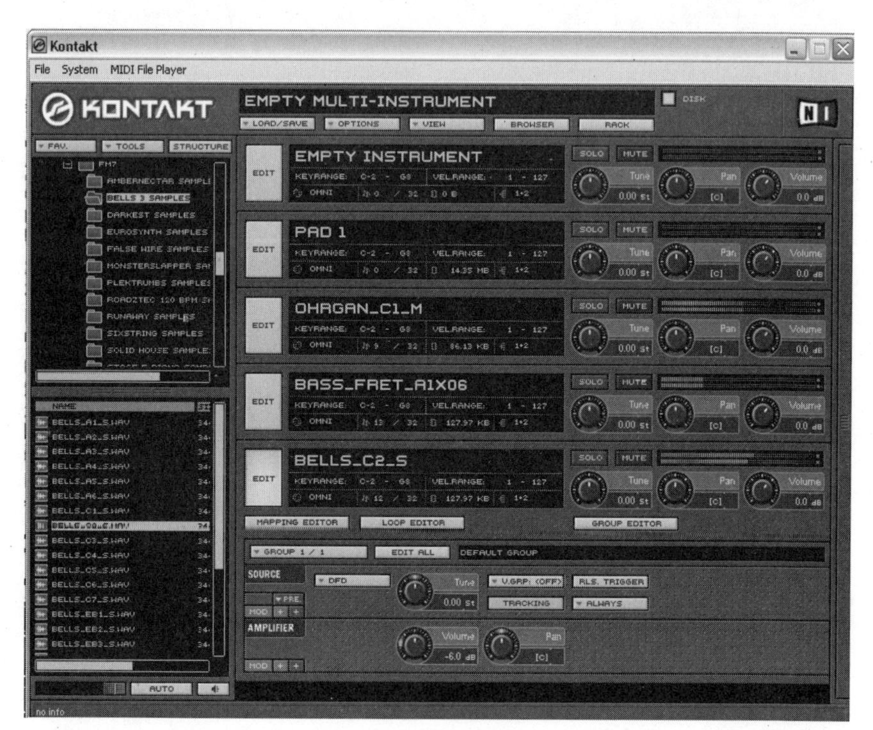

Figure 13.39
Native Instruments Kontakt software sampler.

get you going, including Battery kits and samples from their other products. It can run as a plug-in or standalone, so you can simply load it and play it. $325.00.

B4

Magnificently modeled on the Hammond B3 organ, this is a fabulous-sounding virtual instrument that speaks for itself. $165.00.

Figure 13.40
Native Instruments B4. The Hammond B3 reincarnated.

Applied Acoustics – Lounge Lizard

Simply one of the best electric pianos around. Applied Acoustics use acoustic modeling technology to create an incredibly realistic sound and feel to the Lounge Lizard. $145.00.

Website

http://www.applied-acoustics.com

Figure 13.41
Lounge Lizard. Brilliantly remodeled lazy electric piano.

Spectrasonics Trilogy

Website

http://www.spectrasonics.net

Trilogy is similar to the Stylus drum module, but this time we're dealing with bass. Trilogy is stacked full of acoustic, electric, and synth bass sounds, and they all sound simply marvelous. If you need to improve on the sound the VB-1 is kicking out, then this could be a good option. $325.00.

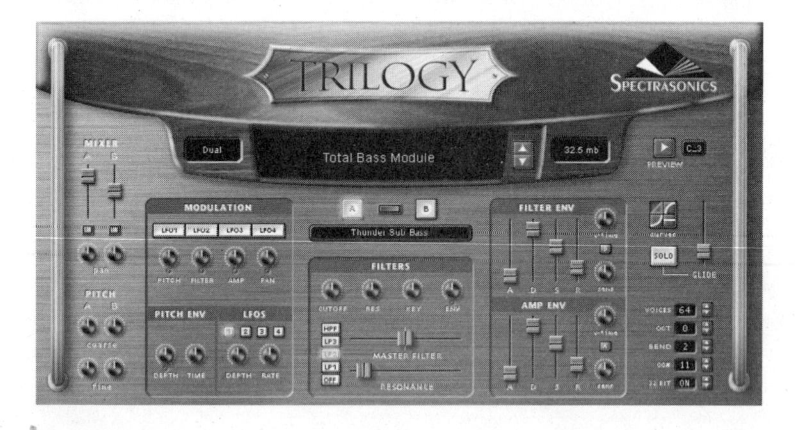

Figure 13.42
Trilogy – the total bass sound module.

Edirol

Website

http://www.edirol.com

Using Roland's synth technology, Edirol have created some high-quality virtual instruments. They have the HQ Hyper Canvas, which is a great bunch of quality GS sounds covering pretty much everything, but more interesting for us is these two:

HQ-QT SuperQuartet

It's a specialized synth with four sounds: piano, bass, drums, and guitar. OK, so the guitar sounds are not really relevant, but piano, bass, and drums are excellent, making for a good quality and simple accompaniment to our guitar recording. $165.00.

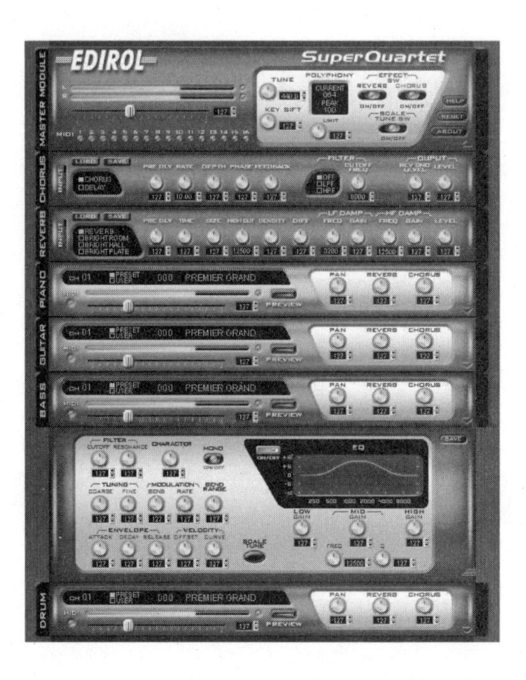

Figure 13.43
SuperQuartet of piano, bass, drums, and guitar – without the 'musical differences'.

HQ-QR Orchestral

Rather than messing around with samples, this software synth has a ton of quality orchestral sounds all ready to go, so if you want to play alongside the London Philharmonic orchestra, now's your chance. $390.00.

Figure 13.44
HQ-QR Orchestral, almost like the real thing.

MIDI controllers

Keyboards, knobs, floorboards - MIDI controllers come in all shapes and sizes. One thing I haven't mentioned is MIDI guitar interfaces. You can use a MIDI pickup to convert your playing into MIDI note information so you can use your guitar to play MIDI sounds from synths and the like. These can work very well, but personally I find them a bit inaccurate and hard work, probably due to my sloppy playing – they certainly take a bit of practice to get the best out of them. I can't seem to get my head around the idea of playing drums with guitar strings, but if you have one, then I'm sure you're a master of it. I would recommend getting a keyboard, though. It's just a really handy bit of equipment, even if you don't play. Simply slapping keys tends to make a better sound than you'd think, and playing drums is far simpler. Anyway, here's a selection of keyboards, knobs, and floorboards to consider.

Behringer FCB1010

Website

http://www.behringer.com

Been playing with this floorboard now for a while, and I really like it (Figure 8.9). It's simple, sturdy, got everything I need to control software, and it's a splendid silver color. Ten footswitches, bank up/down so you can access up to 128 programs, and two expression pedals that can be assigned to whatever MIDI control number you like. $165.00.

Yamaha MFC10

Website

http://www.yamaha.com

Used this one as well, and it certainly does the job, although I found it more complicated and less pretty than the Behringer. Ten footswitches, bank up/down and a single expression pedal. $245.00.

Art X-15

Website

http://www.artproaudio.com

Not entirely sure if this is still available, as it's over 10 years old and I can't seem to find anyone who sells it. It's a shame, because it's the only floorboard I've found that can turn the pedals into MIDI-assignable controllers, meaning that messing around with MIDI-OX shouldn't be necessary. Ten footswitches and two expression pedals. Can't find one on sale.

Evolution

Website

http://www.evolution.com

Evolution's product line has really advanced in the last year. They used to make cheap and nasty MIDI keyboards, and now they make cheap and cool keyboards and controllers. Silver seems to be the color this year and a blue LED display enhances the coolness. Here's a few:

UC-33

I really like this one. A bunch of knobs and some sliders/faders that can control everything, it even has a transport control and assignable buttons. It's not as fancy as some control surfaces - the faders are not motorized, and it is made of plastic - but it's great value for all that control. USB interface. $325.00.

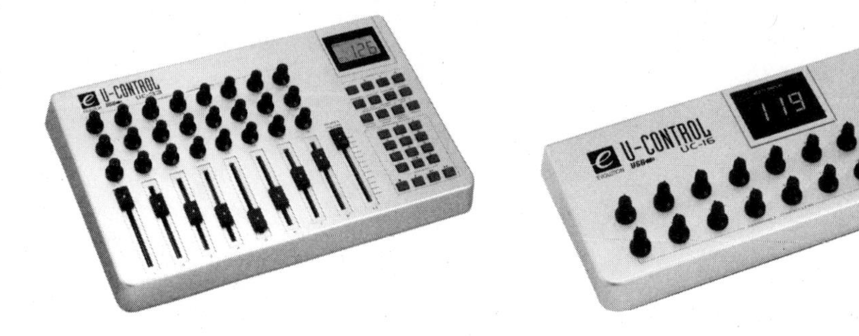

Figure 13.45
Evolution UC-33 and UC-16.

UC-16

Same as the UC-33 but without the faders and a few less knobs. Cool little knob box and just about heavy enough not to slide off your desk. USB interface. $165.00.

MK-225C

Great little two-octave USB keyboard with eight controller knobs. $165.00.

Figure 13.46
Evolution's MK-225C two-octave keyboard.

MK-361C

61-note keyboard with 16 knobs, the largest USB keyboard they do. There is another one halfway between these two, so you've got a good selection. $325.00.

Figure 13.47
Evolution's MK-361C 61-note keyboard.

Edirol

The Roland PC-180 is one of the longest-serving MIDI keyboards designed for use with computers. When Edirol took over the computer side of Roland, they had a chance to update the old favorite, add USB, and introduce a bit more control – which is nice. Silver again with a big blue power LED – a bit of a theme going on.

Website

http://www.edirol.com

PCR-30

Along with eight knobs, you also have eight little sliders, just big enough not to be laughable, all assignable, two and a half octaves. $275.00.

PCR-50

49 keys with the same knobs and sliders, a good-sized controller. $325.00.

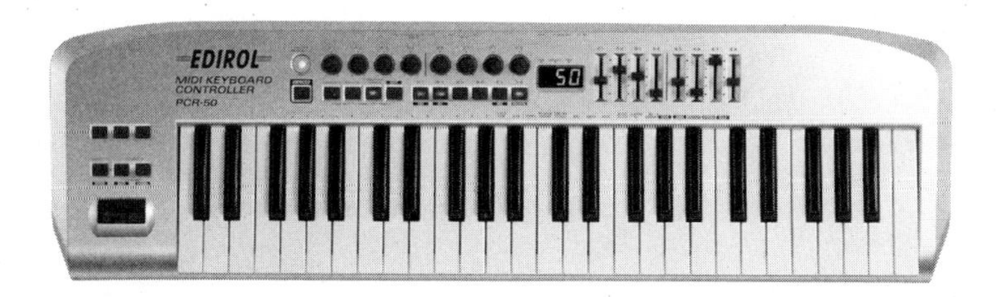

Figure 13.48
Edirol PCR-50 keyboard.

Website

http://www.m-audio.com

M Audio/Midiman

Famed for their audio interfaces, soundcards, and MIDI interfaces, M Audio came quite late to the keyboard market but they have some nice stuff. In particular is the Ozone, which is not only a MIDI controller but also features audio in/out, so it's a real all-in-one solution.

Ozone

25-note USB keyboard, eight knob controllers, and stereo in/out 24-bit audio. Quite a little package and ideal for laptops, and you could probably squeeze the whole thing in your laptop bag. $485.00.

Figure 13.49
Ozone 25-note USB keyboard and audio interface.

Oxygen 8

25-note USB keyboard with eight knob controllers. $245.00.

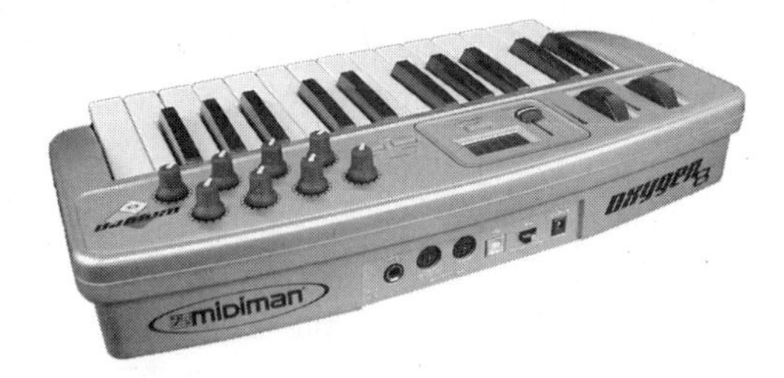

Figure 13.50
Oxygen 8 USB keyboard.

Radium

61-note USB keyboard with eight knobs and eight sliders (sound familiar?).

Figure 13.51
Radium 61 note keyboard.

Kenton Electronics

Kenton have been making MIDI controllers for years, and they have a huge range of sturdy metal products with knobs and sliders. Here's a couple, none of which features USB, so they have to be connected via a normal MIDI interface.

Website

http://www.kentonuk.com

Spin Doctor

Nice purple-colored 16-knob MIDI controller. $195.00.

Control Freak

Eight sliders with tons of built-in presets for pretty much any program going. Solid metal construction makes it a serious bit of gear that'll last you your whole life. There's a larger 'Studio' version available with 16 sliders. $400.00.

Figure 13.52
Spin Doctor (left) and Control Freak.

Akai MPD16

Cool 16-pad USB controller based upon their MPC range of samplers. Great for playing drums and percussion but can be used for anything. $400.00.

Website

http://www.akaipro.com

Figure 13.53
Akai MPD16 USB drum pads.

Website

http://www.roland.com

Roland SPD20

The Total Percussion Pad (Figure 8.6) is an 8-pad drum controller that also contains over 700 drum sounds, so it's much more than just a controller. You can play it with drumsticks so it's a real dream for the frustrated drummers amongst us. Normal MIDI interface. $800.00.

Control surfaces

These are designed to be a real mixer controlling a virtual one. They connect directly to the recording software and take care of all the functions. With motorized faders, they give you real control in a virtual studio. Although products like UC-33 and Control Freak can do similar things, these ones are more professional, better-built, and more expensive. Also don't forget the Yamaha 01X and the Digi002 as control surfaces with lots of extras.

Website

http://www.mackie.com

Mackie Control

Probably the best one to arrive in recent times, it's a smart, stylish controller that's expandable with extra boxes of eight faders. The current parameters being edited are shown in the LCD screen. Complete control over Cubase and Sonar and other programs. $1,950.00 for starters.

Figure 13.54
The Mackie Controller with two expanders.

Steinberg Houston

Designed expressly for Cubase and Nuendo (Figure 8.1), it's a capable controller with all the functions you need, but somehow doesn't feel as good as the Mackie and is not expandable. $1,125.00.

Website
http://www.steinberg.net

Radikal SAC-2K

An interesting and solidly made controller with loads of buttons, knobs, and colorful displays. Comes with eight sliders and is expandable with extra units of eight faders. $1,600.00.

Website
http://www.radikaltechnologies.com

Figure 13.55
The Radikal SAC-2K control surface.

MIDI interfaces

These are really dull, so I won't go into them at all. Suffice it to say that you can get MIDI interfaces with up to eight separate ports and everything in between. If you need to connect lots of external MIDI gear, then check out Steinberg, Edirol, and M Audio for the best selections. Most soundcards come with at least one MIDI port, and most keyboards now are USB, so that's often enough.

Well, that'll do it, I think. There's plenty to choose from if you want to get into music on your computer. You can do it with just some simple software or you can spend as much as you like on interesting controllers and professional software. There's something for everyone and every pocket.

14 What about the computer?

This is the heart of your studio and so really shouldn't be ignored. You've probably got one already and by now have a pretty good idea about how well it's been running these demos. You may be thinking that it's all working rather well, or you might have run into problems and wonder what it's all about. Either way, there may come a time when you want to do more than your computer is letting you do. You might run out of audio tracks, or you might want to add more effects than your computer can handle, or you just want things to run smoother. Then you need to think about upgrading, or more realistically, getting a new one.

Computers vary enormously. With a bit of luck, your current computer has been able to handle everything I've shown you in this book. We've only really dealt with a couple of audio tracks and a couple of effects. Going further, getting the whole studio idea to run successfully may be hard work if your computer is not up to snuff – this, of course, depends largely on what you want to do, as simple programs like Cakewalk Home Studio can run very well on low-powered machines. However, I'm going to talk about the ideal computer, the one you should think about if you do want to go all the way and get serious about your computer-based studio.

What to look for

If you've had a look into getting a new computer recently, you'll know what a dazzling array of choices there are out there. Lots of numbers get bandied around, specifications, promises of amazing things and salespeople spouting all sorts of unintelligible rubbish at you. So, how do you know what to choose or even what to look for? Well, there are three main elements you need to consider when buying a computer – specification, or 'speed', expandability, and quality.

Specification – how fast/powerful is this computer?

Computer power is a combination of three main things – CPU speed, RAM, and hard disk. As a rule of thumb, the bigger the number the better/faster it is and subsequently the more stuff the computer can do.

CPU

The computer's brain, how fast it can calculate things. These are measured in GHz (gigahertz) and you usually have a name of the CPU type (or generation) plus a GHz speed value. For instance, the current Intel CPUs are of the type called

'Pentium' of which the current generation is the 'Pentium 4'. At the time of writing, the available speeds of the Pentium 4 range from 2GHz through to 3.6GHz – the higher the number, the faster the CPU. To make things more complicated, we also have CPUs made by a company called AMD who name their CPUs differently. Their current type is the 'Athlon', and 'XP' is the latest generation. They range from the '1700+' to the '3000+'; however, these numbers do not directly represent gigahertz processor speed. For instance, the 2400+ runs at 2GHz, and the 2700+ runs at 2.17GHz. The problem is that direct comparison of gigahertz speed between Intel and AMD doesn't really work, as they use different technologies. Confusing and annoying, isn't it? In both cases, larger numbers are better. Personally, I prefer Intel simply because the speeds make sense to me, and they did, after all, invent the CPU in the first place. So if this is your first time, or if you find it all confusing, then opt for Intel Pentium 4 at whatever speed you can afford – just makes things simpler.

Figure 14.1
Pentium 4 processor.

RAM

'Random Access Memory' or just 'Memory', although lots of other terms come along, like RDRAM or DDR or RAMBUS and the like, and then you have speeds like 266MHz, 333MHz, and 1066MHz. This is something you shouldn't really have to worry about unless you are planning to build the computer yourself. The type and speed of RAM will be matched to the CPU and motherboard that's inside the computer. The only thing you need to ask is what the total amount of RAM is. The total RAM usually comes in multiples of 128MB (megabytes), so you'd often find 128MB, 256MB, 512MB, and 1024MB (or 1GB). Again, more is better and has a direct influence over how many plug-ins you can run. I'd recommend 512MB if you can manage it, and nothing below 256MB if you can't.

Figure 14.2
A 'stick' of memory.

Hard Disk – or hard drive

This is where all your programs are installed, where you store, or save, all your files and all your audio tracks. The bigger the drive, the more room you have for storing stuff, which essentially equals recording time. You use up roughly 5MB per minute per mono track of 16bit 44.1kHz audio. So an 8-track recording would be 30MB per minute, so you'd get about 34 minutes of 8-track into 1GB (gigabyte). Hard drives commonly come in sizes of 40GB or 80GB, and you can often put two or three in one computer. The more the merrier. I'd recommend at least a 40GB drive, but, if you can, get two so you can have all your programs on one drive and keep a second drive purely for recording audio – much more efficient that way, and safer, too. If for any reason your system breaks down, then the problem is more likely to be with the drive that has Windows and the programs on it rather than your second drive, so anything you've recorded is likely to survive. People also talk about hard drive speeds. These are often access speeds, burst rates, or sustained transfer rates. Most of it is unhelpful. All you should really look for is a drive that has a spindle spin of 7200rpm – that's how fast the drive spins, and 7200rpm is perfect for tons of audio. People may also mention 'SCSI' (pronounced 'scuzzi') hard drives and go on about how much better they are. SCSI drives are completely unnecessary, so ignore them. It's true they perform better than the normal 'IDE' hard drives that I'm talking about, but not enough to justify their huge expense. As a comparison, you could do 150-200 tracks of audio on a normal IDE drive, whereas on a top SCSI drive you could reach perhaps 250 tracks. How on earth you come up with that many tracks is beyond me. Don't believe the hype - IDE drives are plenty good enough.

So, an example specification you might come across would be:

Pentium 4, 2.4GHz, 512MB RAM, 80GB HDD (hard disk drive)

and that would be pretty cool.

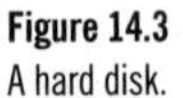

Figure 14.3
A hard disk.

Expandability – what extra hardware you can put in it

Not as easy to see when looking at computers in a shop window. If you are hoping to turn your computer into a studio, then it's vital that you have room to put a decent soundcard. All PCs have 'slots', called 'PCI slots'. These are literally slots on the motherboard where you can put extra cards. These could be network cards, modems, video capture cards, and, what we're interested in, soundcards. So the question you should ask the computer shop is, 'Does it have room for me to install my own soundcard?' A good expandable system will have between four and six PCI slots, of which a couple will be free for your soundcard. Most off-the-shelf computers will already have a soundcard inside. This may be an actual card or something built onto the motherboard. Ideally, if you are going to get a computer for music, then you don't want a normal soundcard installed already. These are likely to be good for multimedia but not necessarily good for music. A computer can have only a limited number of things installed, and similar cards will tend to clash with each other, so we want only one soundcard and we want that to be a quality one for recording. If you are considering the USB route, using an external box that requires no installation – just plug it in – then the expandability issue is not so great. You will need to know, though, how many USB ports there are, so that you have enough to plug in the USB audio box, perhaps a keyboard, and any other normal computer bits like printers. Four USB ports is a good number.

Quality – how well the whole thing is made

Try to avoid buying the cheapest machine you can find. It would be better to get a slower computer that's well-made rather than a fast one that'll fall apart or not work quite as you'd expect. There are some amazing deals to be had, but be wary of offers that are too good to be true, as they usually are.

Where to buy

It's difficult to know exactly what you are getting for your money, and it's also difficult to know whether the computer you buy is going to be as up to the job of being a studio as you'd like. Unfortunately, few computer shops will know anything about running music programs, what sort of requirements it would need, and think that a SoundBlaster soundcard is the best you could possibly get.

I've spent years in music retail, selling soundcards and software, and much of my time was taken up trying to get these things to work in customer's computers that were just not up to the job. The lack of expandability was often one problem, but it was also down to how the computer was installed in the first place. If you buy an off-the-shelf general purpose PC, then it's likely to be filled with all sorts of software and utilities that you might never need but which can get in the way of running more intense software like Cubase. Cubase would like as much processing power as you can give it, but things like office software and virus checkers often take up loads of power by simply existing. The answer for me was completely clear – design and build a computer that's fast, expandable, and not full of unnecessary junk so it will run music software and hardware like a dream. So, that's what I did.

If you want to get a computer for music, then I would heartily recommend getting a pre-configured computer from a decent music shop. Most high-tech music shops can supply computers nowadays and, if they are worth their salt, will install a professional soundcard and the music software for you, test it, and make sure it's running properly. It may cost a little more than buying from a computer warehouse, but you'll be certain that it's up to the job, and if things go wrong you'll have one place to go for help. So many people get stuck in a situation where they have a standard computer from a computer shop, and a posh soundcard from a music shop, and if you can't get it to work, both shops will blame each other, leaving you in the middle with a useless PC. If you get the whole thing from a specialized music shop then, hopefully, you can avoid all these things.

My company, Carillon Audio Systems, does exactly this and I'll give it a quick, shameless plug. We design and build computers expressly for music. They work as studios, all ready to go out of the box. The software's installed for you, the soundcard is installed for you, it's all tested and optimized and runs like a rocket. We even include tutorials on how to get started making music. We support the whole system, so if you ever have any problems, we're there to help. Our computer also looks gorgeous, as we put a lot of time into the design and ruggedness of the computer case. It's also incredibly quiet, quiet enough to record with a microphone alongside the machine. Our systems are not as expensive as you might think and we can custom make them to your requirements or recommend a tried and tested solution that'll do more than you ever thought. If you'd like to know more, then go to http://www.carillondirect.com.

If you already have a computer and you'd like to know how to make it run better for music, then have a look at the appendix on 'Setting up Windows XP for music' and that could improve the performance to no end.

Figure 14.4
Carillon Audio Systems can provide solutions designed for the guitarist.

The great 'PC versus Apple Mac' debate

Got to be the most frequently asked question in the universe when it comes to choosing a computer for music – or many other applications for that matter. It is true that for many years, the Apple Mac was considered to be the best computer available for music, and PCs were generally regarded to be too unreliable to be taken seriously as anything other than a glorified word processor and games machine. Today, this is completely untrue, although there are valid reasons why people would think it still is:

Macs are made by one company: Apple. They have complete control over what goes inside and how well it's made, and they also have complete control over the operating system and how that works with the hardware. This makes the computers very stable and also very consistent in how they work and what they do. PCs, on the other hand, can be put together from bits and pieces from all over the place, from different manufacturers, and Windows XP has the job of getting everything to work together in some kind of coherent manner. This can produce a greater risk of incompatibility and so stability can suffer. However, this is not a fair comparison because of the difference in price. If you buy a bargain basement PC, then this argument may well hold true and you may suffer from odd problems that you get when you buy a rubbish PC. However, if you were to spend the same amount of money on a PC as you would a Mac, then you would have the most amazingly, powerful, superfast workhorse of a machine with go-faster stripes and a built-in coffee maker, and it would be as stable as a rock. Realistically, you could get a decent, stable PC for half the price of the Mac equivalent and both would be able to do a great job of being a studio. The problems arise because there are so many cheap and rubbish PCs out there giving us a bad name, whereas there is really only one Mac to choose from, and it's a very capable machine.

Info

The other advantage of PCs is that there are tons more applications and bits of hardware available for PC than there are for the Mac. You could say that another reason why Macs are so stable is because you can't run anything on them!

It used to be true that all the most professional music applications ran only on the Mac, and that's why you find most professional studios using Macs. However, nowadays there's nothing on the Mac that can't be run just as well, if not better, on a PC.

Pro studios, though, don't really have any reason to trade in their Macs for PCs, but more and more, when it comes to buying a new system, they are turning to PCs.

The debate is essentially pointless because both Mac and PC are equally capable of running professional music software and hardware. So, if you are used to one or the other, and it does what you want, then stick with it. If you are buying your first computer, then I would recommend opting for a PC with Windows XP because it's easy, good value, powerful, and will run pretty much anything you could think of. Either way, though, you can't lose.

Example specification

If you really want me to spell it out for you, I'll give you this example PC specification:

Intel Pentium 4, 2.4GHz, 512MB 40GB system drive, 80GB audio drive, Windows XP.

If you'd like to know what a system like this is capable of, here are some performance figures I got recently while testing Cubase SX on a similar system.

Maximum track count:
184 audio tracks at 16-bit 44.1kHz
80 audio tracks at 24-bit 96kHz

Plug-ins:
With 24 tracks of 16/44.1 audio – 24 EQ, 24 reverbs, 24 full dynamics
With 24 tracks of 24/96 – 24 EQ, 4 reverbs, 4 full dynamics

Polyphony using A1 VSTi:
30 instances with 160-note polyphony

Windows?

Windows XP is by far the best operating system I've come across for music. It's fast, it manages memory and resources far more efficiently, and is generally far more compatible than anything else. Low fuss, low maintenance, easy to use. Windows 98 used to hold this crown, but it can't really compare now. Windows 2000 was indeed very stable but then nothing very much ran on it. XP takes the stability from 2000 (old NT) and the compatibility of Windows 98 and molds it all together very well indeed.

Linux, Unix, or other operating systems are all reportedly very stable and fast and of course not by Microsoft (love them or hate them), but again there's nothing much that works on them so they are no good to us.

XP Home or Pro?

It really doesn't matter. There's nothing special in the Professional edition of XP that helps music programs. It has better network and security support and can run multiple processors, but essentially they are the same, so don't waste your money on Pro unless you need something specific that it offers.

Info

There's an appendix on setting up Windows XP for music at the back of the book, which might help you get the best out of your computer.

Looking back through what we've learned

As we begin to wind up our journey through computer music, I feel it would be a good time to reflect on where we've gone, and consider how you now view the computer in terms of music and what might be possible.

We began by talking about 4-tracks and other bits of recording paraphernalia and drawing comparisons to the computer. We then dived straight in, no parachute, no safety net, and had a go at unearthing what the computer could offer us. We plugged the guitar in and started recording, we talked about drum machines, about digital audio and MIDI and how they complement each other but achieve different things. We've tried out all sorts of interesting software and messed around with music in an attempt to give you a glimpse of what can be done. We entered the often-complex world of MIDI control and came out assured that the hands-on control we all desire is still there and flourishing. We went through the process of creating a finished track and even published it online. Did you think when you picked up this book that you'd come this far?

My sincere hope is that at the very least, I've lit a spark of interest and even excitement about the idea of using a computer with your music. It's your music, you decide how you make it, how you record it, and what you do with it. I can only demonstrate what I believe to be the most important development in recording since Les Paul (the man, not the guitar) invented the multi-track recorder back in 1953.

What the future holds

Software development can move at a bewildering pace. When I wrote my first book *PC Music – The Easy Guide* back in 1998, soft synths and VST Instruments were just beginning to get interesting. Now, even hardware manufacturers are releasing software versions of their synths. Using software effects in real-time was just not possible, and now you can have an entire multi-effects unit in software, in real-time, while everything else is playing back around you. Soundcards were pretty basic, difficult to install and configure, and offered basic connections. Now, we have USB-pluggable audio interfaces bristling with knobs and an assortment of inputs and outputs for whatever you want.

As the processing power of computers bursts through yet another ceiling, we find more complex software, better sound quality, increasingly professional tools, all in the hands of the home recordist. With the Internet as your publisher, there's no limit to where you can take your music.

Sound 'cards' will become less important as new, faster versions of USB and Firewire arrive, giving us all the inputs and outputs we could possibly want, for less and less money. As hard drives get faster and larger, 'DVD quality', that's recording at 24-bit 192kHz, will become the standard. Performance-orientated software will intelligently keep time with your playing – can you imagine a freeform jazz simulator? As the idea of live computer performance with instruments catches on, there'll be a whole range of performance-related products, USB floorboards, integrated MIDI control from the guitar, not just a MIDI pickup, but control over the software. Better control integration with the software has to be around the corner, making it easier to control everything on screen, it's already here but it's just not perfect yet.

Gibson Labs is already working on an audio connection format using networks to connect everything together. They have released a 'Digital Guitar' based upon a Les Paul guitar with an integrated network socket. You can then network up to your computer, your effects, your sound rig, your lighting rig and run everything together. It's still a guitar, it just has a new way of plugging in.

Figure 15.1
Gibson's Digital Guitar.

Line6 have also been busy with their 'Variax' guitar, with built-in modeling that allows the guitar to sound like any guitar you want. No direct computer connection, but the combination of technology is crying out for an easy interface to software. In many ways, Line6 have missed out by concentrating on hardware. A company with this reputation could easily bring the computer and guitar together in very interesting ways. Instead, we have the Guitar Port, which doesn't really do anything useful as far as serious recording goes. These people should get together, I think.

Can you really replace the interaction between guitarist and Marshall Stack on stage? There's no need to replace it. I'm not talking about a new world order, I'm talking about taking hold of new technology and running with it. All this technology, the computer, the software - they're just tools. They can be simply functional, but they can also be very creative in the hands of a creative person. If it allows you to realize the music in your soul better than before, then it can only be a good thing. I hope by now that you understand that you don't have to be a tech head, nerd, or geek, you don't have to 'sell out' anything, you don't have to stop using old gear you're familiar with. It's all just cool stuff we like to mess with along the way to our fantasy musical destination.

Figure 15.2
Line6 Variax – Whatever guitar you want.

If you're still troubled or confused, or just have a question, then please feel free to email me and visit my web page, which is an extension to this book, and if I can help, then I'll be happy to.

robin@pc-music.com
http://www.pc-music.com

Right, I'm off to play with my banjo. Thanks so much for your company, and I wish you all the best with whatever you do.

Understanding the difference between MIDI and audio

I wrote this article some time ago for Carillon customers and thought it would be useful as another explanation of MIDI and audio. Computer music systems use of two very different forms of recording. You will discover as you make music on your computer that the boundaries between these two forms is often blurred. Nevertheless, it is important that you can distinguish between the two, and have an understanding of what each is capable of, in order to get the best use out of your system.

MIDI and MIDI sequencing

MIDI stands for Musical Instrument Digital Interface, and is essentially a computer language which allows different MIDI devices to 'talk' to each other. MIDI is a stream of instructions sent from one MIDI device to another in order to produce a response. MIDI instructions include 'note on', which contains information telling a MIDI device to play a note of a certain pitch at a certain 'velocity' or loudness, 'pitch bend' which tells the device to apply a bend in pitch to the sound currently being made, and 'program change' which tells the device to choose another sound. There are also 128 different 'controllers' available in MIDI, which have many different uses; they could control the faders on a MIDI mixing desk, the depth of effect on a MIDI effects unit, or even the movement of lights on a MIDI lighting rig.

Probably the simplest use of MIDI is to connect the 'MIDI OUT' of a keyboard to the 'MIDI IN' of a sound module. Striking a key on the keyboard sends instructions for that 'event' down the cable to the sound module, which responds by playing a sound. The keyboard itself hasn't made any sound, it has just sent an instruction to a MIDI device that responds to that instruction by generating a sound.

This in itself is marvelous(!), but the best thing about MIDI is that the information sent between MIDI devices can be recorded, stored and edited by a MIDI sequencer.

A 'sequencer' used to be a piece of hardware which could store a sequence of notes and play them back on request. Modern software sequencers can do far more than their name implies, but the essence is still the same. When you play your MIDI keyboard into your sequencing software, all the information on what notes were pressed, how hard etc, is being recorded as MIDI data. No sound is being recorded, just information on how the music was played.

A good analogy would be that of a sheet of manuscript paper. Written music contains no sound of its own, it simply conveys information on how that music should be played. A MIDI sequencer holds exactly the same information and will often even let you print out the score using the recorded MIDI data. To hear the music written (or recorded) on the manuscript you would give it to a musician who would then be able to play it back on their instrument for you. In order for a MIDI sequence to create a sound on playback, the MIDI information must be routed to something which understands it and can play back sound in response.

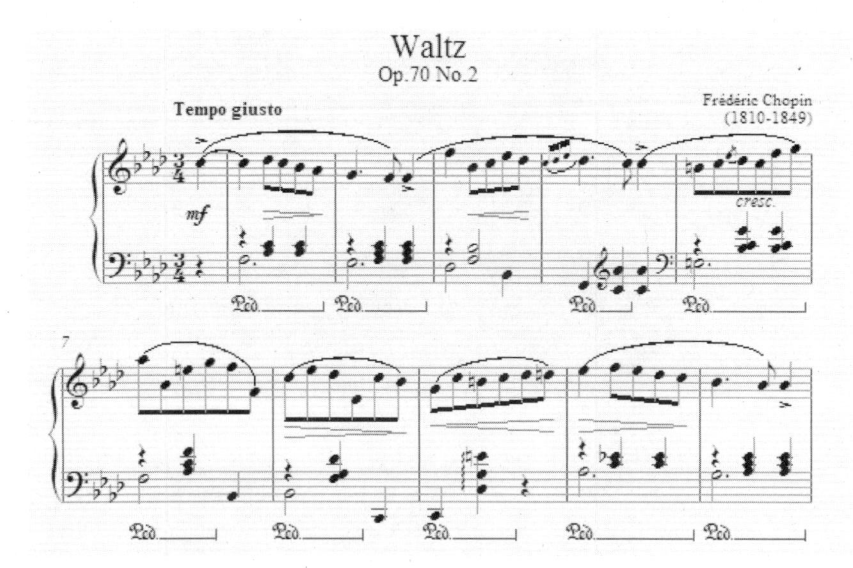

Figure A1
A sheet of music is really just a set of instructions to the musician.

Audio

This is about the recording of sound, stuff we can hear, real live audio. Get a microphone and place it in front of something making a sound, plug that microphone into a recorder of some kind and you'll be able to record that sound and then play the same sound back afterwards. In essence this is what your computer can do. It is often called 'hard disk recording' or 'digital recording' or even 'audio sequencing', and all of these terms are correct in their own way.

A computer, provided that it has the correct equipment attached, can record sound. You could picture the computer as an open reel tape recorder, or a portable multitracker, or a cassette recorder, or any other recording device that you are familiar with, except that a computer records digitally, and can do so much more with the recorded material than was ever possible with tape. Technology has now advanced to the stage where a single piece of recording software can provide all the mixing facilities and effects processing on recorded audio that were previously available only as a collection of expensive studio hardware.

The basic requirement for recording sound is some kind of input for the source to be plugged into, whether that be a microphone, synthesizer or any other kind of electronic instrument. This is where the soundcard comes into play. A soundcard provides, amongst other things, the physical inputs and outputs required for the recording and playing back of sound. They come in many different configurations, from a simple line input through phantom powered balanced mic inputs to multichannel digital connections.

Confusion between MIDI and audio is often exacerbated by the soundcard, which can often provide audio recording facilities, a MIDI sound source and a MIDI interface. In order to deal with this confusion, it is useful to look at a generic soundcard in greater depth so that we can understand the two very different processes going on.

Figure A2 is a crude representation of a generic soundcard. Soundcards can vary a great deal (yours might offer only audio facilities, for example), but it's the concepts we are trying to get across here rather than the specifics.

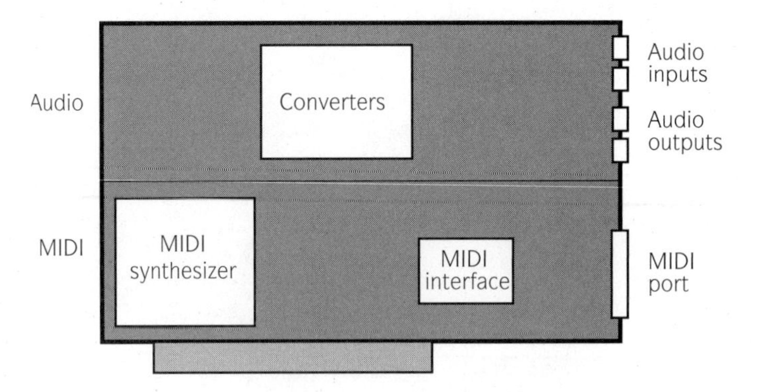

Figure A2
Basic soundcard components.

So, our soundcard provides an audio in and out, a MIDI interface, and a MIDI synthesizer, which is a good representation of the main elements of a computer music system. The audio converters take the incoming analog audio signal and convert it into digital audio, which the computer can understand. On playback they do the reverse. The MIDI interface, which often takes the form of a joystick port on cheaper games type cards, allows us to connect a MIDI keyboard to the computer, and also to route MIDI information out to an external MIDI device such as a synth or sound module.

Lets look at this in greater detail:

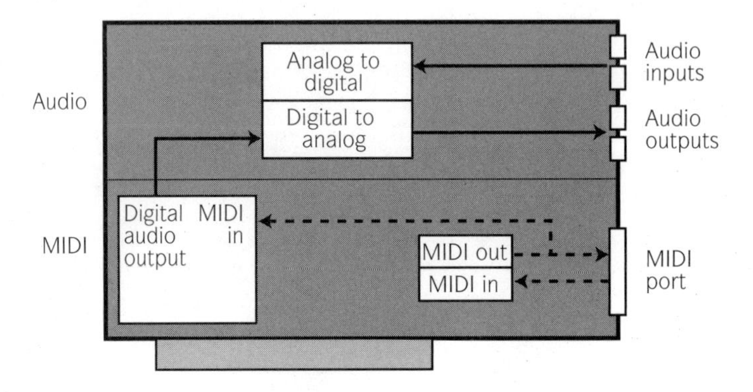

Figure A3
Soundcard data flow.

The audio part of the soundcard consists of two main integrated circuits, or 'chips' if you prefer. One converts the incoming electrical or ANALOG signal from the mic etc. into DIGITAL information which can be understood and stored by the PC. This is called an analog-to-digital converter (ADC). The other circuit does the opposite. It converts the digital information generated by the PC back into an analog signal which can be used by an amplifier and speakers to reproduce sound. This is called a digital-to-analog converter (DAC). So, digital audio is simply audio which has been through an ADC and has been 'digitized'. The quality of the converters has a direct effect on the sound quality of what you're recording, in the same way that something recorded on a cheap and nasty tape recorder won't sound as good as something recorded on an expensive professional machine.

The process of A-to-D conversion is called sampling – this term is often misunderstood because of its association with samplers. A sampler does the same thing as a soundcard in that it digitally records audio, but it stores it in RAM (Random Access Memory) and allows playback of the sound to be triggered via MIDI. It uses the recorded audio as a MIDI instrument, in much the same way as playing a sound on a synthesizer. A computer on the other hand, samples audio and streams it onto a hard-disk, where it can be played back like a tape machine. It's a small difference but an important one to understand. To act like a sampler, a computer needs additional hardware in the form of a sampler card, or alteratively a software sampler program.

What sampling does is to look at (sample) the analog signal many times a second, and returns a single value to represent the amplitude of that signal at each of those times. So, there are two factors involved in sampling which govern the quality; sampling rate and resolution. Sampling rate is measured in hertz (Hz) and denotes the number of times per second that the analogue signal is looked at (or sampled). Resolution or 'bit rate', is the number of values available to represent that signal (i.e. how accurately it can be measured), and is measured in bits.

The most common standard of resolution and sample rate is 16 bit at 44.1 kHz. That's a bit rate of 65,536 (2 to the power of 16) possible values measured 44,100 times a second. This is also known as 'CD quality' because it's the resolution at which CDs are recorded. So, by increasing either the resolution or the sampling rate you can increase the accuracy of the recorded audio. As with many things, the law of diminishing returns comes into play, and it rapidly becomes fruitless to continually increase either bit or sample rate.

MIDI information flows in through the interface from a MIDI keyboard or other controller, and is routed to your sequencer for recording. On playback that MIDI information is routed from the sequencer to the MIDI OUT, where it can either leave the computer and go to an external device, or be directed to your soundcard's onboard synthesizer, whose output is combined with any recorded digital audio, before being converted back into analog sound by the DAC.

Confusion often arises because the output of the soundcards synth comes out of the same output as the audio playback, this is the same with software synths and samplers. You must realize that the soundcard's synth and any software synths are all MIDI devices and so are not actually recorded as sound. This is very important when you come to mix your music down for recording to CD to whatever. Mixing down audio tracks can be done internally by the computer as it digitally combines the digital audio, but if you try to mixdown MIDI tracks you'll find that you can't because they are not actually sound, just instructions. To mix down MIDI tracks, you must first record the output of the MIDI device you are sending the MIDI data to as audio. To do this you simply plug the output of the MIDI device into the input of the soundcard and record it as you would any other audio source. Once this is done then all the music is digital audio and can all be treated and mixed in the same way.

Setting up Windows XP for music

Computers are designed to do a whole myriad of tasks, and Windows XP, an extremely versatile and competent operating system, does this very well. However, sometimes it tries too hard, sometimes it's automated to the point where half your system is spending its time thinking about what you might possibly do next, or it's carrying out some task that you're not even aware of. For normal usage, this is fine. However, Windows XP doesn't often come across software as complicated or demanding as music software, and so what we need to do is concentrate Windows' attention on the single task of running our studio, rather than worrying about whether we want to write a letter or surf the Internet.

If we can free up as much of the CPU's thinking time as possible, then our studio will run more smoothly and we'll be able to squeeze more tracks, effects, and instruments out of it.

There's a lot of talk and websites about 'tweaking' Windows XP, and some of them go into terrible depth and suggest some serious hacking into the system's registry and files. Much of this is unnecessary, and you could also find yourself disabling things that you actually need. Not everyone can afford one PC for music and another for everything else, so I'm going to show the main tweaks that are going to improve the performance of your system without removing all the normal functionality we'd quite like to have.

Background annoyances

The biggest resource hog is all the programs that run innocently in the background waiting for you to do something that might involve them. Of these the most common culprits are virus checkers, media players, screen savers, and other Internet-related software, and you're probably not even aware of them. If you take a look down at the taskbar, to the right, next to clock, you'll probably see a line of little innocent icons minding their own business. Well, these are thieves, blaggarts, and layabouts, sucking resources from your computer like little virtual vampires. They are annoying anyway, so let's get rid of them. Now before you start to worry, there's nothing that we will do that will permanently disable or harm these, often useful, utilities, we're merely going to prevent them from starting up on their own. For instance, if you are about to go online and check your email, then you can manually turn on the virus checker or firewall software, and turn it off again when you're done. Nothing is going to attack you while you're offline and making music.

Here's what to do:
Click on the 'Start' button and select 'Run'. In the box that appears, type 'msconfig'.

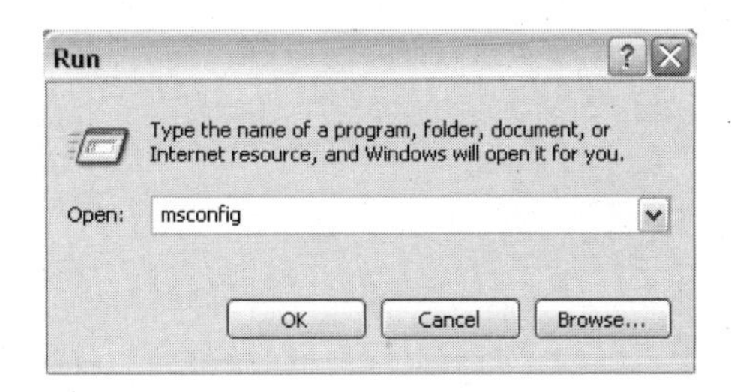

Figure B1
The 'Run' window, found under the Start button.

This will bring up the System Configuration Utility, and you want to click on the tab at the top that says 'Startup'.

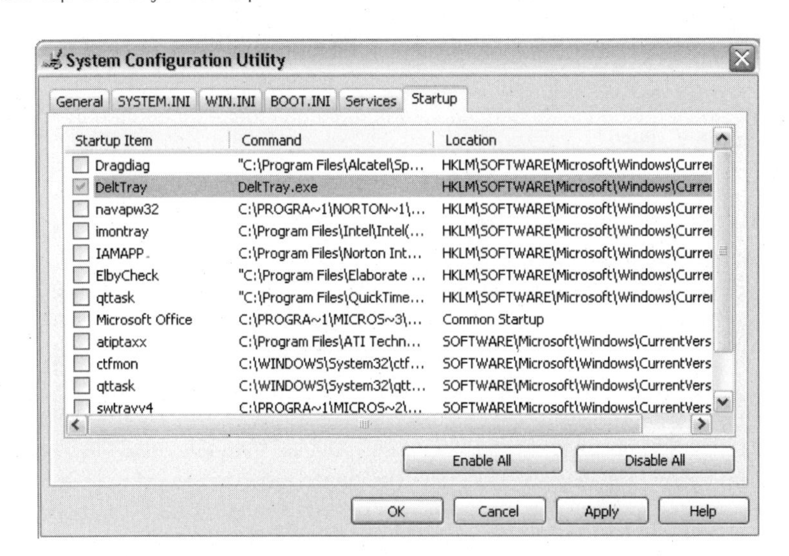

Figure B2
System Configuration Utility.

What's actually contained in the Startup window depends on what software you have on your machine. In mine, I can spot a couple of easy ones like 'Microsoft Office' and 'navapw32', which isn't so obvious, but if you look at the 'Command' column, you can see that it's something to do with 'Norton', which is a virus checker. Now you should be able to disable all of them with no ill effects; however, there may be one or two that would be useful to keep. For instance, I've left the 'DeltTray' on; this is the mixer control panel for my soundcard, and you may have something similar that'd be good to keep. You might also find that you lose some graphical settings after rebooting, as some graphics cards put utilities in the Startup box. If this happens, then you can always re-enable it. When you're done, click 'Apply' and reboot the computer. Now your taskbar should be more or less free of evil icons.

This isn't the only place where Startup items hang out. If you click on the Start button, go to 'Programs' you'll find an item called 'Startup', inside which will be shortcuts that run programs when the computer starts. Would you believe it, if you have Office installed, you'll find another shortcut to it here.

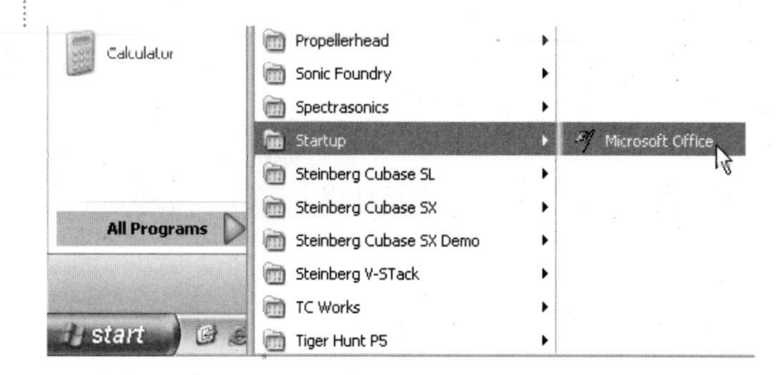

Figure B3
The Startup folder contains shortcuts to programs that start up when Windows XP loads.

Delete anything you find there. The reason programs like Microsoft Office like to run on startup is so that even if they get a whiff of an intention to write a letter or create a spreadsheet, they'll come bouncing in trying to be all helpful before you're even aware you wanted to do anything. Turn it off and Office will load up, on demand, all of about 0.563 seconds slower.

Screensavers

Lovely though they are, screensavers make the computer keep track of the last time you did something so it can bring in the screensaver after the specified amount of time. This does use up some resources; however, more importantly they can have a nasty effect on music software if they kick in while the music software is running. Perhaps you're in the middle of a massive masterpiece, lots of tracks, lots of effects, your computer just about coping with it, and you're practicing your final guitar track, leaving the computer untouched. After a few minutes, the screensaver kicks in and poor computer tries to cope with keeping all the music together and animating a screensaver at the same time. It could be tragic. Also many screensavers use sound that might conflict with the drivers your music software is using, which

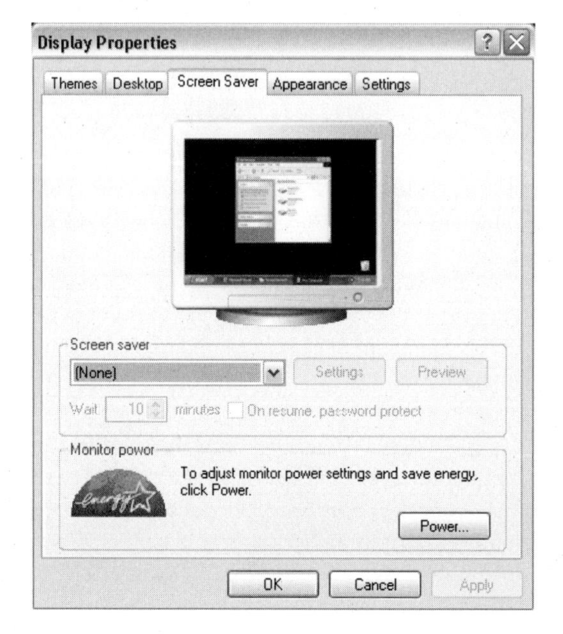

Figure B4
Display Properties – Screensaver. Turn it off.

could possibly cause an unhealthy crash and leave you wondering when the last time it was you saved your masterpiece. I think that we'd best turn them off.

Right-click on an empty piece of desktop and select 'Properties' from the list. Click on the 'Screensaver' tab and select '(none)' as the screensaver.

While we're here, let's look at the power settings. Click the 'Power' button and make sure all the power schemes are set to 'Never'. This prevents Windows from thinking about turning off things to save power – this again could do nasty things to our music software. Other things like Hibernation can be turned off as well.

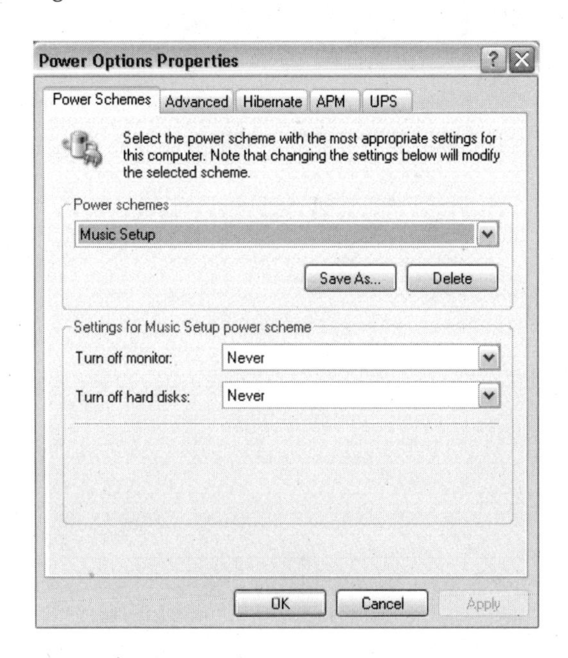

Figure B5
Power Schemes. Don't let anything turn itself off.

Reboot the machine and we've driven a stake through the heart of the background annoyances.

Performance tweaking

There are a couple of things you can do to Windows in general which seem to have a positive effect on the performance of music programs. Most of this happens in the System Properties window. If you open the Control Panel (you'll find it under the Start button), you'll see an icon labelled 'System'; double-click it. Click on the 'Advanced' tab and then the 'Settings' button under 'Performance'.

This is where all the visual effects in Windows hang out. Most people say you should turn them all off so that all the graphical cuddliness of Windows XP is removed and turns it into looking like Windows 2000. Personally, I think Windows 2000 looks rubbish and I much prefer the bouncing XP look. The key option to all this is the last line, 'Use visual styles on window and buttons'. If you leave it ticked XP will still look cool, and if you don't it'll look like old Windows 2000. Two other options I prefer to leave on are 'Show contents when dragging' because it shows windows contents when dragging (!) and 'Use common tasks in folders' – this simply displays the very handy left-hand toolbar in folder windows that gives you

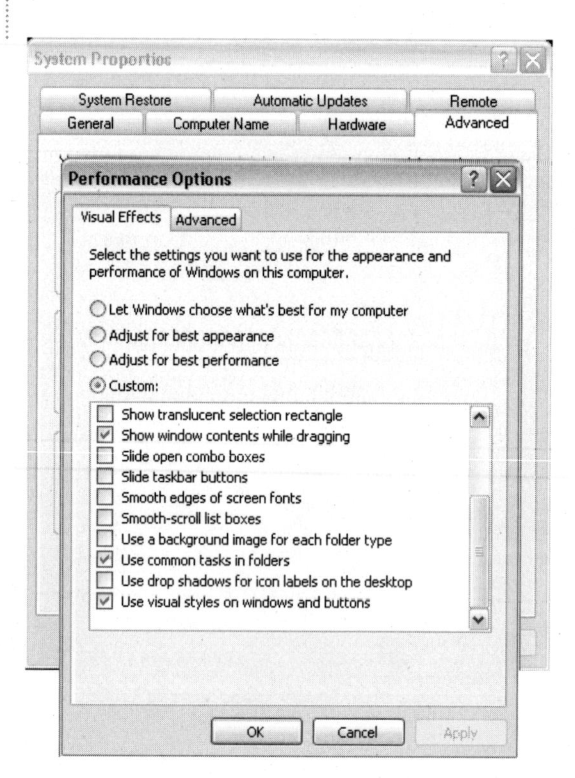

Figure B6
System Peformance – Visual Effects.

access to useful stuff like information on files and shortcuts to things. I find this too useful to remove. These three things are going to have only the tiniest impact on your system. The rest of them are essentially window dressing that you won't notice if they're not there and do free up a tiny bit of power.

Now click the 'Advanced' tab.

Figure B7
Performance Options – Advanced.

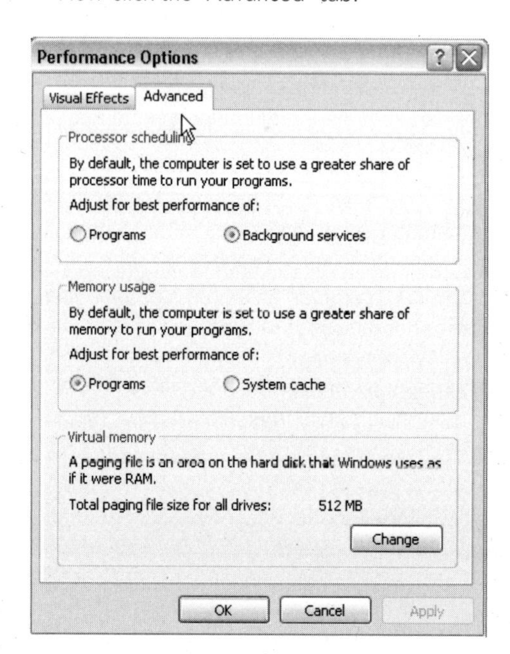

For 'Processor Scheduling', set it to 'Background Services'. This makes Windows concentrate on things like the soundcard drivers, ensuring the best possible performance with your music software. Next the Virtual Memory, click the 'Change' button, select 'Custom size', and set the initial and max values to 512MB. This dictates the size of the Windows virtual memory or 'swapfile', meaning that Windows doesn't have to think about adjusting it. The actual size that should be set is a point of discussion for many people who talk about using equations that include the memory size and all sorts. This is probably all good stuff, but I find that 512MB pretty well does it for everyone. Click 'OK' and get back to the normal System Properties window.

Last few bits. 'Automatic updates' turn off, 'Remote desktop' turn off. 'System Restore' people like to turn off, but I'm not so sure. System Restore is a very useful thing that lets you roll back Windows to an earlier configuration – very handy if you've mucked up installing some drivers, as you can just restore Windows to an earlier time before those drivers were installed. Far too useful to remove completely. If you have two hard drives, however, I would recommend turning it off on the one you use for audio, but keep it on the main system drive, where Windows is. You can do this by selecting the drive and clicking on the 'Settings' button.

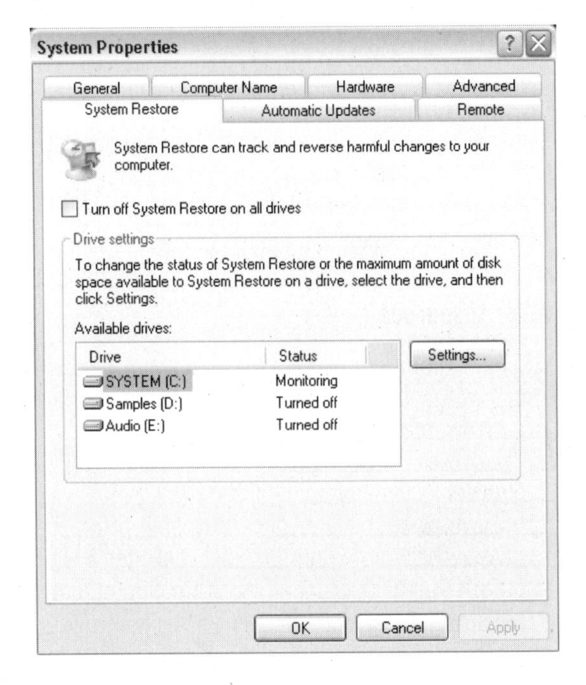

Figure B8
System Restore. Good for getting out of trouble.

That should do it. Your system should be much smoother and cleaner and probably starts up much more quickly as well. Now your computer can concentrate on the real job of making music.

Internet resources

I've included links to all the manufacturers in Chapter 13; however, as a quick reference, here are the links for those whose software I used during the book, as well as other Internet resources you might find useful.

Links to software used in this book

Cubase SX http://www.steinberg.net
Amplitube http://www.amplitube.com
Battery http://www.native-instruments.com
DR-008 http://www.fxpansion.com
SlicyDrummer, Fill-inDrummer http://www.musiclab.com
MIDI-OX, MIDI Yoke http://www.midiox.com
ACID Express http://www.sonicfoundry.com
GT Player http://www.dsound1.com

Other resources

http://www.mp3.com – best place for MP3 resources
http://www.vitaminic.co.uk – good place to air your music
http://www.musicxp.net – for further XP tweaks
http://www.computermusic.co.uk – Computer Music Magazine on-line
http://www.intermusic.com – Future Publishing's website
http://www.pc-publishing.com – publisher of fine books on music and computers
http://www.harmony-central.com – music technology news and reviews
http://www.sospubs.co.uk – Sound On Sound magazine on-line
http://www.kvr-vst.com – for everything about VST plug-ins
http://www.homerecording.com – for everything relating to recording at home
http://www.winamp.com – great MP3 player
http://www.hitsquad.com – Shareware Music Machine has a library of demos, free and shareware music programs to download.
http://www.audiomelody.com – news, tutorials, and downloads of music free and shareware.

Glossary

A/D Abbreviation for analog to digital.

ADSR Attack, decay, sustain, release. See 'Envelope' for detailed explanation.

AES/EBU Professional format for digital signal transfer using a balanced signal, usually via XLR connectors. Stands for Audio Engineering Society/European Broadcasting Union.

Analog In electronics, this describes a continuously variable signal; one which is not restricted to exact values. For example, sound waves are converted into a continuously variable electrical signal by microphones, which generate electricity in response to the varying pressure of sound waves. An analog device is also described as being linear, and as having an output proportional to its input.

Attack The rate at which a sound increases in volume, see 'Envelope'.

Attenuation Making smaller – reduction of signal strength.

Audio Sound waves in air, anything audible, anything you can hear. The normal frequency range of human hearing is from 20Hz to 20kHz, although this typically declines with age.

Audio sequencer A piece of software run on a computer which allows for the recording and arrangement of multiple audio tracks, in addition to MIDI sequencing.

Aux send Short for Auxiliary send. Also known as an effects (FX) send, used for sending signal from a channel to an auxiliary bus, typically to run through an effects processor.

Balance The relative levels of an audio signal in the stereo field.

Balanced cable A cable that uses three wires for connecting audio equipment. The live signal is split over two wires and one half is phase inverted. When re-inverted and combined at the other end, any noise picked up over the cable is eliminated by phase cancellation. Pretty clever, but the connections at either end must also be balanced for this to work.

Bandwidth With audio, it's the range of frequencies utilized by an audio device. In computers it refers to the amount of information that can pass through an interface at one time.

Binary A numbering system based on 2, where there can be two states '0' or '1'.

Bit The smallest unit of digital information represented by '0' or '1'.

BPM Beats per minute – the number of steady, even pulses during one minute.

Byte A collection of 8 bits.

CD quality The digital resolution at which audio CDs are recorded; 16-bit resolution, 44.1 kHz sampling rate. As many other factors are involved in audio reproduction, though, the words 'CD Quality' are no guarantee of actual results!

Channel A single path that an audio signal can travel through from input to output. Also known as a track.

Chorus A modulation effect, created by mixing a small modulated delay with the original sound. Good for fattening up sounds, but can become sickly if overdone!

Compressor Device used to restrict the dynamic range of a piece of audio. A 'threshold' is set, and any signals which exceed this level are reduced by a given 'ratio'. (A limiter is a compressor with an infinite ratio.)

Controller With MID,I it's a device that sends out MIDI information to control another MIDI device.

CPU Central Processing Unit – the brain of your computer.

Cut-off frequency The highest frequency of low pass filter, or the lowest frequency of a high pass filter, or the highest or lowest frequency of a band pass filter.

Cycles per second Unit of measuring frequency, also known as hertz (Hz).

D/A Abbreviation of digital to analog.

Data Information.

Decay The fading of a reverb effect. Also see 'Envelope'.

Decibel (dB) This is a ratio rather than an absolute value, and can be used to describe anything. It's often used in audio to describe the difference in gain or attenuation of the amplitude of sound. For example, boosting a signal by 6dB would mean that the signal has been boosted by a ratio of 2:1. It's a logarithmic scale, and the ratio can be calculated using dB=20logx, where x=ratio.

Delay An effect which creates a distinct echo.

Digital Something that consists of numbers.

DSP Digital Signal Processing – any processing done on a signal once it's been converted to digital, or, Digital Signal Processor – a device whose sole purpose is to process digital audio.

Dynamic range The difference between the quietest and loudest sound.

Effects Various ways of modifying an audio signal.

Enhancer Device used to boost higher frequencies and/or generate extra harmonics to produce a brighter tone.

Envelope How the value of a function varies with time, most often defined by four parameters: Attack, Decay, Sustain, and Release (ADSR). The most common usage of an envelope is to control the volume of a synthesized sound over time:

Attack – the length of time taken from when the note was struck to when the sound reaches its maximum volume.

Decay – the length of time taken for the drop of volume to occur after the sound reaches the maximum.

Sustain – the volume of the sound while the note continues to be held.

Release – the length of time taken for the volume to return to zero once the note has been released.

Equalization (EQ) Shaping the tonal character of a sound by boosting and/or attenuating specific frequency ranges.

Fade The gradual reduction (or increase) in an audio signal's level.

File A collection of data stored on a computer under a single heading.

Filter A device which removes certain frequencies above or below the cut-off frequency.

Frequency The number of cycles per second.

Frequency range The range of frequencies that are responded to, or generated by, a device.

Full duplex The ability of a computer soundcard to record and play back audio simultaneously.

Gain The amount of increase in an audio signal's strength. Usually measured in dB.

General MIDI (GM) A standard which defines which kinds of sounds are assigned to which MIDI patch numbers. It also specifies that drum sounds must appear on MIDI channel 10, and conform to a specific layout across the keyboard. This is useful, as it allows a piece of music created on one GM device to be played back on another and come out sounding correct. The original specification allowed for 128 sounds plus 10 drum kits. Roland and Yamaha have gone further to produce their own expanded versions of GM, which are still backwardly compatible with the original spec. Roland's GS standard offers around 250 sounds, and also adds control for reverb and chorus effects. Yamaha's XG standard goes further still, with over 700 sounds, a few more drum kits and lots of controls for all kinds of effects. Most software sequencers allow you to select a GM sound by name, which makes everything a lot more friendly.

Hard disk Or Hard Drive. It's a rigid magnetic storage device for computer data.

Hardware The physical, touchable parts of a computer or other device.

Headroom The level difference between the optimum level and the point of distortion.

Hertz (Hz) A measure of cycles per second. The higher the frequency, the higher the pitch of a sound. The 'A' above 'middle C' on a piano keyboard is generally tuned to 440 Hz. A doubling in frequency represents an increase of one octave.

High pass filter A device that rejects signal below a certain frequency (cut-off), allowing higher frequencies to 'pass'.

Interface A connection between two different computer components.

I/O Short for Input/Output.

KB Kilobyte – a measurement of 1024 bytes.

Key mapping Defines how samples are assigned to different MIDI note numbers. Essentially, it's the process of mapping samples across a keyboard.

Latency The amount of time between a command and a response in a computer system. Between pressing play and hearing the sound from an audio track, or between striking a note and hearing a sound from a software synth, or between a signal entering the computer and it emerging again.

Level The amount of signal strength.

Loop A section of audio that can play continuously when looped.

Low pass filter A device that rejects signal above a certain frequency (cut-off), allowing lower frequencies to 'pass'.

Memory Part of a computer that stores information.

MIDI Musical Instrument Digital Interface. It's a computer language used to communicate between compatible devices.

MIDI device/module/instrument Something which responds to MIDI information. Usually generates the sound of an instrument in response to a MIDI 'note on' event.

MIDI information A stream of instructions created by a MIDI device.

MIDI interface A connection to a computer that allows it to understand, process, and store MIDI information.

MIDI sequencer A piece of software that can store, edit, and play back MIDI information.

Mixdown Combining the signals from a number of tracks to a single, usually stereo, track.

Monophonic Used to describe a synthesizer/MIDI instrument that can produce only a single note at a time.

MP3 A digital audio file compression format. Turning a digital audio file into an MP3 file reduces it to around a twelfth of its original size. This is particularly useful for Internet distribution, and indeed MP3 is rapidly becoming the de facto standard for audio on the net. MP3 compression is 'lossy', i.e., some of the data is lost during the compression process, so an MP3 file will never sound quite as good as the original (discuss!).

MP3 player A device which plays audio files that are in MP3 format.

Mute Turns off a channel or track so no sound is heard from it.

MTC MIDI Time Code. Can be used to synchronize one or more MIDI devices with their own sequencers via MIDI. MIDI tempo, position, and start/stop can be all be transmitted.

Pan Placing an audio signal in the stereo field by adjusting the distribution between left and right speakers.

Phantom powering A system used to supply the power required by a condenser microphone. Usually 48 volts.

Pitch The perception of frequency by the ear.

Pitch bend Smooth increase of decrease in pitch usually performed by a wheel on a MIDI controller.

Polyphonic Used to describe a synthesiser/MIDI instrument that can produce more than one note at a time.

Polyphony The number of tones, voices, or notes a synthesizer/MIDI instrument can produce simultaneously.

Quantization Moving MIDI notes (in terms of start time and/or length) to the nearest musical division. In other words, it tidies up your sloppy timing! You can now even quantize audio with some software.

RAM Random Access Memory, used to store data that needs fast access on a computer. RAM is volatile, which means that it's only available while powered and loses all data when turned off.

Red Book The specifications for the production of audio CDs.

Reverb Short for reverberation, which is the complex series of reflections of sound inside a building (imagine what it sounds like inside a cathedral as opposed to a completely open outdoor space). Adding reverb to a recorded sound gives it the effect of being in a physical space.

Release The rate at which volume drops after a key is released – see 'Envelope'.

ROM Read Only Memory. Non-volatile memory that cannot be edited. It is used to store essential instructions.

Sample Digital representation of audio.

Sample rate The number of times an analog waveform is measured or 'sampled' per second to convert it into digital.

Sampling The process of converting analog audio into digital audio.

SCSI Small Computer System Interface. This is a protocol for the transfer of data to and from hard drives. Once considered 'de rigeur' for hard disk recording because of its superior speed, IDE (Integrated Drive Electronics) drives are now so fast that SCSI is required only for the most demanding of applications.

SMPTE Society of Motion Picture and Television Engineers. This is the standard for the most widely used form of synchronization for analog machines. It is a code which is recorded to tape (striped), and contains timing information in hours, minutes, seconds, and 'frames'. As you may have guessed from this, it was originally used to sync music to film. For us, it's most useful in that SMPTE can be converted to or from MIDI Time Code, enabling us to sync MIDI sequencers and analog tape machines together.

Software A 'program' or set of instructions for your computer that tells it what to do.

Solo Allowing only a single track to sound.

SoundFont A SoundFont is a data format for sounds to be replayed by your computer via 'wavetable' synthesis. It contains sound samples and instructions to the hardware (or software) on how to articulate these samples. For example, a SoundFont can contain sound samples recorded from a trumpet being played at different pitches. It can also contain various instructions to the synthesizer; for example, instructions to tell the hardware to filter or mute the sounds when notes are played softly, loop information about a sample that allows a short recording to be stretched to a sustained note, or instructions on how to apply vibrato or to bend a note's pitch. SoundFonts can be played via MIDI when loaded into a supporting piece of hardware or software.

SoundFont bank A collection of SoundFont instruments bound together in a single file that can be loaded together and treated as a single MIDI device with 16 parts. There can be up to 128 SoundFonts in a SoundFont Bank.

S/PDIF Short for Sony Philips Digital Interface, a standard for the transfer of digital audio. Usually comes in two formats – Coaxial and Optical.

Stereo Two channels where the placement between left and right can be perceived.

Synchronization The act of linking together two or more bits of gear so that they play in time together.

Synthesis The artificial generation of a sound by electronic means.

Synthesizer A device which can synthesize sounds using electronics.

Tempo The rate at which music flows, measured in beats per minute.

Transport controls Originally for controlling the transport parts of a tape machine. Now used as a generic term for the play/record/forward/rewind/stop controls in any audio related device.

Velocity How hard a key was struck.

Velocity mapping Using two or more samples on a single MIDI note number, each of which is triggered by a separate MIDI velocity range. So the sample replayed on that note changes, depending on the velocity with which the note was played.

VST Virtual Studio Technology. The audio engine created by Steinberg for their Cubase program. It incorporates an environment of mixing, effects, EQ, and virtual instruments.

VST instrument Software synthesizer that runs inside a VST compatible host program.

VST plug-in An effects plug-in compatible with the VST audio engine.

WAV Or wave file. The digital audio file format used by Windows.

Wavetable synthesis Although originally this referred to a type of synthesis made popular by PPG in the seventies, the term has now fallen into widespread use to describe the playback of pre-recorded samples via MIDI with additional subtractive synthesis, i.e., filtering, modulation, etc.

Windows A computer operating system created by Microsoft.

XG Yamaha's version of the GM (General MIDI) format that includes extra sounds, effects, and editing.

XLR A three-wire audio connection used in balanced cabling.

Index

A/D, 227
A1, 94
Aardvark, 177
Ableton Live, 164
ACID, 75
ACID XPress, 76
ACIDized Loops, 77
ADC, 27, 218
adding chords in the Key Editor, 95
adding a Generic Remote, 105
ADSR, 227
AES/EBU, 227
Ahead Nero, 144
Akai MPD16, 103, 205
Alesis SR-16, 44
Alien Connections - ReValver, 193
Amplitube, 4, 12, 38, 107
  as an insert, 128
  presets, 41
analog, 227
analog signal, 219
analog-to-digital converter, 27, 218
AOL, 148
Apple, 152
Apple Mac, 212
Applied Acoustics - Lounge Lizard, 199
applying Amplitube to an audio event, 128
arranging patterns, 67
arrow tool, 92
Art X-15, 202
ASIO, 8
  DirectSound Setup, 10
  DirectX Full Duplex Driver, 9
  Driver, 9
  Multimedia Driver, 9
assign pedals to the transport controls, 121
attack, 227
attenuation, 227
attributes, 139
audio, 217, 227
audio CD, 144
audio data, 31
audio file, 145
Audio Part Editor, 81
Audio Phonics Guitar Tuner, 4, 6
audio sequencer, 227
audio slicing, 79
Audio Stream Input/Output, 8
Audiophile 2496, 173
Autogate, 133
Autolatch, 133 134
automatic updates, 225
automating, 123
  effects, 135
  VSTis, 135
automation, 133, 140
automation subtrack, 134
Autoscroll, 81
aux send, 227

B4, 199
background services, 225
backing track player, 167
balance, 227
balanced cable, 227
band filters, 95
band pass, 95
bandwidth, 227
basic functions of a 4-track, 15
basic soundcard components, 218
Bassic Bass, 90
Battery, 45, 46
  demo, 5
Behringer FCB1010, 103, 202
BFD, 194
binary, 228
bit, 228
  depth, 28 – 30
  rate, 27 – 30
BombFactory SansAmp PSA-1, 193
BPM, 228
BPM slider, 77
buffer, 31
  size, 41
burn audio CDs, 143
byte, 228

Cakewalk, 187
Cakewalk Home Studio, 189
Carillon, 211
cassette, 138
CD, 138
  labels, 144
  quality, 28, 219, 228
  writing software, 144
  writing wizard, 144
CD-ROM, 4
channel, 228, 139
chorus, 228
coding, 139
coding/attributes, 139
compress, 133
compression, 141
compressor, 133, 228

connecting a 4-track to the soundcard, 18
connecting a MIDI keyboard to the computer, 57
Control Freak, 205
control surfaces, 206
controller, 99, 228
controller pane, 66
controlling Cubase, 104
controlling the mixer, 104
controlling VSTis, 108
Cool Edit, 140
copyright, 152
count-in, 61
CPU, 208
CPU performance, 96
create an audio CD, 143
create audio slices, 80
creating MP3s, 145
Creative, 183
Cubase Default Project, 11
    mixer, 93
    Preferences, 11
    projects, 4
Cubase SL, 186
Cubase SX, 186
    demo, 5, 7
Cubase Transformer, 108
Cubasis VST 4.0, 185
cut-off, 95
cut-off frequency, 228
cycles per second, 228

D/A, 228
DA2496, 175
DAC, 27, 219
DAT, 138
data, 228
data compression, 145
Data Mapping, 115
Data Mapping window, 118
DD Sequencer, 51
decay, 228
decibel, 228
default project, 11
delay, 228
Delta 1010, 174
demo song, 12
depth, 130
detecting hit points, 80
device setup, 9 10
Digi001, 179
Digi002, 180
Digidesign, 179, 190
digital, 228
    effects unit, 3
    guitar, 215
    mixer setup, 160
digital-to analog, 27
    converter, 219
digitizing, 27
DirectPro Q10, 177
DirectX, 8, 35
display properties, 222
DMX 6 Fire 24/96, 184
DoubleDelay, 37
DPU, 228
DR-008, 45, 49,194
Demo software, 4
drag and drop, 78
draw, 91
draw button, 134
drum control, 102
drum editor, 65
drum loops, 77
drum machine, 2, 44
drum software, 194
drum sounds, 45, 65
drum stick, 65
drums, 44
DSound GT Player, 5 , 193
DSound Stomp'n FX, 193
DSP, 228
duplicating MIDI events, 67
dynamic compression, 133
dynamic range, 133, 228
dynamics, 132
dynamics processing, 133

Easy CD Creator, 144
Edirol, 175, 200, 203
editing a guitar track, 96
editing slices, 82
effect parameters, 107
effects, 140, 107, 130, 228
    boxes, 3
    patch, 110
    plug-ins, 192
    processing, 34
    processor, 167
    with VSTis, 93
encoding, 146
enhancer, 228
envelope, 229
EQ, 126, 131
equalization, 229
Event Infoline, 68
Evolution, 101, 202
Evolution UC-33 MIDI controller, 120
expansion, 141
export audio mixdown, 139
exporting of audio, 129

fade, 229
fader movements, 123
file, 229
file transfer, 148
Files of Type, 139
filter, 95, 229
Filter menu, 37
Finalizer, 141
FIREstation, 179
Firewire audio, 170
floorboard control,
    in Cubase, 111
    of Amplitube in Cubase, 113
fonts, 62
foot controller, 103
frequency, 229
frequency bands, 132
frequency range, 229
ftp program, 148
full duplex, 229
Fxpansion, 194
Fxpansion BFD, 73
Fxpansion's DR-008, 49

gain, 229
gate, 133
General MIDI, 60, 229
Generic Remote, 104
    Setup window, 105
Get it on CD, 144
getting sound into and out of a laptop, 168

Gibson's Digital Guitar, 215
GigaStudio, 87
gigging with a computer, 164
glitch, 81
Global Quantize, 66
glossary, 227
glue tool, 92
GM, 60
grid, 66
Groove Agent, 195
Groove Quantize, 64
GT Player, 166
guitar effects processor, 166
Guitar Tracks Pro, 188

Halion 2, 88, 197
Halion Strings Edition, 94, 197
Hammond B3, 85
hard disk, 16, 96, 209, 229
hard-disk recording, 2
hard drive, 209
hardware, 26, 172, 229
hardware sampler, 88
HDSP 9652, 178
headroom, 229
hertz, 229
high filters, 95
high pass, 95
high pass filter, 230
hitpoints, 80
Houston, 100
HPD-15, 102
HQ-QR Orchestral, 201
HQ-QT SuperQuartet, 200
html, 149
  document, 149
hypertext markup language, 149

I/O, 230
IDE, 210
IK Multimedia - Amplitube, 192
import option, 78
insert effect, 36
Installing,
  Amplitube, 12
  Battery, 45
  DR-008, 45
  the software, 4
Intelligent Drum Rhythm Compose, 72
interface, 230
Internet, 138
  connection, 147
  music formats, 152
  resources, 226
Internet Service Provider, 148
ISP, 148

jack plug, 17
joystick port, 56

KB, 230
Kenton Electronics, 205
Key Editor, 91
key mapping, 230
Keyfax, 74
Kontakt, 88, 198

laptop, 164
latency, 30, 41, 230
layering, 48
level, 230
level adjustment, 130
limiting, 141
line input, 17
line output, 17
Line6 Guitar Port, 181
Line6 Variax, 215
link, 149, 226
LM4-Mk2, 194
LM7, 5, 58
loading VSTis, 46
loop, 230
loop on/off, 24
looping a drum loop, 79
loops, 4, 77
  in Cubase, 78
Loopstation, 78
Lounge Lizard, 94
low pass filter, 95, 230

M Audio, 173
M Audio/Midiman, 204
Mackie Control, 100, 206
Mackie/Universal - Audio Nigel, 193
making your own MP3s, 147
markers, 61
master outputs, 127
Master X, 142
mastering, 138
mastering software, 140
Mastertrack, 61
Mbox, 180
MCPS, 152
measuring VST performance, 96
Media Player, 144
media players, 220
memory, 230
metronome, 60, 63
  setup, 64
mic input, 17
Microsoft GS Wavetable SW Synth, 44
MIDI, 27, 53, 216, 230
  activity, 57
  control, 99
  controller, 66, 104, 201
  device, 53, 58, 230
  drum kits, 102
  drum pad, 54
  effects processors, 110
  files, 74
  floorboards, 103
  IN, 54
  information, 219, 230
  interface, 55, 230, 207
  keyboard, 89
  merge, 115
  merge options, 72
  OUT, 54
  output, 59
  pickup, 54
  port, 17, 54
  sequencer, 230
  sequencing, 216
  THRU, 54
  track, 58
  Transformer, 109
  Yoke, 5, 116
MIDI-OX, 5, 114
  MIDI device options, 117
  monitoring, 117
mini-jack plug, 17
minidisk, 2

minimum specification, 5
mixdown, 128, 230
  window, 139
mixer control surfaces, 100
mixer, 126
mixes, 4
mixing, 123
  on a computer, 99
  in Cubase, 124
  demo, 124
mixing down in Cubase SX, 139
MK-225C, 203
MK-361C, 203
MME, 8, 31
MobilePre USB, 174
mod wheel, 104
modulation wheel, 104
monitor buttons, 127
monitoring, 30
monophonic, 230
motherboard, 210
motorized faders, 99
MP3, 145, 230
MP3 player, 230
MP3 Pro, 153
MP3.com, 150
MPEG audio layer 3, 145
MTC, 231
multitrack recording, 23
Music Lab, 5
musical instrument digital interface, 27, 53
Musiclab, 196
mute, 127, 230

Napster, 146
Native Instruments, 198
  B4, 86
  Battery, 194
  Pro 53, 86
noise, 133
noise reduction, 141
Noise Reduction plug-in, 141
notch filters, 95
notebook, 164
Nuendo 2.0, 187

O1X, 182
Ogg Vorbis, 153
Omni Studio, 173
on the road, 164
operating system, 6
output routing, 127
Oxygen 8, 204
Ozone, 204

pan, 231
panning, 130, 127
pattern, 49, 51
PatternSelect, 37
PC, 212
PCI slots, 210
PCR-30, 203
PCR-50, 203
performance, 223
  options, 224
phantom powering, 231
Phatboy, 101
phono plug, 18
piano roll, 91
  editor, 89
pitch, 231
pitch bend, 231
pitch-bend wheel, 104
plug-ins, 34
plugging the guitar into the computer, 17
polyphonic, 231
polyphony, 231
PortaStudio, 1
positioning backwards, 130
positioning forwards, 130
Power Schemes, 223
preset patterns, 68
presets, 95
Presonus Audio Electronics, 179
prg, 95
Pro Tools LE, 190
processor, 6
Processor Scheduling, 225
program change messages, 112
programming drums in Cubase, 53
project window, 21
Propellerhead, 82, 84
publishing audio, 146
publishing your music on the Internet, 147
putting your mix onto CD, 143
Pyro, 144

Q, 132
Quantization, 63, 231
quantize column, 66
quantize setup window, 64
Quicktime, 152
Quicktime Pro, 152

Radikal SAC-2K, 207
Radium, 204
RAM, 6, 209, 231
Reaktor, 85
RealAudio, 152
RealNetworks, 152
RealVideo, 152
Reason, 164
Rebirth B-338, 84
record buttons, 127
record enable, 127
record routing, 127
recording,
  a drum track, 60
  with effects, 43
  a second track, 24
  software, 184
  your first track, 20
  your guitar, 15
Recycle, 82
Red Book, 231
Reel Drums, 196
register your web page/site, 150
release, 231
remote desktop, 225
repeat command, 92
resolution, 28, 139, 219
Resolution/Sample Rate, 139
resonance, 95, 132
reverb, 231
REX files, 82
Rhodes, 94
RME, 178
Roland HandSonic, 102
Roland SPD-20, 8, 102, 206
Roland TB-303, 84
ROM, 231
RT Player, 168

S/PDIF, 232
sample, 219, 231
sample formats, 88
sample rate, 27, 139, 231
sampled instrument, 87
samplers, 27
samples, 27
sampling, 219, 231
sampling rate, 28, 219
score editors, 61
screen savers, 220, 222
SCSI, 210, 231
send effect, 36
  window, 38
sends, 126
Sequential Circuits Prophet 5, 86
setting up
  Amplitube, 12
  Cubase SX, 7
  Windows XP, 220
setup, 154
setup with a mixer, 154
SlicyDrummer, 69, 70
SMPTE, 231
soft synths, 84
software, 4, 16, 172, 232
  samplers, 86
  synths, 30, 84
  synths and samplers, 196
  used in this book, 226
solo, 127, 232
Sonar, 189
Sonic Foundry ACID, 5, 76
sound card, 6
Sound Forge, 140
soundcard, 16, 26, 172, 210
  data flow, 218
  MIDI interface, 56
  sockets, 17
SoundFont, 232
SoundFont bank, 232
SPD-6, 102
SPD-20, 102
speaker output, 17
specification, 208
Spectral Band Replication, 153
Spectrasonics Stylus, 196
Spectrasonics Trilogy, 200
Spin Doctor, 205
split (scissors) tool, 97
startup box, 221, 222
Steinberg, 194, 197
  Groove Agent, 73
  Houston Surface Controller, 100, 207
  WarpVST, 192
StepFilter, 37
stereo, 232
stomp boxes, 3
streaming audio, 152
studio setups, 154
synchronization, 232
synthesis, 232
synthesizer, 232
system configuration utility, 221
system performance, 224
system restore, 225

takes, 24
Tascam, 1, 180
tempo, 61, 232
Terratec, 184
The Grand, 198
time signature, 61
timeline, 61
toolbar, 21, 133, 134
TR-808, 84
TR-909, 85
track Info, 21
  column, 58
track mixer, 126
tracks, 21
transformer window, 109
transport, 21
transport control, 13, 121, 232
transpose, 60
TrueTape, 13
TV over the Internet, 153
Twiddly Bits, 74

UA-5, 175
UA-20, 176
UA-700, 176
UA-1000, 175
UC-16, 202
UC-33, 101, 202
undo, 24, 128
universal serial bus port, 55
UR-80, 177
URL, 148
US-224, 181
US-428, 181
USB, 55
USB3, 178
USB audio, 170
  boxes, 169
USB-enabled keyboard, 56
using drum loops, 75
using software effects live, 165

VB1, 89
velocity, 232
  control, 67
  layers, 48
  mapping, 232
  values, 66
virtual bass unit, 89
virtual drum machines, 44
virtual effects, 34
Virtual Guitarist, 73
virtual memory, 225
virtual studio, 161
Virtual Studio Technology, 35
virus checkers, 220
Vitaminic, 151
volume automation subtack, 134
volume fader, 134
VST, 35, 232
  Channel strip, 127
  Channel Window, 126
  Host, 166
  Instrument Automation, 136
  Instruments, 44, 45, 232
  Mixer, 108
  Performance, 96
  plug-in, 232
VSTis, 44, 45, 108

wah automation, 135
Waldorf Attack, 195
Waldorf PPG, 85
wav, 145, 233
Wavelab, 140

wavetable synthesis, 233
WDM, 32
web page, 149
web space, 147
Windows, 233
  Driver Model, 32
  Media Player, 153
  mixer, 42
  soundcard mixer, 20
Windows XP, 31, 212, 213, 220
World Wide Web, 148
write automation, 133, 135

X-over, 133, 134
XG, 233
XLR, 233

Yahoo, 150
Yamaha, 182
  DX7, 85
  MFC10, 202

zip file, 145

16 bits, 27
24-bit, 28
4-track, 1
44.1kHz, 27
8 bus mixer setup, 158
96kHz, 28